Books are to be returned on or before
the last date below.

WITHDRAWN

DEMOCRACY, LAW AND SECURITY

Democracy, Law and Security

Internal security services in contemporary Europe

Edited by
JEAN-PAUL BRODEUR
University of Montreal, Canada
PETER GILL
Liverpool John Moores University, UK
DENNIS TÖLLBORG
University of Gothenburg, Sweden

ASHGATE

Published by
Ashgate Publishing Limited
Gower House
Croft Road
Aldershot
Hampshire GU11 3HR
England

Ashgate Publishing Company
Suite 420
101 Cherry Street
Burlington, VT 05401-4405
USA

Ashgate website: http://www.ashgate.com

British Library Cataloguing in Publication Data
Democracy, law and security : internal security services in
      contemporary Europe
      1. Internal security - Europe 2.Secret service - Europe
      I. Brodeur, Jean-Paul II. Gill, Peter, 1947- III. Töllborg,
      Dennis
      363.2'52'094

Library of Congress Cataloging-in-Publication Data
Democracy, law, and security : internal security services in contemporary Europe /
[edited by] Jean-Paul Brodeur, Peter Gill, Dennis Töllborg.
      p.cm.
      Includes bibliographical references and index.
      ISBN 0-7546-3002-1 (alk. paper)
         1.Secret service–Europe. 2.Intelligence service–Europe. 3.Internal security–Europe.
      I.Brodeur, Jean-Paul. II.Gill, Peter, 1947- III.Töllborg, Dennis, 1953-

HV8194.A2 D44 2002
363.28'3'094–dc21

                                                                                      2002025857
      ISBN 0 7546 3002 1

Printed and bound in Great Britain by Antony Rowe Ltd.,
Chippenham, Wiltshire

Contents

List of Tables and Figure

Tables

Figure

List of Contributors

Jean-Paul Brodeur is Professor in Criminology at *Université de Montréal*, Canada, and former Director of the International Centre for Comparative Criminology.

Iain Cameron is Professor in International Law at the Faculty of Law, Uppsala University, Sweden.

Nicolas Dupeyron is a researcher at the *Institut des Hautes Études de la Sécurité Intérieure*, France.

Peter Gill is Reader in Politics and Security at John Moores University in Liverpool, England.

Andrea Giménez-Salinas is a researcher in Criminology at the UCLM, Spain.

Peter Klerks is Doctor in Criminology and consultant researcher in the Netherlands.

Laurence Lustgarten is Professor at the Faculty of Law, University of Southampton, England.

Lode van Outrive is Professor Emeritus in Criminology and a former MEP for Belgium.

Andrzej Rzeplinski is a Professor at the Helsinki Foundation in Warsaw, Poland.

Shlomo Shpiro is a Doctor in Political Science and a researcher at the Bar-Ilan University in Israel.

Istvan Szikinger is a researcher in Hungary.

Dennis Töllborg is Professor in Legal Science at the Gothenburg School of Law and Economics, University of Gothenburg, Sweden.

Chapter 1

Introduction

Jean-Paul Brodeur, Peter Gill, Dennis Töllborg

When reading academic and other literature on intelligence in different countries, the many common features displayed are rather striking. We encounter the same type of criticism that 'political policing' rather than 'security intelligence' describes what happens, there are similar problems of management and control, deniability is as important in the conservative governed liberal democracy as in the social-democratic hegemony etc. This feeling grew stronger and stronger when those of us researching in the field met on different occasions and read and compared each other's work. Finally we came to a stage where it felt natural to formulate a hypothesis on intelligence: common structures, common dangers?

This was the start of a project involving two symposiums in Gothenburg, financed mainly by the Swedish Council for Research in the Humanities and Social Sciences (HSFR), that led to the production of the book the reader now has in her hands. From the first session, in 1997, we published National Security and the Rule of Law (ed. Töllborg, Centrum för Europaforskning, Gothenburg University). This second book is an attempt to examine more deeply the structures of intelligence policing in ten countries with different political and historical background. England with its Anglo Saxon police tradition, France as the mother of all intelligence policing, Belgium with its rather peculiar policing tradition and of course Canada with all the changes precipitated by the path-breaking MacDonald Commission. Spain, Poland and Hungary are especially interesting as three countries leaving a long dictatorship and, in a difficult time, trying to find their way towards democracy. Germany had a similar background until 1945 and then a split between East and West and has now had to go through the period of reunification, while Sweden and the Netherlands with their long humanistic tradition are interesting as well-known examples of very stable democracies.

It was agreed that all authors reporting on the situation in their respective country would follow a common blueprint and as far as possible, address the same issues. There is in consequence no need to summarise each of the papers as they address in varying details the same issues. Each paper is comprised of a descriptive and of a normative part. The descriptive part consists of an account of the security intelligence apparatus that was developed in that country. This account first begins by providing some historical background against which the security intelligence agenc(y)ies are then profiled. There is discussion of the organisational structure of their various components and the relationships between them, their mandate as it is determined by the law, their budget, their personnel and their methods and powers.

The normative part of the papers does not only bear on what is presently existing but also on what is desirable according to a perspective that tries to balance the fulfilment of an agency's mandate with the respect of fundamental rights. This part of each paper addresses the issues of doctrine, secrecy, accountability, human rights and, when it applies, transition towards democracy. The issue of doctrine deserves special attention. Doctrine is different from mandate in that it provides the key for interpreting the mandate as it is formulated in law and for translating it into operations. For instance, the mandate of all intelligence agencies directs them to protect their countries' national security against espionage, sabotage, terrorism, subversion and the like. In most countries, the intelligence and security agencies' mandate was not changed significantly after the end of the Cold War, although its interpretation was transformed to a significant extent. For Western countries the doctrine of containing the expansion of communism became abruptly obsolete. The troubling problem is that this doctrine was not, at least not before 11 September 2001, replaced by any new coherent worldview that could provide a rationale for their continuing operations. Consequently, accountability now ought to take a broader meaning than it did in the past. It does not anymore refer only to the provision of accounts for various operations in respect to their legality and their observance of basic human rights but also to what we may call doctrinal accountability, that is accounting for the reorientation of the agencies' operations within the new historical context.

As it will be obvious to all readers the papers which are part of this collection do not cover in equal detail the research agenda that we described above. This is due in large part to the fact that researchers do not all enjoy the same access to sources of information on intelligence and security agencies. The most direct source of information regarding these agencies is their own archives and in those of other government units that had some contact with them (for example, the police). These archives are very highly classified and when they are declassified after a long period of time they are of interest mainly to historians. Although they are to a certain extent an indirect source, the public reports issued by various government commissions of inquiry and other investigative bodies on the security and intelligence services are the most informative and reliable sources of knowledge on these services. Countries with strong traditions of research on the so-called intelligence community are generally also countries that have at one time or another instituted governmental investigations into their security and intelligence apparatus. Such examples as the US Senatorial Church Committee or the Canadian McDonald inquiry readily comes to mind. In countries where large inquiries into security intelligence have taken place, the investigative bodies generally recommended that the security and intelligence services publish an annual public report on their activities. Although their content is often relatively uninformative, these reports can yield important pieces of knowledge when they are scrutinised year after year and their content systematically compared.

The other sources of information are the memoirs and recollections of ex-members of these services or of persons who had inside knowledge of their operations. A great number of these books are self-censored and also self-serving, although they occasionally perform a whistle-blowing function, as in the case of the US operative Frank Snepp. Notwithstanding personal contacts that a researcher may harbour with secret agents, the last but not the least source of information is to be found in press reports, particularly when they are filed by investigative journalists. All observers in the field of security intelligence have their extensive newspaper clipping files. The press may be responsible for very important exposes of information as when the New York Times published the Pentagon Papers, and there are also now a proliferating number of newsletters – both paper and electronic – disseminating information on security intelligence.

Taken together, all these sources of information provide many insights into security and intelligence. Yet it is also clear that they would all be found wanting in countries where the operation of the intelligence and security apparatus is shrouded in highly repressive secrecy. Here, where there is no freedom of information and, consequently, no free press, obtaining such information would invite a charge of treason. In spite of the wide disparity in the accessibility of the sources on security intelligence, whenever information does surface it is both interesting and significant that it so often indicates how problems are often of the same nature in various countries, although they may greatly differ in their intensity. It is a widespread view that scandals are the main – maybe even the only – driving force for change in intelligence policing. Even though this impression seems striking, some thought ought to be reserved for discussing why this seems to be such an outstanding feature of this field of bureaucracy.

One common feature between intelligence in different countries – no matter how different their political context and historical background – is the system of compartmentalisation. Compartmentalisation means that the service, as a way to minimise the damages whenever infiltrated, organises in a way that the employees (the desk officers as well as their chiefs) are to have knowledge of only a part of the puzzle. In literature this is well known as the need-to-know principle. In effect, this means that you are only to have operational knowledge sufficient to fulfil your specific task.

A successful implementation of the need-to-know-principle means that the employees internalise this as a professional attitude to the extent that you do not ask – you are really not even interested – in the project of your colleague. Need-to-know becomes a measure of the professionalism both of the employee as an individual and of the organisation as a whole. The other side of this professionalism is, however, seldom discussed. If you succeed in internalising this in the organisation, it will be an effective barrier against everyone – including the supervisory organs, and even the courts. To not tell an 'outsider' and only answer direct and concrete questions from the supervisory organ must mean that necessary knowledge is denied to the supervisory organs, unless they have unrestricted access to the files. This is, of course, reinforced by the parallel facts that the questioned employee might actually not have the answer at the same time as the supervisory organs do not have the professional knowledge to formulate the relevant questions. Ergo, we claim that even disregarding the (political) rationality of deniability, the need-to-know principle is a paradigm cause of the apparent impossibility of controlling these organisations. For creating scandals that may excite the mass media, this is a creative state-of-affairs indeed, but for creating intelligence policing protecting democracy and the ideas of human rights, this must be acknowledged as a main structural problem.

We note that, formally, the mandates of security intelligence agencies changed little as a result of the end of the Cold war but that their interpretation, or doctrine, was significantly transformed albeit in no coherent way. We can see why this may have been the case but the consequences remain no less troubling for that. The situation in the Cold War was frequently characterised as a two person (US/NATO v Soviet bloc) zero-sum (the gains of one side equalled the losses of the other) game. This was a more accurate metaphor for the security situation in the

Northern hemisphere than in the Southern but it certainly dominated security doctrine, structures and methods in Europe and North America.

The changing notion of 'security' itself has contributed much to the new complexity. For example, in the West the idea of 'national security' has increasingly incorporated ideas of economic intelligence. In Europe, the main sources of threats to economic 'wellbeing' are precisely those same advanced capitalist nations who formed the Cold War western alliance. So, while intelligence co-operation continues in some spheres, for example, maintaining 'Fortress Europe', in others it is replaced by competition. There have been other shifts away from the relatively one-dimensional Cold War concept of security (in the West summarised as the 'threat of communism'). Bigo (1994) has shown how these form a 'security continuum' in which genuinely damaging threats of political violence shade into fears around population movements. These are often conflated into the threat of 'transnational organised crime', which is deployed in political rhetoric as justifying all manner of new surveillance powers with their potential for incursions on human rights. While some criminal actions undoubtedly threaten public safety and security, for example, the proliferation of nuclear weapons, the deployment of transnational organised crime, as with 'communism' in its day, demonstrates too often the official tendency to characterise 'criminality' in terms of threats from the 'other'. Thus various foreigners are presented as a serious criminal threat to an otherwise prosperous and legal domestic economy while, in reality, it is precisely the social distortions and dislocations of *domestic* political economies that produce the overwhelming proportion of damaging behaviour.

Now, the security 'game' certainly involves many more players (it has become n-person) and it no longer seems as unambiguously zero-sum. In one sense this is just one part of a more general shift in the view we take of the state and governance. States themselves are seen as less able to exercise traditional sovereignty and their behaviour is more likely to be characterised as 'steering' rather than controlling. Certainly the security arena, although the last resting place of more traditional notions of sovereignty, has not been immune from these shifts. Thus the relatively stable bi-polar security intelligence structures of the Cold War have fragmented and pursue a wider array of competing interests. The Soviet bloc has been replaced by independent states, each with their own security structures, now much more independent of Moscow than hitherto. Within each of those states, a single party no longer co-ordinates the security structure so that turf wars – that have long characterised Western security structures – become more frequent.

Another aspect of this fragmentation of formerly monolithic security intelligence structures is the increasing significance of private sector agencies. These have existed as departments within large corporations or as specialist agencies offering various vetting and espionage services to the former but their significance is now increased by various factors, including, the 'downsizing' of some state agencies in the West and the massive privatisation of state assets in the former Soviet bloc. Thus many former public security personnel now work in the private sector where their value is measured in part by their remaining contacts with the smaller state sector. So, across both public and private sector there are now a much larger number of agencies working in the security intelligence field and – most importantly – with extensive interchanges of personnel and information between them. The only way to describe the resulting structure is in terms of a network (in contrast to the hierarchical structures of the Cold War). The resulting increase in 'grey policing' (Hoogenboom, 1991) presents an immense challenge to proponents of more democratic and rights-oriented security structures. To security practitioners the precise value of the extensive informal exchanges of information and opportunities for sub-contracting within this large security network is that they protect deniability and avoid the irksome bureaucratic procedures established by way of formal international protocols on security co-operation. For outsiders the very fluidity of the network provides an extraordinarily difficult target for inquiries and other traditional modes of increasing accountability.

The attacks on New York and Washington DC on 11 September 2001 took place as the preparation of this collection was being completed. One or two contributors have addressed the consequences of those attacks but we decided that we would not delay completion further in order to provide a systematic update. Rather, we present these papers as what may come to be seen in retrospect as a set of benchmarks of the world of security intelligence prior to September 2001 against which the rapid changes now in train may be judged.

PART I

THE BELOVED LANDS OF UNDERCOVER

Chapter 2

Democracy and Secrecy: The French Intelligence Community

Jean-Paul Brodeur and Nicolas Dupeyron

Introduction

When they compared the police cultures of five European countries – Belgium, France, Germany, Luxembourg and the Netherlands – who had signed the Schengen agreement on transnational police co-operation, Joubert and Bevers concluded that France used covert methods the most frequently and that it had the least open police culture.[1] This conclusion is all the more valid with respect to the French security and intelligence services (SIS), on which little is publicly known, although much is rumoured. Michel Dobry's pioneering study on security intelligence quotes some 95 works, only five of which were written by Frenchmen. The published material on the SIS falls within two broad categories. A first but narrow body of work is theoretically impressive but relatively distant from present SIS field operations: these studies draw on archive material and textual sources and their relevance for understanding the present situation lies in providing the necessary historical and legal background.[2] The second group of studies includes the memoirs of high-ranking ex-SIS members[3] as well as works of popular history.[4] In addition to these sources in the literature, two commissions – *La Commission Nationale de l'Informatique et des Libertés* (CNIL) and the *Commission Nationale de Contrôle des Interceptions de Sécurité* (CNCIS) – release annual reports that can be helpful in monitoring some aspects of the activities of the French SIS. However, none of these commissions have the specific mandate of bringing the SIS into account, the first one dealing with computerised files of every kind and the second one with wiretapping in its narrowest sense. For the purposes of this paper, we have relied on all publicly available written sources. In addition, one of the authors of this chapter works in a French institute devoted to the study of internal security, which operates under the authority of the French *Ministère de l'Intérieur*, the equivalent of the

British Home Secretary. He was thus in a position to informally discuss some of the topics of this paper with various actors within the French intelligence community.

When all is said, however, the world of the SIS in France remains shrouded in secrecy deeper than in Anglo-Saxon countries. For the researcher this secrecy is at worst an insurmountable obstacle and at best a fog in which one must tread with great caution. There are two consequences to this situation. First, it means that secrecy cannot be viewed as an accidental feature of our field of study. In the tradition of Simmel (1996) and Bok (1982), secrecy must become a theoretical object in its own right, as it already is in the work of Dewerpe (1994) and of Couëtoux *et al.* (1981). Second, focusing on secrecy as an object of research in its own right reveals that it does not merely govern the relationships between the SIS and the outside world, but also the *internal* relationships between the members of the SIS themselves. The 'need to know' principle that governs operations is a prime example of the institutional culture of secrecy that permeates security intelligence agencies. As deep as you may be within the so-called intelligence community, you are always someone else's outsider. As Dobry (1997) rightly argued, this situation ultimately means that fuzziness cannot wholly be expelled from the logic of research on the French SIS – and perhaps any other – because it only mirrors the systematic ambiguity that pervades this field of inquiry.

This chapter is divided into four parts. We first describe the security intelligence apparatus, with an emphasis on historical context. We then discuss the control exercised on this apparatus, stressing its limitations. In a third part we focus on abuses of power by the French security apparatus, some well known, others strongly suspected. Finally, based on the present situation we try to extrapolate how the French SIS may evolve in the short term.

The French Security and Intelligence Apparatus

The Historical Background

The police, as an organisation completely distinct from the military, was invented in 17th century France under Louis XIV. Although it would be simplistic to assert that the history of the French police is an unbroken thread running from 1667 to the present time,[5] there are some enduring features to French policing. Two texts quoted below will help show this: one dating from the *Ancien Régime,* when France was ruled by kings, and the other written following the French Revolution, after many French institutions had been transformed by Napoleon Bonaparte into their present shape or something close to it.

The first text describes the duties of the French Police Minister as they were perceived in 1715. It is excerpted from an eulogy pronounced by Fontenelle, the Secretary of the prestigious French Academy of Sciences, when the feared and celebrated Marquis d'Argenson retired as the *Lieutenant de Police* of the realm. We shall only quote the part of the eulogy which is relevant for our analysis:

> To perpetually feed in a city like Paris an immense consumption...to repress the tyranny of the merchants...to hold necessary abuses within the precise bound of necessity which they are always prone to violate; to reduce these abuses to such obscurity as they must be condemned, and not even to retrieve them from it by too glaring a punishment; to ignore what it is better to ignore than to punish, and to punish only rarely and usefully; *to penetrate inside families through underground passages and to keep the secrets that they never imparted for as long as it is unnecessary to use them*; to be everywhere without being seen; finally to move or to check at will a vast and tempestuous multitude and to be the ever active and nearly unknown soul of this great body; these are the duties of the police magistrate. [6]

Before quoting the other text, let us stress how stark the perspective articulated above really is: since 'abuses' – including crimes, as the context makes clear – necessarily occur, the police mandate is the governance of crime rather than its eradication.

The second excerpt is taken from an 1816 letter from Fouché, who was Napoleon's minister of police, to the Duke of Wellington:

> The police is a political magistracy, which, apart from its special functions, should co-operate by methods, irregular perhaps, but just, legitimate and benevolent, in augmenting the effectiveness of every measure of government...In the social order there are invisible strata; things are not always immediately apparent; there is, as it were, a secret world in the midst of the public world; ordinary authority cannot reach it, its sources are out of reach...The peace of the state depends upon the moral attitude of the working classes who compose the greater part of the nation, and who form the foundation of the social edifice, they should therefore be, so to

speak, the object of assiduous care and of the vigilance of a good police.[7]

With his customary acuteness, Michel Foucault aptly summarised the conception of the police conveyed by these texts (and many others): policing consists of the sum of all means necessary to the internal growth of the State's strength.[8] Focusing on the primacy of surveillance and intelligence gathering, one of us referred to this tradition as 'high policing', the phrase being merely a literal translation of the French *haute police* that was used to describe the core of the French concept of policing. There are a number of consequences flowing from this conception:

1. *An instrument of the executive:* The police are much more an instrument of the executive than of the legislative and even of the judicial branches of government. So much so that Fouché viewed the surveillance of the extra-legal no-man's-land as the specific prerogative of the police. In a letter to Napoleon, he wrote: 'the police, as I conceive it, should be established in order to forestall and prevent offences and to check and arrest such as have not yet been foreseen by the law'.[9] This is an astonishing statement with respect to human rights for it negates the fundamental principles that everything which is not explicitly forbidden by the law is permitted and that no punishment should be inflicted unless it is provided by law (*nulla poena sine lege*).
2. *All-encompassing range of action:* As Max Weber emphasised, there is no limit to the nature and the number of goals that the state can set itself. Consequently, police activity embraces all spheres of human action when it is defined as the means to maximise the power of the state.
3. *Between instrumentality and identity:* The relationship between the executive and the police is defined as so close that it becomes difficult for the political analyst to separate what is from the state and what is from the police in the context of policing operations. Considering the extensive police feedback in political decision-making, it is impossible to view police agencies as passive instruments of politicians. Foucault's insight that policing is a form of governance is echoed by both quotes, which vest on the police the duty to control the population taken as a whole.[10] To view policing as a form of governance is much less naive than to assume that a relationship of neutrality and non-interference between the political executive and the police can be found or established, as Porch (1995) seems to argue. Politicians should not interfere in policing on a case by case basis; however, no government

can afford to renounce its prerogative to set policy in respect to policing or the SIS, policy-making being of the essence of governance.

4. *The secrecy complex:* Secrecy is usually conceived of as the protection of the secrets of the state. Although this is correct in many respects, it is also an oversimplification. It cannot be doubted that secrecy protects the state in two basic ways: it first aims to keep its designs and its strengths and weaknesses hidden from its enemies; to a lesser extent, it is also used to cover up wrongdoing by agents of the state, most notably by the police. However, as both texts quoted above reveal, state secrets also include secrets originally alien to a government but that become state secrets by virtue of having been collected by government agencies. Secrecy is highly contaminating: a secret learned is also a new secret that has to be kept. It has to be kept primarily because of strategic reasons: knowing your real or potential enemy's secrets is an advantage largely to the extent that this knowledge remains concealed. It must also be kept for ethical reasons: betraying private (for example family) secrets randomly is a case of malice for its own sake and would quickly discredit any institution. It must finally be kept for social reasons: 'abuses' (deviance) should be condemned to obscurity lest they demoralise those who witness them. Needless to say, as Fontenelle warns us, secrecy should persist only insofar as it is not necessary to dispense with it. However, the dynamics of concealment and disclosure are much more complex than the advocates of transparency generally believe.

There is one last historical element that must be mentioned in order to put the development of the present French SIS in its proper perspective, namely their relatively recent creation. Shortly after the 1940 defeat General de Gaulle led a government in exile from London until the liberation in 1944. Headquartered in London, the French Resistance created its intelligence arm, the *Bureau Central de Renseignement et d'Action* (BCRA). The BCRA was transferred to France after the Liberation and became the seed for the French foreign intelligence community; after many transformations, it settled in 1981 as the *Direction Générale de la Sécurité Extérieure* (DGSE), which is still the French foreign secret service. The history of the French intelligence community from the BCRA to the DGSE is much too complex to be retold here and is detailed in Warusfel (2000). However, the Gaullist stamp on the French intelligence establishment must be underlined, for it is an enduring source of tension within the community. De Gaulle's view was that France without *grandeur* (greatness) was a contradiction in terms. Hence France's constant striving to hold its own among the world's great powers. From the start, this implied a strong foreign intelligence capacity, which severely strained the limited resources of an intelligence apparatus traditionally geared to the defence of France's internal security. Despite spectacular coups such as the recruitment of a KGB colonel (code name: Farewell) as a source,[11] France had to limit its foreign intelligence operations to its former colonies, particularly in Africa. Even today, meeting the often competing demands of internal and external security is a challenge that stretches the assets of the French intelligence community to their breaking point.

The Apparatus

To describe the French security and intelligence apparatus is a challenging task. All French SIS were created by government decree and there is consequently no enabling legislation spelling out their mandate and their powers. Furthermore, beside the five official SIS there are large police organisations such as the French *Gendarmerie* and other agencies such as the Customs service or the *Police aux frontières* (PAF) that have developed an intelligence capacity about which little is known. Every division (*légion*) of the *Gendarmerie* has its own intelligence unit.[12] But most importantly, there have been clandestine units created by the executive to spy illegally on French citizens under the umbrella of national security. The infamous '*cellule de l'Elysée*' (Elysée cell), which operated out of the French presidential palace during the tenure of François Mitterrand and engaged in large-scale wiretapping, is the best known case of such secret surveillance operations.

   We shall describe the officially existing agencies, giving whenever possible information about their personnel and budget, the number of the decree creating them and their mandate. Most of this information is based on a report advocating parliamentary control over the French intelligence community that was prepared by a French MP and presented to the parliament.[13] It is the most recent and reliable source of information that we have on the French SIS apparatus. According to Paecht,[14] the French intelligence community (the five official services and the intelligence unit of the customs service) numbers some *12,779 government employees.*

   There are two intelligence agencies that operate in theory under the authority of the *Ministère de l'Intérieur* (Interior Minister).

Direction Centrale des Renseignements Généraux (DCRG: General Police Intelligence)

The DCRG is part of the French national police (DGPN). According to Berlière,[15] the clause *renseignements généraux* was first officially used between 1907 and 1913 under the French Third republic to refer to police units who were to restrict themselves to intelligence gathering (*police d'observation*) as opposed to launching attacks against the internal enemies of the state as they previously did (*police d'attaque*). The forerunners of the DCRG were then the railroad police (*police spéciale des chemins de fer*, who circulated over the whole French territory except Paris) and the intelligence brigades (*brigades de recherche*) of the Paris police administration (*Préfecture de police*). Of all French police agencies it is the most mythologised, having been accused by French right-wing extremists of spearheading various 'Masonic' and 'Jewish' plots under the Third republic.[16] Its reputation for being involved in all shades of dirty tricks (*basses oeuvres*) goes back to the beginning of the 1900s.

Its personnel now number some 3,200 police; its budget is not known with any degree of precision. Its legal base is formed by decree 85–1057 (2 October 1985, with numerous amendments), which defines its mandate thus:

> The DCRG is charged with the collection and centralisation of intelligence intended for the information of the Government; it participates in the defence of the fundamental interests of the state; it contributes to the general internal security mission. It is charged with the surveillance of gambling establishments and racecourses.

The 'fundamental' interests of France to whom the decree refers are enumerated in Section 410–1 of the new French penal code (*Code Pénal*), which has been in force since 1994. They include: France's independence, the integrity of its territory, its security, the republican form of its institutions, its means of defence and of diplomacy, the protection of its population in France and in foreign countries, the environment and essential elements of its scientific and economic potential and of its cultural heritage. We purposely began our description of the French SIS with the DCRG because we wanted to show the continuity between the historical roots of the French police and its present activities in respect of the scope of its intelligence mandate. Inasmuch as the DCRG informs the French government on all topics relevant to its fundamental interests as they are stated in Section 410–1 of the penal code, there is in fact no sphere of activity that could possibly be excluded from its intelligence-gathering mission. When Brodeur interviewed one director of the DCRG during the 1980s, the latter described the work of the service that he headed as 'general journalism on behalf of the state' (the forerunners of the DCRG during the Third Republic engaged in what was then called 'political meteorology'[17]). In view of the all-embracing nature of the DCRG's mandate as it is specified in decree 85–1057, this description still applies (with possible reservations as to the meaning of 'journalism'). Of all the French SIS, the DCRG enjoys the poorest reputation in public opinion and is believed to be responsible for the most serious abuses, including the death of a homosexual clergyman suspected of being a paedophile. The status of the DCRG agent is akin to that of uniformed police patrolmen: patrolmen are on the frontline and their duties are so diverse that they defy definition; consequently they are also the most likely to be in judicial and deontological trouble (and in fact most public complaints involve police in uniform). Likewise, the agents of the DCRG are the footmen of French intelligence. As we have seen, there is no sphere of activity falling outside their surveillance, which ranges from fixed horse racing to the explosive question of the financing of the French political parties. Between those extremes, occasions for corruption and abuse of power are multiple. Furthermore, the DCRG is deployed over the entire French territory, exposing its members to petty local political pressure. When Brodeur interviewed a head of the DCRG, he was told that in a provincial town his agents were required by a political boss to keep tabs on what time political opponents returned home from the restaurant on Christmas night and what state of inebriety they were in.

Direction de la Surveillance du Territoire (DST: Internal Security)

The DST is also part of the national police (DGPN). However, it enjoys a special status within the DGPN and directly reports to its political authorities. Its personnel number some 1,500 police. As in the preceding case, the information on its budget is limited: it was assessed to have been some 73 million US dollars in 1995.[18] The DST was created in 1982 by government decree 82–1100 (22 December 1982). The DST is basically charged with protecting France's internal security against foreign threats such as espionage and terrorism. It is involved in counter-terrorism in general, whether the source of the terrorist violence is foreign or domestic, since in practice this aspect of the problem often remains ambiguous.

There are three intelligence services under the formal authority of the French *ministère de la Défense* (department of defence).

Direction Générale de la Sécurité Extérieure (DGSE: Foreign Intelligence Service) The DGSE replaced the *Service de Documentation Extérieure et de Contre-Espionnage* (SDECE, known as 'the swimming pool') in 1982, which reported directly to the Prime Minister. It is officially nested within the Department of Defence, but it still answers directly to the Prime Minister's office. Its personnel number 4,100 and its projected budget for year 2000 was 310 million US dollars. In terms of personnel and budget, the DGSE is the most important component of the French intelligence and security apparatus. It was created in 1982 by decree 82–306 (2 April 1982) but started to operate only in 1984. Its mandate is basically to gather intelligence outside of France (espionage) and to counter foreign spies at their home base. As one of its former director, Admiral Pierre Lacoste, acknowledged, the DGSE may also pursue investigations within France.[19]

Direction du Renseignement Militaire (DRM: Military Intelligence Directorate). The DRM was created in 1992 by decree 92–523 (16 June 1992) and is the latest addition to the French intelligence community. It numbers 1,709 personnel and its projected year 2000 budget is 7,2 million US dollars for operations and 9,2 million for infrastructure. Its mandate is to collect signals intelligence (SIGINT) for the French military and is analogous to the US National Security Agency (NSA), the British Government Communications Headquarters (GCHQ) and the Canadian Communications Security Establishment (CSE). However, compared to the latter agencies it operates on a shoestring budget.

Direction de la Protection et de la Sécurité de la Défense (DSPD: Internal Security of the Department of Defence). This agency replaced the Military Security in 1981 (decree 81–1041, 20 November 1981). It is staffed by 1,620 military personnel, with a budget of 12,6 million US dollars. As its name indicates, it is responsible for security within the military and the Department of Defence.

We should mention very briefly the intelligence unit that is under the authority of the French *Department of Economy, Finance and Industry*. It was created in 1988 and its role was enhanced by a 1998 ordinance (17 August 1998). It is part of the customs agency and it collects and processes intelligence for 'strategic' purposes; it is also responsible for the development of a large database (the *Fichier national informatisé de documentation*). The investigation unit of the customs department is manned by 650 persons (including the intelligence unit).

The co-ordination of these various services is under the authority of the *Comité Interministériel du Renseignement* (CIR: the Interministerial

Committee for Intelligence) and of its secretary (the *Secrétaire Général de la Défence Nationale*: SGDN). The Prime Minister chairs the committee and its members are the ministers of Defence, the Interior, Foreign Affairs, the minister of Economy, Finance and Industry, the minister of Research, the minister of Overseas Affairs and Cupertino. The President of the Republic is also represented by two officials. The CIR meets approximately twice a year to discuss intelligence priorities and was rather inactive from 1962 to 1989, when it was allegedly revived by Mr. Pautrat, an energetic prefect. In addition, a subcommittee of Cabinet directors from the above ministries and of heads of the various intelligence services meets more frequently.[20] Whether or not the French intelligence security apparatus is efficiently co-ordinated is a controversial issue in France. Most insiders and external observers seem to believe that co-ordination is far from being optimal and that a fair share of conflict between the various agencies still persists.[21]

It is interesting to note that it was far less difficult for MP Paecht to get specific figures on personnel and manpower from the French Department of Defence than from the Ministry of the Interior, that is responsible for the police. This points to a difference between the organisational culture of the two main corps comprising the French intelligence establishment. The military culture is rigid and very sensitive to rank, whereas the police culture is imbued with the discretionary exercise of power and therefore closer than the military to the slickness of the civilian politicians' ethos. The French military tend to be suspicious of the cloak and dagger world of intelligence. This suspicion was exacerbated when President Mitterrand appointed an admiral, Paul Lacoste, as the head of the DGSE in 1982. Under orders from the President and the Minister of Defence, Admiral Lacoste had a DGSE team sent to New Zealand to destroy the Greenpeace ship *Rainbow Warrior*, which was used to hinder French nuclear testing in this part of the world. When the whole affair was disclosed by Edwy Plenel, a French journalist, Admiral Lacoste was left alone by his political masters to face the scandal.

The tensions between the police and the military feed into what is referred to in France as the 'war' between the various policing organisations. This war is believed to be particularly acute in the field of security and intelligence where, it has been argued, it is deliberately fostered by the political authorities.[22] Undeniably, the competition between the various agencies is often fierce. However, it must be stressed that France is not unique in this regard and that police in contact tend everywhere to be police in conflict. There is a rather simple explanation for this, at least in the field of intelligence. Granting that knowledge is power, agencies that specialise in the search for information will tend to accumulate this power rather than to share it.

Accountability and Control

Strictly speaking, the concepts of accountability and control are distinct but they complement each other. Accountability is an information process whereby an agency is under a legal obligation to answer truly and completely the questions put to it by an authority to which it is accountable. Control, on the other hand, refers to the measures – systemic reforms and individual sanctions – taken on the basis of the information provided by an agency. For the sake of brevity, we shall conflate these two complementary notions and refer to them under the single heading of control. However, it should be pointed out that there is a crucial aspect of accountability that must be considered as part and parcel of the notion of control: true accountability is directed to an *external* authority. Being accountable only to oneself is being accountable to no one. Therefore, SIS which are only accountable to the executive branch of government are not truly accountable since the relationship between the state and the police apparatus is not external, the police in France being a form of governance. That being said, we will address three issues: what control is not, what it should be and whether or not the French SIS are under control.

What Control is Not

The issue that we are addressing here is basically normative. We are not simply asking, what is the nature of control in the context of the French SIS, but rather: what are the prerequisites for a type of control which would prevent the SIS from infringing civil rights? Hence we begin by reviewing types of control that are effectively exercised but that in fact provide no guarantee for the respect of civil rights.

Control If control means compelling others to act in a certain way and then checking if and to what extent they have followed orders, then the French SIS actually suffer from an *excess* of control. Political authorities do use the SIS to fulfil their ends and to this extent are at least partially controlling them. Furthermore, the French bureaucratic tradition implies that the high-ranking officers within an organisation weigh heavily on their subordinates. However, not only are none of these controls favourable to the respect of civil rights, they are actually detrimental to it, as demonstrated by the numerous scandals afflicting the French intelligence establishment.

Control in conflict It might be retorted that the view just presented is too simplistic and that there is no single, prevailing source of control but really several competing ones. The multiplication of the sources of control may maximise the mathematical amount of control, but conflicting controls may actually neutralise each other. Finally, it is far from evident how conflicts between the SIS hierarchy and their political masters could in any way be beneficial to civil rights.

Secret control Whatever may be the variety of controls exercised upon the French SIS, they share a basic feature: they are all exercised under the tutelage of state secrecy. Notwithstanding the fact that secrecy may be used to cover-up abuses perpetrated on behalf of the state, it is also incompatible with civil rights, for it deprives citizens of their fundamental right to know under what circumstances they may be put in harm's way by the state.

What Control Should Be

Control exercised in order to safeguard civil rights should be *legally based, independent of external interference, effective* and *democratic*. These features, which are not exhaustive, should be obvious and need no justification. Their meaning will be explained below in our discussion of whether control over the SIS, as it now exercised in France, exhibits these features.

Legal base This factor underlies all others. Yet, not only is there no legislation providing for direct external control of the SIS, but there is no enabling legislation for any of these agencies. They were all created by government decree. This is a fundamental and crippling factor for any external form of control. The decrees do provide a juridical base for the SIS, but this base is overextended, as for instance is the case of the mandate of the DCRG (general police intelligence), and its definition was never the object of a public debate.

Independence This is a very controversial question in France. According to one position, the officials of the two existing controlling bodies are appointed by the executive and thus enjoy a small degree of independence. According to the opposite point of view these officials are either chosen or elected by independent bodies such as the French *Cour de Cassation* (High

Court) and the government has no alternative but to formally confirm their choice. There is presently no clear-cut way to decide the issue. One's conclusion about the independence of the controlling bodies is directly related to one's assumptions about the direction of the flow of power within the French political structure.[23] Still, after the regal presidency of de Gaulle and of Mitterrand, a strong case can be made to the effect that the French pyramid of political power hangs from its top instead of resting on its base.

Effectiveness As previously explained, there is no body in France that is solely devoted to the control of the SIS. No SIS has an inspector such as the Australian inspector general of the domestic security service, who reports to Parliament, and none is overseen by a watchdog committee like the Canadian Security and Intelligence Review Committee. However, there are two administrative commissions that play an indirect part in controlling the SIS.

First, the *Commission Nationale de l'Informatique et des Libertés* (CNIL: commission on computerisation and liberties) was created by law No. 78–17 (6 January 1978). The commission is composed of 17 members, appointed for 5 years. They belong to the Parliament, the judiciary, various state councils or they are appointed on the basis of their known competence in the field covered by the CNIL's mandate. Three members of the commission are directly appointed by the ministers in council. Furthermore, according to section 9 of the CNIL act, a government commissioner appointed by the Prime Minister sits on the CNIL and can compel it to reconsider a decision through a second deliberation within ten days of the first deliberation, thus putting a check on the Commission's independence. The CNIL's mandate is to control the applications of computerisation to the State's nominal data banks: it keeps an inventory of existing databases and insures that their content is not in violation of civil liberties (the right to privacy). It has a limited regulatory power and also acts as an access to the information commission, and in this regard processes citizens' complaints. The CNIL reports every year to the President of the Republic and to Parliament. Covering the whole field of the State's databases, the CNIL consequently also exercises its jurisdiction over the SIS databases. In describing its mission on its website, the CNIL explicitly mentions its role in respect to the DCRG databases. The commission operates under the strict rules of secrecy that prevail within the French government and its power of public disclosure is thus very limited. Also, it cannot change the security classification level ('confidential', 'secret', or 'top secret') of any item of information. According to section

413–9 of the new penal code, the level of classification is determined by a decree from the State Council (*Conseil d'Etat*).

Second, the *Commission Nationale du Contrôle des Interceptions de Sécurité* (CNCIS: wiretapping) oversees three kinds of wiretaps in France. There are wiretaps authorised by the judiciary, that is the *juges d'instruction.* These magistrates are charged with heading criminal investigations (the closest approximation would be a US District attorney responsible for a particular investigation or, more to the point, an Italian judge fighting terrorism or the Mafia). A *juge d'instruction* may order wiretaps in the context of investigations for which he or she is responsible and so cannot be said to be an impartial authority. Judicially authorised wiretaps are said to be the most excessive in their number. According to a 1995 report by the French *Conseil d'Etat*, these magistrates authorised some 10,000 wiretaps during the previous year.[24] In addition, there are administrative wiretaps (*écoutes administratives*). In France, the departments of Defence and of the Interior and the Customs service are awarded a quota of *telephone land lines* which they can *simultaneously* tap in the course of one year (in 1997, 330 lines were available for Defence, 1,190 for the Interior and 20 for Customs; one line can be used for several successive wiretaps in the course of one year. There were over 4,500 wiretaps authorised for year 1995 and 1996).[25] Finally, there are what are called in France 'wild wiretaps' (*écoutes sauvages*), essentially unauthorised and extra-legal wiretaps conducted by government units under the authority of the executive. Created in 1991, the CNCIS is the authority controlling all *administrative wiretaps*, including electronic surveillance conducted by the SIS. Its chairperson is appointed by the President of the Republic upon a recommendation from the High Court and the State Council. In 1996, it authorised 4,623 applications from the various police services (1,756 in respect to terrorism, 1,320 in respect to organised crime, 1,241 in respect to national security, 297 in respect to economic intelligence and 43 in respect to subversive groups) and refused only 26. Since the CNCIS only provides aggregate figures on electronic surveillance without specifying which service had recourse to what number of wiretaps, it makes international comparisons with other SIS impossible. Like the CNIL, it operates under the state secrecy constraints and is helpless with regard to state authorised 'wild' interceptions of communications.

Democratic character SIS which are democratically controlled are accountable to the people and their elected representatives. Thus, democratic control implies a certain amount of *public* transparency and it also implies *parliamentary* control. Both these features of democratic control are completely lacking in France. All operations of the SIS are covered by unimpeachable state secrecy and, occasional revelations brought about by investigative journalism or media leaks excepted, very little information on the activities of the French SIS ever reaches the public. As for parliamentary control, it is presently non-existent. MP Arthur Paecht presented a well-informed report to the French Parliament on this topic in 1999.[26] It reviewed parliamentary control in Austria, Canada, Germany, Italy, the UK and the US and presented recommendations for the development of a framework of parliamentary control in France. The French intelligence community negatively received the report and its proposals now seem to have been shelved.

In sum, the control of the French SIS is not firmly grounded in law; while conclusions about its actual degree of independence vary, most observers agree that the French traditions in government run counter to the principle of independence from the executive; the control is severely limited in its effectiveness, no independent body having a specific mandate to control any of the SIS; finally, inasmuch as democratic control implies public openness and also accountability to Parliament, it must be concluded that there presently is little of it in France. That the traditions of the present Fifth Republic hinder the functioning of democracy in respect to the SIS has recently been explicitly recognised by ex-Minister of Defence and of the Interior, Paul Quilès.[27]

SIS Abuses

There is overwhelming public evidence that the French SIS are responsible for seriously abusing their power. For example, the responsibility of the DGSE for bombing and sinking the *Rainbow Warrior* was established beyond doubt by a series of articles published in the French daily *Le Monde* by Edwy Plenel and Bertrand Legendre in September 1985. Two members of the DGSE's action service were even tried and sentenced to prison in New Zealand. No less than eight books on the affair were published in the three years following the affair.[28]

On the basis of the many scandals that have plagued the French SIS since the 1965 Ben Barka case, it can be asserted that grave violations of civil rights were indeed committed. However, it is much more difficult to go beyond the individual cases of wrongdoing in order to assess the extent or the depth of the deviant practices exemplified in each particular scandal. In countries like the US or Canada, there is a tradition of appointing independent boards of inquiry to hold public hearings and to examine whether the acts of wrongdoing alleged in a particular context form an isolated case or are just the tip of an iceberg of submerged practices of the same type. No such public boards of inquiry are ever appointed in France. In the rare case where a commission is appointed, its report is not made public and its recommendations not followed. For instance, the Mauroy socialist government appointed in 1981 Robert Schmelk, a judge from the High Court, to chair a commission of nine members chosen from Parliament and the legal establishment. Its terms of reference were to study the interception of private communications through wiretaps. The Commission submitted its competent report in 1982; it was immediately classified as 'confidential-defence' and vanished from the public sphere until it was gradually leaked in the press.[29]

From April 1985 to March 1986, journalist Edwy Plenel was the target of systematic electronic surveillance conducted by a group of irregulars operating from the presidential palace and whose chief was publicly commended by President Mitterrand himself. Plenel took his case to court and, with the assistance of his lawyers, used the legal proceedings to gain access to a portion of the documents produced by this rogue outfit. Plenel wrote a book about what he found, providing valuable insights into the scope of the operations conducted by this group, who came to be known as the *Elysée cell* (Plenel, 1997). Elected President in 1982, François Mitterrand was, according to Plenel a man obsessed by secrecy: he had fathered an illegitimate daughter whom he saw regularly and he wanted to keep his health condition from the public (he had prostate cancer, from which he eventually died). Mitterrand surrounded himself with a praetorian guard recruited from the DGSE – the *Groupe d'Action Mixte* (GAM) – and the French Gendarmerie – the *Groupe de Sécurité de la Présidence de la République* (GSPR) – who also used the *Groupe d'Intervention de la Gendarmerie Nationale* (GIGN) as a reserve force. This protection force numbered some 161 men.[30] To this force was added the *Elysée cell* itself, an intelligence unit specialising in wiretapping. Its core consisted of five military from the *Gendarmerie* and six civilian police, plus 4 secretaries. The cell had devised codes for its 300 targets. Its computerised database (code name 'TPH') contained 1,022 nominal files.[31] The cell had two main targets, Edwy Plenel from *Le Monde* and a writer named Jean-Edern Hallier, who published a magazine called *L'Idiot international*. Both were the objects of elaborate surveillance operations. The wiretapping of all of Plenel's telephone lines resulted in the writing of some 650 reports of private communication interceptions (*everything* that concerned Plenel, including a passing illness of his wife, was recorded). The surveillance of Hallier produced some 800 nominal files. The list of the cell's 'subjects' reads in this case like the who's who of the French political and cultural elite: one former president (Giscard d'Estaing), one future president and former Prime minister (Jacques Chirac), one future Socialist Prime minister (Laurent Fabius), one future Minister of the Interior and right-wing strongman (Charles Pasqua). The list is endless, as everyone receiving telephone calls from Hallier was put on file.

The wide-ranging character of this operation is indisputable. Nor can it be denied that it was extra-legal and based on the sole authority of the presidency. But there is a further question that can be raised: how much were its targets actually harmed by it? After all, most of them enjoyed an apparently undisturbed career. One of its prime targets, Edwy Plenel, is presently the chief editor of the prestigious daily *Le Monde*. This question, which is far from being rhetorical, is very difficult to answer for it implies exploring a complex set of emotions, like anger, embarrassment and even shame. Plenelís book makes it clear that he was psychologically scarred by the whole ordeal. Furthermore, as he himself notes, he was lucky to live a fairly quiet life that offered few hooks for blackmail. But what about all the others whose conversations were also intercepted and have remained silent?[32] Whatever may be the cases of individual damage, the damage inflicted upon the institutions and particularly upon the intelligence community was significant. Generally speaking, the legitimacy of the French SIS has been steadily undermined by the succession of scandals.

There is finally one shady aspect of the SIS activities which has been the object of persistent public allegations but is difficult to document. It is the involvement of members of various SIS in cases of corruption. For instance, the installation in 1987 of recently legalised slot machines in various casinos generated the payment of illegal commissions to political authorities which agents from the DCRG section in Marseille not only ignored, but were rumoured to have profited from. The institutional involvement of the DCRG in the surveillance of gambling activities makes it vulnerable to accusations of corruption as gambling is, in France as anywhere else, infiltrated by organised crime. The best known case involving financial corruption is the notorious case of the *avions renifleurs* (literally: sniffer airplanes).[33] In 1967, General de Gaulle prompted the creation of a national company – *Entreprise de Recherches et d'Activités Pétrolières* (ERAP), which became the petroleum company presently known as Elf-Aquitaine – that was to secure France's energy independence by prospecting for and exploiting oil resources at home and abroad. Early on ERAP was tied to the French foreign intelligence service (then known as the SDECE and later the DGSE) in order to promote French interests in Africa, economics just being another way of doing politics. Between 1976 and 1978, ERAP (now Elf-Aquitaine) spent some 145 million US dollars to test a revolutionary prospecting technology that was basically a complete hoax. Instead of the conventional methods of detection and drilling, the company was persuaded that radar-like equipment could be installed inside a commercial plane that could then 'sniff out' unexploited oil fields from the air. As it turns out, the hoax brought little profit to the 'inventors' of the new technology, one of who eventually went bankrupt. In fact, most of the money was diverted to Swiss accounts in what appears to have been an elaborate swindling operation whose real beneficiaries were never identified with certainty, since there was no police investigation of the case.[34] Two ex-members of the SDECE, who were well connected with former colleagues from the service now working in the private security unit of Elf-Aquitaine, served as intermediaries between the French petroleum company and the members of the improvised consortium that attempted to sell them the counterfeit technology. These two persons had actually been expelled from the SDECE and Elf-Aquitaine, whose behaviour in this whole affair is highly suspicious, never bothered to check their credentials. It would be a mistake to discard this whole affair as too outlandish to be significant. It raises the whole issue of the connection between the SIS (national security) and national interest within the global economy. Is it, for example, unreasonable to hypothesise that there may be connections between US petroleum companies and the US intelligence and security apparatus in the Middle-East? We believe not, particularly in view of the multiplication of revelations about the ECHELON surveillance project in Europe, which is in great part run by the US NSA.

Future Trends

The future trends in respect to the French SIS do not differ to any significant extent from what they are in other countries, with one exception. This has to do with the French state tradition of secrecy, which weighs more heavily in that country than in other democracies. The French *Conseil d'État* recommended in 1995 that an independent mechanism be created to regulate the use of the stamp of state secrecy, which is abused in France in order to cover up deviance from agents of the state. In March 1998, the French government created a national commission to control the classification of government information as falling or not under the blanket of state secrecy (*Secret défense*). This was a hopeful start but it is still premature to assess the results of this very recent policy. But at this point a close examination of the legal texts creating the Commission already reveals that it is going to be chaired by the head of the CNCIS, who also oversees administrative wiretaps. This concentration of power in the hands of a single commissioner, who already has his hands full with the regulation of electronic surveillance, was a bad omen for the diligence of this new body and for its independence. Up until 1999, a single individual, *conseiller d'état* D. Mandelkern, did hold both positions. They are held by two different persons now.

Other trends are common to the SIS of other countries as well. First, the overlapping between political and common criminal investigations is wider in France, where it always was a constituent part of policing, than in other democratic countries where it is in its incipient stages. As was stressed above, the *Renseignements Généraux* (DCRG) were from the beginning involved both in political policing and in criminal investigations. The much-publicised fight against Corsican secessionist terrorism is a telling example of the intertwining of politically motivated delinquency with organised crime.

The second trend is the rush for so-called 'economic intelligence' which is partly a euphemism for the time-honoured craft of industrial espionage. In the post-Cold War world, France and Japan are considered by their Anglo-Saxon allies as predators searching for technological knowledge. Without surprise, the view from France is exactly the opposite. It feels that its industrial secrets are at risk of being stolen by competitors and that it is not aggressive enough in the global fight for technological know-how. For instance France, like the other countries of Continental Europe, is extremely critical of the ECHELON program of electronic surveillance, which is run jointly by the UK and the US.

The last trend is less a trend in itself than a problem that must be solved by the French SIS: how will they adapt to the global economy of knowledge, which is bound to impact on policing and, some say, will transform it. At first sight, it would seem that a police culture that is characterised by 'high policing' would have a distinct advantage in adapting to the knowledge economy. Without disputing this claim, we wish to mention three problems. First, there is a crucial difference between knowledge and intelligence. What is called 'knowledge' in a scientific culture is shared information that was validated by a community of peers. Furthermore, it is frequently asserted that the exponential growth of knowledge during the 20th century was in part due to the public character of most of it (with the exception of military technology): a whole research community has more chances to solve a problem than an isolated team. In contrast, the cult of secrecy that prevails in the intelligence community – and most notably in France – hinders both the validations of intelligence and its growth in quantity and in quality. Second, recent police theorists argue that the police and the SIS will increasingly act as a clearing house for intelligence, thus dispatching relevant information to external organisations and private enterprise, which will possibly reciprocate.[35] However, the ghetto mentality that prevails in the French intelligence community has not prepared it for this development. Lastly, much remains to be done in the mastery of the new technologies of intelligence and particularly in computer science and in the quality control of the intelligence product. Péan quotes two entries (*blancs*) from the DCRG files.[36] Reading them, one cannot help but get a strong impression that an undergraduate student working from open sources could undoubtedly have done as well, if not better. It is to be hoped that the quality of intelligence, which is not a problem specific to the French, has since then made a great leap forward.

Notes

[1] Joubert and Bevers (1996), p. 536.

[2] Berlière (1994); Dewerpe (1994); L'Heuillet (1997); Warusfel (2000). Dewerpe (1994) is typical of this kind of work. The title of his book is *L'espion* (the spy) and its subtitle is: "an historical anthropology of state secrecy". It aims to provide an epistemology of the discourse of the SIS. This work is theoretically challenging but has limited bearing on the present juncture of security intelligence. Other studies such as Warusfel (2000) are much closer to the present trends and developments in the French intelligence community and are necessary readings for anyone trying to assess the current situation.

[3] Beau (1989); Barril (1984); Bonnet (2000); Burdan (1990); Commissaire Diamant (1993); Lacoste (1997); Le Roy-Finville (1980); Marion (1991); Melnik (1988); Ockrent et Marenches (1986); Rougelet (2000).

[4] Faligot et Krop (1985); Calvi et Schmitt (1988); Guisnel et Violet (1988); Harstrich et Calvi (1991); Lenoir (1992) and (1998).

[5] For example, the French police are viewed today as a prime example of a centralised apparatus, since there are only two police forces in France, the *Police Nationale* and the *Gendarmerie*. What is little known outside France is that this centralisation which resulted in the abolition of the municipal police forces only occurred in 1941 under the Vichy government.

[6] Quoted in and translated by Brodeur (1983); our emphasis. For a full quotation and commentary, see Brodeur (1983).

[7] Quoted in Radzinowicz (1956) p. 555.

[8] Foucault (1994), p. 721. Interestingly enough, Foucault quotes a very similar definition of policing, which originates from German 18th century's *Polizeiwissenchaften* (police science). The true opposition may not be between the French and the British concept of policing but between the views held on the Continent and in the British Isles.

[9] Quoted in Radzinowicz (1956), p. 566, our emphasis.

[10] Foucault (1994), p. 720.

[11] Bonnet (2000).

[12] Paecht (1999), p. 16.

[13] Paecht (1999).

14 (1999), p. 15.
15 (1994), pp 196–198 and 218, note 11.
16 Berlière (1994), pp 198–99 and 218, note 14.
17 Berlière (1994), p. 197.
18 Paecht (1999), p. 16.
19 Bouchet et al. (1997), p. 149.
20 Renouard (1997).
21 Warusfel (2000).
22 Porsch (1995).
23 On this debate, see Bouchet et al. (1997).
24 France, *Conseil d'État*, 1995, p. 79.
25 CNCIS (1996); Bouchet et al. (1997), p. 144. These figures can be compared to the number of wiretaps in Canada, a country that has approximately half the population of France. All authorisations for wiretaps are granted by the judiciary in Canada. According to yearly official reports released by the Canadian Solicitor General, there were from 1974 to 1998 some 14,304 wiretaps authorised in the course of criminal investigations, this number including both renewals and new authorisations. For this period, the number of yearly authorisations varied between a maximum of 325 and a minimum of 149. From 1976 to 1999, 4,335 additional authorisations were granted to the Canadian SIS, this number including again both renewals and new authorisations (yearly maximum: 247 and yearly minimum: 78). By comparison, there were some 10,000 judicially authorised wiretaps in France in 1994 and the CNCIS authorised over 4,500 wiretaps in 1995 and 1996. Granting that the number of judicial authorisations was similar in 1995 and 1996 to 1994. There are at the present time over 14,500 wiretaps judicially and administratively authorised in France each year. This is 25 times more than the yearly total in Canada, when the maximum yearly figure is chosen (572 authorisations). There is in one year more wiretaps in France than there were in Canada from 1974 to 1998 for the purposes of criminal investigations. It must be added that according to a 1986 study of the Law Reform Commission of Canada, Canada used electronic surveillance of its citizens proportionately 20 times more than the US. This proportion may now have changed, but the fact remains that Canada does not use wiretapping moderately. Canadian parsimony in the use of electronic surveillance cannot then be the explanation for the huge discrepancy between France and Canada.
26 Paecht (1999).
27 Quilès, (2000), p. 49.
28 Derogy et Pontaut (1986); Du Morne Vert (1987); Dyson (1986); King (1986); Lecomte (1985); Luccioni (1986); Maniguet (1986); Sears and Gidley (1986).
29 Guisnel and Violet (1988), p. 269–273.
30 Plenel (1997), p. 25.
31 Plenel (1997), p. 192.
32 Plenel (1997), p. 305.
33 See Péan (1984) and for a more recent and extensive discussion, see Lascoumes (1997).
34 On the white-collar crime aspects of this scandal, see Lascoumes (1997).
35 Ericson and Haggerty (1997); Dorn (1998).
36 Péan (1986), annexe 4.

Chapter 3

Intelligence Services in Belgium: A Story of Legitimation and Legalisation

Lode van Outrive

Introduction

1998 was a historic year for the intelligence services in Belgium. After one and a half centuries the two services, the civil and the military, were legalised and legitimated. Several other laws with direct or indirect influence on the functioning of the services were voted during the same year. However, to really understand these events we first have to look at the historical evolution.

General Historical Background

The *Sûreté de l'Etat* (State Intelligence Service) was an inheritance from the time of the French and the Dutch occupation (1794–1830). A provisional Government proclaimed the foundation of Belgium on 26 September 1830. A National Congress was installed on 4 October and it had to draw up a Constitution, which was voted on 7 February 1831. On 15 October 1830 the provisional Government nominated five *Administrateurs-Généraux* and one of them became the General Administrator of the *Sûreté Publique*. A Governmental Decree of 16 October allowed him extensive power over general police, prisons and borstals, passports, mail censorship, public transport, except for mail delivery, as well as controlling theatres and insanitary factories.[1] A Royal Decree of 9 January 1832 'reduced' his competence to 'the surveillance of the execution of the laws and the provisions on the general police'. This permitted him to have access to all the authorities and to requisition of all the other police services for the execution of his mission, and also to control in a very arbitrary way the foreigners staying in Belgium. In fact his power was rather enlarged and remained very discretionary.

The Constitution did not provide for the creation of a State intelligence apparatus. In 1884 some parliamentarians denounced the illegality of the earlier Royal Decree: a law had to define the special mandate of a higher civil servant. The Minister of Justice then argued that the Parliament already voted on a budget for the public intelligence service on thirty-five occasions.[2] Hence, during the debate in the National Congress in January 1831 there was no mention of a parliamentary control of the service, only of the control on the General Administrator by one or other minister, a member of the executive power. However, from time to time and already in 1834 and 1839, some ministers and parliamentarians were asking to legislate about the intelligence service. The reaction of the General Administrator was: 'Do not do it, in the end the service will be given the mandate it already has.'[3] Meanwhile, in the course of the first years after 1830, the head of the service introduced several successive proposals to enlarge his competencies. The aim was to get the same mandate for its agents as the judicial police officers, so that they could make judicial investigations and arrest people, of course always under the control of a inquiry magistrate like it is granted in the Napoleonic continental system of administration of penal justice. He did not succeed.[4] It may be said that in this first period the intelligence service was an instrument of a liberal-conservative and catholic bourgeois regime, concerned only with the consolidation of the new Belgian State.[5]

The *Sûreté de l'Armée* (Military Intelligence Service) was founded by Royal Decree on 1 April 1915, ergo during World War One. The commissioners, inspectors and agents received the same mandate as the judicial police officers. The agents of the State intelligence services were not given this competence. On 16 October 1916 the new military intelligence became a *Service Militaire de Sûreté*, divided into two sections: 'the military intelligence service' and 'the intelligence service of the army on the battlefield'. The service was formally dissolved on 30 September 1919, but in fact survived within the general staff of the Belgian Army. In December 1919 the service received the task of 'counter-espionage in all its forms and the surveillance of subversive groups within the army'.

Just before World War Two, on 8 March 1940, the two intelligence services, the civil and the military, were transferred to the Army and to the Ministry of War. On 20 July 1946 the two services were split up again with the military service maintained as a part of the General Staff of the Army, now with three sections: 'Military Intelligence'; 'Military Counter-espionage'; 'Analysis and Exploitation of the reports of the military attachés in foreign countries'. The agents could no longer act as the judicial police officers – they lost this mandate. Since 1964 the service has been called *Service Général de Renseignements et de la Securité (SGR).*[6]

Finally, on 5 June 1990, after a report from a Parliamentary Inquiry Commission on the fight against crime and terrorism – which was very critical of the functioning of the intelligence services – the centre-leftist government decided on a political program of order maintenance, security and the fight against crime in the *'Plan de la Pentecôte'* (Plan of Pentecost). This plan also included a reorganisation of the intelligence services and an intention to legislate. It took nearly nine years to realise the project. On 30 November 1998 Parliament voted a comprehensive law on the two services and finally gave them an explicit legal base. The real discussion of the Bill took place in the Senate and not in the House of the Representatives.

Even before this, a law from 18 July 1991 established a *Comité permanent de controle des services de police et de renseignements* (permanent controlling Committee on police and intelligence services) linked to Parliament. The one that interests us we call the 'Comité R' (R from *renseignement*: intelligence). Since 1993 the Comité R investigates the functioning of the intelligence services, at the request of ministers or of Parliament, or on its own initiative or even upon requests from private persons. After years of parliamentary discussion, a Law of 1 March 1999 seriously modified the one from 1991: the mandate of the Comité R was reduced, and control on the committee intensified.

Evolution of the Missions

Definition of the Missions

It is interesting to note the evolution of the mission between 1964 and 1998. In 1964, a General Director Administrator, Caeymaex, wrote a kind of general doctrine on the *Sûreté de l'Etat*. First of all he noted that it was not an institution but a function in which not only the intelligence agents and the police forces participate, but any civil servant. Security problems can occur in all areas of society.

Caeymaex distinguished four activities:

• the fight against internal subversion, effective or potential, of Belgian or foreign origin;
• counterespionage: a) to detect spies who collect military, political, economic, technical or scientific information, as well as persons

who plan sabotage in order to destabilise the State and b) finally to prevent any foreign interference in the Belgian decision making process;

- protection of important persons;
- control on political behaviour of foreigners staying on the Belgian territory.

It took a further fifteen years to have the missions of the military *SGR* defined in a Royal Decree of 19 December 1989:

- security: a) to formulate territorial security provisions for use by the armed forces who have the mission to protect the secrecy and b) to inspect and investigate buildings and investigate persons;
- intelligence: to collect any information of strategic, tactic, international importance;
- nuclear security: a) to control people working in the nuclear branch, b) to inquire into national and international traffic of nuclear materials, c) to physically protect nuclear equipment and d) to represent Belgium in the international inspectorate on non-proliferation.[7]

In 1994 the Comité R extensively described the three missions of the intelligence services, distinguishing two principal missions and some particular tasks.

Intelligence as a defensive activity The first task is to guarantee the confidentiality of some information, the security of documents, installations, equipment and the second to verify the reliability of persons who have access to the data. The conception of the military intelligence and control tasks ought to be limited to the military interests.

There is a difference between external and internal security. The former are the activities undertaken by Belgian agents working in foreign countries to protect the State sovereignty or its scientific, economic and military potential that could be in danger. Because of espionage aimed at clandestine exportation of goods, knowledge or information essential to the well-being of the State, but also because of interventions in order to influence decisions in favour of foreign interests and because of sabotage. External security also includes activities undertaken because of attempts to create unrest, aimed at destabilising or bringing down the national authorities; activities depending on military threats and activities caused by harm done to the Belgian interests in foreign countries. Internal security refers to 'subversion' (see below).

Intelligence as a preventive activity   Here the main task is the duty to inform government on activities that could endanger the security of the State. This involves two phases: a) collection and b) analysis of intelligence and also two aspects: a) administrative police and b) judicial police.

This preventive activity may only be related to threats to the structures or the organisation of the State. It does not involve a mandate of judicial police officer for the agents; the judicial police and the *parquets* (investigative magistrates) have to track down and prosecute all the crimes against the State security, enumerated in the Penal Code.

Intelligence means long term activity. Police forces participate in the same function, but in a more specific way and when a concrete event takes place. A clearer delimitation of tasks and more co-ordination between all the services and forces is needed.[8]

Additional intelligence distinctions are made:

- strategic intelligence: biographical, economic, sociological, political, technological, telecommunications intelligence to prepare national or international decisions (of the UN, NATO, WEO) or to support operations of military authorities;
- operational intelligence: military means, doctrine, armament, infrastructure, equipment and training for planning important military campaigns and operations;
- tactical intelligence: knowledge on all kinds of aspects of the military and paramilitary enemies, characteristics of the population, etc. which could help the military decision-makers in the field.[9]

Particular missions   This includes close protection, conservation of historical documentation of the army and issuing of weapon permits to foreigners. The Law of 30 November 1998[10] drew almost completely upon the analysis of the Comité R. In the commentary on the law we find large parts of the text of that Comité R. so we have only to mention the most important articles of the Law

The mission of the Sûreté de l'État is, first, to collect, analyse and handle intelligence in relation with every activity which threatens or could threaten the internal security of the State, the external security of the State, international relations, scientific or economic potential as defined by the ministerial Committee, or any other fundamental interest of the country, as defined by the King at the suggestion of the ministerial Committee. Second, it executes security inquiries along the guidelines of the ministerial Committee; third, it executes the tasks of close protection along the guidelines of the ministerial Committee; fourth, it executes any other mission commanded or provided by the law (art.7).

Caeymaex mentioned the mission of 'protection of important persons'. The Comité R does not mention it explicitly, but now it is a part of what is called 'close protection'. This seems to become an always more important mission. It means protection of very important people (VIP) or of certain special persons estimated to be in danger and who need special police protection.

Some opposition members in the Senate demanded that law should always lay down any new mission, because privacy could be in danger. Art.8 of the European Convention of Human Rights urges that these missions and the list of organisations and persons under security control should be published. Even the Parliament should be informed, because the citizens ought to know beforehand when their activities represent a danger to the State security. The Ministers of the Government replied that such a provision is not necessary and that even the European Court of Human Rights did not think it necessary that for example lists of organisations or persons under security control should be published.[11] To reply on to the former remark, in the Law many terms are defined, based on the 1994 Comité R report. The Law maintains the principle that the police forces can also do some intelligence work (art.14). During the discussion it was said that the difference is that the police forces collect information referring to specific situations of disorder.[12]

The mission of the Service Général du Reseignement et de la Sécurité is, first, to collect, analyse and handle intelligence in relation with every activity which threatens or could threaten the integrity of the national territory, military defence planning, accomplishment of the missions of the armed forces or the security of the Belgian citizens in foreign countries or any other interest of the country, as defined by the King at the proposition of the ministerial Committee, and to immediately inform the competent ministers; also when government asks for it, to advise them on the definition of the policy of defence. Second, it takes care of the military security of the military personnel, installations, weapons, ammunition, equipment, plans, writings, documents, computer systems and communication. Third, it protects secrecy in relation to the first two and, fourth, it executes security inquiries in line with the provisions of the Ministerial Committee (art.11§1).

In the course of the discussion some members of the Senate objected, in vain, that the missions of the military intelligence are similar to those noted during the period of the cold war and that one has to modernise the missions referring to international humanitarian and peace operations.[13] It is clear that a certain overlapping of the missions of the two services is not avoided.

Protection of Scientific or Economic Potential

This mission was mentioned already in 1964 by Caeymaex. In the 1995 and 1998 reports of the Comité R, this is said to become a more and more important, but also difficult, activity. However, neither the Government, nor the Parliament defined this task explicitly. Instead the Law of November 1998 allows the Ministerial Committee to exclusively define the matter. The Law just says *the scientific or economic potential: it is the safeguarding of the essential elements of the scientific or economic potential* (art. 8 4°). Of course, this is a real tautology, and the Comité R has proposed to set up a co-ordinating body, including those ministers and private companies most concerned.[14]

Subversion and Terrorism as Key Terms

Two key terms always came back in the discourses on security and intelligence: subversion and terrorism. In the June 1981 report of a Parliamentary Inquiry Commission on private militias and the police services, 'subversive organisations' were defined as those:

> ...which because of their fundamental aims, their action methods and their behaviour will bring down, destroy or change the structure of the legally established State or paralyse its functioning by illegal means...Groups which promote subversive ideas without using illegal means or which use illegal means without clearly promoting subversive ideas ought to be considered as potential subversive and merit the same attention.[15]

But in the same year the Minister of Justice, in charge of the civil intelligence service, defined subversive organisations as *each movement or group which tries to destroy the State or the structures of the State in an illegal way.* This definition is again larger.[16] 'Subversion' is associated with 'extremism': 'to collect intelligence on any possible threat against the legal democratic order, for example on extremist organisations which even operate during social agitation.'[17] In the Law of November 1998, the term 'subversion' is no longer maintained but replaced by that of 'extremism':

> racist, xenophobic, anarchist, nationalist, authoritarian or totalitarian conceptions or views, either with a political, ideological, confessional or philosophical character, in theory or practice contrary to the principles of democracy or of human rights, to the good functioning of the democratic institutions or other foundations of the State (*'l'Etat de droit'*, art.8 1°c).

With such a large definition one no longer needs the term 'subversion'.

A term, very often connected with subversion, is 'terrorism' or 'terrorist groups'. In the same 1981 report of Parliamentary Commission those terms are defined as 'an organisation of which the members are guilty of criminal activities or are suspected having committed or could commit such crimes in order to reach their political aims'. But the Commission never succeeded in knowing which specific organisations the intelligence services referred to. Some leaks in the press about the gendarmerie's list of subversive or terrorist organisations – all mixed up – revealed that organisations such as *OXFAM* or *Mouvement pour la Paix* as well as some trades unions were listed as such.[18]

In September 1984 a governmental definition of terrorism became even broader: to manifest sympathy was also suspect.[19] The Law of November 1998 defined terrorism more narrowly as 'the use of violence against persons or material interests for ideological or political reasons with the aim to reach the objectives by way of terror, intimidation or threats' (art.8 1°b).

Missions in Practice: The Targets of the Intelligence Services

The activities of the intelligence services always were a kind of a reaction to national events, but also in accordance with international trends, situations and even connections and influences.

The First Years After 1830

The main mission in these early years was to protect the Belgian National State against political refugees coming from France and Germany, republicans, socialists and anarchists, Saint-Simonists and Fourierists.

Before World War One

The mission now changed to focus on protection of the power base of the bourgeoisie. Because of an elitist voting system (*suffrage censitaire*) Parliament and the Government were truly bourgeois bodies. We can understand why from 1840 on, it was the expanding socialism which became the target of the intelligence service.[20]

Between the Two World Wars

During this period the main aim was protection against the enemies of the Belgian State, specifically communists and Flemish extremists. From 1918 until the 1930s there was a close collaboration with the French intelligence services. Also information on socialists and, increasingly, on communists was exchanged with other European countries.

On 14 October 1936 Belgium became 'neutral' and 'independent' again. Officially the link with the French services was interrupted not to provoke the Germans, but in practice co-operation went on, certainly with some agents of the Belgian intelligence services. Some connection with German intelligence people did already exist. The communists remained the first targets.[21]

In March 1940 the intelligence services were immediately charged to draw up two lists of suspects which should be arrested in case of war. In the night of 9 May 1940, when the Germans invaded Belgium, more than 5,000 persons were arrested: anti-fascists as well as German refugees, Rexists (extreme right Walloon people), Flemish nationalists. Many files were destroyed, but at the end of 1940 lists on nearly 325,000 foreigners, including 38,000 Jews living in Belgium, fell into the hands of the German Gestapo. After the beginning of the German war against the USSR, the existence of a list of communists permitted their arrest and deportation by the German Gestapo.

After World War Two

After the war the Belgian intelligence remained under a strong British and American influence. Hence the focus remained the same as during the war. In June 1944, the intelligence services started to investigate and arrest people who collaborated with the Germans. But the ordinary police forces – the gendarmerie and the judicial police – were also co-operating in the same task. Any way, the civil intelligence fought against every extremist, left wing or right wing, but the military intelligence, surely under American influence, considered the communists rather than the ex-collaborators as their main target, and the right wing groups rather as its allies in the fight against the communists. All this did not prevent the services from closely monitoring social movements – strikes, union actions and activities, unrest – just as they had before World War Two.

After 1945 civil intelligence, too, was more oriented towards the communist target. Consecutive governments participated increasingly in the American and Western (NATO) anti-Russian mood. From 1949 on, secret agreements were set up between several Western countries, i.e. a common policy of 'stay behind': clandestine networks of resistance to serve in the case of a Russian invasion and occupation with intelligence, communication and sabotage. The intelligence services were involved in this American 'strategy of tension'.[22]

During the Late 1980s and in the 1990s

The two intelligence services were always watching the Belgian federalist or anti-unionists and anti-Atlantic and anti-American movements, those of the extreme right and the extreme left. But they continued also to watch all the important socio-economic, political and ideological conflicts inside Belgium.

After many parliamentary and press complaints that the intelligence services were excessively targeting left wing and unionist movements or people and even collaborating with right wing informants and infiltrators, the socialist Minister of Justice in the beginning of the 1980s ordered civil intelligence to start mapping out the very active Flemish and Walloon extreme right movements in Belgium. It was also mentioned that these had tried to infiltrate the intelligence services. More recently it was also revealed that in that time extreme right-wing organisations had many adherents in the Army and in the Gendarmerie.[23]

In October 1995 a newspaper revealed a list drawn up by the military intelligence with 80 so-called 'subversive' organisations classified into different categories: extreme left, radical greens, extreme right, radical Flemish, terrorist organisations, third world, pacifist, anti-militarists and foreign or international organisations. Civil intelligence was supposed to have used a list of nearly 200 items. The matter was subject to parliamentary and media criticism. Since this revelation the list is supposed not only to have become smaller but also to be revised every six months and subjected to ministerial approval.[24]

In a 1995 year report of the Comité R we find an overview of the new targets: economic information, uncontrolled mass immigration, proliferation of Nuclear, Bacteriological and Chemical (NBC) weapons and of nuclear technology, vital and vulnerable civil infrastructure such as nuclear installations, computer and communication systems and transport, organised crime and corruption, fundamentalism, extreme nationalism, extreme left and right movements, terrorism and sects. In fact the new formulation of targets means 'extremism' in any form.[25] Most recently 'organised crime' became a very important target of the intelligence services 'because it also destabilises the democratic political system'.[26]

On 1 December 1998 the president of the military committee of NATO, General Klaus Naumann, declared at a conference in Brussels, *NATO today and tomorrow*, that NATO is working on a new 'strategic concept' in the context of the new geopolitical situation. The General identified four dangers: instability of Russia, the ethnic conflicts and the instability in the periphery, the absence of control and spread of nuclear, bacteriological and chemical mass destruction weapons and cyber attacks on some resources, such as water or information systems.[27] Maybe with this he pointed out new targets for the military intelligence services?

Methods are Changing

When scandals were revealed, almost every time we would see a discussion on the use of certain methods of investigation: wire-tapping, interception of radio communications, infiltration, provocation and the use of informants.

Many Suspicions

Parliament often noted that the services were suspected of using illegal means to get information, but it was nearly impossible to verify and control these allegations. Once the Law of 8 December 1992 on the protection of privacy was voted, and because the intelligence services are not police forces, they fell under the law and had to let their information gathering be controlled by the 'Committee on the Protection of Privacy'. The results of a Comité R inquiry showed that some practices were illegal. Hence, a new legal arrangement was badly needed.

Information is Finally Available

The head of the *Sûreté de l'État* gave an overview of the methods used by his service to a 1988–1990 Parliamentary Inquiry Commission.
– *Personal files*: 800,000. Their content, however, was not up-to-date.
– *Open sources*: press articles, which seem to deliver nearly 90 per cent of the information.
– *Informants*: persons do this work to earn money or to get protection. A distinction is made between 'weak' and 'protected' ones. A procedure to screen, register, protect and keep them secret existed, but was not always respected. In 1997 the Comité R made a very precise analysis of the use of informants by the intelligence services and noted many deficiencies. The rules should be the same for all the services and police forces involved in public order maintenance, security and crime fighting.[28]
– *Allied foreign intelligence services*: can deliver important information. The execution of international treaties allows informal contacts. Meetings of the TREVI working groups and of 'the friends of TREVI' (the U.S., Canada, Switzerland, Morocco) offer treasures of information.
– *Surveillance*: on a grass roots level, like wire-tapping and interception, provocation, etc.
– *Infiltration*: This is said to be a difficult and rarely used method, therefore normally not done by security agents themselves.[29]

In 1994 the Comité R mentioned another source of information: 'human sources'. It means cost-less information procured by the police forces and other administrative departments or authorities.

The same Comité R analysed the use of 'open sources' in 1996 and found out that they were not very well exploited. The intelligence services lack funds, analysts, contacts with the external world and its sources such as public and private libraries and databases. New sources such as 'internet' are not explored.[30] As to the access to data belonging to other public administrative departments, the Comité R noted that this is used only in an informal way and that regulation is needed.[31]

Since 1995, in the context of the policy of openness, the new Administrator General of the *Sûreté de l'État* declared on several occasions that the number of files on persons had to be drastically reduced. At the end of November 1995 941,206 persons were on file, of whom 46 per cent were older than 70 years of age, and 239,470 persons between 70 and 80. The number of files ought to be reduced to some 100,000 to 150,000.[32] In September 1998 150,000 were already screened. The people of the civil intelligence service thought that they could retain only 140,000 personnel files.[33] Four categories are used: to be destroyed; to be transferred to the State archives; to be kept; to be re-examined. In the future, files not consulted in the course of 10 years will be re-examined. A kind of selection criteria similar to this was formulated by the *SGR* already in October 1995, but not applied.

Close protection becomes increasingly important. Twenty three out of the 48 articles of the Law of November 1998 on the intelligence services deal with this mission (art.22 to 35). Whereas the civil intelligence service normally works under the authority of the Minister of Justice, the whole matter of 'close protection' is now placed under the Minister of Home Affairs. It is a so-called matter of order maintenance. Only the intelligence agents in charge of this mission have large judicial police competence and can requisite the assistance of police forces. However, still there are no specific control measures for this very specific and important task.

About Very New Methods

In the course of the discussions in the Senate on the new Bill of November 1998, the Minister of Defence made an interesting overview of the new and future methods and the problems they bring with them. Internet involves problems of confidentiality and security; civil satellites compete with military ones and spy satellites can suddenly change the geo-political scene. Moreover, corporations and other private organisations have access to data systems formerly held only by public and official agencies. A mix-up of civil and military matters, discussions on 'secret', privatisation of information apparatuses are increasing. Because of the high costs not all the people, organisations, companies and even states can afford direct access to all kinds of information systems. Hence, they become dependent on others. At the same time, cryptographic systems are developing in such a way that anybody can use them in an uncontrollable way. Hence, it becomes very difficult to transform the increasing mountain of information into useful data and to find qualified analysts. In such a situation, there is a danger that one has so much confidence in technical means so that one forgets the human ones. The increasing possibility to manipulate data and information is a dangerous evolution. The vulnerability of the information systems allows for a new kind of (computer) aggression. The information and communication technology is so powerful that it can become a new weapon for aggression and destruction.[34]

Recently the Comité R reported on the participation of the intelligence services in the satellite intelligence programmes. Still the *Sûreté de l'Etat* does not participate but is interested in the American 'Global Positioning System' to detect and follow mobile targets, also in audio-interception systems by satellite. The *SGR* participates already in the Satellite Centre of the West European Union (WEO) in Torrejon Sweden and in the military programmes *Hellios II* and *Trimilsatcom*. But the military intelligence service has more needs.

The Comité R was very critical. The SGR has no direct access to the images and is fully dependent of foreign decision making and goodwill. A collaboration with the big European countries is highly necessary. But the use of 'positioning systems' has to be regulated by law.[35]

At the same time, the Comité R ignore what is going on in this area on the European level and manifestly in co-operation with the US. On 7 May 1999 the European Parliament accepted *the Lawful Interception of Communication Council Resolution* (ENFOPOL) concerning the new technology which could permit the police and intelligence services to intercept any form of telecommunication, included satellites. This began in 1990 with the American COMINT project. Since 1993 American and European delegations met each other in the *International Law Enforcement Telecommunication Seminars* (ILETS). Since the same time the Council of the European Ministers of Justice and Home Affairs (JHA) has been involved: the fight against serious and organised crime, 'the European Information System' (EIS), and mutual judiciary assistance are the covers. All this occurred in complete secrecy. On 23 November 1995 the same ministers signed a *Memorandum of Understanding* on the interception of telecommunication with explicit reference to the development of the new generations of satellite communication. Discussions in the Council, for example on 27–28 May 1999, are dealing with the power and the right of interception of the communications, rather than on transparency, democratic control and respect of human rights and privacy. The *Daily Telegraph* of 10 June 1999 also mentions another problem: 'In time the two technical systems – one designed for national security and the other for law enforcement – will merge, and in the process finally eliminate national control over surveillance activities.'[36]

Schengen Information System 'Is Not Used'

In September 1997 the Comité R stated that the intelligence services did not use the opportunity to participate on the 'Schengen Information System' (SIS) and secondary 'Sirene system': the procedures are too heavy and unusable. Moreover they have their own international information channels. But the Comité asks: are they subject to control in order to protect the privacy? [37]

State Secrecy and Human Rights

An essential characteristic appeared to be the traditional secrecy of the functioning of intelligence services. During a long time the heads of the services followed this policy. On 1 September 1993 a new head of the civil security was nominated. He started a certain policy of openness.[38] The Comité R insisted on secrecy, but thought that the services could never decide themselves on a policy of secrecy or openness.[39]

About State Secrets

The Law voted in November 1998 by Parliament contains a chapter on secrecy (art. 36 to 43). We do not find any really new ideas in it. One thing is, however, quite new: Art. 19 allow the heads of the services or their representatives to communicate with the press. That is quite new.

During the discussions in Parliament the problem of the significance of the concept 'secret' popped up again. There is no general definition of 'State secret', only a piecemeal approach in all kinds of regulations. The Comité R made an effort to harmonise, specify and enumerate all that is understood by 'State secrets'. It also noted that the violation of some security secrets by intelligence agents is sanctioned more drastically than the violation of privacy. [40]

Classification of Secrets

Finally on 11 December 1998 Parliament voted a Law *relatif à la classification et aux habilitations de sécurité* (classification and security clearances).[41] It is interesting that we got a definition of classification: 'to procure a degree of protection by law or by international treaties or agreements' (art.2).

The classification contains three degrees: *VERY SECRET, SECRET, CONFIDENTIAL* (art.4 al.1). 'The subject can be information, documentation, data, material or stuff, under any form of which the inappropriate use can be harmful to a certain number of interests.' (art.3 al.1)   There is always the same vague enumeration in accordance with the list of the missions of State security, for example: 'any other fundamental interest of the State' or 'the functioning of the decision-making bodies of the State'.

Important matters, such as 'Who decides on the classification and declassification and how to do it', and 'who can attribute a degree of classification are not defined by law' (art.7). Hence, of course, some authors were very critical indeed:

> If privacy is one of the interests which is protected by the classification, it is certainly not of primary interest to the defence or the security of the Nation and is only of a lower level of classification. The specific protection of privacy has to be fully applied...The Law of 1992 on the protection of privacy aims at the protection of a fundamental right...and it cannot end in a weakening of this protection. Moreover we have to remember that a classification measure excludes the possibility of consultation of personal data, provided by the Law of 1994 on the publicity of the administration. If a person loses this means of control, he or she must count on a perfectly rigorous application of the protective principles of privacy.[42]

Always a Problem of Protection of Privacy

But the problem of the protection of human rights and privacy is not new.[43]

> The Comité R thinks that several investigation methods used by the intelligence services do not guarantee the full respect of the constitutional liberties of the citizens. Indeed, several methods used seem to make an intrusion on the private life of the individuals.[44]

> In the current state of the Belgian legislation, the national intelligence services do not dispose of any possibility to proceed in a legal way to listen to or intercept private telecommunications, even military ones, even in a foreign country and even in war time.[45]

It seems that the government of that time did not wish that the law should be applicable to video surveillance, inquiries on third persons, etc. All that would limit the action of the services. Following the advice of the *Conseil d'État* the law has to mention the 'forbidden' ways to collect data.[46] The same authority noted that if for the common citizens the rule would have it that 'what is not forbidden is allowed', this is not the case for intelligence services as State organisms: the principle of legality (art.22 of the Constitution) provides that the means to be used ought to be clearly defined in the law. Moreover, the services can use special means and again violate the privacy of persons. The Government and the political majority in Parliament did not follow this advice. Instead they argued that the services have to react to unexpected situations and that the 'enemy' and foreign intelligence services, who are in fact 'private persons', otherwise would get advantages. It was also underlined that these services have very special aims. The permission to wiretap and to intercept should however be procured by a special Law 'on administrative wire-tapping'.[47] Still, as of November 1999 this Bill had not been voted on.

Under the influence of the jurisprudence on art. 8 of the Convention of Human Rights a Law of 1 December 1998 changed the Law of 8 December 1992 on the protection of privacy. Now it is in an explicit way applicable to the treatment of data by the intelligence services. At the same time a whole series of automatic exceptions was provided to facilitate the work of the intelligence services. But again the critics are quite right:

> Why this long list of exceptions? Why this automatism? Is the Committee on the Protection of Privacy not hindered in using its right to control? An independent authority that could create a balance between the private and the State interests and check the 'proportionality' is not provided. The intelligence services can collect all information that seems 'useful' and must no longer be 'necessary' as provided in the Law on the protection of privacy. The regulation of the transmission of data between the intelligence services and the judiciary and administrative authorities, and of internal and external use of data, is very loose. The access of some one to the data collected on him is now only indirect and the intelligence services can veto it. Finally the new Law of 1 December 1998 takes away more than it gives. [48]

Also a Problem of the Right to Defence

How to object to something that is in essence secret, an infiltration, a provocation, an unlawful method? Even the right of defence seems to be in danger. National and European jurisprudence is very severe for the national authorities that invoke secrecy and confidentiality of witnesses or documents: defendants should have the right to object directly against anonymous witnesses. Hence, there is a legislation gap. Control authorities

– judges, the Comité R, Parliament – have to be very vigilant to assure the respect of fundamental liberties.[49]

Difficult External Relations

Intelligence services have to maintain a certain number of external relations: not only with the police and the judiciary but also with equivalent foreign services.

Difficult Relations with Law Enforcement Agencies

Since the beginning, from 1830 on, relations with the police force as well as with the judiciary were rather bad.[50] When the Judiciary Police was founded in 1920 as another police force with national competencies it immediately installed 'political sections'. The rivalry was now promoted in a structural way. The Gendarmerie participated all the time in the intelligence work by way of its 'political information sections'.[51] The Parliamentary Inquiry Commission in its report of 30 April 1990 criticised the lack of co-operation, co-ordination and communication between the two intelligence services as well as between the services and the police forces. The commission recommended structural measures to organise the interactions by law.

The Comité R also gave some attention to the problem of the relationship between law enforcement and the intelligence services. A report notes that in the past the activities of the two agencies had different aims, different rules and different methods. Intelligence services collected information to assist the policy makers in matters of national security. Police and judiciary agencies collected information in order to prosecute. The quality of the information was different as well. The intelligence services collected 'rough' information. Information gathered by police and judiciary people had to be very reliable, because it has to be used as evidence before the Court. Even sources and methods were different: police and magistrates got their information from interviews, short-term informants, physical and electronic surveillance. Intelligence information came from observation, interception, long term informants, open sources and information from foreign services.[52]

In June 1996 government took some structural initiatives. Two protocols were concluded: one between the intelligence services and the judicial authorities on 15 December 1997; another between the services themselves on 20 February 1997. Moreover, the Law of November 1998 legalised all that: legal assistance, automatic and other exchange of information, technical supply and also regular encounters. Magistrates ought to take care that security information is not used before the Court (art.20).[53] However, still the communication between the services and the magistrates is not really organised and remains too coincidental.

Less Problematic but Nearly Uncontrolled International Relations

In 1994 and 1995 the Comité R obtained information on the international telecommunication networks and the international contacts of the *Sûreté de l'État*. They are no more than *de facto* constructions.

Since the 1970s there was the TREVI co-operation with six monthly meetings of higher civil servants of the police and intelligence services. Since the Amsterdam Treaty of 1997 the collaboration between police and intelligence services is dealt with in the Treaty of the Union, but not yet in the Community Treaty. It is only a matter of 'common interest', of the Council of the 15 E.U. ministers of Justice and Home Affairs (JHA). Real Union legislation was not yet possible.

There was no information about the external international relations of the *SGR*.[54] In the course of the debate in the Senate in June 1998 on the new Bill, the head of the military intelligence service declared that there is a growing general and bi- or multilateral collaboration between the services of the NATO and other countries and even repartition and specialisation of tasks between the national intelligence services.[55] What kind of division of labour is going on is not mentioned.

Much informal co-operation was being developed. We know that the informal meetings and *de facto* networks are generally more important than the formal ones. More and more police, customs, civil and military intelligence and immigration services meet with each other on an international level and the boundaries between their competences, just as the borders between external and internal security seem to fade.[56] The same goes for the techniques that are used. The intelligence services have enlarged their working area and have become interested in major (organised) crime solving, in the control on legal and illegal immigrants and illegal trafficking of human beings.[57]

Control Structures in Evolution

After a whole period of *de facto* autonomy, in 1991 Parliament itself took a remarkable initiative establishing a permanent controlling body. It was directly modelled on the Canadian Security Intelligence Review Committee (CSARS-SIRC).

A Period of Autonomy

Since 1830 the intelligence services had enormous autonomy. Even when a royal decree gave more controlling power to the Minister, he delegated the whole accountability to the Director General Administrator.[58] This happened again and again in the course of one hundred and fifty years. After every 'scandal' the head of the service was replaced and the service moved around back and forth between the Ministries of Home Affairs and Justice.

In the course of World Wars One and Two the two services fell under the authority of the Minister of War. After new difficulties with the activities of agents, in 1947 and 1948 and again in 1950, 1958 and 1980, several members of Parliament asked for a legislative provision and certainly for more control on the intelligence services.[59]

A Remarkable Initiative of Control and Accountability

On 5 June 1990 the new centre left Government announced in its *Plan de la Pentecôte*: 'The State security will be subject to external control'.[60] On 18 July 1991 Parliament voted a law on a controlling body: the already mentioned Comité R. Until the end of 1999 the Comité R had five full time commissioners, mostly magistrates, and a team of five investigators from the police services. The investigators have judicial police competence. The committee is only accountable to Parliament and is set up as an autonomous body. Their mission is 'to guarantee the defence of the rights which the Constitution and the law grant to the citizens; to take care of the co-ordination and the efficiency of the intelligence services' (art.1). It acts on demand of the House of representatives, the Senate, or at its own initiative or upon requests from private persons (art.32). The Comité R inquired into the activities and methods of the intelligence services, their internal regulations and directives, all the documents which regulate the actions of the members of the intelligence services. A report on any closed inquiry is sent to the competent ministers and to the two houses (art.33). These authorities also receive a yearly report and can even ask for any file or document if the confidentiality and the privacy of persons is respected (art.36). Private persons can complain to the committee about activities of the intelligence services (art.40). The agents are obligated to communicate secrets to the Comité R, except if they are part of an ongoing judicial inquiry. The commissioners and the investigators can urge the police forces to assist them (art.50). The Comité R recruits its own personnel and has to provide its own internal regulation.[61]

Comité R obtained an enormous competence and an important power of interpretation of its missions. The politicisation of the board – the members were in fact designated by the political parties – however had a very negative effect on its functioning.

A Royal Decree of 21 June 1996 put an end single ministerial authority over the intelligence services. A *Comité Ministériel de Renseignement* (Ministerial Committee for Intelligence) and a *Collège de Renseignement* (Intelligence College) were installed. The former is composed of the Ministers of Defence, Justice, Home Affairs, Foreign Affairs and Economic Affairs and decides on the (political) security policy; the latter, an administrative body, is composed of higher civil servants and takes care of the co-ordination and execution of that policy, the co-ordination between police and intelligence.[62] This way not just one minister, nor the security services themselves, any longer defines the security policy.

The Law of November 1998 contains very few articles on control (art.5, 6 and 10). The general accountable authorities are the above mentioned *Comité ministériel* and the *Collège de reseignement*. The executive authority over the *'Sûreté de l'État'* is a subtle bicephalous construction of co-decisionmaking between the Ministers of Justice and Home Affairs. It is a matter of political equilibrium in controlling police and intelligence in pluralistic or multi party governmental coalitions. The *SGR* is nevertheless under the executive authority of the one Minister of Defence.

Very soon the Comité R was subject to criticism, because of internal conflicts and a too broad interpretation of its competences. But Parliament failed to maintain enough contact with the Comité R. For almost nine years it discussed the matter and finally on 1 March 1999 a Law was voted to modify that of 18 July 1991. The competences are reduced to a real control on the functioning of the services and no longer on matters of political and legal initiatives (art.2 al.2). The number of permanent commissioners is reduced from three to one (art. 20 1°). Inquiries on the Comité's own initiative must be controlled by the Senate (art. 24). The members of the executive power, the ministers, obtain more control on the inquiry reports (art.27 and 28). The Senate will be in closer and structural contact with the Comité (art.40).[63]

Control in Practice: The Intelligence Services as Targets

During the last years the intelligence services have become even more subject to control and inquiry. Most of all on the proper initiative of the Comité R, but more than once after one or other journalist revealed some 'scandal' or 'failure', several times clearly after a certain leak.[64]

It was after a recommendation of the Comité R that the list of 'subversive' organisations and persons, as well as that of the subjects of information gathering and observation, had to be proposed by civil intelligence in line with certain criteria, and afterwards be approved by a Committee of Ministers. The Comité R had to urge the military intelligence to follow the same procedure.

The Comité R inquired into the way in which the military security in the beginning of 1994 handled information on the political situation in Rwanda. Sensitive information that mentioned some military intrigues against the Rwandese President, the armament of Hutu extremists, and as well as the hostility against the UN and the Belgian army detachment, was in the hands of the intelligence services several months before April 1994, when the President, and later ten Belgian para-commando soldiers, were murdered and when the genocide of Tutsis and dissident Hutus broke out. It appeared that information was not taken seriously, not organised and not passed on to the authorities. It also appeared that these authorities were not really interested, did not take them seriously and gave no instructions to the security services. However, the inquiry and the results were contested by some members of the board of the Comité R[65] and a Parliamentary Inquiry Committee took over the affair.

Over many years cases of illegal wiretapping by the intelligence services were revealed from time to time in the press or in parliament. On 21 September 1995 a newspaper revealed that the military intelligence operated a centre for wiretapping and radio communication interception. The Army staff and the Minister of Defence said that all that happens in a NATO context. 'To respect human rights is not a matter for military people', the general said.[66] The Comité R could not but state that the wire-tapping and the radio interception system was illegal: '...It is only allowed in the course of a judicial investigation and with the permission of a judge...We urgently need to have a law to legalise and...organise control before and after...and privacy has to be protected. Meanwhile the army can invoke 'an emergency situation' not to be prosecuted.'[67]

In March 1996 a Deputy asked the Comité R to inquire into the so-called reorganisation of a 'stay behind' network by the 'human intelligence' section of the military intelligence. The Comité R did not detect such a network, but discovered nevertheless that since April 1993 some army reservists were organised in 'the military defence of the territory' to keep an eye on 'sensitive points' and on foreign groups and immigrants which could possibly undertake terrorist activities, who are spying, or are involved in sabotage, terrorism or subversion, actions against military targets, the NATO, the Army.'[68] The Comité R was of the opinion that the military intelligence has too broad a conception of threat and that a clear distinction has to be made between a military threat and a threat coming from terrorist and subversive groups.[69]

In 1994–1995 the Comité R made a very extensive inquiry into the safety of the communications of the national intelligence services. The report was very critical of the Belgian situation: there was no certification structure to verify the quality of the Belgian or foreign protection systems; there was no legislation on the cryptographic systems; the control of communication is *a priori* and not *a posteriori*; the coding systems are too provisional and not waterproof and the protection of privacy is not guaranteed.[70]

Another inquiry in the course of 1995–1996 had bearing on the use of informants by the intelligence services. The Comité R detected many problems: no consideration of the ethical aspects; the privacy of the citizens is not guaranteed; there is a problem of reliability and evaluation of the informants; there is a real risk of provocation; the payment is not controlled; there are no provisions for physical protection; there are no precise guidelines, no codification system, nor training of the intelligence agents to cope with informants. The situation was even worse within the military intelligence than within its civil counterpart.[71]

Close protection is one of the tasks of an intelligence service. The Comité R verified in 1994–1995 how this task was executed by the services. The report concluded that the ministerial guideline of 1994 is old-fashioned, that there is illegal use of police powers and that the agents are too old. 'But notwithstanding all these defects the "protection" service was able to execute their tasks in a decent way.'[72] The Law of November 1998 provides a new regulation of 'close protection'.

On many occasions the Comité R complained about the lack of co-ordination between the civil and the military intelligence services. It appeared in each inquiry the Comité undertook. It noted that systematic provisions on co-operation are lacking; an imbalance exists between the tasks of the two services.[73] Again the Law of 1998 provides some arrangements.

At the end of June 1998 the Comité R detected that since the 1980s both intelligence services collected information on 15 members of the

Green Party in Parliament. But the data would only refer to press articles and was collected in the period before the Greens entered Parliament. Nevertheless the head of the civil intelligence refused to reveal the content of the files.[74]

Conclusion

It took until 30 November 1998 until the State intelligence services was regulated by law. How could it take such a long time until the repeated requests from the Parliament was satisfied?

There certainly is not just one reason that can explain this phenomenon. First the situation perhaps became more difficult as international co-operation increased. Furthermore, since the middle of the 1980s, successive Parliamentary Inquiry Commissions analysed manifest failures and mistakes of police and magistrates. But at the same time the security services came into focus as well. Moreover, for some journalists the intelligence problem became a favourite subject: the conflict between the intelligence and law enforcement, between the two intelligence services, and not in the least between the head of the civil service and some ministers or the Americans were phenomena which attracted the attention to the problem of security and intelligence. Of course the ever-greater emphasis placed on the protection of human rights and principally on the protection of privacy in the 1980s and the 1990s was another important element. And finally, once the Comité R started its inquiries in 1993 and detected many cases of blatant mismanagement, irregularities as well as illegalities, there was no way back.

But we might just as well look on it from another side. As we said, since 1830 Parliament very regularly asked to legislate but the Governments refused just as regularly. Why did Parliament itself take no initiative? Certainly some attempts were made, but not by important deputies or political groups. This has of course something to do with the real functioning of our democratic system and with the relations between the Government or the executive power on the one side and Parliament or the legislative and controlling power on the other. But perhaps it has mainly to do with the birth of political parties and with the growing power of party leaders of the majority and their friends, comrades and colleagues in the Government. If the dominance of that kind of collective is not new, it was and is still increasing. The democratic principle is that Parliament controls the government, but *de facto* it is just the other way around. And in such a context it is not too difficult for governments to keep under their control as much as possible the police, the intelligence and even law enforcement generally as very strong governmental instruments. They have an important interest in endorsing the concept of the strong centralised State, which they can incorporate. So they keep the power of Parliament as small as possible, and Parliamentary majority most of the time follows the Government and even more so the party leaders. Remember the discussions and the decision-making process about the organic Bill of 1998 and about the diminished competence's of the Comité R in 1999: all indications of the turnabout of the relations between the constitutional bodies and of the dominance of the executive power: to keep controlling and decision making power are always the most important targets.

Nevertheless, within the government the coalition partners disagreed for a long time on how to regulate the intelligence services. The socialists were in favour of as much control over the services as possible, but by the Government rather than by Parliament. The Christian Democrats were in favour of significant autonomy for the services – their man was then the head of the civil intelligence service – to be laid down by law. Finally, after nearly nine years, a kind of compromise was reached, but with a victory for the executive power and with an executive authority equilibrium between the Ministers of Justice and Home Affairs, who in each coalition government belong to different political parties.

This 'governmental democracy' also marks the kind of legal regime Belgium has achieved. To a very large extent it is a legitimation of an existing practice and/or of what important members of the executive power wanted. They attend to the legal integration of the intelligence services within the Governmental State structures. Moreover the solution of the problem is a very legalistic one: now we have a law. Parliament is rather the loser. It could not obtain that new missions and new methods should be defined exclusively by law; that it must be informed of the categories of persons, organisations and groups under security control, which was a most valid claim; that they could keep a good eye on the respect for human rights and on the protection of privacy. Just as in the past, it will have no control over all kinds of committees or working groups the ministers install. It has no guarantee whatsoever of receiving more information in the future on activities, manpower, budget, international involvement, nor on technical means and instruments, which will probably evolve tremendously in the next years. It appears to become true that in the future 'what is not forbidden by the Government or the competent Minister, is allowed' and Parliament will be kept in the dark as before.

But it must also be said that Parliament did not really exploit the existence of the Comité R. Interest and communication was rather low. The fact that in the beginning Parliament did not object to the politicisation of the nominations of the members of the board and of the team of investigators by the party headquarters boomeranged afterwards. Many Deputies were convinced that changes were necessary, but did not succeed in finding an acceptable majority solution. Parliament manifestly contains too few members with knowledge of and interest in the security and intelligence questions. And the government is of course not too unhappy with this situation and maybe even encourages it. If better communication structures between Parliament and the Comité R were established by the Law of 1 March 1999, the possibility increased that the executive power, the government, interferes.

In fact the Comité R did some excellent work, but finally the Government benefited more from it than Parliament. The Comité R gave attention to many new challenges: the important protection of the economic and scientific potential; the new methods of communication and the problems of the protection of human rights; the uncontrolled international relations of the services, etc. The Comité R believes in legislative solutions for the functioning of the intelligence as well as for the protection of human rights. But its ideas about the combination of both are not always clear and the government was not asking for it.

There is probably still a problem of interaction between the intelligence and the law enforcement authorities. The Gendarmerie as well as the Judicial Police organised political sections that participated in the intelligence work and even almost took over the job after each World War. If we should believe a Minister of Home Affairs the information he received in the 1990s from the Gendarmerie was very similar to that he got from the intelligence services. A theoretical explanation of the difference is given but sounds so abstract. In the 1830s the *Sûreté de l'État* claimed more competence, that is, a judicial police mandate for its agents, but only got it during and before and after periods of war. Now the agents in charge of close protection will have it, and nothing prevent these agents from executing other tasks with that competence. And what about the control on that? First a protocol was drawn up organising some co-operation between the intelligence and law enforcement in terms as nice as they are vague. The Law of November 1998 legalised it. But we do not know what it means in practice and how it works. We do not know either if there is any systematic or rather occasional transfer of intelligence information to the police and judicial agencies, which is not accessible to the defence or the parties before the Court. But it was mentioned that a legal vacuum exists, an absence of an arbitration system for the right of defence in a case of State secrecy or of confidentiality of witnesses or evidence: these are real problems concerning the respect of human rights. From recent viewpoints we learn that more and more the two functions overlap, that they are complementary to one another and have to collaborate in the most intensive way, not in the least on the international level. Do we have to give up the very traditional separation between the two functions: intelligence and law enforcement?

To me it is very clear that the military *SGR* is much more important than the civil *Sûreté*. For a long time as well as according to the new Law, the military service has almost the same competence's as the civil one and can redo what the other was doing or do that it did not do. It is the dominant service and is very autonomous because it is working under the umbrella of NATO. Only one Minister (of Defence) is accountable and not two, as it is the case with the civil service. And when there is almost no public control, it is quite logical that little is known about the functioning of this *SGR*. Is the very secret functioning of the military intelligence service in connection with the US services perhaps the reason why we did not know that already since the 1970s a British-American spy satellite, the 'Echelon Network', was tapping telephone, telex and e-mail communications, on industrial and business affairs as well as on the activities of human rights organisations? This is what the report 'Appraisal of the Technologies of Political Control' made by the British audit firm Omega and published by the European Parliament in September 1998 revealed only very recently.[75] And we also noted that what is going on the EU level about the use of the new communication methods is not too transparent either.

Everybody who observes the enormous chaotic collection of the most heterogeneous terms in the field of security and intelligence must be either impressed or cannot take it seriously. Many terms are perfectly interchangeable and are used the one for the other, such as: security or secret services and intelligence services; State security and public security; counterespionage and counterintelligence; information and intelligence; the latter term sometimes has a military connotation. The significance and interpretation can change in time, like that of 'subversion', a term which finally disappeared in the Law of November 1998. All kind of associations of terms is possible. The missions of the civil and the military services overlap and it does not appear to be so difficult to transfer a mission from one service to the other. Finally even a key term like 'State secret' seems to be indeterminable.

We cannot but get the impression that the agents themselves and eventually the executive authorities can interpret as they like. Can we not note that nearly every political, economic, or social situation or activity can be defined as a danger or even as a threat to State security? Moreover, intentions or attempts are considered to be as dangerous to the State security as real or effective actions: 'threatens or could threaten'. Finally we have to conclude that it is really a political matter and that in some circumstances those who are in power may use these flexible terms to inculpate and eliminate some of their political enemies. They have an important discretionary power to decide whether an activity is real terrorism, organised crime, Mafia, espionage, etc. or rather a threat to certain vested political and not so democratic power interests. It is just a matter of political definition of the situation. At that moment we can have many doubts about the respect of human rights and privacy and how people can get effectively the rights they have in theory. We have strong indications that because of the evolution of all kinds of new technologies the methods will change very quickly and that no serious external control over their quality and their use is prepared or provided, certainly not on the European, international or global level. The fifteen EU Ministers dealing with satellite communication manifestly do not worry all that much about the protection of human rights and privacy.

We cannot deny that nevertheless some small 'formal' gain is made in the field of respect of human rights and protection of privacy. But it is perhaps more on the level of discourses that on that of practice. So the law permits the intelligence services to have access to all 'useful' – and not 'necessary' – data and no longer respect the law on the protection of privacy: many exceptions are provided by law, so the arrangement is legal. We have rather the impression that the authorities and agencies finally succeeded better in guaranteeing their own security and protection and that of their activities and data, than that of the rights of individuals. Moreover always the same problem arises: to have rights does not mean to really obtain them. No common citizen understands the very diversified and complex procedures on the right of protection of privacy.

Finally the duty of the intelligence agents to maintain secrecy is very explicit and the sanctions the law provides in case of violation are very severe. It is another guarantee for a certain protection of privacy, but at the same time it is an instrument in the hands of the authorities to keep close control over their intelligence services and agents.[76]

Notes

[1] Padectes Belges, 'Administration de la Sûreté Publique', T.IV, (s.d.), p.433.
[2] Annales Parliamentaires de la Chambre des Représentants, 4 Décembre 1884, pp.153–170.

3   Archives Generales du Royaume, 'Police des Étrangers', D.G., N° 93.
4   Carpentier, C. and Moser, F. *La Sûreté de l'Etat, Histoire d'une déstabilisation* (Bruxelles: Quorum, 1993) pp.16–17.
5   Van Outrive, L., Cartuyvels, Y. and Ponsaers, P. *Les Polices en Belgique, Histoire Socio-Politique du Système Policier. De 1794 à nos jours* (Bruxelles: Evo Histoire, Eds. Vie Ouvrière, 1991) p.46. Keunings, L. 'Les Grandes Étapes de la Police Secrète en Belgique au XIXième siècle', *Rev. Trim. du Crédit Communal*, 43, 3 (1989), pp.3–30.
6   A separate 'nuclear security'-service exists (Law of 4 August 1955 and Royal Decree of 14 March 1956). A project to integrate the service in the 'Sûreté de l'Etat' is now in execution since December 1998.
7   Caeymaex, L. 'Attributions, Missions et Méthodes de la Sûreté de l'État', *L'officier de Police, Revue de la Fédération Nationale des Commissaires de Police et Commissaires de Police Adjoints,* 9 (1964), pp.30–41. Caeymaex, L., 'La Sûreté Publique', *Répertoire Pratique Du Droit Belge*, T.IV (1972), pp.620–25.
8   Ibid. pp.24–35.
9   Comité, Rapport 1997, pp.118–20.
10 Moniteur Belge, 18 December 1998, pp.40312–22.
11 Senat de Belgique, Session de 1997–1998, 9 Juillet 1998, 'Projet de Loi Organique des Services de Renseignement et de Sécurité, Procédure d'évocation, Texte Adopté par les Commissions Réunies de la Justice et des Affaires Étrangères', 1–758/11. Senat de Belgique, 'Rapport fait au nom des Commissions Réunies de la Justice et des Affaires Étrangères par Mme Lizin', 1–758/10, pp.54; 56–58.
12 Ibid, pp.34–35.
13 Ibid, pp.23 and 53.
14 Comité, Rapport 1998, p.71 and 102.
15 SEVI, *Het Labyrinth, private milities en politiewezen doorgelicht, met het officieel rapport van de commissie Wijninckx* (The Labyrinth, an analysis of private militias and of police; with the official report of the Commission Wijninckx) (Brussel: Sevi-Publicatie, 1, 1982), p.168.
16 Carpentier, C., Moser, M. and Ibid, pp. 165–66.
17 Documents de la Chambre des Représentants de Belgique, 59/8 (1988), p.281.
18 Ibid, pp.166–67.
19 Van Outrive, L. *et al.* Ibid. pp.276–77.
20 Archives, Ibid., N°111.
21 Van Outrive, L. *et al.*, Ibid. pp.112–13.
22 Van Doorslaer, R. and Verhoeyen, E., *L'assassinat de Julien Lahaut, Une Histoire de l'anticommunisme en Belgique*, (Anvers: Epo, 1987), pp. 173–75.
23 De Morgen, 22 September 1997, p.5.
24 De Morgen, 16 October 1995, p.3.
25 Humo Magazine, 17 October 1995, pp.46–53.
26 De Morgen, 20 December 1996, p.9.
27 De Morgen and De Standaard, 2 December 1998.
28 Ibid, pp. 141–173.
29 Carpentier, C., Moser, F. and Ibid., pp.66–70.
30 Comité, Rapport 1994., pp.40–41; Rapport 1996, pp.204–16.
31 Ibid, 1997, pp.280–81.
32 De Morgen and De Standaard, 21 November 1995; De Morgen, 25 March 1995, p. 24.
33 De Morgen, 21 September 1998, p.2.
34 Senat de Belgique, Rapport, Ibid. pp.5–8.
35 Comité, Rapport 1998, pp. 149–68.

[36] Busch, N. 'Interception capabilities 2000: the abolition of privacy?', *Fortress Europe?* 58, (1999), pp. 10–13 and 14.

[37] Comité, Rapport 1998, pp. 128–129.

[38] SEVI, Ibid, p. 12.

[39] Comité, Rapport 1997, p. 275–76.

[40] Chambre des Representants de Belgique, 'Projet de Loi relatif à la classification et aux habilitations de Sécurité et Projet de Loi portant création d'un organe de recours en matière d'habilitations de sécurité', Mai 29th, 1998, 1193/10–96/97. Annexe: 'Les devoirs de secret auxquels sont tenus les membres des services de renseignement', pp. 48–107. (Analysis made by the Comité R)

[41] Moniteur Belge, 07.05.1999, pp. 15752–60. La 'habilitation de sécurité' is better known under the name of 'NATO clearance': every person who is in contact with military matters has to be checked on security: to be trustful, confidential and loyal.

[42] Poulet, Y. and Havelange, B. 'Secrets d'Etat et Vie privée: ou comment concilier l'inconciliable?, dans Comité Permanent de Contrôle des Services de Renseignements et l'Institut Royal Supérieur de Défense, *Secret d'État ou Transparence?* Colloque 20 janvier 1999, p.68.

[43] Different laws prohibit the use of any mean to intercept military or civil telegraphy or telephony, radio messages, any telecommunication in order to protect privacy.

[44] Comité, Rapport 1994, p.42.

[45] Ibid. rapport 1996, p.38.

[46] Poulet, Y. and Havelange, B., Ibid. 84.

[47] Senat de Belgique, Rapport, Ibid. pp. 16–23. There was no agreement to include the item 'administrative wiretapping and interception' into the November 1998 Law on the intelligence services. So a special legislation is needed. Until now, July 1999, a Bill of June 1998 was not voted by Parliament.

[48] Poulet, Y. and Havelange, B., Ibid. pp.88–97.

[49] Krywin, A. and Marchand, Ch. 'Le secret d'Etat et les droits de l'Homme', dans Comité Permanent de Contrôle des Services de Renseignements et l'Institut Royal Supérieur de Défense, *Secret d'Etat ou Transparence?* Colloque 20 janvier 1999, pp. 55–61.

[50] Archives Generales du Royaume, 'Police des Étrangers', D.G., N° 156.

[51] Van Outrive, L. *et al.* Ibid. pp. 153–54, 164–66.

[52] Comité, Rapport 1994, pp. 36–39.

[53] Ibid., pp. 36–38

[54] Comité, Rapport 1995, pp. 148–49.

[55] Senat de Belgique, Rapport, Ibid. pp.66–69.

[56] Chambre des Represantants,' Rapport de la commission d'enquête parliamentaire sur la façon fut organisée la lutte contre le banditisme et le terrorisme', Nos 59/8, 30 Avril 1990, pp.157–159.

[57] Bigo, D. *Police en Réseaux-L'expérience Européenne*, (Paris: Presse Des Sciences Po 1996), pp. 101–05, 303–36.

[58] Carpentier, C., Moser, F. and Ibid. p.27.

[59] Van Outrive, L. *et al.* Ibid. pp. 169–70, 235, 241.

[60] Carpentier, C., Moser, F. and Ibid. pp. 160–63.

[61] Moniteur Belge, 26 July 1991, pp. 16.576–16.597.

[62] Senat de Belgique, Rapport 1996, Ibid. pp.12–13.

[63] Moniteur Belge, 3 April 1999, 'Loi modifiant la loi du 18 juillet 1991 organique du controle des services de police et de renseignements', 1 March 1999, pp.11161–68.

[64] Here we have to mention the research-journalist Walter De Bock and the newspaper De Morgen.

[65] Comité, Rapport 1996, pp. 126–31.

[66] De Morgen, 27 October 1995, p.1.
[67] Comité, Rapport 1997, pp. 98–100.
[68] Ibid, pp. 108–14.
[69] Ibid, pp. 130–32.
[70] Ibid, Rapport 1995, pp.103–06; Ibid. Rapport 1996, pp.64–5; Ibid, Rapport 1997, pp.202–03.
[71] Ibid, Rapport 1997, pp.156–65.
[72] Ibid, Rapport 1996, pp.82–5.
[73] Ibid, Rapport 1997, p.182.
[74] De Morgen 22 juni 1998; De Standaard 23 juni 1998.
[75] Ceustermans, C. *Justitie bespiedt Brits-Amerikaans spionnagenetwerk*, (Justice is spying on a British-American network), De Morgen 14 December 1998, p.1.
[76] These analyses end in 1999. A most recent and very interesting report from the 'Comité Permanent de Contrôle des Services de Renseignements' (Rue de la Loi 52 1040 Bruxelles; e-mail comiteri@skynet.be) is the <Rapport d'activitiés 2000> which contain analyses about the growing role of the private intelligence enterprises, the still more important protection of the scientific or economic potential, the new relationship between the intelligence services and the law enforcement agencies after the reform of the Belgian police system, the Echelon network and international satellite intelligence programs, the intelligence work during the Euro 2000 football event, the military intelligence work on the situation in Kosovo.

PART II

FROM DICTATORSHIP TO DEMOCRACY

Chapter 4

The Spanish Intelligence Services

Andrea Giménez-Salinas

Introduction

The Spanish intelligence service in its current form dates from 1976 (following the end of the dictatorship of Franco). Before that, intelligence activity outside Spain was much reduced, not co-ordinated and poorly developed. This was due to the fact that, first of all, during Franco's era, Spanish intelligence services were fragmented into more than ten services[1] and their activity was very limited and mostly focused on obtaining information within Spain to control any threats to Franco's regime. At the time, the obsessive objective was to avoid the overthrow of the established order. The main targets were students, catholic institutions, separatist groups and mass media (especially, written media) (San Martin, 1983:128). On the other hand, Spanish politicians were less interested in the notion of national security. Two facts contributed to the absence of a notion of national security: first, during Franco's era, there was no common notion of national security since the regime used to identify its own security with national security. Obviously, the opposition did not share such identification. Second, historically, there has been a lack of political discussion in Spain. Such discussion has been replaced by a clash of ideologies exclusively aimed at achieving power and obtaining privileges at any price, based on conspiracy, secrecy, or *Coup d'état* mentality. These ideologies have contributed to a conspiratorial view of history where security services are adored and feared simultaneously (Cachinero and Trujillo, 1993:121).

    At the end of dictatorship one of the big changes made by former Prime Minister Adolfo Suarez was the legalisation of the Communist Party in April 1977. The Communist Party was the principal opponent to Franco, and with its legalisation, intelligence services lost one of their main targets. The change of regime led to an evident need to reorganise the intelligence services. Such reorganisation began with the creation of the Ministry of Defence[2] by virtue of a Royal Decree of 1977. This Royal Decree also created the Spanish intelligence service: the *Centro Superior de Información de la Defensa* (CESID). The CESID is a military intelligence service under the direction of the Ministry of Defence and is the product of the merger of the *Servicio Central de Información* (SECED) and the General Staff Intelligence Section: *Servicio de inteligencia del Alto Estado Mayor* (SIAEM). The CESID mandate was to gather, evaluate, interpret and provide the Ministry of Defence with defence information following the priorities of the *Junta de Jefes de Estado Mayor*.[3] Nevertheless, CESID was not exempt from contradictions and its mandate was excessively vague. It was necessary to find a quick definition for the first institutionalisation of a Spanish intelligence service under the direction of a democratic government, and more important, without introducing radical changes that would disturb the army (Agüero, 1995). The CESID was composed of three divisions: internal intelligence (with the experience of the SECED[4]), counterintelligence (with the experience of the SIAEM) and external intelligence which was later developed because of the limited expertise of Spanish intelligence services in such area. The main issues in Spain during the period 1977–1985 were terrorism and internal threats to democracy. CESID did combat terrorism, however it was only after the failed *Coup d'état* of February 1981, that CESID was instructed to detect any threats to democracy. As a matter of fact, CESID did not detect coup plots such as *Operación Galaxia* in 1978 and the events of February 1981 but was able to detect further conspiracies.

Throughout its first years of existence, CESID was characterised by an absence of direction and definition of its functions, as well as by keeping personnel close to Franco's regime. Consequently, CESID was not in a key position during the transition to the democratic period. Nevertheless the *Coup d'état* of 1981 made a break with the past: CESID clarified its mandate in order to detect conspiracies to the democratic transition, changed its image and did succeed in detecting a planned *Coup d'état* in October 1982.

During the socialist era (1982–1996), the CESID carried out its internal and external activity to a level comparable to that of other west European intelligence services. External developments were the great challenge in this period. The membership of Spain in NATO and the European Union implied the necessity to obtain and exchange international information and to expand the CESID abroad. The expansion began in other member-countries of such organisations (including the USA). Later came South America, Northern Africa, and finally East European countries and the Middle East. This period of expansion and consolidation was suddenly interrupted by several scandals that became public after the chief of the operations department of CESID stole some documents about the activities of the GAL.[5] The blast of these scandals led CESID to suffer the most difficult time of its short history.

Even though internal affairs are quite different in every country, the end of the Cold War brought a similar international context to all intelligence services, which have experienced the same changes and problems. There was a need *to reorganise* information in order to increase its intelligence value. Also, given the substantial changes in the international arena, intelligence services operate under much more severe conditions. Spanish authors have characterised this situation in the following terms: first, risks are undefined in terms of origin, persons, etc. This is one of the issues that have changed the most. Problems may not be defined in military terms, rather in economic ones. Second, problems and actions have become global. Security problems may be identified in all orders of life (communications, culture, economy, etc.) and such problems may not be solved by the action of only one State (Calderón Fernandez, 1988).

As Cachinero and Trujillo say:

> there is a new frame of international relationships where the two poles have been replaced by ambiguous conflicts and new and remote references, and in which, cultural, religious, tribal and psychological components of protagonists, in other words, the strictly human characters, have a relevance and signification that fall beyond the detection and evaluation of computers and satellites[6] (Cachinero and Trujillo, 1993:120).

Arms smuggling, especially mass destruction weapons coming from the late Soviet Union, organised crime, drug-traffic and terrorism are neither problems independent from each other nor simply national problems. Such problems are often related one to each other and demand global solutions. Likewise, these problems may not be solved nor combated by only one or two countries, on the contrary, they are international problems that require international co-operation to be solved. Intelligence services were historically national redoubts with great reluctance to open their activity and findings to foreign services. Dangers need now an international response, and intelligence services must also co-operate and open themselves to foreign services.

The need for a reorganisation of the Spanish intelligence service to face internal and external challenges has been discussed in the Spanish Parliament and there seems to be agreement among most political parties and the Government. Such reorganisation, necessary for the CESID to overcome the political scandals in which it was involved, will certainly be orientated towards making the Spanish intelligence service capable of coping with all these challenges.

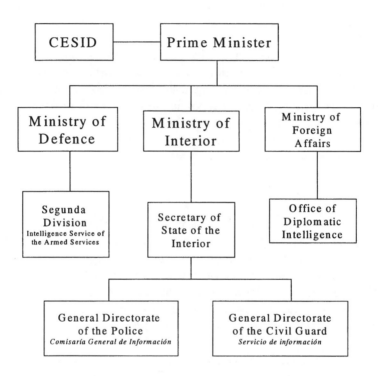

Figure 4.1   Spanish Intelligence Community

The Spanish Intelligence Service Model

The Spanish Intelligence service model is composed of one national intelligence service (CESID) that has internal and external competence and depends on the Ministry of Defence and other intelligence services which depend on the Ministry of Interior, the Ministry of Foreign Affairs and military. The competence of such services is to obtain operational information to carry out their functions. The co-ordination among all the information services is not assured by one institution, but is rather executed by the ministries involved. The following classification summarises the services existing in Spain and their respective competence (see also Figure 4.1).

Internal security information is provided by CESID, the intelligence service that works in counter-intelligence and counter-terrorism and the intelligence services of the several police forces operating in Spain. Each police force has operational duties and these services must gather and analyse information related to public order and security inside Spain, as provided for by Law 2/1986, that describes the mission of the Spanish police forces:[7]

- *Cuerpo Nacional de Policía* (CNP)
- *Guardia Civil* (GC)
- *Ertzaintza* (The police of the Basque Country).

Regarding external and military information, the Foreign Service information office (*Oficina de Información Diplomática*) takes care of institutional relations with the media and obtains information from the media and other open sources. Second, the director of CESID is specifically the 'national delegated authority', who is appointed by NATO to protect classified information. Third, each branch of the military also has an intelligence service. All such intelligence services are co-ordinated by the intelligence division of the *Estado Mayor de Defensa*.

Centro de Información de la Defensa (CESID)

Mandate

Since 1982[8] CESID has been a department of the Ministry of Defence and supplies the information required by the Prime Minister in order to carry out its functions of managing and co-ordinating government action in defence and military matters. CESID has a double dependency. From an organic standpoint it depends on the Ministry of Defence. However from a functional standpoint, it depends on the Prime Minister. The Director of CESID reports to the Prime Minister.

The present mandate of CESID is:

- to obtain, evaluate and disseminate information;
- to prevent external dangers and threats against the independence or integrity of the Spanish territory;

- to prevent external dangers, threats or aggression against the Spanish weapon industry and market and to secure the national interest in those economic and technology sectors having a particular connection with defence;
- obtaining information regarding internal conspiracies that may threaten the integrity and stability of the fundamental institutions of the nation by anti-constitutional means;
- counter-intelligence in order to prevent foreign intelligence services from threatening the national security and interests;
- co-ordination of the action of other institutions that use encrypted methods and procedures, guaranteeing their security, and the promotion of the acquisition of material as well as the preparation of specialist personnel.[9]

Structure

In order to comply with its mandate, CESID is divided into the following sections:

- External intelligence
- Counter-intelligence
- Internal intelligence (including anti-terrorist section IC-4, which is focused on the terrorist organisation ETA and on the groups supporting ETA and its political party) and
- Economy and technology.

CESID also has the following administrative departments:

- General Sub-Directorate of Administration and Services,
- General Sub-Directorate of Personnel Matters (in charge of the selection, education, training and administration of personnel),
- Operational Support Division (carries out special activities that require special procedures and methods),
- Security department,[10]
- Legal adviser, and
- Technical office.

The budget of CESID in 1997 was approximately US$118,880,000 (EL PAIS, May 5, 1997).

Personnel

The composition of CESID personnel has changed significantly since the Service was created. In 1981, 90 per cent were military personnel (Jaime-Jimenez, 1997:7). By 1995 that percentage decreased to 55.[11] The Director General has always been a member of the army. However, Prime Minister Aznar has recently declared his intention to appoint a civilian as Director General in the near future, probably as part of the service reorganisation.

CESID currently employs approximately 2,000 persons, of whom 960 come from the military forces, 676 from the public civil administration and 374 from police forces. The biggest expansion took place between 1983 and 1987 when the number of employees of CESID increased by 1,500 (EL PAIS, 23 August 1997). Nevertheless, it was only in 1995 when a Personnel Statute[12] for CESID was enacted. This established common rules for all the employees of CESID without making any distinction about their origin. That is, all personnel have the same status regardless of origin. The terms of such Statute are published in a Royal Decree: the admission, selection, education and training of personnel, the different kinds of personnel, rights and duties of such personnel and the disciplinary regime. The detail of jobs, the personnel register and the personnel evaluation remains classified information.

Employees working in the CESID can be permanent or temporary (maximum of seven years) personnel. Temporary personnel succeeding to comply with the profile in a minimum period of three years, may become permanent personnel of CESID provided they get through the evaluation period. The term of office of the CESID's director general shall not exceed five years, as provided for in the statue. This is a consequence of the political scandals involving the previous director general who remained in office for more than 14 years.[13]

Operations

The way CESID operates does not differ markedly from other intelligence services. The external network is composed of representatives of the CESID in the Spanish Embassies or Consulates abroad. This network complements the diplomatic and military services network. The internal network is formed by the delegations that the CESID keeps in the Spanish provinces in accordance with its information targets. CESID also collaborates with other national and international information and intelligence services to exchange documents and information. CESID obtains its technical information from:

- communication interceptions, which need judicial authorisation (sometimes such authorisation could not be obtained quickly enough and some political controversy was created);
- coded and encrypted messages;
- satellites;
- surveillance, including the identification and detection of persons and electronic surveillance;
- access to personal and confidential information kept in the files of the Administration, with no restriction; and
- searches made with judicial authorisation in homes etc.

The operational group is in charge of gathering information through special means. Such means must observe the law if the activity is carried out in Spain. If abroad, the means employed must be reciprocal with the methods used by foreign services in Spain.

Other Intelligence Services

The Ministry of Interior also has its own intelligence services. Each national police force has one department that carries out research and obtains information related to national security. Police forces are ordered to obtain and analyse all information that may be of interest to public security and to the maintenance of order. The CESID and police in effect share functions regarding interior information but the CESID does not have an operational capacity for action. Further duplication happens with the security services of each police force. All police forces have created intelligence services with the same objectives and duplicate (or even triplicate) effort, resources and expense.

Comisaria General de Informacíon (CGI)

The CGI depends on the General Operational Sub-Directorate (*Sección General Operativa*), which in turn depends on the General Direction of Police. The CGI is the department that manages the information obtained by the national police force (*Cuerpo Nacional de Policía*). The CNP is the police force with the mandate to control foreign immigration, and fight illegal gambling and drugs.

The CGI has also to manage the reception, treatment and development of information regarding public security and to use such information in the course of its functions and objectives within the national territory. The fight against terrorism is a priority for the CGI.

The divisions inside the CGI are as follows:

- Internal Information (UCII): The primary task of this division is to investigate terrorism and street violence, especially in the Basque Country.
- External Information (UCIE): The main departments of this division are the Arab and Islamic, as well as those for the protection of technology and international co-ordination.
- Intelligence (UCI): This division obtains and analyses information about terrorism and economy.
- Operational Support (UCAO): This division obtains information by covert technical means.

This structure is repeated at every administration level of the territory. There are information brigades in every autonomous community and, in certain towns, the operational brigade also has an information section. These divisions are mainly involved in the fight against terrorism, even though the *Guardia Civil* has overall more significance.

Intelligence Service of Guardia Civil

The *Jefatura de Información e Investigación* (JII) of the *Guardia Civil* works under the direction of General Sub-Directorate of Operations that reports to the General Directorate of the *Guardia Civil*. The *Guardia Civil* is a rural police, compared with the CNP, with competence to control weapons, explosives and smuggling. It is also in charge of frontiers and harbours. The *Guardia Civil* is a military force with a double dependency. It depends on the Ministry of Defence in personnel matters and for certain military missions and on the Ministry of Interior in public security matters. The two ministries have joint responsibility for the selection, education, and training of its personnel.[14]

JII has an intelligence service, a judicial police service and a tax service.[15] In practice the three services overlap their activities. The intelligence service inside the JII is the department that centralises all the information. It is divided into the special operational group (*Grupo de apoyo operativo*); the counter-intelligence group (*Unidad contra-inteligencia*), and two special units, the main objectives of which are, first, terrorism matters, one in charge of the terrorism of ETA and the other for other terrorist groups. Second, this division is also decentralised to the different territorial levels, where every unit has the duty to refer to this division all the information it obtains.

Ertzaintza

The *Ertzaintza* is the police force of the Basque Country, the region that gave birth to the terrorist group ETA and in which it is mostly active and has all its political support. *Ertzaintza* was created in 1936, when the Basque Country for the first time was granted autonomy by the government of the Republic in the middle of the Spanish Civil War. Upon the establishment of the democratic regime in Spain, and the reintroduction of the autonomy of the Basque Country, *Ertzaintza* was recreated in 1980.[16]

    Ertzaintza did not assume competence to fight against terrorism. The Basque Government did not want to assume such responsibility, and the Central Government did not want to transfer it. Nevertheless, when ETA killed some members of this police, both governments agreed that *Ertzaintza* should also be involved in the fight against terrorism. In 1989 the co-ordination body of the police resolved that the different police forces operating in the Basque Country could share such competence. (Jar Couselo, 1995:179–180). From that moment it was necessary for *Ertzaintza* to set up an intelligence department. This is located in the criminal division and is also independent from the judicial police unit. The intelligence department employs 260 agents.

    AVCS (*Unidad de Adjuntos al Viceconsejero de Seguridad*) was a special group separated from the *Ertzaintza* that never appeared in the organisation chart and that reported to the vice-president of security of the Basque Government. This group was alleged to be the political police of the Basque nationalist party (PNV) (Jar Cousuelo, 1995:248–252). Its existence was much criticised. As a result thereof, it was finally integrated in the intelligence department located in the criminal division of the *Erzaintza*.

Control and Accountability

The Reform of the Services

As mentioned, the Spanish intelligence services model is concentrated basically in one service (the CESID), with some other intelligence services that depend on other ministries. Yet the organisation of the intelligence services is neither centralised nor concentrated in one service in order to avoid the danger of concentration of power in one institution without political control. The price for such division is the lack of co-ordination between the intelligence services and the waste of resources. There is no institution that officially co-ordinates the activities of the different services. Members of each service attend meetings held on a weekly basis to exchange information about terrorism and other matters. The Socialist Government intended to create an administrative body that could co-ordinate all such services. Its name was to be State Intelligence Centre *Centro de Inteligencia del Estado*. However, the idea did not succeed (ABC, June 19, 1995).

One objective of the Conservative Party in the elections of 1996 was to reform the intelligence services. As mentioned, the CESID was very directly involved in the political scandals that appeared in the last years of the socialist government. Such reform again reached the front page of newspapers due to some recordings made by the CESID of telephone conversations held in one of the offices of *Herri Batasuna*, the political party that supports ETA, without any judicial authorisation.

The main points of the reform, according to the program of the Conservative Party, were:

- to change the name in order to create an independent service, which would not be linked to the Ministry of Defence;
- to create a co-ordination centre that would exclusively report to the Prime Minister or Vice-Prime Minister. The functions of this centre would be to define the priorities of action of the services, to co-ordinate their actions and to supervise their budgets proposals. External and internal intelligence departments would be distinguished;
- to transfer competence of the CESID to the services of the Ministry of Interior and armed forces, especially in internal security, terrorism and drugs traffic;
- to create a military intelligence centre, the responsibility of the *Estado Mayor de la Defensa*. His centre will concentrate the intelligence divisions of the armed forces;
- to ensure that the Spanish Parliament controls the intelligence services. Such control would be made by a joint Commission of Congress and Senate, the deliberations of which would be kept secret.

Control and Accountability

The control of the intelligence services is ensured by four different means:

Executive control The Prime Minister personally appoints the Director of CESID and is responsible for such appointment before the Spanish Parliament. The Government also controls the activity of CESID by establishing its operational direction. In practice, CESID submits a permanent plan to the Ministry of Defence and the Prime Minister for approval. Although the Government is the only institution that has control over the activity of the CESID, such control has rarely been effected.

Parliamentary control Parliament has a general competence through hearing the Minister of Defence and the Prime Minister and by creating investigation commissions. The Parliament has also the power to request information classified as secret if one quarter of its members so approves, but they are not allowed to reveal any information contained in those documents.

A specific commission named *Comisión de Secretos Oficiales (CSO)* has been created to control classified information, but it does not really have a permanent control of the activities of CESID. The Commission is composed of members of the Parliament who are not experts in the subject. The Parliament does not have a permanent commission to control the activity of CESID. Consequently, the Government may abuse its privileges under the Law of Official Secrets to declare secret many activities of its security forces, extending the scope of such law to information that should not be classified secret. This was the case when the Socialist Government in 1996 declared secret information about the activities of the terrorist group GAL, which was a group active in the mid-eighties in Southern France (ELMUNDO, March 14, 1996).

Budgetary control The *Tribunal de Cuentas* (Accounting Court-TC) is a special court that directly reports to the Parliament, the competence of which is to control the accounting and economic administration of the public sector, including intelligence services.

The intelligence service budget is approved by the *Ley de Presupuestos Generales del Estado* every year. Nevertheless, it contains an important item of confidential expenses (*gastos reservados*). Before 1995, there was no control over these monies. The absence of such control was at the origin of one of the political scandals of the Socialist Government, in which senior officials of the Ministry of Interior were accused of using such money to pay themselves an extra salary.

A law was enacted in 1995 aimed to control better the disbursement of such expenses. The Law allows the Ministries of Defence, Justice, Foreign Affairs and Interior to have confidential expenses and to defray expenses for the 'Security and Defence' of the State. These expenses do not need any documentary justification but the directors of the departments authorised to administer these expenses must dictate internal rules to ensure they do relate security and defence of the State.

These confidential expenses are kept secret and also have a particular accounting system. Their amount must be specified in the annual general budget but what they are actually used for is kept secret and protected by the Law on Official Secrets. Directors of the Departments who are responsible for these confidential expenses must periodically report to the Prime Minister, to the President of the *Tribunal de Cuentas* and to a parliamentary commission on a bi-annual basis, so that the commission may prepare an annual report about the administration of such confidential expenses.

Judicial Control Intelligence services are also partially controlled by the courts. If any illegal action has been committed by such services, criminal courts are obliged to prosecute the persons responsible for such action. This control, fundamental in a democracy, is formally applied to all actions. Nevertheless, such control may be reduced by the possibility that the Government declares some documents secret. As mentioned above, the Socialist Government declared secret many documents and all the future information about the GAL, and anti-terrorist procedures, methods and structures, CESID or police. Such declaration, which was made just two days before the general elections were won by the Conservative party, meant that the documents could not be transferred to a criminal court (EL MUNDO, 14 marzo 1996).

Documents can be classified secret by the Law of Official Secrets (LSO) 9/1969 modified by Law 48/1978 and its Regulations (RSO). The law on official secrets is an exception to the general principle of openness of the public administration. Certain activities and information need to be kept secret and protected from potential disclosure to unauthorised persons, since such disclosure may put national security in danger. The LSO protects national security and the criminal and military codes impose serious sanctions on the publication of official secrets. Nevertheless, the LSO was published before the Spanish Constitution, and some of its provisions are not appropriate for a democratic State.

The LSO defines as classified any information, document, data, acts or objects that can damage or endanger the national security and the defence of the State. This broad definition allows great flexibility in practice. The Council of Ministers is the competent body authorised to classify, although the LSO also admits the competence of the *Junta de Jefes de Estado Mayor*.[17] The Spanish Government may specify the period of classification and the personnel authorised to have access to the information (art. 4 LSO and art. 3 RSO). The institutions that may have access to the classified documents are the Parliament (Congress and Senate) and the Ombudsman. The commission of Official Secrets and one or more parliamentary groups with more than one quarter of the total members of the Congress may request information about classified documents through the President of the Congress.[18] The Ombudsman is the only institution with limited access to secret information,[19] although the Council of Ministers (*Consejo de Ministros*) may forbid such access.

The LSO establishes two categories of secrecy, secret matters and reserved matters. Such a distinction has become obsolete in relation to the NATO terminology (the LSO is almost 30 years old). Under the LSO, the distinction depends on whether the knowledge of the relevant matter may damage or puts in risk the security and defence of the State (Cousido González, 1995:35).

The LSO 9/1969, modified by Law 48/1978, does not specify any judicial control of classified documents. It mentioned only that the institutions that have access to classified information are the Congress and the Senate. The absence of provisions allowing the courts to have access to classified information has been criticised. These critiques increased when a judge of the *Audiencia Nacional*[20] who was investigating the activities of the GAL, asked the CESID and the Ministry of Defence for some classified documents[21] that could be used as a means of evidence for the clarification of the origin of the GAL. The judge lodged an appeal before the Court of Conflicts against the Government asking for the clarification of his competence to have access to classified documentation. Although the Court of Conflicts may not be considered an adequate institution to solve this issue,[22] its decision was very controversial (Lozano, 1998:446), since it decided that the courts could not have access to classified documents. The courts could only ask the Council of Ministers to withdraw the classification (the art. 4 of LSO). This does not mean that the classification decision is entirely out of judicial control since the decision of the Council of Ministers may be subject to an appeal before the Supreme Court (*Sala 3 del Tribunal Contencioso-administrativo*).[23] The Supreme Court may then control such decisions and review the documents classified by the Council of Ministers, to determine the appropriateness of such decision. Consequently, ordinary judges may only know the contents of secret documents once such documents have been disclosed by the Council of Ministers.

There has been much controversy about this decision, since it has been considered that it attacks the right of defence and the right to bring evidences before the court. The Ombudsman shared this opinion in his report of 1995 to the Parliament.[24] The procedure established by the Court of Conflicts offers a limited right of defence to the citizens, because there may be an immunity zone that remains out of the jurisdiction of the courts. The Ombudsman advised the LSO should be reformed in order to guarantee an unlimited right to defence to all citizens.

The decision of the Court of Conflicts must be understood in the context in which it was issued. The Spanish Criminal Code includes a chapter regarding crimes against national defence. The disclosure of secrets and information related to the national defence is a crime and has been the excuse used not to present classified documents to the court. In the GAL case, secret documents were highly relevant as they would have been the means of evidence necessary to prove the involvement of the Socialist Government in the origin of the GAL. Neither the court nor prosecutors have had access to classified documents as a means of evidence.

The possible breach of the right of defence has been the argument used by the Supreme Court in its decisions[25] regarding the appeals lodged against the decision of the Council of Ministers not to disclose documents. The Supreme Court has pondered the right to defence and the national security and in certain cases has revoked the decision of the Council of Ministers and disclosed some documents based on the pre-eminence of the right of defence.

A draft of a new LSO has been discussed by the Conservative government but has not been introduced into the Spanish Parliament. The draft LSO attempts to modify the main problems created by the existing law. In the draft, the definition of official secret is modified in order to strengthen the concept of national security and to specify the circumstances allowing the government to classify the documents. The draft LSO also follows the categories of classification used by NATO (top secret, secret and confidential). The Council of Ministers is competent to declare top-secret matters, the ministries are competent to declare secret and confidential documents. The act of classification becomes a more formal act. Such classification must be justified and the concept of secret is more detailed. The draft LSO also regulates the effects of the classification of the documents and the institutions that have access to the classified documents.

It establishes a maximum period of classification of 50 years for top secret and secret documents and 25 years for confidential documents.

The draft LSO clarifies certain aspects that are not defined by the existing LSO, but it does not increase judicial control of the activities that the government carries out regarding national security. In this regard, the draft LSO merely follows the criteria enacted by the Court of Conflicts in the aforementioned decision.

Conclusion

The Spanish intelligence services have not changed since the transition to democracy. Neither the consolidation of democracy, the end of the cold war, nor the scandals where the CESID has been involved have motivated a reform of the Spanish intelligence services model. After the crisis of CESID at the end of the socialist government, the Conservative Party announced important changes that have not been implemented. Yet recent controversies about spying on the political party that supports ETA have brought the debate about CESID again to the front pages.

CESID should no longer have a dual dependency on the Prime Minister and the Ministry of Defence. It is also necessary to create a co-ordination institution that would report to the government and that can control the different intelligence services, both internal and external. This institution must co-ordinate the services in accordance with the priorities marked by the government, although this is a difficult task under the current Spanish security model. Duplicating activities is not necessarily negative, since it may prevent the manipulation of the final decision.

The control of the intelligence services is the most urgent issue regarding the Spanish intelligence model. The lack of constitutional provision for the activity must be counteracted by a strict control of the activity. First, executive control must be more effective in establishing the mandate of the different intelligence services. This control should begin with the specification of the permanent plan: this is an annual document that must set forth the intelligence objectives for every year. It must include the needs for information established by the government, and the services must control the information sources and the creation of new sources. Second, the actual lack of parliamentary control must be changed by the creation of a permanent commission of members of the parliament. Third, judicial control must comply with the principles and rights granted by the Spanish Constitution. Criminal judges must have access to classified documents to ensure the right of defence and to control the activity of the intelligence services, with appropriate measures to prevent possible dangers from such access. The procedure created in United States of inspection in camera (without the parties being present) of the documents to evaluate if the information is relevant to the national security is an option. Another option is the creation of an *ad hoc* court.

These control mechanisms must be complemented by the definition and limitation of the activity of the intelligence services and by a new regulation of secret matters. Secrecy cannot be an excuse for carrying out illegal activities not legitimated by national security. The secrecy ensured by the LSO must also be revised in accordance with constitutional principles. The concept of national security is too ambiguous to grant a blank cheque to the security services. The reasons for classifying documents as secrets must be well defined and not left to the services' interpretation of national security.

Notes

[1] The intelligence service of the Armed Forces (one for each branch); the General Staff Intelligence Section; *Brigada Central de Información*; the *Brigada Político-Social of the Cuerpo Superior de Policía*; the *Servicio Central de Documentación* (SECED) who was in charge of the co-ordination of the mentioned services; *Servicio de Información de Excombatientes* (the war veterans service); *Servicio de Información de la Guardia de Franco* (Franco's Guard service); and the *Servico de Información de la Organización Sindical Verticalista* (the unions service). Only the General Staff Intelligence Service and the SECED were really intelligence services even though their task was mainly to gather information, rather than conduct intelligence activity (Jaime-Jimenez, 1997).

[2] The Ministry of Defense is the product of the merger of three ministries of the dictatorship. The Army, the Navy and the Air, in order to ensure the direction and co-ordination of the policy of security and defense in one institution.

[3] This department assists the Prime Minister and the Minister of Defense in military matters (art. 20 of the Royal Decree 1883/1996, of 2 August, on the basic organic structure of the Ministry of Defense).

[4] SECED was mainly in charge of controlling the opposition forces in the education, union and religious sectors. See more information about the functions of SECED in Sainz de la Peña, J.A. and Marquina, 1996.

[5] The Socialist government supposedly created or supported the antiterrorist group of liberation and the CESID was also implicated. One of the judicial investigations into those supposed to be responsible for the actions of the antiterrorist group of liberation (GAL) is finished. The former Minister of Interior (José Barrionuevo), the Secretary of State of Security (Rafael Vera), the Civil Governor of Vizcaya (Julián Sancristobal) were sentenced to ten years of prison and prohibited for twelve years from being a public servant. The crimes committed were misappropriation of public funds and kidnapping a supposed ETA member (STS2/1998 of 29 July).

[6] Personal translation.

[7] Art. 11 of the Organic Law 2/1986 of State Police Forces.

[8] Order of the Ministry of Defense 135/82, of 30 September.

[9]   Art. 3 of Order 135/1982, of September 30, articles 4 through 7 of Royal Decree 2632/1985, of December and article 5.3 of Royal Decree 1883/1996, of 2 August.

[10] This department was reinforced after the scandal where Colonel J. A. Perote, Chief of the department of special operations had a leading role. Mr. Perote stole some secret documents of CESID and leaked them to the press. Mr. Perote was sentenced to jail for this affair.

[11] Appearance 212/001710 of the Director of CESID before the Defense Commission of the Congress.

[12] Royal Decree 1324/1995, of 28 July.

[13] He resigned in June 1995, after the affair 'Perote'. The documents disclosed by Colonel Perote proved that the CESID unlawfully listened to telephone conversations of relevant and popular persons, including the King of Spain. The deputy Prime Minister and the Minister of Defense also resigned due to the scandal originated by the publication of such conversations.

[14] Art. 14 Organic Law 2/86 on Security Forces and Bodies.

[15] This service gathers a lot of information about drug smuggling.

[16] Royal Decree 290/1980, of 22 December, on the Miñones and Miqueletes of the Diputaciones Forales of Alava, Guipúzcoa y Vizcaya.

[17] Even if the law admits the competence of the *Junta de Jefes de Estado Mayor*, the law of 1984, on defence functions reduces the functions of this institution and converts it to a consultant body.

[18] Art. 2 of the resolution of 3 June 1992 about the access by Congress to official secrets. The resolution also regulates the different methods to transfer information in case of secret and reserved matters.

[19] Art. 22 Organic Law 3/1981, 6 April, regulating the Ombudsman.

[20] The Court in charge of judging terrorism, drug trafficking and crimes that are committed in more than one province in Spain.

[21] The judge asked for some documents about the use of reserved expenses by CESID. The judge believed that such funds were used to finance illegal antiterrorist actions.

[22] This Court of Conflict has the mandate to solve conflicts of competencies that may arise between the judicial and administrative institutions. The main point of the question was not a conflict of competencies but an interpretation of the LSO, that is a pre-constitutional law. The law does not establish the accessibility of the judges to the secrets of the State, but the Constitution recognized the right of defense (art. 24) and the submission of the Administration to the law (art. 9.1 and 103.1) and to judicial control (art. 1061).

[23] Art. 58 Organic Law on the Judicial Power, 6/1985.

[24] The Ombudsman said in his report: It is difficult to guarantee the right to an effective access to justice by this solution. There is an immunity zone outside the scope of judges and tribunals. Likewise, it cannot be guaranteed that all means of evidence may be used in the court process, since there is a dark zone where the courts cannot have access unless so authorized by the council of ministries or the *Junta de Jefes de Estado Mayor* (Annual report of the Ombudsman, June 26, 1996 – serie A, num. 7, p. 9).

[25] Supreme Court decisions 4513/1997, 4514/1977 and 4515/1997, of 4 April.

Chapter 5

National Security in Hungary

Istvan Szikinger

The Present Structure

After extensive debate the Hungarian Parliament enacted in 1995 a comprehensive Act on National Security, consolidating the existing network of intelligence agencies. Act CXXV of 1995 made no fundamental change to the structure which had been in force since a government decree in 1990, with one remarkable exception. The new law separated the Special Service for National Security from the National Security Office, transforming the latter into an independent agency. This left five separate services responsible for national security, with the possible addition, in the near future, of one more agency to co-ordinate the community and to fulfil new demands coming from the country's recent NATO membership.

The overarching mission of these agencies is to protect Hungarian national security through open and covert intelligence gathering within the framework established by the Act. National security is understood to include the protection of national sovereignty and of the constitutional order (Section 3). More specifically, the services are to:

- detect efforts to undermine the independence or the territorial integrity of the country;
- reveal and eliminate covert attempts to subvert or to threaten the political, economic and military interests of the country;
- acquire intelligence on other countries relevant to governmental decision-making;
- reveal and eliminate any covert attempt to change or disturb, by unlawful means, the constitutional order and undermine the respect of basic human rights, representative multiparty democracy or constitutional institutions;
- investigate and elucidate terrorist acts, weapons and drug trafficking and illegal trade of controlled goods and technologies.

The specific powers and responsibilities of each of the five agencies are defined in sections 4–8 of the Act. The Intelligence Office is to gather intelligence on foreign countries that may be useful in setting government policy. The Office may also engage in counterintelligence activities to protect national security interests abroad. It has the responsibility to gather intelligence on transnational criminal organisations, potential threats to the country's economy, etc. Finally, the Office has administrative authority in the field of data encryption.

The National Security Office, on the other hand, is to:

- reveal and eliminate any effort of foreign intelligence services that may undermine or threaten the sovereignty of the Hungarian Republic or its political, economic, military or other important interests;
- reveal and eliminate covert activities aimed at changing or disturbing the constitutional order or the Hungarian Republic by unlawful means;
- reveal and eliminate any terrorist activities of foreign powers, organisations or persons;
- reveal and eliminate covert efforts to threaten the economic, scientific/technical or monetary security of the Hungarian Republic, as well as the illegal traffic of drugs or weapons;
- provide protection to the central state and governmental institutions and facilities;
- provide protection to, and control over persons under its jurisdiction;
- perform security checks on persons applying for immigrant or refugee status or for Hungarian citizenship or visa;
- uncover, prior to official investigation, offences against the state, offences against humanity, desertion, mutiny and other acts endangering the Armed Forces' combat-readiness;
- uncover offences or acts of terrorism against national, ethnic, racial or religious groups if and when the crime has either been reported to the National Security Office or uncovered by it;
- participate in uncovering and preventing the illegal trade of internationally controlled goods and technologies, and in the monitoring of the legal trade of such goods and technologies;
- participate in uncovering and preventing the illegal trade of military goods and services, and in the monitoring of the legal trade of such goods and services.

The Military Intelligence Office gathers, analyses and distributes information on all aspects of foreign military and security activities. It also collects data about the illegal trade of weapons and about terrorist organisations that may threaten the security of the Armed Forces. The Office is also responsible for the security of Hungarian military personnel and facilities abroad.

The Military Security Office's mission is to detect and neutralise foreign intelligence activities, as well as any attempts to interfere with the Hungarian Republic's constitutional order through illegal means. Simply put, the Military Security Office has responsibilities equivalent to those of the National Security Office, the difference being jurisdictional.

Finally, the Special Service for National Security serves as an auxiliary to all other agencies legally authorised to access secret intelligence, including police forces. It provides them with means of communicating data and the technology necessary for covert communications interception, within the limits of the law. The Service is also the administrative authority regarding data protection and security. Its members sometimes carry out specialised expert activities in that field, but the Service is not allowed to engage in intelligence activities without the explicit request of other agencies. All services are offered free of charge to authorised agencies.

Table 5.1   Budget of Hungarian Intelligence Agencies (Amounts in millions)[1]

AGENCY	1997		1998	
	HUF	USD	HUF	USD
National Security Office	2,793.9	13.6	4,075.7	24.8
Information Office	2,583.9	12.6	3,183.9	15.5
Special Service	3,757.6	18.3	4,218.2	20.6
Military Information Office	3,420.7	16.7	4,868.2	24.2
Military Security Office	732.0	3.6	1,056.0	5.2
Total	13,288.1	64.8	17,402.0	90.2

The Act on National Security provides no details on the internal structure of the five national security agencies. All of the agencies, including the civilian ones (the Information Office, the National Security Office and the Special Service) are managed by 'Directors General' with the military rank of general. Regional and local units are set up as seen fit by government.

Each of the agencies has its budget determined by the government, as shown in Table 5.1. Taken together, national security expenditures represented 0.52 per cent of the national budget in 1997 and 0.66 per cent in 1998. However these figures do not represent the entirety of the expenses: it is estimated, for example, that about 10 billion HCF (50 million USD) was spent on technology necessary for the interception of mobile phone conversations (in the future a substantial portion of this expense should be assumed by the phone companies themselves).

There is no official information about the staffing of any of the agencies. Based on data from the budget, and with knowledge of the average salary level, it can be estimated that about 3,000–4,000 officers work for the civilian services and 2,000–3,000 for military security agencies.

Hungary is not part of any international treaty on the co-operation of national intelligence services. So far exchanges of information and joint operations have been conducted under unpublished protocols and occasional or coincidental arrangements between the agencies concerned. According to reliable sources, the most common causes for joint international efforts seem to include the fight against the traffic of weapons and internationally regulated dangerous substances, transnational organised crime and terrorism. Other inter-agency co-ordinated activities also focus on the trade of internationally controlled goods and technologies. That being said, it is public knowledge that bilateral co-operation does not preclude the interference of conflicting interests.[2]

The legal status of intelligence officers was defined by the 1996 Service Relations of Officers of Armed Organs (Agencies) Act (no. XLIII). The Act defines the rights and duties of all officers serving in agencies operating under a military structure and uses the phrase 'armed organs' even though it also covers state and local fire brigades. 'Armed organs' also include the border guard service (under military responsibility while performing police activities), the prison service, customs and finance departments, civil defence and national security agencies. Basically, 'armed organs' have in common a military style organisation and a rule of unconditional obedience; however, the drafters of the Act stipulated, somewhat disingenuously, that consistent regulations were necessary to respect the professional nature of all the services. Section 3 of the Act also defines 'service relationship' as a particular type of legal connection between the state and the officer, in which both parties are bound by duties and rights specific to the service. Members of the 'armed organs' are to perform their duties with the understanding that their work requires willing, lifelong commitment in an environment characterised by strict discipline, risk to life and limb and the restriction or suspension of some individual rights. All officers, including those working in civilian national security agencies, are soldiers in terms of criminal law, meaning that they are subject to special provisions within the criminal code.

This militaristic approach is also responsible for one of the most objectionable provisions of the National Security Act, one that is also reinforced by the Service Regulations Act: it is the duty of all agents to comply with any unlawful order given by their commanding officers. Section 27 of the National Security Act requires that members of the intelligence services carry out unlawful activities if so instructed by their superiors. Violations of the law must be reported, but must be carried out regardless – unless the act obviously constitutes a criminal offense. The vocabulary used here is important: note that the Act stipulates 'activities' and not single acts. This wording is unique to the security services and does not apply to other 'armed organs', where the singular 'action' is used. Further, the addition of the word 'obviously' is also peculiar to national security officers: in their case the activities have to be obviously illegal to warrant reporting. In short, it is clear that the Legislator has determined that national security required a higher degree of tolerance for criminal behaviour on the part of its agents, clearly allowing more headroom for state delinquency in this area than in police or other armed organs. This approach is only made more questionable by the fact that, in practice, almost all activities of intelligence agencies may constitute crimes if due legal justification cannot be offered. The result is that in everyday activities officers are left without the most important, perhaps the only, way to distinguish between legitimate and illegitimate means.

'Danube-gate' and its Aftermath

In January 1990 the Danube-gate scandal rocked the otherwise peaceful process of negotiated transition to democracy in Hungary. Nicknamed after the Watergate scandal in the United States, the case soured the relationship between the incumbent Communist Party and the new constitutionally acknowledged opposition on the eve of the first free elections. In short, it was revealed that secret intelligence activities had been directed against legal political parties and other legitimate organisations opposed to the government. At the time the components of the state security service were officially part of the Hungarian police. The hypocrisy of the ruling elite, who while showing a tolerant and open facade had been secretly employing the state police to undermine the opposition, probably caused their electoral defeat to be even greater than had been expected. It also underlined the urgency of addressing policing and state security matters in the new constitutional environment.

As a result, Parliament established a special Investigative Committee with the mission to investigate the causes of the scandal and to make recommendations for the future. One consequence was the resignations of the Minister of the Interior and of most of the leadership at the State Security Service of the National Police. It is important to note that the investigations were limited to Section III/III of the Service, which had traditionally dealt with the fight against 'internal' enemies of the system, and whose officers had actually engaged in the acts of political spying. Other sections of the State Security Service were never under investigation, although it is obvious that the conclusions of the Committee could also be applied to Foreign Intelligence (III/I), Counterintelligence (III/II), Military Security (III/IV) and the Technical Service (III/V). Not to mention that 'ordinary' criminal and uniformed police had also been under the same command structure and the same legal framework. The Committee's Report (29/1990 [III.13] OGY hat. melléklet) put the blame on the former leadership of the Ministry of the Interior for neglecting to amend the rules and regulations relating to political and criminal intelligence work and thus failing to insure their conformity with constitutional provisions. Even in the days of communist rule, Hungary had been party to international covenants on human rights, while at the same time devising domestic standards for the restriction of basic rights.

At any rate, as the Committee pointed out, a complete revision of the Constitution had come into effect on 23 October 1989, and had eradicated any remaining legal justification for the collection of information about political opponents by the security services. Direct political interference prevented the state security services from introducing even modest reforms before the transition to democracy. Yet, even after the comprehensive constitutional amendments, reports on rival political formations prepared by official intelligence agencies had been distributed not only to members of the government but also to Communist Party brass. The Committee emphasised that one of the most dangerous remnants of the Cold War within the intelligence community was the still pervading totalitarian take on the concept of 'enemy of the state', whereby 'official' enemies are selected, become permanent targets of security activities and just like in wartime are given no quarters, their protection by 'due process of law' being suspended.

In addition to condemning the old state security system, the new Parliament also decided to introduce changes into the legislation dealing with the collection of confidential information. A Provisional Act on Authorisation for Gathering Intelligence (no. X from 1990) was adopted, covering the relevant activities of all intelligence agencies, including criminal police. Section 1, paragraph 2 of the Act defined the phrase 'special means and methods' (in short, 'special means') as:

> any means or method applied without the knowledge of the person concerned, which may violate the rights to privacy of the home or of personal secrets, confidentiality of correspondence or personal data protection.

The Act further stipulated that 'special means' could only be used when the circumstances could justify it and when no other means of gathering the information were available; all data not directly relevant to the goals pursued were to be deleted from the record. Section 5 of the Act also required that special means be discontinued once the goal was reached or when it became obvious that it would be impossible to reach. In addition, if the application of special means failed to confirm suspicions and no criminal proceedings were launched, the person who had been under surveillance had to be informed of that fact, and all data had to be deleted. On the other hand, no special authorisation was needed to adopt special means, with the exception of communication interception using specialised equipment, interception of postal communications and the secret search of private residences. In these cases a warrant from the Minister of Justice was needed. While this still leaves all control within the hands of the executive, it must be mentioned that none of the agencies actually enabled to use special means were subordinated to the Minister of Justice.

This outline clearly shows that the Provisional Act, as approved by the outgoing Communist-ruled Parliament, failed to provide adequate measures for the protection of individual rights. Still, taken in combination with constitutional reforms, it offered a promising development towards the establishment of a state respectful of the Rule of Law. Ironically, the post-transition Parliament, far from improving or even supporting the modest advances in the Provisional Act, proceeded instead to repeal all of its more progressive aspects. The author of the only Hungarian monograph on security intelligence, far from a radical critic, still concluded that on the whole the laws meant to replace the 1990 Provisional Act actually lowered the post-transition constitutional standards.[3]

The new constitution did not require the reorganisation of the intelligence community's legal framework. The 1989 amendment to the Constitution, in addition to enhancing existing human rights provisions, included a special chapter dealing with the armed forces and the police. It stipulated that new regulations on police organisations and activities had to be spelled out in a specific act of Parliament. Section 40/A, paragraph 2, says that:

> the fundamental function of the police is to safeguard public security and defend internal order. The enactment of the law on the police and the detailed rules connected with national security require two-thirds of the votes of the Members of Parliament present.

Undoubtedly, references to the police task of defending 'internal order,' which was the terminology of the legislation in force at the time, should have been interpreted as a confirmation of the existing integrated structure of public and state security. It should be mentioned that this structure was quite unique in socialist countries, where separate intelligence service was the norm. On the other hand, the legal situation of state security units had already changed several times in our country before 1989.

Historical Background

1949 saw the creation of an independent state security organisation that ostensibly reported to the government but was in fact directed by the upper leadership of the Communist party. The extreme arbitrariness of the activities of that security apparatus came to light with the 1956 uprising. With the uprising suppressed, the socialist regime consolidated its power and the police and state security organisations were integrated in an effort to increase their transparency. In practice however, political police remained independent within the unified structure. It was left under the direction of the Minister of the Interior, where one Deputy Minister was responsible for ordinary policing and another for state security. Each county police chief had a deputy responsible for state security within his jurisdiction, who could receive instructions from above and act without the chief's knowledge or specific authorisation. This independent subsystem is a very good example of direct party interference with policing; political interest superseded the demands of public order or criminal investigations.

This structure also made it easy to disguise politically motivated operations as ordinary police matters. For instance, members of the opposition were often searched and detained under pretence of public security imperatives, simply to prevent them form attending important meetings or electoral gatherings.

Acutely aware of these sophisticated means of political oppression, during the transition the Opposition had demanded the separation of state security from police organisations and the clear definition of their respective jurisdictions and powers. Under added pressure from the Danube-gate affair, the communist government finally decided to reorganise the system. The authoritarian state security organisation was disbanded by government decree (26/1990 [II 14] MT r). It was replaced by four separate agencies under Cabinet supervision: the Information Service was given the task of collecting intelligence, while the National security Office would engage in counterintelligence and protect the constitution. Operating in parallel were the Military Information Office and the Military Security Office.

The drafting of the new comprehensive Act on national security began immediately after the 1990 democratic elections.[4] But for political reasons, including a change of government in 1994, the first version of the Bill was not introduced in Parliament until February 1995 – only to be quickly withdrawn by the government to allow for further political modifications. It was finally put on the House's agenda in October 1995.

It must be emphasised that most of the objections to the Bill were not the result of fundamentally different political positions. Quite the contrary: as pointed out by the Minister without portfolio in his introduction of the Bill, there actually was widespread consensus on the matter. The Minister also praised his predecessors, quite an unusual stance considering the very sharp political turn taken by the country with the 1994 elections. Blaming the first democratic Cabinet for any and all problems had become the explanation of choice for the new government, yet as far as national security issues were concerned, any hint of that attitude seemed to disappear. The real opposition to the Bill came not from political parties but from groups within law enforcement agencies and the military, who managed to influence the legislative process to a great extent in an attempt to protect their interests. A major controversy developed around the issue of the participation of national security agencies in the fight against organised crime. Organised crime had not traditionally been under the responsibility of state security agencies, but having lost their political policing mandate and faced with a change in the international order, the newly created units sensed they might be on the brink of irrelevance and were looking for new ways to justify their existence. Organised crime appeared to be just the ticket. Unfortunately police and other law enforcement agencies were already active in that field, with the power to use 'special means,' and were not about to give it up. The rather intense cover-pulling resulted in major conflicts at the party political level as well.[5]

From the beginning and even at the time of the Provisional Act, four principles had been underlined as bases on which to organise national security activities. First, the services must be deprived of their party political connections in order to avoid their involvement in political struggles. Second, intelligence agencies must protect the security of the state and the constitutional order under government authority. Third, in contrast with the state security ideology of the past, the services should be concentrating on concrete threats to the interests of the Hungarian Republic and avoid any form of witch hunting leftover from the old totalitarian 'enemy of the state' doctrine. The fourth principle dictates that intelligence agencies only restrict individual rights where it is unavoidable, and only to the extents required by national security interests.[6]

Lustration

Of course, as was the case with other countries that went through a transition from dictatorship to democracy, Hungary had to face demands to do justice to the victims of the old regime's political police and to deal with perpetrators who had participated in the system of oppression. The term 'lustration' is often used to designate the investigation and removal from office of politicians and civil servants who have engaged in oppressive activities in the past. Parliament's approach to this delicate matter was hesitant at best.   After turning down several proposals, the Act on Investigating Persons in Certain Important Positions of 1994 was finally adopted (*Évi XXIII. Törvény egyes fontos tisztségeket betöltő személyed ellernőrzéséről*, hereinafter: Lustration Act). A comprehensive amendment was made in 1996 (Act LXII of 1996), following a Constitutional Court ruling that several provisions of the original Act were unconstitutional (60/1994 XII. 24.] *AB hat*). The Court found that the Act was flawed for neglecting to impose uniform criteria for the selection of groups and individuals whose past would be investigated. Another significant finding reprobated the absence of a right of victims of the old state security apparatus to be told about the secret measures taken against them. Most importantly, the Constitutional Court made it very clear that Section III/III was not alone in having acted in violation of basic constitutional principles and that the other units had also engaged in oppressive tactics in defence of the former dictatorship. The 1996 amendment to the Lustration Act did introduce important changes in keeping with the Court's findings. However, some provisions of the law still come short of full compliance with the ruling: for instance, investigations are still exclusively focused on Section III/III. This is likely to contribute in preserving the myth of the lone black sheep of internal political security in the otherwise lily-white herd of the honourable professional agencies of the former totalitarian state.

As amended, the Lustration Act provides for the investigation of the past activities of persons in important positions within the public service. Those having participated in political oppression are asked to resign their posts. This includes having served as internal security agents or having collaborated with internal security by informing on others, as well as membership in the fascist Arrow-Cross party (which contributed to the destruction of democracy in Hungary before and during the Second World War), or in military groups responsible for the suppression of the 1956 revolution. Further, following the spirit of the law, one can also be blamed for having received reports resulting from unconstitutional activities. The members of the Commission created to carry out the investigations are judges, but act independently from the judiciary and make administrative decisions. If the Commission finds that the individual was involved in the activities mentioned above, it will call for his or her resignation. The reason for one's resignation does not have to be revealed, but it is not against the law for one to mention it as the cause of his or her departure. As long as the individual complies with its request, the Commission keeps its findings confidential. Failure to comply, however, results in full publication of the information – but there is a right of appeal before the courts.

In other words, the Commission is powerless to enforce its decision and once a politician's unacceptable past has been declared, there is no further recourse. Among those called to resign their positions were then Prime Minister, Mr. Gyula Horn and Speaker of the House, Zoltán Gál, as well as many other leading personalities of the Socialist Party. Most of them were found to have received reports based on illegally garnered information, but Prime Minister Horn had actually been a member of a military unit involved in the repression of the 1956 uprising. The Prime Minister readily admitted the facts but declined to leave his position, arguing that his politics, past activities and military service were known to voters before the election. Many other politicians who had held important functions during the totalitarian regime also refused to resign. Needless to say, the spirit of the Lustration Act has been somewhat undermined by this attitude.

Another important aspect of the Lustration Act's implementation has been the creation of the Historical Office, as provided by the 1998 amendment. The Office is tasked with depositing the files accumulated by Section III/III over the years, together with other sources relevant to the Commission's investigative work. The entirety of the information is to be made available to those who were victimised by the actions of the old state security apparatus, with the exception of files still kept by the current national security agencies, as well as any document which may inform them of the identity of the agents who had been spying on them.

All in all, the lustration 'experiment' has not resulted in the removal of any of those supporters of the previous totalitarian state security system still active in the reorganised intelligence community. Essentially, the security organisations have managed to weather the political transition with only whatever minimal sacrifice was needed to create the appearance of reform.

The Doctrine of National Security

As previously mentioned, one fundamental principle underlying the reform of national security agencies was the eradication of the totalitarian concept of 'enemy of the state'. This made it necessary to adopt an entirely new approach for the restructuring of the intelligence community and the elaboration of national security strategies. To that effect, in 1993 Parliament adopted a Resolution stating the Principles of Security Policy of the Hungarian Republic (11/1993 [III.12] *OGY hat*). The Resolution states that national security policy must ensure:

- the defence of the sovereignty and of the territorial integrity of the state,
- the internal stability of the Republic, including the undisturbed functioning of all democratic institutions and of the market economy, as well as the full realisation of political, civil and human rights (including religious, ethnic, national and minority rights), the protection of life, property and the welfare of the people living in the country, and
- the protection of conditions favourable to the organisation of economic, political, cultural and other relations and institutions of co-operation with other states.

It was emphasised that in practice, national security interests are common to all countries in Europe and that no state would be able to guarantee its own security independently from its neighbours – and certainly not at their expense. Consequently, the Principles are based on the idea that antagonism, isolation and competition would be counter-productive to the consolidation of our standing within the continent. Quite the opposite, relations of co-operation must be developed and maintained with our neighbours and other countries in the region. It follows, then, that the Hungarian Republic must leave behind its tradition of designating official enemies of the state.

As to particular risks associated with such co-operative activities, the Principles point out that traditional military factors have lost much importance within national security matters. On the other hand, economic, social, human rights and other such new dimensions have become increasingly crucial. Obviously, the European Union is the main influence on all international relations on the continent. The Hungarian Republic will therefore make substantial efforts to join that community. What is more, participation in international institutions may further Hungary's integration into various multilateral agreements and conventions promoting, among other things, the protection of national security. Of paramount importance in the field are institutions such as NATO, the CSCE (later, OSCE) and the Council of Europe.

Hungarian national security depends primarily on the overall state of affairs in Europe, but special consideration must be given to some important characteristics of our immediate neighbourhood. Considerable dangers may arise from the continued underdevelopment of most neighbouring economies, compounded by the complications associated with the recent introduction of the free market model. In addition, past regimes left legacies of accumulated social problems, as well as old and new tensions between states, all of which adds to the risk factors. The Parliament's Principles on Security Policy also point to the growing threats of transnational organised crime, illegal immigration and refugee crises, and conclude that in addition to continued participation in international efforts to address these problems, unilateral steps may become necessary. With the caveat, of course, that these steps be provisional and kept in line with strict international legal standards.

Finally, the Resolution emphasises that political and diplomatic efforts should always be predominant in the protection of Hungarian national security. At the same time, it recognises that the maintenance of armed forces adequate to the defence of the country remains an important element of our national security policy. However, the Principles do not cover the specific duties to be performed by the national security services. The document is also short on details in matters of internal security, setting specific goals but with little explication. Evidently, defining intelligence targets and fields of activity within the country proved too sensitive so early in the transition and with the Danube-gate scandal still fresh in everyone's mind. And indeed it is very difficult to identify clear areas where the conduct of secret intelligence activities would not clash with the values they are supposed to protect. While any extremism clearly beyond the limits of legality may be a legitimate target, the very nature of a democratic system is to open the door to all kinds of political movements usually prohibited by dictatorships – and traditionally targeted by their intelligence services. Little wonder, then, that a population freshly freed from totalitarianism might look dimly upon the apparent return of any form of internal 'security' activities.

Before exploring possible internal security endeavours, one preliminary question must be considered, that is, whether internal security activities are of the same nature as those involved in the protection of external security. Assuming that the nation is to be protected from all threats, regardless of their source, the answer must be negative. In essence, the idea that citizens can be protected against threats stemming from within the state by the same organisations active in the repression of external threats, and using the same methods, is a contradiction in terms (not to mention, a practical conundrum). Undeniably, even in a democracy some behaviours must be suppressed in order to safeguard the very existence of the democratic order. However, by no stretch of the imagination should this ever include acts outside the scope of criminal law. Considering that simply planning to commit a criminal offence in itself constitutes a crime in most cases, conventional police prevention and investigation would seem to be entirely adequate methods of protecting internal security. William Stanley, along with José Manuel Ugarte, rightly argue that the failure to distinguish between the realms of national defence and internal security leads to a doctrine that places absolute priority on the protection of the nation as a whole. Such a doctrine, widespread in Latin American countries, usually results in increased disregard for individual rights and the definition of entire classes of persons or opinion groups as threats to the security of the nation. Ultimately, the next logical step is taken and a war is declared against the deviant groups, who are transformed into enemies of the state.[7]

By setting general internal security goals without further explanation, and more importantly without any idea of the means and methods considered appropriate to their pursuit, the Hungarian Parliament made no difference between internal security work and the countering of external threats. One author who endorsed the official perspective on this issue made it very clear: 'our security policy has been built on dealing with internal security and military tasks as an undivided whole'.[8]

Yet it is important for an emerging democracy such as ours to set itself apart from the old regime by reorganising its national security agencies. A change in rhetoric consisted in parting with the old terminology of 'internal enemy' and even, at a later stage, 'alternative organisations'. Obviously, groups promoting alternative political views and challenges to the government should not only be tolerated, they are in fact essential aspects of any constitutional democracy. Therefore, beyond the rhetoric, a substantial modification of policy regarding the identification of threats to national security was also adopted: following the German pattern, one new central mission of domestic security is the protection of the constitution (*Verfassungsschutz*). According to explanations submitted by the government to Parliament regarding the necessity and the contents of the 1995 National Security Bill, 'protection of the constitution' means the monitoring and investigation of illegal activities aimed at the subversion of the constitutional order. The services are also given the task to counter illegal attempts to influence government institutions or officials. The logic is that since these activities are usually conducted in secrecy and under the cover of entirely legal enterprises, ordinary police work is not enough to keep them in check. This, in conjunction with the severity of the dangers involved and the possible damage to the fundamental values of our constitutional democracy, justify the call for the 'special means' of the security services. The actual, concrete tasks relevant to this policy have not been described but strict compliance with the constitutional framework is required.

This argument is less than convincing since police already have the powers to use the noted 'special means'. Following Danube-gate, the separation of police from security agencies was proposed as a way to safeguard against the concentration of power. But, instead of introducing a corresponding division of tasks, parallel competences were created and caused much confusion as to the respective duties of each organisation in the area of subversive activities. Between the risk of encroaching on police jurisdiction and the privacy restrictions imposed by the constitution, the services are left with little to no leeway at all in which to conduct internal security activities.

One example of information gathering on ethnic and national minorities cogently illustrates how desperate the agencies are to justify their existence in spite of an obvious lack of real need. The case has to do with the establishment and functioning of minority self-government, as provided for by the 1993 Act on National and Ethnic Minorities (no. LXXXVII). The Act sets out three ways in which ethnic minority governments can be established, with the prerequisite that official representatives voluntarily declare themselves to be members of a given national or ethnic minority (no official record may legally contain this information). In the first instance, a local government established by general elections may declare itself to be an ethnic minority government if a majority of its elected representatives are from a single national ethnic group. This is also the case if at least 30 per cent of the representatives have been elected as candidates for a minority. Finally, electors may directly vote to establish an ethnic minority government. The duly formed administration, of course, must still represent the entirety of its constituents and perform the normal duties of any equivalent government, but it is thereby also authorised to act on behalf of the minority represented. This involves no substantial new powers but allows for a more effective representation of minority interests.

Now according to the report of the Minority Ombudsman for the years 1995–96 (accepted by Parliament by resolution 54/1997 [V. 21] *Ogy hat*), Presidents of the Greek, Croat, German and Serb national minority governments requested an investigation into the data collection activities of the National Security Office. Enclosed in the investigation report was a document marked 'strictly confidential', a study of the national minorities living in Baranya County (Southern Hungary) complete with annexes about the regulations concerning minority self-government and lists of names of elected officials. Needless to say, the information contained in the document came from open sources and was in the public domain. Still, minority leaders concluded that their communities might have been monitored by national security agencies as enemies of the state. The Minister without portfolio, who is responsible for the operation of the services, confirmed that the document had been produced as part of national security work. However, since the signature of the competent official was missing (it was apparently a draft), the study could not be regarded as a state secret or as the product of covert internal security activity. The Minister also admitted that there had been long-term data collection concerning national and ethnic minorities, but never included the use of 'special means' that would have required a warrant (wiretapping, bugging, secret searches). According to him, the entire operation was aimed at protecting the minorities against provocation or subversion by extremist groups. He substantiated his statement with references to wars in states of the former Yugoslavia. Apparently, the National Security Office was especially concerned about the risk of hatred between ethnic groups in Hungary being instigated by conflicts in their respective motherlands.

The Ombudsman concluded that the operation had indeed originally been launched in order to protect minority groups against improper influence from forces bent on escalating the national conflict in the former Yugoslavia. Yet from the beginning of the activities in question in 1992 to the 1996 report, no intelligence confirming these suspicions was ever found. Furthermore, the Ombudsman could not find any form of link between the protection of the minority groups and the acquisition of already public data on the self-government statutes or the lists of elected minority officials, and there was no legal basis on which to carry out the information gathering. It also appeared doubtful that information gathering on Bulgarian, Roma, Greek and German minorities had anything to do with the war in the former Yugoslavia. Finally, the Ombudsman pointed out that it might have been more productive, if protection was a priority, to inform ethnic groups and minority governments about the possible dangers they faced, and possibly to openly ask for information confirming or disconfirming the provocation hypotheses. Recommendations were made to immediately terminate the operation. For his part, the Minister without portfolio steadfastly supported it, praising its professionalism, and contested some of the Ombudsman's findings.

The case glaringly highlights the fundamental contradictions that surround the internal activities of the national security services. The author of the present paper cannot but note that the same reasons, namely the protection of the organisations being monitored, were also given to him by the state security agencies as he conducted his investigations in relation to the Danube-gate scandal (as a member of the Ministry Committee). But it is now quite obvious that the monitoring of ethnic minorities resulted in the very situation it was supposed to avert: increasingly tense relations with the central authorities. On the other hand, the Minister's position is understandable: if such operations proved to be unacceptable in a democratic state, would there be anything left for the services to do?

Secrecy

The Johannesburg Principles provide a comprehensive framework for the achievement of a reasonable level of national security in keeping with the fundamental values of democratic society, where constitutional order always favours human rights above bureaucratic expediency. According to principle 11:

Everyone has the right to obtain information from public authorities, including information relating to national security. No restrictions on this right may be imposed on the ground of national security unless government can demonstrate that the restriction is prescribed by law and is necessary in a democratic society to protect a legitimate national security interest.

Other principles define some of the terms used in this field and can help determine the limits of secrecy. For instance, principles 12 and 13 dictate that blanket invocations of national security interests are unacceptable justifications for the denial of due disclosure. Secret matters and issues must be kept to specific and narrow categories in keeping with the primary importance of the public interest in access to information (Johannesburg Principles, 1995).

The Hungarian constitution is entirely compatible with this international standard. Article 61 stipulates that everyone has the right to freely express his or her opinion and to access and distribute information of public interest. Only a majority vote from the representatives can modify laws related to this freedom. For its part, the Constitutional Court has also rendered a number of judgements adopting the same basic standards as the Johannesburg Principles. It ruled, for instance, that freedom of information is key to a healthy public life in a democratic society and that laws restricting freedom of expression should be interpreted restrictively (30/1992 [V. 26] *AB hat*). It also reasoned that:

Freedom of information, the openness of public power, the transparency of the activities of the state and of the executive branch, are prerequisites to the right to freely criticize and to freedom of expression. Therefore, this fundamental right – with consideration to legitimate constitutional limits – benefits from at least as much constitutional protection as its 'mother' right, the freedom of expression. The open, transparent and accountable nature of state administration and the public nature of the activities of the executive branch are fundamental requirements of democracy and are guarantees that the state operates under the rule of law. Without the test of the public, the state would become an 'alienated mechanism,' its operations incalculable, unforeseeable and expressly dangerous, since when the state operates in the dark it poses an increased danger to constitutional liberties (60/1994 [XII. 24] *AB hat*).

The Hungarian Parliament confirmed and concretised the constitutional standards with Act LXIII of 1992, the Protection of Personal Data and the Publicity of Data of Public Interest Act (Data Protection Act). Item 3 of section 2 defines the concept of 'data of public interest' as information possessed by institutions or persons fulfilling state or local government duties or other public duties as defined by legal rules, and that does not qualify as personal data. Access to this information cannot be restricted, unless it falls under the category of state or service secrets according to specific statutes. Information can be so categorised by expressly authorised agencies or officials of the state, provided it is necessary to national defence, national security, criminal investigations, crime prevention, central financial or foreign exchange policy, foreign affairs, relations with international organisations or court proceedings. On the whole, the provisions of the 1992 Act are in compliance with international standards, provided that appropriate legislation clearly defines the relevant powers of the state and of the security services. However, a 1995 amendment (Act no. LXVI) substantially derogated from the standards created by the original Data Protection Act. According to the present wording of paragraph 5 of section 19:

> Unless an Act provides otherwise, data generated for internal use and in connection with the preparation of decisions shall not be public within thirty years following their inception. Upon request, the head of the relevant agency may permit access to the data even within the above time limit.

Act LXV of 1995 on State and Service Secrets defines the particular conditions for classifying and protecting confidential information. State secrets have to fall in one or more of the categories listed in the annex to the Act. However, in itself, subsumption under one of these categories does not automatically and immediately qualify the data as a state secret. Actual qualification has to be made with regard to potential dangers linked to the eventual disclosure of specific sets of data, the interests of national defence, national security, criminal investigations, crime prevention, central financial or foreign exchange policy, foreign affairs, relations with international organisations or court proceedings (section 3, paragraph (1) of the Act). Categories of service secrets have to be determined by the authorised officials of public agencies before any data is classified. The length of time for which data will be kept secret is determined by the authorised classifier, within the limits of preset time periods devised for each type of secret. The maximums are 90 years in the case of state secrets and 20 for service secrets. The Act on State and Service Secrets also contains provisions regarding the data qualification procedure, including a requirement that revisions be done every three years following the original classification. The Data Protection Ombudsman is given responsibilities in matters of freedom of information and has to be consulted prior to relevant policy decisions (e.g. before modifying the scope of service secrets classification). The Ombudsman also has the right to request the change of status of specific data.

The National Security Act, on the other hand, clearly fails to meet the international standards already mentioned. For instance, paragraph 1 of section 42 declares, without any further explanation, that all data acquired from outside data processing systems, data forwarded to other agencies and notes put into outside agencies' files by the national security services constitute state secrets. This provision violates the spirit of the Johannesburg Principles as well as the corresponding domestic statutes and the constitution, with the only justification that the data is important or being used by the national security services.

Section 62 stipulates that all data obtained by secret means and methods qualify as state secrets. The same applies to the identity of persons co-operating with the intelligence agencies. The very performance of such activities, as well as any technical details are also state secrets. The only way such data can ever see the light of day is through their use as evidence in a court of law. Contrary to the Provisional Act on Authorisation for Gathering Intelligence (no. X from 1990), which had made it mandatory to inform those concerned when there remained no particular interest in keeping the intelligence activities secret, the present National Security Act categorically excludes any such communication.

In addition to the indiscriminate classification of all data gained through processing systems or clandestine activities of the services, the National Security Act also creates a general authorisation to hide any other data. Section 48 provides the Director General of a national security agency with the authority to reject information requests based on the right to consult and correct personal data. The same goes for data of public interest. Needless to say, 'data of public interest' is whatever information remains after all other means to classify it have been exhausted. The given legal justifications for such a retrograde position are the need to protect national security and to respect third parties' rights.

Summing up, Hungarian national security legislation does not satisfy the elementary requirements of constitutionalism concerning freedom of information. In clear violation of international and domestic standards, the security services are forbidden to communicate data acquired in the course of performing their duties, even if there is no particular reason to keep the secret. Any other information may also be classified based on sheer invocation of national security interests or the protection of third parties.

Control and Accountability

Government, through its authorised officials, controls each of the national security services. Military services fall within the responsibility of the Minister of Defence, while civilian agencies report to another Minister who, in order to avoid any conflict of interest, may not be Minister of Defence, the Interior or Justice. In practice a Minister without portfolio fulfils these duties. Before the 1995 Act on National Security, oversight of the intelligence community was exercised by the Cabinet. The Act, for one thing, substituted 'control' for 'oversight', clearly signalling the executive's desire to directly manage the services. It is questionable, however, whether this active involvement can really be justified, in light of the assurances that the 'enemy of the state' doctrine was a thing of the past. If the services truly react only to concrete violations of national security interest, why would they need to be told what to do? The security agencies are the ones equipped with the necessary network to detect threats and to produce the information needed for policy decisions. Yet, the Minister's direct management of the services implies that he already knows what the threats are – but if this were the case the services would be superfluous.

The Minister responsible determines the tasks, oversees the activities and regulates the functions and organisation of the security services. He is empowered to issue general policy as well as specific instructions directly to the heads of the services. General Directors maintain operational power over their services but may be instructed, in writing (sections 10–11 of the National Security Act), to launch specific investigations. However, the Minister cannot take over day to day operations or terminate specific investigations. His written instructions are meant as a guarantee that any substantial intervention on his part is put on record.

The National Assembly exercises parliamentary oversight over all national security services through its National Security Committee, the President of which must be an MP from one of the opposition parties. In parallel, the Defence Committee has powers of oversight over the military agencies. The responsible minister has to inform the respective Committees on the general activities of the intelligence agencies regularly and at least twice a year. Government must also provide information about policy decisions regarding the national security services, via the responsible minister. The Committees have the right to:

- request information from the Minister and the General Directors about the national security situation of the country and the activities of the national security services;
- request information from the Minister of Justice, the Minister responsible for civilian national security services, the Defence Minister and the General Directors concerning authorisations to use special means;
- examine the complaints of unlawful activities of the national security services.

Furthermore, the Committees have a right to be informed of the contents of files and information reports prepared for the government. Finally, if the National Security Office launches an investigation including secret data collection against a Member of Parliament or against a member of his family, the responsible minister must report it to the Committee (the MP involved, however, is not to be notified).

On the whole, one can conclude that the powers of the National Security Committee enable it to carry out its supervisory duties effectively. However, all sessions of the Committee dealing with substantial issues of national security are secret. When confidential data is involved, no-one outside the Committee may be informed of the details of the proceedings or the decisions – and of course this is usually the case. Not even the individual whose rights may have been violated can be informed of the relevant files and investigations. The fact that the President of the Committee must be a member of the opposition is a positive development, but it must be kept in mind that there was never any real disagreement between political parties as to the role and functions of the security agencies. What is more, since compliance with unlawful orders and the consequent carrying out of illegal activities is required by law, a fair amount of confusion remains. When the Committee declares that no violation of the law has occurred, it could simply be saying that the officers fulfilled their duty to obey unlawful orders.

Another form of Parliamentary control is exercised by the four Parliamentary Commissioners who were elected in 1995. One of them is responsible for monitoring the services' compliance with constitutional provisions and basic rights. He is assisted by three deputies, one for general duties and one each in the fields of data protection and minority rights. It is not part of the functions of the Commissioners to issue binding orders, their weapons being limited to persuasive arguments made in public recommendations. What is more, the legislature clearly shielded the national security agencies from too much scrutiny on the part of the Ombudsmen. According to the Appendix to the Ombudsmen Act of 1993 (n. LIX), the Commissioners do not have access to information concerning the administrative organisation, internal regulations, facilities or staffing of the intelligence services. Other information has also been denied to the Ombudsmen, with the justification that sources must be protected or that it falls in the category of international intelligence. So in practice there is hardly any security document that cannot be withheld from the Ombudsmen for one reason or another.

Yet despite these strong limitations on their powers, the Ombudsmen still manage to monitor the security services; for one, the Commissioner for Data Protection investigated a good number of problems related to national security. In his recommendation 7/A/1996, for example, he pointed out that the collection of data on persons nominated to important positions raised serious questions of legal necessity and justification. In many cases the very purpose of the security checks remained unclear. The Ombudsman recognised that some provisions of the law were obscure but argued that this in no way justified interpretations restrictive of individual rights. He concluded that violations had occurred in 797 cases, which is the majority of the security services' interventions. None of the individuals submitted to security checks had been informed of the fact, even though Act X of 1990, which was in force at the time, clearly required disclosure upon completion of the investigation. The recommendations of the Ombudsman have been accepted by the Minister and the persons concerned were subsequently informed about the security checks.

Finally, in addition to the National Security Committee and the Ombudsmen there are other bodies playing limited roles in monitoring the security agencies. One of them is the Prosecutor, who also has general supervisory powers in terms of the application of the law. However, the functions of the secret services have traditionally been considered to fall outside of the judicial system. The courts constitute another monitoring body as far as national security is concerned, but due to the high level of secrecy it is practically impossible to legally challenge the intelligence community's interventions or omissions. The Constitutional Court focuses on the constitutionality of legislative acts, but individual violations of basic rights may occasionally also be adjudicated, on the basis of constitutional issues in the original case.

National Security and Human Rights

Traditionally, the national security interest is an accepted justification for the limitation of individual rights. But such restrictions should remain within strict boundaries if potential arbitrary abuses of power are to be prevented. Hungary is party to a number of international agreements and conventions outlining the extent to which interference with fundamental rights and freedoms can be justifiable. Each of these agreements and conventions were elaborated with due consideration to the national security question.

Article 17 of the International Covenant on Civil and Political Rights protects the privacy of the family, the home and the correspondence of persons, along with their character and their reputation. It does stipulate, however, that this protection may not interfere with lawful actions taken by the state. It is then perfectly logical that the lawful character of such activities be open to review, in keeping with the Covenant. Further legal guidance is found in the European Convention for the Protection of Human Rights and Fundamental Freedoms. Article 8 of the Convention covers the rights most likely to be endangered by the activities of national security agencies:

1   Everyone has the right to respect for his private family life, his home and his correspondence.
2   There shall be no interference by a public authority with the exercise of this right, except such as is in accordance with the law and is necessary in a democratic society in the interests of national security, public safety or the economic well-being of the country, for the prevention of disorder or crime, for the protection of health or morals, or for the protection of the rights and freedoms of others.

In addition to these standards, the Hungarian constitution also determines boundaries for the acceptable restriction of rights. The most important principle can be found in section 8, paragraph 2, where much is made of the German phrase *Grundgesetz* or 'core legal principle': in the Republic of Hungary fundamental rights and obligations can only be modified by an act of Parliament, and without imposing any restrictions on essential individual rights.

Without questioning the values of such an approach it must be noted that rights cannot be divided into an essential, untouchable nucleus and an optional adjunct. The Hungarian Constitutional Court (like its German counterpart) developed a doctrine free from an overly literal interpretation of this section of the constitution, and avoided the trap of having to determine a rigid boundary between essential and non-essential rights. It is a complex, comparative perspective according to which restrictions of individual rights are deemed constitutional only insofar as they can be shown to be absolutely necessary to the protection of another right or constitutional value, and only if they are appropriate and strictly proportional to the objective being pursued (for example, 11/1992 [III. 5].). The Court also ruled that in a state governed by the Rule of Law (*Rechtsstaat*), in addition to an institutional framework of protection available to the people, all state agencies must also be established and maintained in ways that guarantee the respect of basic rights. In fact, no institution can perform its duties democratically unless it has the built-in capacity to protect constitutional rights (36/1992 [VI. 10] *AB hat*), and among others the freedom of information.

In effect, the legal norms and regulations enabling the Hungarian security services hardly satisfy these requirements. Section 62 of the National Security Act stipulates that not only does the intelligence gathered by 'special means' constitute state secrets, but so does the very conduct of such activities, unless used as evidence in criminal proceedings. In other words, the persons targeted by the services may never know about it, even if no national security or other official interest justifies maintaining confidentiality. This exclusion of all information, irrespective of its importance to state security or the legality of its collection, constitutes a clear step backwards. With its provision for post facto disclosure of all closed investigations, the already mentioned Provisional Act of 1990 was much closer to satisfying constitutional standards. But this new legislative situation, in practice, deprives victims of illegal interventions of their right to take legal action against the services.

This also contradicts section 70/K of the Hungarian constitution, requiring that decisions restricting individual rights be open to judicial review. While judicial control over the executive branch at state and local level seems to follow the German model and satisfy elementary requirements of the Rule of Law, the possibility of challenging official statutes and formal, written decisions of the authorities, is of no help when it comes to the unwritten directives often governing in practice the operations of the intelligence services. Such directives and 'Measures,' as opposed to formal decisions or resolutions, do not fall under the purview of the courts. Civil litigation against the police is possible, but violation of the law by officers has to be proven. In the case of national security agencies this is practically hopeless given the wide discretion and the high level of secrecy that characterise their operations.

The National Security Act of 1995 defines and strictly limits the movement of information between the security services and the citizens, but not between the different agencies of the state. In the course of fulfilling their tasks and in the absence of any special legal provisions the national security services are entitled, upon the submission of the purpose of their investigation, to access data from any government organisation, including those secretly collected by police. They are also authorised to closely monitor these organisations and to access their administrative documents. Requests made by security services must be satisfied even if the data are incomplete or insufficient. Conversely the police, border guards, Customs and Revenue Service, the courts, prosecutors and the Prison Service can, in the fulfilment of specified tasks, also request information from data collected by the security services.

Most secret information gathering methods can be used without the need for a warrant. The services may use informants or secret agents and use false identification documents to cover for fronting organisations. Monitoring persons or events in public spaces, as well as the use of technology to store and process data (as opposed to interception) do not require special authorisation either. Entrapment schemes are legal as far as they do not cause personal injuries. National security officers have the right to disguise themselves as members of other law enforcement organisations, provided that prior notice is given to the Minister responsible and to the chief of the service concerned at the national level. In other words, a form of reunification with the police can take place at anytime and without legislative approval, even though exactly what powers disguised agents actually have remains obscure. At any rate, the separation of police from security services was meant to protect basic constitutional values: provisions in the Police Act of 1994 (no. XXXIV, article 69) is abundantly clear on this matter. Police were given the exclusive competence to conduct criminal investigations in accordance with the Code of Criminal Procedure. Yet, even before a reasonable suspicion can be said to exist, national security agencies can act in advance of any official criminal investigation and may start gathering intelligence about possible criminal activities if state security or other fundamental values are endangered. As already mentioned, however, planning to commit such offences is already criminal in itself, and any reasonable suspicion that a conspiracy or verbal agreement to commit concrete acts against the state or against fundamental constitutional values should trigger police intervention. Intervention at an even earlier stage is clearly impossible without inflicting disproportionate restrictions to individual rights. Again, the services are caught between probable violations of rights and a duplication of what the police already do.

Another constitutionally dubious institution adds to the confusion in the police–security services relationship. The law allows for agreements with perpetrators of crimes where immunity is offered in exchange for information; this is perceived as a form of 'plea bargaining' in Hungary. Like police, national security agencies and the Special Service may make individual deals with offenders. According to the law (section 55 of the National Security Act), the agencies must obtain the designated prosecutor's approval, and show that national security would be better served by immunity with information than punishment of the offender. But of course before investigations are conducted any identification of individual perpetrators remains speculative. In addition to individual rights what is at stake here is the courts' prerogative to determine guilt. Serious interrogations also remain concerning the actual manner in which the services determine whether or not to offer immunity. Only one restriction exists: no agreement may be concluded with persons guilty of murder.

According to sections 56–62 of the National Security Act, warrants must be obtained prior to the following activities:

- secret search of dwellings and the recording of the operation by technical devices;
- monitoring and recording of events taking place at a private residence by technical devices;
- interception of mail and the recording of the content by technical devices;
- interception and electronic monitoring of communication via phone lines or similar ways of conveying messages.

The application for a warrant to use these special means must be submitted by the head of the competent National Security service, and must include:

- the location where special means are to be used, the name of the persons involved and any data available for their identification;
- he description of the special means intended to be used and the justification for that use;
- the day and hour of the beginning and the end of the use of the specified special means;
- demonstration that national security interests are involved.

Where the general functions of national security protection are involved, warrants are issued by the Minister of Justice, while in the case of crime detection and prevention the warrants must be issued by a judge. In both cases the warrant is valid for a maximum of 90 days, but upon special application by a Director General, in duly justified cases it may be renewed multiple times. The person targeted will not be informed of the monitoring or of the circumstances in which it is being conducted.

When the inevitable delay of normal warrant applications and approval is deemed deleterious to the success of the national security service's operations, the Director General may order a secret search or the use of special means for a period of 72 hours or until a proper warrant can be obtained from the Minister or from a judge. However, the warrant application must be submitted simultaneously with the order. Finally, emergency orders may be used only once in the same case, unless new data emerge which shows an immediate threat to national security.

As already pointed out, security services do not have the power to conduct criminal investigations. However, officers may take measures to prevent crimes or to arrest offenders within their jurisdiction (sections 31–36 of the National Security Act), and they are empowered to use force when so doing. Handcuffs may be put on a person in order to prevent him from injuring himself or others or from escaping arrest. Officers also have the right to carry and use firearms. The use of weapons is legally justified where necessary to avert direct threats or attacks against life or bodily integrity. They may also be used to prevent or interrupt a series of offences, including the forcible change of the constitutional order, destruction of public property, espionage, genocide, causing a danger to the public, terrorist attacks and airplane hijacking. Weapons may also be used to interrupt illegal attempts to learn state secrets, violence against persons or goods and to avert direct attack or threat of attack against the premises of the national security services.

In sum, the intelligence services regained clear cut police powers with the 1995 legislation. Conversely, police have been given authorisation to use intelligence gathering methods. So instead of the separation of the police and national security functions, the result has been their duplication and overlap on almost all levels. This is, needless to say, an ominous development, and not only in terms of the constitution. In fact, such overlapping raises many problems in the basic division of powers, not to mention the skyrocketing costs resulting from the maintenance of redundant organisations (see Table 5.1).

The National Security Act, though the constitution does not make this expressly compulsory, essentially follows the German model in its definition of which basic rights may be restricted in the course of fulfilling national security functions. They include personal liberty, privacy of the home, person and correspondence, protection of personal data, access to and possession of information of public interest. The measures employed must not cause harm that would be obviously disproportionate to the lawful objective of the operation. Among the appropriate legal secret or coercive measures, the one selected should cause the least restriction to individual rights, and the least harm to the person concerned while still allowing successful completion of the operation.

Conclusion

Hungarian law and practice confirms the thesis that national security actually supersedes the Rule of Law.[9] It is still surprising to see how the old political police managed to sail smoothly through the political transition and the Danube-gate scandal. The present agencies openly admit to operating in continuity with the past, and to using the old files as valuable sources of information. Only one section of the party-state apparatus, the internal branch of the secret intelligence service (III/III), has clearly been disbanded and abandoned. However, many aspects of the old political policing functions have been preserved under the new heading of 'constitutional protection' (*Verfassungsschutz*).

There is some, though weak, parliamentary control over the activities of national security agencies; however, control on the part of instances of civil society is completely lacking. One especially dangerous development is the concentration of intelligence, police and administrative authority within the intelligence community.

Notes

[1] Pardarvi, Marta, *Oversight of National Security Services in Hungary*, manuscript, Budapest 1998, based on the data of the national budget.
[2] Dezső and Hajas (1997) pp. 137–138.
[3] Nyíri (1997) pp. 5–13.
[4] Katona (1995) pp. 5544–5545.
[5] Szikinger (1995).
[6] Katona, (1995) pp. 5543–5544.
[7] Stanley (1996) pp. 37–38.
[8] Lénárt (1996) p. 65.
[9] Töllborg (1997) p. 21.

Chapter 6

Security Services in Poland and Their Oversight

Andrzej Rzeplinski

Introduction

Two statutorily defined security services exist in Poland: the Office of State Protection (UOP) and Military Information Services (WSI). The definition of security services is specified in Article 4.2 of the Law on UOP of 6 April 1990:

> Attached to the Council of Ministers a Board for Security Services (Board) shall operate, as an agency to prepare opinions and advice in matters of programming, supervision and co-ordination of operations of the Office of State Protection and Military Information Services (Security Services), and of activities performed by the Police, Frontier Guards and Military Police, and aimed at protection of state security...[1]

This means that secret operations for the purpose of state security may be undertaken – as auxiliary or main activities – not only by UOP or WSI but also by the Police, Frontier Guard and Military Police as well as other government bodies referred to in other parts of this article.

A definition of Security Services is also included in the Standing Orders of the Sejm of the Republic of Poland, which established a Committee for Security Services in 1995 (see below). According to Article 74f:

> appropriate regulations of the Rules of the Parliament are applied to the Committee for Security Services as well as Members of Parliament selected for this Committee. Security Services in the understanding of the Rules hereof are Office of State Protection and Military Information Services.[2]

Office of State Protection (UOP)

The communist security service (SB)[3] was dissolved on 10 May 1990 when the Law on UOP was enacted. All SB functionaries were dismissed by force of the law (Article 131.1); some who anticipated the dissolution of SB had joined the then Civic Militia prior to that date. For this reason, the Law on UOP provided for dismissal of all militia officers who had been functionaries of SB before 31 July 1989 (Article 131.2). A further provision (132.2) authorised the Council of Ministers to specify the procedure and conditions of employing former SB functionaries in the newly-formed UOP and other services subordinated to the Ministry of Internal Affairs. At the moment of dissolution, SB had 24,000 functionaries. Employment in the newly formed security services of each and every former functionary of SB was thereby submitted to external oversight.

On 21 May 1990 the Council of Ministers issued Resolution No.69 which specified the conditions of employment in UOP or other organisational units of the Ministry of Internal Affairs for all former Security Services functionaries applying for such employment. Based on that resolution, on 8 June 1990 Prime Minister Tadeusz Mazowiecki appointed the Central Qualification Commission of ten members, chaired by the Head of the newly formed State Security Offices.[4]

The Commission was composed of deputies, senators, a representative of the police officers union, the deputy Chief Commander of the Police and Vice-Minister of Internal Affairs. Only the last, soon to be dismissed, represented the *ancien regime*. The Chairman of the Central Commission appointed a Commission for Central Staff that examined the qualifications required by former functionaries of SB to be admitted to UOP. The central and 48 provincial commissions were composed of deputies, senators, a representative of the UOP, Chief Commander of the Police, representatives of the police officers union and, to quote the Prime Minister's enactment, 'persons trusted by society'. Over 140 deputies and senators took part in the Commission's proceedings. The Central Commission examined appeals against decisions in cases examined by commissions in the first instance.

The Law on UOP provides in Article 15 that 'Qualified to serve in the UOP is a Polish citizen with immaculate moral and patriotic attitude...'. A negative opinion issued by the classification commission prevents a person from entering UOP and other police services for that person's lifetime. Of over 24,000 functionaries of the dissolved SB, 14,034 submitted to qualification proceedings. Commissions in the first instance approved 8,658 persons (62 per cent). Of the 5,376 rejected persons, 4,755 (89 per cent) of former SB functionaries appealed to the Central Commission which sustained the negative opinions in 1,243 cases. The cases of the remaining 5,112 persons were sent back to provincial commissions which sustained negative opinions with respect to 1,719 persons.

Accepted, therefore, were 10,451 persons or three-quarters of those who submitted to the qualification procedure. Of course, the criteria of classification applied by different provincial commissions varied. As a consequence, over a half of former SB functionaries were disqualified as potential candidates to Office of State Protection in some provinces (e.g. 56 per cent in Bielsko-Biala), while in Gdansk or Warsaw negative decisions were only taken in 7 per cent of cases. The Central Commission started its work on 31 of July; the work was completed on 18 September 1990, and a report was duly submitted to the Prime Minister.

The head of UOP was not obliged to employ all those former SB functionaries who had been accepted by the Commission. This would not have been possible, as the new Office of State Protection was to have a staff of about 7,000.[5] In sum, every other approved SB functionary was re-employed in state security. A considerable proportion of those who did not submit to the qualification procedure at all could receive an earlier old-age pension. In 1998, functionaries of the former SB constituted about one half of the composition of UOP; the rest were new.[6] Each year between 1994 and 1996, the UOP admitted 'from several to about a dozen, nay as many as several dozen' approved former SB functionaries who had failed to get a job with it in 1990.[7] Now the situation has changed. In 1998 UOP dismissed more than 500 of its agents, almost all of them had joined the service before 1989.[8] On the other hand it has to be noted that a number of the newcomers are children or cousins of former SB officers.

The basic mandate of communist security services was civilian intelligence and counterintelligence. Functionaries of those services, constituting respectively Department I (Intelligence) and Department II (Counterintelligence), often emphasised their separate character and superiority over other SB officers. The two services also played the role of political police, counteracting the opposition against the communist regime in Poland[9] and abroad, and in their purely professional functions were subordinated to, as well as controlled and supported by, the international actions of KGB. In 1989, the Intelligence Department employed about 1,000 officers. It was a powerful agency, suitable for at least a regional empire and, during the verification of 1990, 'only two or three officers (among the total of 1,000) were verified negatively. However, 25–30 per cent of those who remained had to quit the service despite a positive verification'.[10]

About 200 former SB functionaries refused to accept the negative opinion. They complained to the Ombudsman, Sejm deputies, and to other authorities, including a complaint by Mr. Wieslaw Kall, lodged in 1995 with the UN Human Rights Committee on violation of Article 25 of the Covenant. Late in 1996, the Committee found the complaint admissible but on 14 July 1997 decided that Poland had not violated the applicant's right to access, on general terms of equality, to public service.[11] In 1996–1997, a group of deputies from the Democratic Left Alliance (SLD) representing this group, tried to quash the ban on employment in UOP with respect to all those who had received a negative opinion, in effect aiming to rehabilitate the former SB.

The attempt was made at a session of the Commission of Administration and Internal Affairs of the Sejm on 10 April 1996. The Minister of Internal Affairs, present at the sitting, feared the discrediting political effects of this action and consequently kept his distance. Additionally, the 1990 Head of the Office of State Protection made a statement and was supported by the Chairman of the Commission and by other deputies representing the opposition. As a result, the post-communist attempt at rehabilitating security services functionaries failed for the time being. Another attempt at rehabilitation of SB officers disqualified in 1990 was made in September 1996 by several deputies of SLD, representing the interests of those functionaries. They proposed, actively supported by a representative[12] of the Ombudsman (RPO), that the Head of UOP and the Minister of Internal Affairs abandon the regulation concerning the prohibition of work of SB functionaries in institutions involved in state security. The proposal was rejected by one vote.[13]

Since the beginning UOP has had six chiefs, both political dissidents and career security officers.[14] Such frequent changes are a clear indicator that UOP is closely dependent on political changes. The head of UOP is appointed and recalled by the Prime Minister in consultation with the President, Board of Security Services and Parliamentary Committee for Secret Services (Article 4a of the Law on UOP). The Head's duties include:

- identifying and counteracting threats to the security, defence, sovereignty, integrity and international position of the State;
- preventing and detecting crimes of espionage and terrorism, as well as other crimes against security of the State, and investigating their perpetrators;

- preventing and detecting crimes directed at economic foundations of the State and investigating their perpetrators;
- preventing and detecting crimes of international nature or scope, including illicit manufacture and possession of as well as trade in arms, ammunition and explosives, drugs, as well as nuclear and radioactive materials, and investigating their perpetrators;
- identifying and counteracting violations of state secrets;
- preparing reports and analyses vital to national security for the supreme bodies of the State and public administration;
- cryptographic protection of state and professional secrets which are transmitted by electronic devises for state institutions and public economic and financial organs.

The Head of UOP is empowered also:

- to order, after prior authorisation of the Public Prosecutor General, interception of communication, clandestine purchase or confiscation of objects deriving from the offence, or those whose manufacture, possession, transport or trade is prohibited, and also handing over of profit (Articles 10, 10a, 10b of the Law on UOP);
- to protect official secrets and determine the circulation of confidential and secret information in the Office (Article II b.1, 2 the Law on UOP);
- to reveal, after authorisation by Chief Justice of the Supreme Court, to a public prosecutor or to a court confidential data on agents or secret informants in cases of crimes against life (Article 11.b.4 the Law on UOP);
- to determine tasks concerning operation of the UOP, e.g. to lay down 'norms of equipment and armament', 'rules for establishment and administration of operational fund', as well as other rules concerning the salary, rewards and service apartments of functionaries of the Office (Article 16, 16a; Article 18.5,6; Article 21.2; Article 22 the Law on UOP).

Military Information Services (WSI)

After the Second World War, military counterintelligence was named the Headquarters of Information (GZI) divided into local branches. As with civilian communist secret services of that time, the GZI was part of a Soviet-type criminal organisation of political police directed against any non-communist thought of military and paramilitary servicemen.[15] After 1956 the GZI was reorganised into the Military Internal Service (WSW) who played the role of military counterintelligence as well as a military police.

Until 1991 Military Intelligence was known as the Second Department of the General Staff of the Polish Army. The Second Department dealt with strategic military intelligence and had no counterparts within the country. In divisions of the army there were only Reconnaissance troops, and in regiments there were officers who dealt with so-called 'shallow intelligence', directly serving the needs of the army. In October 1991, the Military Information Services (WSI) were established, which combined military intelligence and counterintelligence departments.[16] The WSI was at first subordinated directly to the Minister of National Defence. Unlike UOP, there was no verification of former communist functionaries of the military secret services after 1989. There are no data regarding the number of former functionaries among the current staff of WSI. Unofficially it is said that there are 'about 1,600' of them altogether.[17] Since October 1991 the WSI has had five chiefs: the nature of their dismissals and appointments was distinctly political.

The activities of the WSI are regulated by the above-mentioned Articles 2.1 and 4.b.3 of the Law on UOP and Article 15.1 of the Law on the General Duty to Defend the Republic of Poland that states:

> Military Information Services are responsible for identification of and counteraction against dangers to the country's defences and violations of state secrecy on matters of national defence, and also prepare information and analysis relevant for State defence for State agencies.

Agencies Competent to Supervise and Review the Security Services

President of Republic of Poland

The President's competencies with respect to Security Services follow from the Constitution under which he is to guard the security of the State (Article 126.2 of the Constitution of 2 April 1997). The law on UOP says that when information gathered by the Office '...may be of major importance to state security, Head of the Office of State Protection is duty bound to immediately transmit it to the President of Republic of Poland and to the Prime Minister...' (Article 11.2 of the Law on UOP). This means that the

President has the power to order Head of UOP to collect information of such importance.

During the presidency of Lech Walesa there were no conflicts between his administration and UOP apart from the several months of 1992 when the Cabinet of Jan Olszewski was in office. Walesa was not supported, by his own choice, by any specific political party or other influential group of interests. This kept UOP from making alliance with any political party although it seems obvious that many of them were still loyal to their former comrades from the Communist party who had transferred in 1990 into the Social Democratic Party.

The administration of the President elected in December 1995 took control over the UOP immediately. There were no noticeable conflicts between UOP and the administration of the President, yet UOP underwent a most profound process of 'purging' with respect to executive posts[18] and young anticommunist officers left. The President and the leftist Cabinet pursued a policy of political revenge for the historic defeat of Communism in 1989. Some leftist deputies tried to offer general 'amnesty' for former servicemen, as was mentioned above.

This situation led to calls by some anticommunist opposition leaders for a total purge of all UOP and WSI officers who had been in service before 1990. They called for 'option zero' and recalled the Czech example of 1990. They argued that the Czech model of reorganisation of Security Services (a total removal and non-verification of former communist functionaries) was the best means of achieving non-political security services.[19] They called also for the preparation of a law that would make communist security services criminal organisations but after parliamentary elections in September 1997 that option was rejected by the new coalition. Dismissal of all those who had served the longest time in the SB and were no longer useful for the UOP was preferred.

The cohabitation of the new centre-right coalition and the post-communist President offered the latter much less power over the UOP. The President tried to expand his power over secret operations through the WSI and through his National Security Council. This meant that a military agency could operate beyond its military field; it also meant expansion of the staff of National Security Council that was granted the legal power to act as an intelligence agency.

Prime Minister and Minister Co-ordinator for Security Services

In the spring of 1996, a government draft was submitted to the Sejm, which provided for considerable extension of the Prime Minister's part in controlling UOP. The draft was entitled 'Law on the Board for Security Services attached to the Council of Ministers and on amendment of several statutes'. It referred to the following aims of this legislative initiative:

- to remove the Office of State Protection from the structure of the Ministry of Internal Affairs and to establish subordination of civilian security services to the Prime Minister (...);
- to secure to the Prime Minister legal instruments of co-ordination and supervision of the activity of civilian and military security services;
- to secure the removal of UOP from the organisational and financial structure of the Ministry of Internal Affairs;
- to secure to the Prime Minister actual and effective supervision over UOP with due respect to the prerogatives of President of Republic of Poland.

The pretext for this change was the scandal involving Prime Minister Oleksy (see below). More important still, however, was the wish to strengthen the position of Prime Minister at the expense of the President's prerogatives irrespective of what was stated in the draft and of the fact that Prime Minister and President were rooted in the same parliamentary faction. The President was a victim of his policy as the chairman of a Constitutional Committee of the National Assembly in 1993–1995 when he was in favour of making the President's power rather symbolic under the new Constitution.

The law on the UOP was amended in August 1996 and on 1 October 1996 the UOP was removed from the Ministry of Internal Affairs and subordinated directly to the Prime Minister. Within his supervision of UOP, the Prime Minister defines detailed tasks for the Office. So the civilian security services in today's Poland are subordinated directly to the Prime Minister; the military security services to the Minister of National Defence; and all operational activities of the Police (for example, to fight organised crime) to the Minister of Internal Affairs and Administration. Subordination means supervision, that is the right to inspect and to give binding orders. The Constitution of April 1997 strengthened the position of Prime Minister among executive agencies, making him the 'supervisor' of the 'work of members of the Council of Ministers' (Article 148.5). Internal policy is the task of the Council of Ministers (Article 146.1).

On behalf of the Prime Minister, supervision over the UOP is performed by the Minister Co-ordinator for Security Services (Minister without portfolio). The prerogatives of the Minister Co-ordinator on behalf of the Prime Minister include, among other things:

- appointment and dismissal of Head of UOP (Article 4a.1, Law of UOP);
- approval of annual plans of action for UOP (Article 4b.2);
- appointment and dismissal, at the request of Head of UOP, of his deputies (Article 4a.4);
- establishment and dissolution of local UOP branches (Article 5.2);
- definition of annual 'directions for UOP actions' (having consulted the Parliamentary Committee for Security Services) (Article 4b.1 and 2);
- awarding (and removing) officer ranks, with the exception of a General, who is nominated and dismissed by the President at the request of the Prime Minister;
- definition of the manner of transfer of information to UOP from the police and the Frontier Guard (Article 6a);
- creation of conditions for co-operation of special services with the Police, Frontier Guard, WSI and other services (Article 4b.3);
- appraisal of the appeals of officers dismissed from service by a decision of Head of UOP (Article 33.2).

The role of Minister Co-ordinator for Security Services and the extent of his power over the Head of UOP were not too clear. The reason for the post was obviously to avoid any direct responsibility of the Prime Minister for current events in civilian and military services. Despite the absence of an explicit consent to such procedure in the Law on UOP, the former Prime Minister appointed the first Minister Co-ordinator. In fact, the new Minister took over the whole of the Prime Minister's powers to supervise security services. Between November 1996 and October 1997, however, the post-communist coalition's Minister delegated more power in practice to the Head of UOP and subjected him to less accountability for his decisions. The Minister protected the consolidation of old career officers in the UOP. His oversight of military services in practice did not exist.

The policy of the following Cabinet was similar. On 7 November 1997, the Prime Minister issued an ordinance granting to the Minister Co-ordinator the powers to, for example, 'exercise current supervision and oversight over the operation of security services (civilian and military) and over actions carried out by the Police, Frontier Guard, Military Police and other units to protect the security of State' (paragraph 2.2.b), and also to 'supervise special duties and missions in the area of security of State' (paragraph 2.3).[20] Thus the Minister of Internal Affairs and Administration was deprived, by force of that ordinance, of the powers to supervise the operation of his subordinate forces – the Police and Frontier Guards – in the area of state security; the same can be said of the Minister of National Defence and his powers with respect to Military Police.

The new Minister, Janusz Palubicki, a well-known political dissident who carried out the longest hunger strike in prison in 1984 (104 days) and was one of the leaders of Solidarity, seemed to have three different focuses. The first was to prepare and pass through the Sejm a law on access of victims of communist security services (both civilian and military) to their files and removing those files from the archives of the newly established UOP and WSI.[21] The second focus was to cut off leaks from UOP and increase discipline of the demoralised agency. The third was to dismiss officers with the longest careers in the communist SB and to move the service away from politics.

Board for Security Services

Under amendments to the Law on UOP, approved in 1996, a Board for Security Services was appointed as a consultative and advisory body with respect to the programming, supervision, and co-ordination of the actions of UOP and WSI with the activities of other services – the Police, Frontier Guard and Military Guard. According to Article 4b.3 of the Law:

> The Prime Minister, in order to assure the required co-operation of security services may, upon consultation with the Board, give binding directives to the Minister of Internal Affairs and Administration concerning this sphere – with regard to the operation of the Police, Frontier Guard and military units subordinated to him; to the Minister of Justice – with regard to the operation of the Central Administration of Prison Service; to the Minister of National Defence – with regard to the operation of Military Information Services and Military Police; as well as to the Head of the Office of State Protection – with regard to the operation of the Office of State Protection.

In October 1996 the Prime Minister charged the Minister of Internal Affairs with the task of organising the Board for Security Services and ten posts were created. The Board is chaired by the Prime Minister and its members are: Minister of Internal Affairs and Administration, Minister of Foreign

Affairs, Minister of National Defence, Head of Office of State Protection, Secretary General of National Defence Committee, and Chairman of the regular committee of Council of Ministers competent in matters of external and internal security of State (Article 4.3). Also the President of Republic of Poland may appoint his delegate to take part in proceedings of the Board (Article 4.3).

The Board for Security Services commenced its activities on 1 January 1997. It gives opinions to, supervises and co-ordinates the work of UOP and WSI as well as actions carried out by the Police, Frontier Guard and Military Police to protect state security (Article 4.2 sentence 1). The Board's duties include in particular the formulation of appraisals and opinions in cases of:

- appointment and dismissal of Head of UOP and Chief of Inspectorate of Military Intelligence;
- definition of directions and preparation of plans of activity of security services;
- preparation of detailed draft budgets of UOP and WSI before their examination by the Council of Ministers;
- preparation and modification of central plans for the protection of state agencies and institutions and of the national economy;
- performance by security services of their tasks in accordance with the directions and plans of their activity;
- co-ordination of the work of security services with Military Police, the Police, and Frontier Guard, and their collaboration in the area of protection of security of State;
- co-operation of State agencies with security services (Article 4.2 sentence 2).

The Minister Co-ordinator for Security Services may invite chairmen of appropriate parliamentary committees to attend sessions of the Board for Security Services. The determination of tasks, detailed rules for functioning of the Board, issues concerning participation in the sittings of representatives of security services and other units, as well as the scope of activities of the Secretary of the Board are among competencies of the Council of Ministers.

Heads of Provinces

The Law on UOP (Article 14) authorises heads of provinces (16 since 1 January 1999) who represent the Government locally, to demand from local branches of the UOP reports and information on the state of security in their respective provinces. The problem prior to 1999 was that there were fewer local branches of the Office (14) than provinces (49). This meant that those officials only enjoyed a symbolic power to control the work of such branches. Now the two areas are coincident there is at least the potential for greater influence.

Parliamentary Oversight

Parliamentary Committee for Security Services   Until 1995, the only instrument of parliamentary oversight of security services was approval of the budget and acceptance of the report on the carrying out of that budget. The instrument was extremely weak. The expenditure on civilian and military security services was shown so as to prevent any detailed analysis. A separate Defence Department within the Ministry of Finance, which drew up the draft budget, protected the interests of those services. The formal supervisor of security services, Committee of Administration and Internal Affairs of the Sejm, received no answers to its questions about the ways in which security services disposed of the budget.

The Senate has been quite passive in this area, since 1993 in particular, despite having a Committee in Human Rights and the Rule of Law. The first and second terms of the Sejm (1991–1993 and 1993–1997 respectively) attempted to gain insight into the work of UOP, especially its files, and not only in situations of political scandal such as the case of the Enquiry Committee appointed in June 1992 after the defeat of Prime Minister Olszewski's operation of screening all deputies and ministries in terms of their alleged collaboration with the communist secret services.

In the autumn of 1994, in an atmosphere of mutual suspicion between the post-communist coalition in power on the one hand and the opposition parties and political associates of the President on the other as to the uses of UOP secret operations in partisan political struggles, the deputies' initiative finally emerged, supported by the main parliamentary factions, to appoint a Committee for Security Services. The argument of the motion for amendment of the Sejm's regulations and for appointment of the Committee was that it should, first of all, give opinions on the major legal acts pertaining to security services, the directions of the work of such services, their reports, and also analyse their budget, in particular, reviewing the interdependence between the expenditure and efficiency of their operations.

Ultimately, the Sejm did amend its Standing Orders, and appointed the Committee for Security Services on 27 April 1995. The Committee can have up to seven members. Several months later, on 29 September 1995, the Sejm appointed seven members of the Committee, three of them from opposition parties. These provisions were amended in January 1998. Five members of the Committee were elected, all but one having experience of the services, two of them represent the opposition. Every six months the Chairperson of the Committee is changed, alternating between the governing coalition and the opposition. This latter rule is a political agreement, not a rule in the Standing Orders.

The chairpersons of the clubs of deputies nominate candidates for the Committee; alternately, this can be done by a group of at least 35 deputies, which would be nearly 8 per cent of the entire house. Nominations are lodged with the Presidium of the Sejm. In practice, the candidates are checked by the security services before election. This offers the services the opportunity to eliminate any candidate not only because of his past conduct, allegedly improper from the point of view of national security, but also anyone who might ask too many inconvenient questions as the services' parliamentary overseer.

If members of the Committee require access to secret information regarding defence, the Armed Forces, and state security, the Speaker of the Sejm approaches the Minister of National Defence or the Minister of Internal Affairs and Administration for approval. In matters concerning the security services, the Committee participates in proceedings related to draft budgets and other financial plans of State, and to consideration of reports on their implementation, and presents its opinion to appropriate committees. At the end of one of the corridors in the Sejm building, several isolated and specially guarded rooms have been assigned to the Committee. Sessions of the Committee are held in camera; joint sessions, however, held together with other committees, may be open to the public. The minutes of the latter sessions are published. The Committee may issue a communiqué to the press, radio and television concerning its proceedings upon consultation regarding its contents, where appropriate, with the Minister of National Defence or the Minister of Internal Affairs.

The Committee also: passes opinions on draft legal acts pertaining to security services and on the direction of their operations; examines annual reports submitted by Heads of those services; passes opinions on candidates nominated to the posts of Heads and deputy Heads of security services; appraises the co-operation between civilian and military security services and between those services on the one hand and other agencies of state administration; examines complaints against the activity of security services.

Little information as to the Committee's activity is available, for example, we do not know who among its members started to represent the interests of security services, and how quickly this happened. The Ministers seem not to pay much attention to the Committee, for example, it was ignored in March 1996 by the Minister of National Defence who was to appoint a new Chief of Military Intelligence. It is not known how successful deputies have been in obtaining specific budgetary information or other data from the services.

So far, bulletins from two sessions of the Committee have been published. They both dealt with joint sessions with Security Services Committee of the *Bundestag* in June 1997. During both sessions, attended by invited deputies from other committees of the Sejm, chairmen of the Committee for Security Services stressed the importance of their work. The German parliamentarians clearly performed the function of instructors. The sole moment of real interest was a question asked by Member of the *Bundestag* Hartmunt Büttner about the social perception of communist security services – in the context of perception of STASI in Germany – and another one, 'What prevails in Poland: the notion of "militant democracy" (*Streitbare Demokratie*), or perhaps rather the old-time animosity or resentments?' Committee members representing SLD tried to give the answer but were at a loss how to handle it. According to the then Chairman of the Committee Andrzej Zelazowski, the history of Poland after World War II was allegedly 'quite different' from that of the German Democratic Republic.

More about the Committee itself and about security services can be learned from communiqués published after some of its sessions, especially during the third term of the Sejm. To quote the 'Detailed Proceedings in the Security Services Committee' of 28 January 1998:

At the end of each session the Committee shall determine the general scope of information that may be disclosed to the public by Presidium of the Committee. The contents of such information may be determined in consultation with heads of appropriate Cabinet departments or Head of services if necessary (Para. 2.a). Unless otherwise decided, members of the Committee may reveal the general range of subjects discussed during a session, and present their opinion of them, providing that the principles of protection of State secret are maintained (Para. 2.b). The communiqué for the media (...) is an expression of the common position of the Committee members and is adopted by majority of votes (Para. 3).

On 25 March 1998, after appraisal by the Committee of the report on UOP activity in 1997, a Committee member K. Miodowicz told journalists that in the Committee's opinion, the Heads of UOP had been subordinated to the (post-communist) SLD-PSL coalition and actually ruined the Office: there was a breakdown of operational activities in the priority areas of intelligence; generational exchange of UOP officers had been stopped; and organisational changes had been abandoned. Promoted were chiefly old officers of former SB, and the young staff were dismissed; recruitment of new functionaries had been blocked.[22]

Another Committee member, Jerzy Ciemniewski, added that the Committee 'found it hard to appraise the merits' of UOP activity,[23] which may indicate that Committee members only know what the services are willing to tell them. As is only natural, the opposition deputy Z. Siemiatkowski, responsible within the former Cabinet for the services' functioning in that period, defended himself saying that 'activity of the UOP during last year and the preceding few years was what the Office's budget and fees permitted'.[24] Characteristically, none of the deputies made any mention of violation by security services of fundamental freedoms, and in particular of non-authorised wiretaps or illegal spying on legally operating opposition parties in 1991–1997, although at least one criminal proceeding was already pending at that time.[25] What is stressed in parliamentary criticism of security services, especially of their operation in 1996–1997, although the same might be said about the entire 1990–1997 period, is the reality of UOP described as follows:

> Drink-sodden faces, empty vodka bottles in office rooms, and the (scandalising post-communist) 'NIE' weekly as the favourite reading matter (...) Many employees are said to be mediocrities incapable of any serious work. They are meek and obedient for fear that they might get fired (...) What counts is showiness, such as arresting two kids who traded in T-shirts with the picture of Hitler: the operation was carried out by several dozen functionaries (...) Our peasant versions of James Bond do not speak foreign languages and know nothing about computers. Instead, they gather information about everybody. The information is then used depending on who wins and takes over after the next elections.[26]

The public never get any information about WSI; it is, however, quite indisputable to me that the situation is as tragic there.

Enquiry Committees On 22 December 1995, after the outbreak of scandal around Prime Minister Jozef Oleksy, the work of the Committee for Security Services was moved to the background by the appointment of a twelve-member Sejm Enquiry Committee. The scandal began when one of the 'presidential' ministers[27] of President Lech Walesa submitted documents on Oleksy's alleged collaboration with KGB (since 1983) and then with the FSB (until at least the beginning of 1995) to the Military Prosecutor General.[28] The Enquiry Committee consisted of 12 deputies (seven from the coalition and five from the opposition). Its task was to investigate whether any public official or secret agent had broken the law while collecting information on the Prime Minister, including the denunciation by the Minister of Internal Affairs to the Military Prosecutor's Office.

The Committee was to establish whether the UOP officers who carried out secret operations in the case of alleged espionage by Prime Minister Oleksy had or had not infringed the law, and in particular, whether the entire scandal was or was not a mere political provocation in which the officers participated. The Enquiry Committee had unlimited access to witnesses but its members complained about blocked access to documents, although the Sejm's resolution instructed the Minister of Internal Affairs to turn over all documents pertaining to the Oleksy case. For more than four weeks, the Committee summoned high ranking secret services' officers and public officials to testify at hearings. The Committee's proceedings were secret. According to the Committee's first report, accepted by the Sejm on 1 February, no violation of law by a Ministry of Internal Affairs official was found. But the Committee, politically divided, was not ready to submit the final report. It interrogated several other officials and several times postponed the voting on its final opinion. The report was only accepted by the Sejm on 19 February 1997. In the meantime, on 22 April 1996, the military prosecutor decided to discontinue investigation in Oleksy's case concluding that there was not enough evidence to accuse Oleksy of espionage for the Soviet Union and Russia.

The final report of the Enquiry Committee confirmed that the actions and operations of the then Minister of Internal Affairs Andrzej Milczanowski and UOP could possibly constitute a breach of the law. Some time earlier, on 5 February 1997, the Democratic Left Alliance (SLD) that was then in power submitted to the Speaker of the Sejm a motion to impeach Milczanowski, accusing him, among other things,[29] of failure properly to supervise the activities of the UOP and of revealing State secrets during the plenary session of the Sejm in December 1995.[30] Despite this motion, two SLD ministers (of Justice and Internal Affairs) decided to publish a so-called White Book containing files of the criminal investigation conducted by the Military Prosecutor's Office.[31] After September 1997, the new party in power – Electoral Action Solidarity – has been trying to indict both former ministers for revealing State secrets in that book.[32]

Parliamentary interpellations   Although not exactly parliamentary oversight the institution of interpellations and parliamentary questions play an important part in the political game that invariably goes on between each and every opposition and coalition in power. Parliamentary debates are transmitted on public radio and television, and the more interesting interpellations (in which category questions about the alleged blunders and illegal actions of functionaries of security services belong as a rule) also receive press coverage. As elsewhere in the region, the issue that kindles the greatest passions among parliamentarians is alleged collaboration by individual parliamentarians or other persons from political elites with the security services of *ancient regime* or with their contemporary counterparts; the way in which former functionaries of *ancient regime* have established themselves in various agencies of public authorities and in the economic sector; as well as illegal wiretaps, burglaries of offices of political parties, and attempts made by functionaries of civilian security services to intimidate politicians from specific opposition parties, especially those lacking parliamentary representation.

In February 1998 several opposition deputies asked deputy Prosecutor General Stefan Sniezko about the manner of clearing up 'by the Prosecutor's Office of the cases of wiretaps and surveillance of opposition politicians by security services since 1993, and of illegal turnover of financial means by the Office of State Protection'.[33] Answering the first question, Prosecutor Sniezko said, '(You want to know) if there are wiretaps, if I can vouch for the statement that nobody is listening to your conversations. Let me tell you this: I do not know, but I do not think so, either (I do not think your wires are tapped)'.[34] The question was answered in detail by Minister Palubicki (see the following point). Answering the second question, Prosecutor Sniezko said that the case of violation by UOP of economic regulations was investigated by the Prosecutor's Office, but he maintained he had no time to inquire about the details, having only received the deputies' questions four hours before his pronouncement.[35]

The other interpellation on 19 March 1998 was made by a deputy from the SLD, now an opposition party – Jerzy Zakrzewski. He inquired whether a conservative, Konstanty Miodowicz, deputy from AWS and Head of counterespionage within the UOP in 1992–1995, chairing the

Parliamentary Committee for Security Services during the first half of 1998, had a secret job with UOP (which is forbidden by law) and a service flat in Warsaw provided by UOP. The question was based on an article in a scandalising pro-opposition weekly 'NIE'. Minister Co-ordinator for Security Services Janusz Palubicki responded that any answer to a question thus formulated would be tantamount to disclosure of a State secret. Therefore, answering a question from another opposition deputy Janusz Zemke, he stated that no members of the Sejm in the present term had any service relations with UOP, and added that security services were not carrying out any operational work within the Parliament: they would never take up any such work, not even if they believed that a parliamentarian was involved in activities against the Constitution. This could only be done most formally and openly:

> first, the Prosecutor's office should move for setting aside of the parliamentary immunity. Were the motion granted and the immunity set aside, only then would the Prosecutor's office and, upon its request, perhaps also the Office of State Protection undertake actions with respect to persons whose immunity was set aside. Sending UOP functionaries or associates to the Diet or Senate with the task of secret gathering of information is out of the question; personally, I would consider such action a glaring violation of the aim stated in the Law.[36]

Further on, Minister Palubicki said:

> Security services should never pursue illegal operations with respect to citizens, and I am most particular about it. Thus it is also clear and obvious that the services may never pursue illegal operations with respect to the Parliament. This is simply unthinkable.[37]

Another Member of Parliament, Mr. Miodowicz, took the floor during that debate; he denied having a secret job with UOP and a service flat provided by the Office. Throughout the debate, the coalition was represented by Mr. Miodowicz, and the opposition by about a dozen parliamentarians from SLD; otherwise, the hall was empty. As we have been told by a coalition deputy, the coalition intended 'in revenge' to make an interpellation to Minister Palubicki about the collaboration and service of some SLD deputies with communist security services.

Another issue is a 'big count' of policemen now in service who once were members of SB in People's Poland. The question was posed by a deputy from a rightist coalition party – ZChN (Christian National Union), Marian Kaminski. It appears there are about 3,000 such policemen (among the total force of about 102,000). The Right demand their dismissal from the Police. The Post-communist opposition within the Parliament – but also a considerable part of the coalition in power – argue that such former members of Security Service who are now policemen were approved in the summer of 1990 when the Service was screened and the new UOP formed. Unable to find a job with the Office with its much-reduced staff, they joined the Police and especially its logistics departments (surveillance and interception of communications) where their professional skills are well utilised. The matter is pending and its ending can hardly be anticipated; yet, as most such cases in Central Europe, it will probably end up in nothing at all, without a final 'yes' or 'no' decision.

Other parliamentary actions   Beside general parliamentary debates on security services, there is also another route for the legislative oversight of these services: public debates organised by different deputies' clubs. Naturally, it is the opposition parties that take the greatest interest in this particular form of oversight. A meeting of this kind was organised by post-communist SLD on 28 June 1998. The topic was formulated as a question: 'Is there democratic oversight of security services in Poland?' Deputies of the coalition in power ignored the meeting and Minister Co-ordinator for Security Services, Janusz Palubicki who said that, thus formulated, a question challenges the existence of such democratic oversight.[38] The opposition criticised the fact that the Board for Security Services never held any sessions (it had met only once since September 1996), and that the Security Services Committee of the Sejm acquired no information about the intended model of those services. Also criticised was the dismissal during the preceding months of about 500 UOP officers of long standing and provisions of the Screening Law and the draft Law on Institute of National Remembrance, which offered to citizens full access to the archives of communist security services. More to the point was the criticism made by Deputy J. Zemke, who complained about a lack of oversight of the use of wiretaps and prying by security services. The point is, however, that the accusations of Mr. Zemke must necessarily pertain also to the period when his Party wholly controlled the UOP. When it was in power in 1995, his party – himself included – was definitely against the introduction of judicial review of operational wiretaps carried out by security services, despite the lobbying for this solution by human rights organisations and the

Helsinki Committee in Poland on the occasion of the big amendment of the Law on UOP.[39]

Public Prosecutor General

The Public Prosecutor General is the main organ of the Public Prosecutor's Office and the post is held by the Minister of Justice. Under the Law on UOP (Article 10.2), it is the Prosecutor General who gives the final consent to inspection of correspondence and to the use of other technical means of secret interception of communications in cases where prosecution of an offence is specified in the Law or is one which Polish authorities are obliged to prosecute under an international agreement. Having acquired the Prosecutor's consent, the Head of UOP is obliged to 'inform him on a current basis' about the 'results of actions performed' (Article 10.1). The Head of UOP is also statutorily obliged to hand over to Public Prosecutor General all materials gathered in the course of secret interception of a person's communications if information about that person's offence was confirmed.

> In urgent cases when delay might lead to a loss of information or destruction of evidence of a crime, the Head of Office of State Protection may order mail inspections or the use of technical means ..., simultaneously approaching the Prosecutor General for consent to such actions. (Article 10.2). 'If the Prosecutor General fails to give the consent referred to in 10.2 above within 24 hours, the Head of Office of State Protection shall order an immediate stop on mail inspections or the use of technical means, and a formally recorded destruction by a commission of materials thus gathered.' (Article 10.3). 'If information about a crime (...) is confirmed, the Head of Office of State Protection hands over to the Prosecutor General the materials obtained in the course of actions referred to in points 1 and 2, together with a motion for institution of criminal proceedings.' (Article 10.5).

The Public Prosecutor General also approves controlled purchases carried out by security services in cases against organised criminal groups or cases of corruption. The Prosecutor is to be informed on a current basis about 'actions conducted and their results' (Art. 10.a.1). The Public Prosecutor General does not approve but should be 'notified without delay' of the start of secret surveillance, dislocation, storage of and trade in objects deriving from offences committed by organised groups. The Prosecutor is informed about the course and results of such actions; he may also order their discontinuance (Article 10.b.2).

That is the law but in practice secret interference with the freedom of communication is subject to only superficial formal supervision by the Prosecutor General; as far as we know, this happens only at the moment of his approving the start of such actions. The number of such decisions taken each year proves too large for the review to be effective. As has been revealed in the Sejm, the Prosecutor approved 1,000 secret operations in 1994[40] and 3,000 in 1995. Data are lacking as to the number of 'matters of utmost urgency' when the operation was launched without a prior consent of the Public Prosecutor General and the proportion of such cases where the Prosecutor ultimately refused his consent. Nothing is known, either, about the procedure for destroying materials that failed to provide evidence of offences.

The application for consent to the office of Public Prosecutor General must necessarily be formal. In 1995 the Prosecutor's Department had no prosecutor initially to examine applications signed by the Minister of Internal Affairs. Estimating the average number of workdays at 200 a year, the number of applications filed in 1995 must have been 15 a day on the average. The Public Prosecutor General could but sign them without examination. He probably took special interest in some of them; this, however, hardly changes the general situation. According to a practice developed in 1997, the Prosecutor only examines UOP applications concerning foreigners. Those concerning Polish citizens and those submitted by the Police (90 per cent approximately of the total of about 2,000 – the figures are secret) are handled by a Deputy Prosecutor General, that is the National Prosecutor. Approval by the National Prosecutor and not by the Public Prosecutor General is *contra legem*. It is not my intention to criticise this practice, though, as it at least guarantees a better examination of individual cases by prosecutors.

This is, however, just the beginning of the necessary supervision. From the available data it follows that the applications – especially those submitted by the Police – tend to be improperly drawn up, and the secret gathering of information itself carelessly carried out. In a considerable proportion of such cases, the entire operation, which is invariably most expensive, yields no results whatsoever. The absence of the legally required supervision by the Prosecutor General or an authorised prosecutor over the effectiveness and legality of secret operations must be criticised. It was only in 1997 that a team of prosecutors was established within the National Prosecutor's Office to examine the grounds of such applications and to maintain a register.

According to generally voiced beliefs, security services and the police tend in many cases to tap telephone lines without the required Prosecutor's consent. The latest data on this subject were revealed by a 'head of communications district X in a smaller town':

> 'It is not true', said Mr. X, 'that the Minister and Public Prosecutor General must necessarily approve each and every instance of installation of line tapping as is required by the law. Anyway, the provisions are violated again and again. The functionaries come and go as they like.' The provisions are violated not only in Mr. X's district. His colleagues, heads of neighbouring communications districts, experience the same. None has ever closed up the 'exterritorial room' – they all knew the officers would be back sooner or later. And they did come back, everywhere in the neighbourhood. Some as early as 1993, the last one in the spring of 1995... (Tapped are the lines of) 'the small town elite', he (Mr. X) says, chiefly of managers of State and private enterprises and local higher functionaries of the administration. Next, of activists of the present opposition ('Those of today are not the same as before the elections.') And finally – of persons suspected of offences. Mr. X is not worried about the very fact that the police or UOP are entitled to tap the lines in his exchange station. 'What I mean is that this procedure should not remain unsupervised and arbitrary', he says. 'How am I to know, for example, that an officer or technician does not use our installations for completely private purposes? ...In a small town where all people know one another, you simply have to open the door to an officer who wants to see the installations. Such is the mentality, shaped for many decades'.[41]

Criminal proceedings against functionaries suspected of service offences remain but a theoretical form of supervision by the Prosecutor over the operation of security services. Criminal cases – of which there are several a year – are typical of police services in Poland. They concern drunken driving and corruption (service secrets being sold to third persons, so-called 'businessmen' as a rule). In 1993, ten criminal proceedings against functionaries of UOP were pending; in 1994, there were 12 such cases; and in 1995 and 1996 – eight cases each.[42]

Until September 1998 there were well-formulated provisions of Articles 125–126 of the Law on UOP, adopted on 6 April 1990. They penalised those types of interference with civil rights and freedoms that are typical of police and security services. The first provision forbade a functionary of UOP from exceeding his service powers to the detriment of the citizen's personal interests. The statutory penalty for this act was up to two years' imprisonment (or up to five years if the infringement resulted from the functionaries acting against his superior's injunction). The other provision penalised the use by a functionary of UOP of violence, unlawful threat, or moral cruelty to obtain explanations, depositions or statements. Here, the penalty was up to five years' imprisonment. The provisions were quashed hastily, without a public debate and at the very last moment when the new Penal Code was adopted in June 1997. Functionaries of UOP and the Police (the Police Law contained similar penal provisions) had for a long time been against articles 125–126. The more general provisions of the Penal Code would suffice here, they argued. Yet the very way in which the two Articles were abolished – without consultation with experts and members of the Codification Committee – proves that they were necessary.

Judicial Review

Apart from bringing a functionary of UOP before the court, the law in force offers extremely few possibilities of judicial review of the operation of security services. Thus the Law on UOP (Article 11.b.4 as amended August 1996) provides that, in the case of refusal to release an employee, functionary or person who assists such employee or functionary in performing operational and investigative actions from the duty to preserve State secrets, or refusal to grant access to documents or materials constituting State secrets despite a demand to this effect made by the prosecutor or court in connection with criminal proceedings in the case of an offence specified in Article 109 of the Penal Code (war crime or crime against humanity) or of crimes against human life or transgressions against life and health resulting in a person's death, the Head of UOP shall submit the demanded documents and materials together with an explanation to the First President of the Supreme Court. If s/he finds that it is necessary for correctness of criminal proceedings that the motion of the prosecutor or court be granted, the Head of UOP is obliged to release the employee or functionary concerned from the duty to preserve the State secret, or to grant access to documents and materials constituting such secret.

The right to inquire into the secrets of UOP, and thus also to review the correctness of secret information thus gathered, has been vested in the Screening Court established by Law of 11 April 1997. On a demand of the Screening Court, the Head of UOP shall hand over all the gathered documents and materials needed for screening proceedings and concerning persons in whose cases the proceedings are pending (Article 11.b.5). The problem is that judges – ill disposed towards the Law – prevented the Screening Court from being formed.

Under the Law, the Court was to start once the judges had selected its 21 members. But, from over 2,100 judges of provincial courts and courts of appeal, only twenty applied for appointment. Subsequently, the law was to be amended.

Ombudsman

On 23 August 1996, the Commissioner for Civil Rights Protection (Ombudsman) submitted his *Standpoint on the Principles and Practice of Interception of Communications*[43] to the Prime Minister. The Ombudsman took interest in this issue in 1995 as a result of public pronouncements and letters received from representatives of Helsinki Foundation for Human Rights, letters from citizens, and press reports. Using his statutory powers, the Ombudsman took up the case. The Ombudsman may clarify a case of alleged violation of personal freedoms through either independently conducting an investigation or requesting that competent agencies examine the case.

In carrying out an investigation, the Ombudsman may examine a specific case on the spot; demand provision of the files of that case; and order the preparation of opinions (Article 13.1). However, if the case constitutes State secrets which is true of all cases of wiretaps, 'provision of information or grant of access to files to the Ombudsman follows the principles and procedure laid down in provisions on protection of State and secret services' (Article 13.2). If the Ombudsman finds that a constitutional freedom has been violated, he may demand restitution, administrative, civil or criminal proceedings or may move for cassation (Articles 14 and 15).

In the above case of wiretaps, the Ombudsman approached the ministers of Justice, of Internal Affairs, of National Defence, and of Telecommunications for information about the principles and procedures of using wiretaps. Each of the Ministers duly provided the information required. Some fragments of the answers bore the clauses 'secret' or 'secret of special importance'. In his information, the Ombudsman omitted the secret issues stating that 'the non-secret information and materials suffice for a general appraisal of the situation, especially from the viewpoint of consistency with international standards'.[44]

In his report the Ombudsman stressed that operational wiretaps are supervised by heads of the police and security services and by authorised functionaries respectively. The supervision follows a secret procedure. All that is known is that Military Intelligence prepared periodic reports on cases of interference with the freedom of communication.[45] The Minister of Telecommunications, in turn, informed the Ombudsman that, due to the technological progress in telecommunications, he is no longer able to supervise any illegal wiretaps used by the police and security services. The Minister said there could be no safe technical protection against the use of illegal wiretaps. The Ombudsman criticised this argument that the state of technology could release the Minister from the duty to watch over telecommunication networks and to prevent violations of secrecy of correspondence.

The Ombudsman accepted at face value the information provided by the Minister of Internal Affairs that the use of wiretaps by the police and civilian security services resulted in no violations of civil liberties by his subordinates. What in our opinion should have made the Ombudsman much more cautious are the following arguments: the low professional and moral standards of functionaries of security services[46] and police;[47] the large number of operational wiretaps, especially those used by the Police; the fictitious nature of external supervision by the Prosecutor General of the legality of wiretaps; the absence of review of effectiveness of such actions on part of parliamentary committees; and the failure to provide to the person concerned the possibility of checking what information about him or her, if any, has been gathered and what has happened to such data after the gathering of information has ceased.

In the absence of effective means of legal protection, the Ombudsman himself admits he is helpless in the face of any possible abuses of wiretaps by the police and security services: 'To acquire full knowledge about the extent of wiretaps, one would have to gain access to data on the numbers of cases, persons, telephones, and extensions of the period of interception'.[48] From the Ombudsman's 'Standpoint' it follows that not even he is provided with general statistics of such cases. Judging from the context, he does not find reliable the number of operational wiretaps in 1995 (1,314 cases) quoted to him by the police and UOP.

Concluding his 'Standpoint', the Ombudsman formulated nine critical remarks on the quality of the law, its accessibility for persons concerned, absence of judicial review of wiretaps, secrecy of the very principles of supervision within individual services, and secrecy of statistical data on wiretaps. He concluded with the following observation: 'It is not for the Commissioner for Civil Rights Protection to suggest detailed solutions to the Government or Parliament. His task is to inform about violations of civil rights and about a threat of such violations'.

Despite the Government's efforts towards a greater consistency with international standards binding on Poland, the Ombudsman concludes that 'As regards the current principles and practice of using wiretaps, one might – in the light of the above facts – speak of a threat to the right to secrecy of correspondence'.[49]

Dismissed officers of the communist security services have several times approached the Ombudsman for protection. They could not accept that some newcomers in 1990–1995, without experience in their new job, many of them the former political dissidents they used to spy on or academics from universities were quickly promoted. The criticism drew the Ombudsman's attention to the fact that statutory requirements in this matter were not met by the promoted persons, suggesting that promotions were of a political nature. The author of a letter to the Ombudsman quoted the name of a director in the UOP who in the period 1990–1995, was promoted from the rank of private soldier to the rank of colonel despite the fact that, according to statutory requirements, a functionary should wait at least 20 years for such a promotion. In 1997, answering the Ombudsman's letter to the Minister of Internal Affairs, Zbigniew Siemiatkowski admitted that as regards UOP and the Frontier Guard, some of their functionaries were promoted several times without respecting the period of service which is binding. He denied, however, that this was related to any preferences as to a 'definite political option'.[50]

Internal Supervision of the Services

Irrespective of the Minister's supervision, UOP has an Inspection Department. If necessary, the Head of UOP appoints a special team of inspectors to clarify a specific issue. This happened in 1996 in connection with the scandal of former Prime Minister Oleksy and his alleged collaboration with KGB and FSB after control over the security services was taken over by SLD. A special team of inspectors was formed to examine the case of alleged illegal actions of UOP officers involved in exposure of the scandal back in 1995. The Committee is said to have found such infringements but no records of its proceedings have been kept. What might constitute a specific form of oversight of security services is depriving those services of powers with respect to huge quantities of personal files and other documents prepared and gathered by communist security services. This operation would not just be a symbolic break with the former regime. In Poland, in the context of screening, representatives of security services use two conflicting arguments – conflicting as they are addressed at different groups as need arises. On the one hand, it is argued in discussion with advocates of screening that the screening procedure is doomed to failure since most of the personal files have been destroyed. On the other hand, facing those who advocate the formation of special archives of documents prepared and gathered by communist security services, representatives of the present services argue that this would pose a dramatic threat to today's security of the State. Thus either the record no longer exist, and any scraps that are still left concern completely unimportant persons, or the records still remain the foundation of the security of the State! On 24 March 1998 the Council of Ministers accepted a draft law which provided for separation of such documents in special archives; for creation of a special agency modelled after the Hungarian and German ones; and at the same time for a grant of access to their personal files for all victims of secret gathering of information by communist security services.

Public Perception of Security Services in Poland

A survey of a representative national sample of adult inhabitants of Poland (n = 1,088), carried out on 12–17 July 1997 found that only ten per cent declared considerable knowledge of the area of activity of UOP. Forty-three per cent knew nothing about the Office. Respondents were against the gathering of information by UOP with the use of methods interfering with their private life. The following techniques were found 'completely inadmissible': 'inspection of private correspondence' (63 per cent of respondents); 'bugging and observation in private lodgings' (58 per cent); 'bugging and observation in institutions and workplaces' (43 per cent); wiretapping (43 per cent); the use of paid informers 'from among Polish politicians or businessmen' (43 per cent); the use of paid informers 'from among foreign politicians or businessmen' (41 per cent); the use of paid informers 'from among ordinary foreign citizens' (36 per cent); and the use of paid informers 'from among ordinary Polish citizens'(25 per cent).[51]

In mid-1996, UOP was perceived as an institution entangled in politics. This was the opinion shared by 69 per cent of respondents. The distribution of answers was quite similar irrespective of the respondents' political preferences. Those who voiced this opinion were most frequently university-educated persons, managers, and white-collar workers.[52] A similar negative opinion on the UOP was found in a survey carried out in December 1997 by the Centre for Opinion Surveys.[53] Forty-six per cent of respondents believed that UOP 'serves the interests of those in power'; 17 per cent that it 'pursues its own interests'. Answering another question, 66 per cent said that UOP was used in political games, and 43 per cent that it violates the rights of citizens. Despite such negative opinions of UOP, the largest proportion (44 per cent) of respondents was against the 'zero option' if it were tantamount to liquidation of the Office. Thirty-three per cent declared for that option.

Thus citizens do want the security services; but they want those services to stay away from them.

Notes

1   Uniform text, Journal of Laws, 90.30.180.
2   Amendments, Polish Official Gazette 195.23.271; 96.43.419.
3   Security Office (UB) in 1944–1956 and Security Service (SB) in 1956–1990. See: Andrzej Paczkowski (ed.). Security Machine in 1944–1956. Henryk Dominiczak, Security Agencies in People's Poland 1944–1990, Warsaw, 1997, Bellona: p. 439.
4   Data on the work of the Central Commission from: *Biuletyn Biura Informacynego Kancelarii Sejmu No 2476/II kad. Komisja Administracji in Spraw Wewnetrznych* (No 102). Session of April 1996 on 'matters submitted by citizens to the Commission and the Ombudsman and related to the classification proceedings of 1990 with respect to functionaries of the Ministry of Internal Affairs'.
5   In 1995, according to 'Information on implementation of the Budget', UOP employed 'more than 5,700 officers and about 600 civil servants'. Later on, any information on such figures has been secret. See: Security services. *Rzeczpospolita*, 24 June 1998, No. 146, p. 1.
6   In an interview for *Gazeta Wyborcza*, Minister of Internal Affairs Zbigniew Siemictkowski stated that 'the proportion of old and new functionaries of the Office of State Protection is 51 to 49'. *Gazeta Wyborcza*, 22–23 June 1996.
7   After Minister of Internal Affairs, Biuletyn Biura Informacyjnego, op.cit, p. 23.
8   Security services. *Rzeczpospolita*, 24 June 1998, No.146, p. 1.
9   Przemyslaw Kubiak: 'What was the relation between SB and Lady Punk? The Counterintelligence department decided the list of radio hits.' *Super Express*, 4 December 1996, p. 1.
10 'We served only the State', interview of A. Kubik with General H. Jasik (On the staff of SB since 1970. Chief of the UOP Intelligence Department. Connected with President Walesa. Dismissed at the beginning of 1996.) *Gazeta Wyborcza*. 17 January 1997, p. 16.
11 Case No. CCPR/C60/D/552/1993.
12 The representative was a positively verified former SB officer. In the 1980s he kept the scientific circles under surveillance.
13 The representative was a positively verified former SB officer. In the 1980s he kept the scientific circles under surveillance.
14 Andrzej Milczanowski (August 1990–December 1991), Solidarity Trade Union leader, jurist. At the beginning of his career he was a public prosecutor. In 1992–1995, Minister of Internal Affairs; now a notary; Piotr Naimski December 1991–June 1992), physicist, a political dissident, now a private person; Jerzy Konieczny (June 1992–June 1993), lawyer and chemist, University professor of forensic sciences, now owner of a private company; Gromoslaw Czempillski (June 1993–February 1996), a career officer of intelligence since 1970, colonel promoted to the rank of general in 1995, now retired;

Andrzej Kapkowski (February 1996–November 1997), officer of counterintelligence since 1968, promoted to the rank of general in 1997, now retired; Zbigniew Nowek (November 1997–), former activist of an independent student movement.

[15] Adam Marcinkowski, Zbigniew Palski, Victims of Stalinist Repression's in the Polish Armed Forces. *Wojskowy Przeglad Historyczny* 1990 No.1–2 pp. 168–184.

[16] Military Police was made a separate agency in September 1990; before it had been part of the WSW.

[17] Security services. *Rzeczpospolita* 24 June 1998, No.146, p. 1.

[18] To quote acting Chief of UOP Colonel Andrzej Kapkowski in a press interview, 'The Oleksy scandal must necessarily end; I hope the Office will then be normalised. The scandal crowned a most vehement political struggle in Poland and overlapped the presidential elections. Today, it's over. The Office is unlikely to break down altogether just because several of its officers are guilty of transgressions and will be called to account', *Rzeczpospolita*, 22 May 1996, p. 16.

[19] The Czech example shows that this is not true. As Prime Minister, Vaclav Klaus used the State Information Service to spy on his political opponents.

[20] Dz.U. No. 136 item 924.

[21] On 24 March 1998 the Government submitted to the Sejm a Bill on Institute of National Remembrance [Sejm Papers No.252]. The Bill offers to citizens' free access to personal files gathered by communist civilian and military security services and dating roughly 1944 to 1990. Victims of those services would also have access to names of their oppressors (SB and WSW officers and secret informants). More than 142 km of files produced in that period would be transferred to the Institute. The Institute was originally established in 1945; it was then called the High Commission to Investigate German Crimes. In 1950 it was renamed High Commission to Investigate Nazi Crimes and in 1991 became the High Commission to Investigate Nazi Crimes – Institute of National Remembrance. The post-communist opposition are against citizen access to the files of the communist regime.

[22] UOP picked to pieces, *Gazeta Wyborcza* 26 March 1998, No.72, p. 3.

[23] Ravage and games, *Prawo i Gospodarka* 26 March 1998, No.67 , p. 1.

[24] Ibid.

[25] See: UOP against the Opposition. [Interview with Prof. Lech Kaczyllski, President of Supreme Board of Supervision 1992–1994.] 'Zycie' 22 May, No.119, p. 6. Kaczyllski said, 'I witnessed approval by the Government of the security services' report from activities against legal Opposition. [...] The entire report [prepared by the then Head of UOP Prof. Jerzy Konieczny] seemed to have been written specially to justify the services' interference with the course of elections'. See also: Surveillance of the Right. Establishing the fact. The files have grown to 20 volumes so far. *Gazeta Wyborcza*, July 23rd 1998, No.171, p. 3. In the winter of 1998, I was told by several AWS deputies that they have been spied on, as members of an opposition party, as late as the end of September 1997, that is after the elections. The operation was allegedly conducted not by UOP but by military intelligence (sic!) which would indicate a complete anarchy within the services.

[26] Remont w UOP [Redecoration in the UOP], *Tygodnik AWS*, 1998 No.48, p. 13.

[27] Under a temporary constitutional provision of 17 October 1992, ministers of internal affairs, defence and foreign affairs can be appointed without formal approval of the President. This meant that in the leftist Cabinets of 1993–1995, ministers representing the opposite of the coalition in power were appointed. They were called 'presidential' ministers. The provision was abolished in the Constitution of 17 April 1997.

[28] Oleksy denied the allegation and suggested that it was a revenge of the former President

[29] See 'East European Constitutional Review', Winter 1997, Vol. 6, No.1, p. 22.

30   Sejm of the 2nd term (1993–97) failed to prepare an indictment for the Tribunal of State on time. Sejm of the 3rd term did not hurry to decide on the indictment.

31   The White Book. Records of an investigation conducted by Prosecutor's Office of Warsaw Military District concerning motions of Minister of Internal Affairs of 19 December 1995 and 16 January 1996 (Ref. No. PoSl 1/96). Warsaw 1996 *Centrum Informacyjne Rzadu*: p. 464.

32   This, however, is not the end of stories of alleged collaboration of high-rank post-communist leaders with KGB/FSB. In 1996 some weeklies (e.g. *Wprost, Gazeta Polska*) and newspapers (e.g *Zycie*) suggested that also President Aleksander Kwasniewski and Leszek Miller had been among such collaborators.

33   Minutes of the 11 session of Sejm, pp. 48–55.

34   Ibid, 53.

35   Ibid, 56.

36   Ibid, 143.

37   Ibid, 148.

38   See press reports: Aleksander Frydrychowicz, SLD disclosing the political nature of UOP, *Trybuna* 1998, 29 June, No.150, pp. 3, 5; Pawel Wrollski, UOP scrutinised by SLD. A political seminar on Polish security services, *Gazeta Wyborcza* 1998, 29 June, No.150, p. 3; Anna Marszalek, Plans to merge civilian and military intelligence. The Opposition on democratic oversight, *Rzeczpospolita* 1998, 29 June, No.150, p. 2.

39   For this reason, in the early half of 1995, during intense parliamentary work on amendment of the Law on UOP, extension of the uses of UOP secret operations under Article 10 included, as an expert of a Sejm Committee, I spoke for a regulation requiring approval by a court of such operations (as is the case in the Czech Republic under § 10 of the relevant statute). Despite an initial informal acceptance of this solution by heads of the Ministry of Internal Affairs, they finally declared for the Public Prosecutor's supervision; my suggestion was not even supported by opposition deputies. Also representatives of the National Council of the Judiciary and the Supreme Court who participated in the Committee's proceedings opposed the suggested solution, obviously reluctant to add to the load of judges. Representatives of the Ministry of Internal Affairs quoted the difficulty of keeping such operations secret. The argument was not only offensive to judges: it was also false. UOP proved an agency guilty of many instances of leakage, not only in connection with the Oleksy scandal. It soon turned out, too, that in order to start secret surveillance of Prime Minister Oleksy, the Minister of Internal Affairs was forced to infringe in mid-1995 the provision of Article 10 of the Law on UOP, failing to approach the Public Prosecutor General for consent to that operation. The Minister could not apply to the Prosecutor because he was the Prime Minister's trusted associate and party colleague.

40   Response of Minister of Justice to a parliamentary question by deputy Lidia Bladek concerning the review of legality of wiretapping, Shorthand report, 46th session of the Sejm in the 2nd term, part II, p. 51.

41   W. Markiewicz: Permanent tapping has been restored to telephone exchange stations, *Polityka*, May 11th 1996, pp. 28–29.

42   M. Kozural; The problem of discipline within the UOP. *Gazeta Wyborcza*, 5 October, 1996.

43   A threat to the right to privacy resulting from inspection of mail and the use of technical means enabling secret gathering of information and fixing of evidence. *Biuletyn Rzecznika Praw Obywatelskich* 1996 No.3 pp. 9–23.

44   Ibid, p.10.

45   Ibid, p. 17.

46 In January 1998, in the face of widespread drunkenness of functionaries on duty, blood alcohol testers were installed in offices of UOP.

47 See T. Bulenda, A. Kremplewski, P. Moczydlowski and A. Rzeplinski: Between Militia and Reform. The Police in Poland 1989–1997. A report submitted in March 1998 within an international project *Police in Transition* co-ordinated by Hungarian Helsinki Committee.

48 A threat to the right to privacy resulting from inspection of mail and the use of technical means enabling secret gathering of information and fixing of evidence. *Biuletyn Rzecznika Praw Obywatelskich* 1996 No.3 p. 20.

49 Ibid, p.23.

50 Swierczakowska H., Promotion to higher ranks. *Gazeta Policyjna*, 1996 No.21, p. 3.

51 Center for Opinion Surveys. Society on the Office of State Protection. Survey report. Warsaw, August 1996, p. 13.

52 Ibid, p. 9–10.

53 CBOS survey of 11–16 December 1997. Random sample of 1,066 Polish citizens.

PART III

SECURITY INTELLIGENCE IN
STABLE DEMOCRACIES

Chapter 7

Security and Intelligence Structures in the Netherlands

Peter Klerks

It's called service, remember? You're cleaning the political drains. It's the dirtiest job democracy has on offer. (John Le Carré, *Our Game*)

Introduction

In Holland the security and intelligence services have managed to avoid the limelight for most of the post-war period. Shortly after the Second World War the foundations for the present structures were laid. Three separate military intelligence services were formed to continue the work of the pre-war services, but with a new orientation on NATO and the United States. Signals intelligence (communications intercepts) became a prominent and very expensive task that was executed under the control of naval intelligence in close co-operation with the Anglo-American monitoring organisations.

Foreign intelligence remained a small and very secretive espionage service of which little became known until it was formally disbanded in 1994. Holland of course also developed its own stay-behind ('Gladio') structures, strongly influenced by the British and later the US services. They too were formally disbanded in 1993.

Also after the Second World War the *Plaatselijke Inlichtingen Diensten* (PIDs, local police intelligence services, recently renamed the Regional Intelligence Services), often dating back to the 1920s, were reinstalled for domestic security purposes. In 1948 however the *Binnenlandse Veiligheidsdienst* (BVD) in The Hague was established to achieve better co-ordination, standardised security investigations and procedures, and also to improve international contacts.[1] The BVD still exists today, and most of this chapter is dedicated to this organisation since it is the most relevant Dutch intelligence and security service from a political and civil liberties point of view.

Organisation

Binnenlandse Veiligheidsdienst (BVD, Domestic Security Service)

Legal basis Currently, the BVD operates under the *Wet op de inlichtingen – en veiligheidsdiensten* (WIV, Law on the intelligence and security services, enacted in 1987 and revised twice in 1993). However, recent jurisprudence by the European Commission is about to lead to a total overhaul of Dutch intelligence legislation. The intelligence service's legal foundation began to shake when a group of ten individuals who had sued the Dutch state for unlawfully registering them in intelligence files (which were uncovered after a burglary by activists in the military counterintelligence offices in Utrecht in the mid-1980s) were each granted a thousand guilders in damages.[2] But what is more important in the Commission's ruling is that the Dutch legal situation and safeguards do not fully comply with the European Convention (ECRM). Following this juridical key event, the Dutch Council of State (*Raad van State*) confirmed in its rulings in two other cases (Van Baggum and Valkenier) that the current intelligence legislation in certain respects does not comply with the requirements derived from the relevant European Convention and jurisprudence.[3] As a consequence, a revision of the legislation is currently under preparation with a bill presented in parliament in early 1998.[4] In the following paragraphs, the expected changes in the current legal situation will be indicated.

The second law governing the BVD's operations is the Security Investigations Act of 10 October 1996 (Stb. 1996, 525), under which the security service is charged with investigating candidates for sensitive positions both in government and key industries, as well as with repeated security screenings of employees on such posts.

Once the new intelligence bill is passed into law (which is expected to happen in 2002), the BVD's name will change to *Algemene Inlichtingen – en Veiligheidsdienst* (AIVD, general intelligence and security service). Simultaneously, the military intelligence service will be renamed the *Militaire Inlichtingen – en Veiligheidsdienst* (MIVD, military intelligence and security service).

Political and strategic co-ordination of both services will be effected (just as it is now) through the function of the Intelligence Co-ordinator, an intermediary between the ministers involved (the Prime Minister and the ministers of Foreign Affairs, Defence, Justice, and the Interior) and the services. The co-ordinator will be responsible for running daily affairs.

The newly named AIVD will be charged with:

- investigating those organisations and persons whose goals or activities give reason for serious suspicions that they constitute a danger to the continuation of the democratic rule of law, or to the security or other weighty interests of the state;
- carrying out security investigations as detailed in the law on vetting procedures;
- promoting measures to protect the mandate, including the securing of data when secrecy is demanded by the interests of national security and of those parts of government services and private corporations that in the judgement of ministers are of vital interest to the maintenance of public life;
- conducting investigations into other countries in relation to subjects designated by the Prime Minister, Minister of General Affairs in agreement with other Ministers involved: in the interest of national security insofar as topics of a primarily non-military relevance are concerned, and concerning vital economic interests of the Netherlands.

Under the new legislation the application of all sorts of operational methods and techniques, including the opening of mail, breaking into computer systems, the use of forged identities, the setting up of front stores, the carrying out of criminal acts, the theft of certain items from the homes of individuals and the like, will be subject to approval by the minister of the Interior or the head of the service, depending on the level of intrusion into the private domain of individual citizens. This means that the proposed legislation actually sums up a limited number of operational methods that the intelligence and security services are allowed to apply.[5] This explicit enactment of all sorts of operational methods is a direct consequence of the requirements of European jurisprudence.

The acceptance by parliament of changes in the constitution, necessary to allow the police and the domestic security service to covertly enter private homes and to engage in all sorts of other intrusions without ever informing the targets did not go without some political fireworks. Shortly before defending the constitutional amendments in Parliament in early 1998, the minister of the Interior sent a letter to the leaders of the four largest Dutch political parties strongly advocating unobstructed wiretapping as an essential tool of criminal investigation as well as in the fight against terrorism.[6] The text of this letter, which appears to have played a key role in the approval of the new law, is said to have been proposed by the BVD itself. In it MPs were warned that if the bill were not passed, the BVD would lose one of its most powerful tools and could no longer operate effectively. To clinch the argument, the BVD let it be known that it could certainly no longer guarantee that 'friendly' foreign intelligence services would not break the law and do their own clandestine bugging and tapping, instead of turning to the BVD for assistance. In the same debate the minister of the Interior used similar arguments to defend burgling homes without ever informing the occupants afterwards.

Also under the new legislation, the Service will be entitled to provide information it has collected to any person or institution that has an interest in it, including foreign intelligence services, and all this without explicit approval of a political authority such as a minister or an oversight body.[7]

Size On 31 December 1998, the BVD formally employed 563 persons, 188 of whom were women and 55 were 'allochthonous' (i.e. people who themselves or their parents are of foreign birth).

Structure The current BVD is divided into six Directorates, which each have a number of departments, plus one Project.[8]

The first Directorate is the small Strategy and Planning Directorate (SJZ), comprising the Directional Secretariat, the Cabinet and Judicial Affairs department, the Strategy, Planning and Co-ordination department, and the Internal and External relations department.

The second and third Directorates are Democratic Rule of Law (DRO) and State Security (SV). Both of these consist of a Director's office, a Quality Management Bureau, and a number of teams.

The Security Directorate (BC), established on 1 January 1999 consists of a Director's office, a Policy and Expertise department, a Security Promotion department, plus two department Security Investigations 'A' and 'B'. This Directorate is tasked with all security investigations ('vetting' clearances) as well as with the preventive advisory security activities aimed at selected governmental and corporate institutions. This Directorate also houses the Integrity reporting centre, through which the BVD each year receives some 15–20 reports, mostly by civil servants and accountants, on incidents and suspicions regarding integrity violations in government organisations.

The Special Intelligence Means Directorate (BI) consists of the following departments: Director's office, Technology, Operational Tasks, Open Sources Information, Foreign Relations, and Special Missions.

The Directorate for Management, Advise and Central Facilities has the following departments: Director's office, Quality Manager, Personnel, Finances and Economy, Information and Organisation, Security, Registry Documentation and Archives, and Auxiliary Services.

Finally, the Foreign Intelligence Project is established to prepare for the foreign intelligence activities which the new AIVD will undertake under the new legislation. In due course, the Project is to become a full Directorate.

Day-to-day operations are carried out *via* projects so that many BVD employees – in contrast to the old situation during the cold war – no longer have formal fields of substantive expertise or 'favourite targets'. Flexibility and improvisation are the buzzwords of today, just like in most organisations.[9]

Budget   The overall BVD budget for 2000 was 94.2 million guilders (approx. 38 million US dollars), of which Dfl. 67.3 million is for personnel, Dfl. 26.7 million for material expenses and Dfl. 0.2 million for retaining fees paid to former employees who were phased out over the last years.[10] An average of Dfl. 4 million is booked under 'secret spending'. About one third of this is earmarked for clandestine operations abroad. The BVD's budget is scheduled for an annual increase of Dfl. 5 million until at least 2004.

Mandate and tasks   Formally, the BVD now has three main mandates, investigating threats, vetting and protective security as detailed in 'legal basis' above. Currently, the security service operates mainly in the domains of protecting fundamental rights involving the democratic process and the rule of law, countering organised crime, anti-extremism and anti-terrorism, investigations into proliferation of non-conventional weapons and illegal arms trade (for example, missile technology), and of course counter-espionage.

Operationally most activities concentrate on issues such as rightist extremism and xenophobia, conflicts between left and right radicals, intra-ethnic conflicts, and the interference of foreign powers with their (former) countrymen who live on Dutch soil (such as the Iranian regime).[11] In proliferation issues and clandestine arms trade investigations especially, the BVD co-operates closely with the MID and the *Economische Controle Dienst* (ECD). As an example of political and religious extremism that causes great concern in Holland as well as in neighbouring countries, the Algerian Islamic extremist networks can be mentioned here. As far as counterespionage is concerned, the main targets are still the Russian and Chinese secret services, although their targets in the main are no longer political or military, but economic. Other countries, such as Libya, are also said to engage in covert operations under the guise of 'Islamic Call Society'. The BVD also has other institutes carry out research projects on its behalf. The RISBO Institute of the Erasmus University in Rotterdam for example recently did a study on the (former) Russian community in Holland to look into possible long-term security risks. In the early and mid-1990s, BVD attempts to recruit asylum seekers as covert sources repeatedly made the newspapers, but judging on the current absence of any such reports, these practices have either been discontinued or are now carried out in a more subtle way.

In 1998 and 1999, the BVD's involvement in the monitoring of environmental activists, particularly those operating under the banner of 'Green Front' became clear.[12] Activists employing peaceful means engaged in a number of blockade protests against the construction of a new high-speed railroad that they claim will damage the rural landscape in some areas. The BVD, together with regional police forces established a co-ordinating centre (CICI) for monitoring the environmentalists.

Also, the BVD is increasingly involved in the fight against organised crime. The service investigates the relationship between organised crime and ethnic organisations and the possible involvement of foreign powers, as well as certain forms of illegal arms trade and the production and trafficking of synthetic drugs such as XTC. In such activities, the BVD works in close collaboration with foreign security services. The service is also involved in investigating so-called 'contra activities' by criminal organisations who employ offensive counterintelligence methods such as charting covert police surveillance teams, breaking their radio encryption, and committing burglaries to obtain compromising material on sensitive operations, or who attempt to intimidate and blackmail law enforcement officials. Other BVD tasks include the monitoring of football hooliganism: police intelligence squads keep the local problematic groups under surveillance, but during major international events such as Euro 2000, the BVD will be charged with monitoring possible disturbances of the public peace on a larger scale.

Another recent field of BVD involvement is the protection of societal integrity and the countering of corruption, for example through the investigation of possible weaknesses in key positions in government institutions, and of money laundering practices that could harm the rule of law or public governance. The BVD in 1996 published a manual to serve as a guide on organisational integrity, and extensive screening methods have been developed for governmental organisations such as local governments, police forces and ministries to detect where organised crime could gain influence. As a result, nowadays, one can encounter BVD advisors who organise seminars on the integrity of civil servants on behalf of a burgomaster or a chief of police, or who work as consultants and trainers on a project to reinforce a climate of reciprocal care and alertness among the staff of the ministry of Transport.

Other BVD officers still work in more obscure areas, such as the investigation of sects like the Scientology Church, but so far these have not led to serious security concerns or prolonged surveillance of such groups.

Operational means and methods   In general, the BVD produces threat analyses balancing the nature of the threat, the resilience against that threat and the interests at stake. Such analysed information is then presented to stakeholders, who are also advised to undertake certain actions.

The BVD's officers have a mandate to approach almost any holder of registrations of personal data to obtain desired information, and in most cases they will be able to obtain data from government and semi-government organs. As far as other, private data collections are concerned, the BVD's access is at the discretion of the official or the management in charge. Regular legal limitations to the furnishing of information to third persons do not apply in case of requests made by BVD officers. It is understood that in most cases, the BVD gets what it needs.

The so-called 'integrity of society' is an increasingly important theme for the BVD. It therefore established a co-ordination point some years ago, where civil servants and others can report violations and threats in relation to integrity. In an average year, this centre receives about 25–35 such reports. In a similar vein, political parties have in the recent past approached the BVD with requests to check its files for possible information on candidates for representative bodies. In most such cases, this concerned members of ethnic minorities who were rumoured to be connected to undemocratic organisations such as the Turkish Grey Wolves, or to drug trafficking organisations.

The BVD, together with the ministries of Justice and Foreign Affairs also has a role to play in ensuring the safety of international bodies residing in the Netherlands, in particular the UN tribunal for war crimes in The Hague.

Doctrine During the cold war, the BVD as well as the other Dutch secret services was firmly embedded in the familiar anti-communist doctrine that governed most of the western world in some form until the late 1980s. Then, in 1989, the new Social Democrat Minister of the Interior Ms Ien Dales started a reform process that would take the BVD through a turbulent period of reorientation and change. The traditionally invisible head of the Service was replaced by the flamboyant and outspoken career civil servant Mr Arthur Docters van Leeuwen, a member of the progressive liberal party D66.[13] In the summer of 1990 the partial publication of the reorganisation paper for the BVD, based on an audit by a private organisation management bureau, offered sufficient material for debate. The paper summarily described an organisation in near total chaos, working along inefficient lines with no clear strategic concept or operational criteria and unable to live up to modern expectations. Later press publications quoting disgruntled and frustrated employees seemed to confirm this depiction.

Under a partly renewed and modernised management the BVD underwent a drastic reorganisation, reviewed its goals, targets and procedures, and was trimmed down from about 700 to some 560 employees, while its annual budget remained roughly the same. At the same time a veritable public relations offensive started. Mr. Docters van Leeuwen became more familiar to the television audience than any of his predecessors and the organisation repeatedly intervened in public debates issuing warnings and presenting its views.

In 1992 the *Binnenlandse Veiligheidsdienst* published its first unclassified 'threat analysis' in which the security service's considerably widened interests were made explicit.[14] The report states that corruption of civil servants, terrorism, arms proliferation, sabotage of vital infrastructure systems and services and theft of high-grade technology, but also organised crime together form the new diffuse panorama of dangers that Holland has to prepare for. The threat analysis was received rather negatively in the press. Most criticism was directed at some rather blunt remarks that suggest a connection between 'bloodshed' and Islamic immigrants. This was judged to be rather unfair toward the Islamic community in Holland, which has so far never given any substantial support to fundamentalism.

In October 1992 the BVD published its first annual report. This gave some details on the functioning of the security service and on the amount of attention given to various issues such as vetting for security clearances, preventing unauthorised disclosures of state secrets and preventing and fighting political violence.[15] In later reports a number of specific target groups and categories are depicted and their potential threat assessed, such as Iranian intelligence activities against dissident refugees in

Holland, and the various ethnic groups originating from former Yugoslavia. The service has since 1992 continued to publish an annual report of approximately seventy pages every year. During the last year, increasing co-operation was reported with more exotic services such as the Jordanian GID and the Bosnian AID.

In the period 1994–1996, answering to increasing pressure to reinforce the protection of economic and financial targets against espionage, the BVD engaged in a review of its policy in relation to corporate interests. Its staffers subsequently began to conduct a large number of interviews with the management of major companies. These interviews provided more fuel to the opinion that economic espionage forms a substantial threat for certain vital Dutch interest. It is hardly surprising therefore that more recently, one can recognise an increased effort in the field of economic intelligence within the BVD. An example worth mentioning here could be the work of the BVD's liaison officer in Singapore, who apart from collecting information on narcotics trafficking appears to spend most of his time on gathering economic intelligence in the region.

Accountability   Since 1952 a permanent closed commission on the intelligence and security services consisting of the leaders of the main parties in parliament has been responsible for intelligence oversight. Since 1967 this commission has produced brief activity reports. Until the late 1980s the commission only met once every four months or so. After the Law on the intelligence and security services came into effect in 1988 these meetings became somewhat more frequent.[16] On average parliament devotes about one plenary session each year on the BVD. Certain specific issues are sometimes discussed in brief.

Apart from the oversight commission the services are also controlled by departmental staff, by the minister, by Parliament as a whole, by the National Ombudsman (who in principle has access to all information on request) and by the magistrate.[17] In spite of all this, the accountability of the services is still judged to be rather poor. During a debate in January 1993, it became clear that a majority in parliament was in favour of some form of augmented control over the security services. Discussions on what specific form this should take have been going on ever since.

Under the new Intelligence and Security Services Bill presented to parliament in early 1998, the National Ombudsman will be tasked with handling citizen's complaints. Also, the bill envisages the establishment of a new oversight commission, which will among others play an advisory role to the minister regarding internal complaint practices. This new oversight commission will consist of three members, who are appointed for a period of six years by the Prime Minister and ministers of the Interior and of Defence. Under the new procedure, a complainant with a grief against the security intelligence services will first have to present his complaint to the minister in question, who will have to react within ten weeks, advised by the oversight council. Following this, the complainant may present his complaint to the National Ombudsman, who may withhold the reasons for his decision in the interest of state security 'or other weighty interests of the state'. In case the Ombudsman makes a recommendation, the minister has to inform him within six weeks of the consequences of that recommendation. Lastly, the minister has to inform the standing parliamentary commission on intelligence and security services on the details of such exchanges with the Ombudsman.

The number of intelligence-related complaints presented to the National Ombudsman has remained rather low over the last few years. In 1997 for instance, a total of only five reports were brought out: in two instances the complaints were ruled to be unfounded, one complaint was founded and two partly founded. Most of the complaints involved citizens who attempted in vain to get access to security service files supposedly held on them. In 1998, the Ombudsman did not bring out any reports on the BVD: the reason was that not one credible complaint was lodged.

Relation with criminal intelligence services The parliamentary enquiry commission (the so-called Van Traa commission that investigated covert policing methods in 1994–1996) concluded that security service operatives should not be allowed to participate in police teams, but the cabinet in 1997 maintained that while the BVD does not carry out strict policing tasks, is has to co-operate operationally with the police and the public prosecutor's office, so that no actual changes were necessary.

Co-operation between law enforcement and the security service has in fact been quite intensive in the Caribbean area and Surinam, as well as in relation to Kurdish political activism (PKK) and violent criminals originating from former Yugoslavia.

International operations and relations Formally, Holland has no separate foreign intelligence organisation.[18] In 1992, following a series of leaks on financial mismanagement and other problems in the *Inlichtingendienst Buitenland* (IDB, Foreign Intelligence Service), the Cabinet decided to dismantle the service altogether. The official end of the IDB came on 1 January, 1994. The IDB's tasks and some of the staff were taken over by the BVD and the Military Intelligence Service, as well as to some extent by the police National Criminal Intelligence Service (CRI). In 1998 and 1999, the BVD and the MID have each been involved in recruiting about ten new employees, who were then given operational training which will allow them to operate under cover abroad. The annual operational costs of these two new foreign intelligence branches is estimated at a total of about US$3 million.

The IDB also had an important task in processing the raw political and economic intelligence that the *Marine Technisch Informatie-verwerkingscentrum* (TIVC, Naval information processing centre) produces. This very sensitive task has been taken over by Military Intelligence as well. The TIVC is the mini-equivalent of the American NSA, a very secretive service that is officially not an intelligence service at all. It has a secret budget of somewhere between 100–150 million guilders and its products appear to be responsible for much of the credit that Dutch intelligence claims to have traditionally enjoyed in the international secret services community. Under the new legislation currently discussed in Parliament, the 'searching' of air waves and communication networks is based on a legal basis, with the Minister approving a broad set of key word categories once every year.

The BVD itself currently maintains operational relationships with close to 60 services from all over the world. Among these, traditional allies such as the British, German and US services obviously take a leading role. Still, new fields and new challenges have made the 'domestic' security services' officers venture out to such exotic places as Morocco, South Africa, Thailand, Venezuela and Cyprus.

One of the BVD's concerns abroad is the precarious situation that exists in the territories of the Dutch Antilles and Aruba, a string of small semi-independent islands situated in the Caribbean reputed to be a money launderer's paradise. The local political elite has been massively corrupted for decades, which has repeatedly led to painful and risky conflicts between local law enforcement and judicial authorities, often supported by the Dutch government, and shady businessmen and local power holders. In the late 1980s, the jeopardised files of the Antilles security service (*Veiligheidsdienst Nederlandse Antillen*) were salvaged by bringing them on board a Dutch war ship, and the Dutch security service has been involved ever since in a training and support program to try and rebuild some sort of dependable security structure.

To maintain its vital international relations, the BVD maintains five permanent liaison officers in Amman (Jordan), Singapore, Washington, Moscow, and Caracas (Venezuela), plus two travelling liaisons operating mostly in Europe.[19] The BVD's liaison officer in Amman is reportedly most active in the fields of counterproliferation, Islamic fundamentalism and antiterrorism investigations related, for example to the PKK and the radical DHKP-C (former *Dev Sol*) party. Until recently, the BVD maintained a liaison office in Ankara. Although the Dutch minister of the interior responsible for the BVD has repeatedly assured MPs that in co-operating with the Turkish MIT intelligence service the BVD naturally restricts itself to legitimate activities, several MPs and commentators voiced concern over such arrangements. This may have contributed to the liaison's relocation to Jordan in 1998.

Over the last years, the BVD has been rather active in promoting contacts with security services from new democracies among middle European countries such as Poland, Hungary, the Czech Republic and Rumania, where it claims to also have had some beneficial influence in introducing modern concepts of intelligence oversight and the primacy of elected officials in the decision-making process.

Militaire Inlichtingendienst (MID, Military Intelligence Service)

In the mid-1980s some light was shed on the activities of the military secret services.[20] Some documents were leaked and a massive number of documents became available through a series of activist burglaries of military and intelligence offices. They were reproduced and analysed in a number of publications which portrayed the secret services' outdated world view: social democrat reformers, some of them leading politicians, administrators and mayors, had until recently been registered and surveilled by the military and civilian services.[21] Soldiers' trade unions, peace groups, anti-nuclear and other progressive organisations were closely monitored and infiltrated, and to some extent manipulated.

All this led to some reforms. In 1987, the military intelligence branches were formally merged and 'modernised', but MID personnel was hesitant to accept the unification of the 'grey, green and blue' traditions. Chaotic and inconsistent management has resulted in a less-than-optimal performance in relation to the Dutch military's involvement in peacekeeping and peace enforcing operations in the Balkans.[22] Intelligence consumers off-the-record complained of the MID's poor products in comparison to what other NATO partners delivered. Added to that, the MID suffered several embarrassing revelations in the late 1990s when senior MI officers appeared to have been involved in an extensive cover-up operation in relation to the Srebrenica debacle, aimed at saving the face of the Dutch military. Also in the late 1990s, concerned military officers voiced internal dissent over the MID's apparent hesitation to investigate indications of extreme-right and racist misbehaviours within the Dutch military apparatus, in particular among units participating in UN peacekeeping missions.[23] After a change of management in mid-1999, the MID is currently undergoing a drastic reorganisation, which in 2002 should result in a modernised military intelligence apparatus employing some 800 staff.

For the purpose of this chapter however, it is important to recognise that most of the tasks of the military intelligence and security services are aimed at maintaining the integrity and operational capabilities of the armed forces. Therefore, they seem of less political relevance than those of the BVD which is primarily aimed at the civil society.

Apart from the BVD and the police intelligence services, the MID (soon to be renamed the MIVD) is the only Dutch intelligence service in formal existence under the law. Its budget and strength remained classified until 1998, when the first annual report came out. On 31 December, 1997, the MID had 807 employees with a total budget of 115.4 million guilders (approx. US$ 58 million).[24]

Signals Intelligence

The blanket interception of telecommunications of any nature, for example telephone traffic via satellite or transmissions on specific bands or channels, is carried out by the signals intelligence department of the military intelligence service. The BVD can also request access to such 'electronic vacuum cleaner' information when this is deemed necessary. The use of such facilities is also arranged in the new intelligence bill, whereby the services only need permission for such monitoring at the moment that the content of specific communications of identifiable persons are analysed in detail.

Police Intelligence Services

Within each of the country's 25 regional police forces as well as in the national auxiliary force, a separate 'special branch', the *Regionale Inlichtingen Dienst* (RID, regional intelligence service) has been established, staffed with anything between 5 and 45 officers and electronically connected to the BVD through the 'Riddle' network. In their tasking, these RID's carry out a mix of local public order intelligence work working as police officers to investigate, for example soccer hooligans or locally-operating activists, and full-blown political intelligence work directed by the BVD. In this latter capacity, they answer only to the director of the BVD and not to local authorities. This arrangement, which through the years has proved to be full of risks such as lack of professionalism on the one hand and an over-eagerness on the other, was maintained through all the reorganisations until the present day. The motivation for this obviously was that the central BVD had to maintain some form of local presence in every city and region, while at the same time the operational capabilities and knowledge of the local police often came in handy to supplement the BVD's own. All the same, many of the transgressions and blunders blamed on the BVD in the past were in fact carried out by police officers working under the BVD's orders.

Neither the BVD's officers nor any police officer working under the auspices of the BVD have (in that role) judicial powers to investigate criminal acts. Theoretically at least, this constitutes a strict separation between the executive powers of the state (mainly the public prosecutor's department and the police) and the intelligence services. In practice, the 'two hats' still tend to get confused.[25]

Criminal intelligence structures   The focus of this book is political intelligence structures, so the substantial criminal intelligence structures present in the Dutch police forces will not be discussed here. At the moment, this poses no real analytical problem since most of the criminal intelligence activities, with the exception of certain investigations into the Kurdish PKK and perhaps the Surinamese drug cartel, lack any political dimensions. This has been notably different in the past, when for instance in the late 1980s and early 1990s several police teams as well as the criminal intelligence departments were deeply involved in investigations with explicit political dimensions. At the time, they charted nearly the entire Dutch activist scene in a prolonged attempt to uncover the RaRa group that claimed a number of firebombs and explosive attacks against targets identified with the Apartheid regime and later the asylum policy. The RaRa group has not been heard of since the last bomb attempts in the early 1990s.

Koninklijke Marechaussee (Kmar, Military Border Police)

The *Kmar* has traditionally carried out the classic intelligence tasks of monitoring border traffic and keeping tabs on suspect foreigners as well as on Dutchmen travelling to Warsaw Pact countries. Organisationally, it has long been unclear whether the *Kmar* in fact also had own intelligence branch, apart from the general intelligence-collecting tasks that every border guard routinely carries out. As this intelligence outfit was not formally recognised or chartered in any law until 1994, what its precise activities were remained obscure. In the 1980s and early 1990s in any case, *Kmar* personnel had been known to investigate and monitor anti-militarist activists who were involved in sabotaging installations at the time. An overlap with the *Kmar*'s elite operational unit, the *Brigade Speciale Beveiligingsopdrachten* (BSB, special security tasks brigade), is most likely. Under the new legislation, the *Kmar*'s intelligence branch will be on a comparable footing with the police RIDs. Furthermore, *Kmar* personnel are also deployed on additional covert surveillance operations as well as on the screening of employees working at civil airport facilities.

Implications for Human Rights and Civil Liberties

The Dutch secret services have over the last decade not been engaged in activities that would constitute gross human rights violations, at least no such activities have become part of the public record. There have been violations of civil liberties however, and this paragraph aims to establish whether these violations in fact constituted illegal acts (meaning that they were not justified by the need to maintain law and order or to protect other legitimate interests).

The Right to Privacy: Intrusive Measures

One of the most obvious civil liberties that a secret service would come into conflict with is the right to privacy. This right is explicitly recognised in the Dutch constitution (albeit with an emphasis on personal data), and the fact that a number of laws make it illegal to interfere in the public domain, for example by tapping a phone without a warrant, provides some protection of the individual's privacy. Also, the working of article 8 of the European Convention to which the Netherlands is a signatory ensures that jurisprudence has developed over the years to guarantee at least to some extent that a person's personal domain is respected.

Secret services, and especially the security service (BVD) routinely monitor the doings and communications of thousands of people who for some reason or other are considered a threat to the security or other interests of the Dutch state. The legal procedures and powers of the BVD have been detailed earlier in this chapter, and it is obvious that different opinions exist on whether or not such intrusions are justified in individual cases. Most often this boils down to the matter of one's definition of what actually constitutes a threat, and to what proportion such perceived threats would provide grounds to intrude in a person's privacy. It is not exactly clear how seriously the current oversight on such decisions is carried out. Formally, several government ministers decide on which telephone and audio taps the BVD is allowed to set up on a case by case basis, while the broader directives and strategic direction of BVD operations are discussed in the parliamentary oversight commission in which the four chairpersons of the largest political parties participate. We know from the recent past (1980s and earlier) that such oversight was in fact almost non-existent, with ministers signing off routinely on dozens of bugging orders without ever reading them, and meeting only once every few years to discuss intelligence policy. The parliamentary oversight commission did little better, with its meetings lasting only a few hours every year during which not all members were present and the BVD's chief practically had the field to himself, entertaining MPs with 'war stories' and technical gadgets. Quite possibly, the current members take their task somewhat more seriously: the fact is we still do not know. The oversight commission's annual reports are never more than a few pages long, and of such a superficial nature that little substantial information can be derived from them.[26]

Not that much is in fact known of the BVD's operational capabilities. From what is known, it can be derived that the number of wiretaps that the service is capable of operating at any one moment must be at least one hundred. In fact the number may be substantially higher, with only the need to actually listen to the recordings limiting the capacity. This calculation is based on comparisons with police phone tapping practices about which much more is known, but such comparisons are somewhat risky since one has to realise that the police have to actually listen to the recordings and make notes of what is said, while the security service can to some extent just record a greater number of conversations and filter out those that it deems of interest, possibly even after a specific incident has occurred. Furthermore, the widespread use of E-mail and the Internet in Holland, while offering all sorts of problems related to undetected message exchanges between clandestine persons and organisations, spreading propaganda and rumours and potentially dangerous information on lethal weapons and so on, has also been welcomed by the BVD as a blessing in disguise since it offers to a security service many new ways of keeping an eye on suspected groups and monitoring their daily communications.

As far as covert surveillance is concerned, the BVD uses both physical surveillance carried out by covert observation teams and remote video surveillance of certain objects. Again, there are clear limits to the physical capacity of surveillance teams, when one realises that it takes at least a team of six to carry out an effective covert surveillance of a mobile target.

Video of course largely enhances the surveillance capabilities: a single operator can observe a specific object and register all relevant things happening, especially if he is aided by sophisticated computer-controlled monitoring technology. Lastly, the option of registering the movement and whereabouts of persons and objects through the use of both active and passive tracking devices and mobile telephone signals analysis is one that is intensely used by the BVD.

As to one of the other information-gathering methods, the use of informants and infiltrators, there used to be quite a lot of reports on that until about five years ago. At the time, the security service was clearly using these tactics a good deal in its efforts to keep track of the various social movements and of political refugees. Several times a year, someone would come forward in the media with an account of how he or she had been approached by BVD agents to work for them, or in some cases even with stories about their experiences with actually working as an agent for the BVD. Also, during the 1980s quite a large number of such BVD agents were unveiled and sometimes questioned by activists. This again produced greater insight into what the service was interested in, as well as to what lengths the service was apparently prepared to go to obtain information or influence what was happening. Quite a number of these cases turned out to be agent-provocateurs, who were actually offering arms and explosives to activists or who engaged in violent activities in an attempt to lure others into dangerous adventures. It is clear that these things constituted clear violations not only of a right to privacy, but also of the right to peaceful political dissent.

Over the last few years however, with the cold war long gone and most social activism reduced to mere rituals that are few and far between, the BVD has clearly sought and found other targets. As a result, when it comes to BVD activities in the field both the near-absent press reports and the absence of experiences among what is left of the social movements are indicative of a much more discrete and limited *praxis* in the late 1990s when it comes to social and political activism. The rather small number of complaints, and the near-absence of complaints relating to intrusive surveillance, is another indicator pointing in the same direction.

When it comes to respecting civil liberties certain foreseeable developments, such as the need under the new legislation to notify at least some of the BVD's targets subjected to bugging and other measures after a period of five years or more, are likely to further increase the acceptance

within the security establishment that some amount of accountability will
have to be accepted.[27]

Security Screening

An obvious point where the interference of security services can directly
influence people's lives is security screening (vetting). Holland now has
about 50,000 jobs outside the military for which some form of clearance is
required. In 1997, a new law came into force regulating the procedures
through which such clearances are obtained. On average, about 35,000 such
security investigations are carried out every year, many of them repeat
procedures. Over the last years about 250 to 400 people have been denied a
clearance each year, mostly on the grounds of them having criminal
records. Some 5–15 per cent of those denied access to a job at first instance
use their right to appeal, which in only one or two cases each year is
successful.

The Military Intelligence Service in 1997 carried out nearly 18,000
security vettings, which resulted in 43 applicants being turned down
because of a criminal record.

The Archives

One of the few ways of learning about the doings of a secret service is by
reading its files. This privilege is limited to few mortals outside the realm
of the secret services themselves, but in some countries time works in
favour of those having the patience to wait.

In Holland, with the end of the cold war the BVD chief Mr. Arthur
Docters van Leeuwen in late 1990 announced his intention to destroy most
of his organisation's archives, since they had become useless. Also, the
BVD's concern for privacy protection reportedly inspired this sudden urge
to get rid of about two-thirds of the BVD files (an estimated 300,000 files).
In the months following a group of researchers, journalists, activists and
privacy protectors organised in the *Vereniging Voorkom–Vernietiging*
(VVV, Association to Prevent Destruction) started over 1,000 judicial
proceedings to stop the destruction process. They claimed that a decision
with such political impact could not be decided by some selected scholars
and civil servants alone. The VVV's activities led to the formal
postponement of the planned destruction, although it later became clear that
in spite of the official ban on destruction, parts of the BVD archives had
still been destroyed during the period 1991–1994. This same situation, only
worse, was found at the archives of the foreign intelligence service

(formally disbanded in 1994) and the Military Intelligence Service. In both these cases, the illegal destruction of the files was so complete as to leave nearly nothing of value to historians or people seeking access to their own files. A parliamentary commission set up to investigate this destruction reported in April 1998 that they had been carried out on the orders of the services' leadership in spite of clear governmental assurances in Parliament that the preservation and integrity of the archives would be maintained and nothing of value would be shredded. In the winter of 2000, the Council of Culture after an extensive investigation in the BVD's archives advised the Cabinet not to proceed with destroying the files on the grounds that historic interests were insufficiently taken into account, and that the proposed selection made by the BVD was not clear enough to allow for a clear and transparent decision-making process.[28] The minister of the Interior thereupon ordered the BVD's own historian, Dr. D. Engelen, to carry out a research into the structure of the archives.

The various positions in the 'open intelligence files' debate are quite clear. The intelligence and security services and most of the government establishment maintain that any publication of classified information, no matter how antique and perhaps futile, could potentially jeopardise current operational methods and means and the identities of information sources and agents, and could also undermine the credibility of the services *vis-à-vis* (potential) informants. This explains the fierce attempts to prevent outsiders gaining access to the files, even to the point of breaking the law by illegally destroying the archives. Those seeking access to the files vary in their position between pleading for some limited form of temporary access to really old documents and demanding full access to all files.

Those demanding access to files can broadly be divided into three categories: those who believe they have been registered at one time and who now want to see their own files or those on the organisation(s) they belong(ed) to; historians and other academics who want to study the past, and believe they may find interesting material in the files; journalists and other publicists who want to write about topics related to intelligence and who want to use the files for that purpose. The division, however, is not always a clear one to make: some historians are perhaps former communists and have mixed motivations for their interest in the past, while other academics are in fact themselves (former) intelligence contacts and thus professionally motivated.

The BVD tried all it could to withhold information and obstruct legal attempts to gain access. In spite of these obstructions though, the efforts of the VVV have not all been in vain. Most of their members (some

300 persons and institutions) had by 1997 obtained some form of access to their historical files, varying from just a few scraps to hundreds of pages. Nearly all information on working methods and on third persons in the dossiers had been deleted however, and many people were quite disappointed at what they saw. The poor quality of the reports and the large number of factual errors led to both amusing anecdotes as well as concerns and grief over jobs missed and opportunities denied on the basis of goof-ups, prejudices and bureaucratic nit-picking. At the time of writing appeals and further proceedings are still under way, and more information from the BVD's files can be expected to become available in the near future. At the same time, the legal naivete of some historians has recently resulted in very restrictive jurisprudence that makes it nearly impossible to obtain access to any intelligence dossiers for academic or journalistic purposes.

The Secret State

One of the functions of a secret service in any society is that it gives those in power the possibility to keep certain things outside the realm of public scrutiny if so desired. This is the domain of the 'state interest'. In the Dutch constitution, this *belang van de staat* is referred to in article 68, where it is cited as the only exclusionary ground for the government to withhold information from members of Parliament. The concept is contested in Parliament from time to time. For example, the parliamentary enquiry into investigative methods in 1995–1996 reported that it had spent much time discussing the 'state interest' concept with government ministers, and had found that very diverging interpretations of it were possible. It urged that Cabinet and Parliament should address this issue in depth to settle the matter of interpretation and use in the context of parliamentary inquiries. The commission felt that certain crucial information had been withheld from it, and that parliamentary enquiry commissions should be allowed access to information that upon publication could endanger persons and issues that affect the interest of the state, provided that the information in question would not be given to all members of parliament. The government however remains opposed to any compromise in such delicate matters.

As to the question of what sort of matters could be classified under the 'state interest' label in a modern, open democracy, three examples can be given. The first one is again derived from the parliamentary enquiry mentioned earlier. One of the operations investigated by the commission was the organising by covert police officers of a fake fruit juice factory in Ecuador, as part of a secret drug trafficking operation involving the importation of thousands of kilos of cocaine. Obviously, the official version was that the juice factory was intended as a front store to lure drug barons into the trap set by the cunning Dutch police. There were a great number of illogical and unexplained elements in this and other related operations however, that neither the commission nor other police investigators managed to clear up. Several of the main players (mostly seasoned covert police operators) suggested that there was a lot more behind it, including political ramifications, but that they could never provide information on that since this would end their career and possibly endanger their life. Therefore, the memories of those involved that testified under oath showed such surprising flaws that it makes one question their ability to work as police investigators. Analysis of available information (including some 'inside sources') and logical deduction suggests that the whole South American operation stood in the context of a larger covert scenario directed by US players, presumably the Drug Enforcement Administration and possible the Central Intelligence Agency. This would explain several of the loose ends, including the availability of millions of dollars of investment funds and the presence at crucial moments of shady figures with Texan accents. The 'state interest' in this case would have been the international dimension: the hiding of the American role and the exact arrangements between the US and Dutch governments, and possibly the political implications such as the mingling in the internal affairs of several countries in the Latin American region.

At the time of writing, new information is surfacing which indicates that the BVD had an information source in the cocaine trafficking network discussed here. A respected Dutch newspaper claims to possess a 1997 confidential BVD report, which asserts that some of the police officers involved managed to make a profit for themselves amounting to hundreds of millions of guilders. This however has not so far been substantiated. One BVD informer believed to have supplied such information was assassinated shortly afterwards in 1997. In a parallel case, Amsterdam police officers in 1999 entered a flat after neighbours had reported a water leakage, only to uncover a huge arms cache containing very sophisticated military equipment.[29] Detectives managed to trace some of the guns as having been bought by US and Jordanian intelligence organisations in the 1980s and 1990s. One of the arrested suspects, a former Dutch special forces operator and suspected cocaine trafficker who could be linked to the stash by fingerprints found on the weapons, turned out to be an informer for a public prosecutor as well as for the BVD. It is as yet too early to assess the implications of these and other exposures, but some tough questions certainly seem justified when investigating arms and narcotics trafficking in the Netherlands.

A second example would involve military aspects, traditionally a sensitive subject in any country. Dutch governments have since the 1950s had a close relationship with consecutive Israeli governments, and part of this relationship was the willingness of the Dutch to support covertly the Israeli military in times of crisis. In the 1967 war for example, large parts of the Dutch military apparatus were cannibalised in a frantic effort to feed spare parts and ammunition to the strained Israeli army and air force. Although thousands of people on all levels of Dutch society were in the know, nothing had ever been published about this episode until the mid-1990s. These close ties have resulted in the Israeli air line El Al maintaining an extensive presence at Schiphol airport, closely guarded from nosy unwanted visitors (which includes virtually all non-Israelis, including airport security officers and other authorities). Under a unique arrangement, El Al avoids all contacts with Schiphol management and deals directly with the Ministry of Traffic. Within the El Al perimeter, the Israelis have absolute authority to do anything they deem necessary. El Al has always been a virtual part of the Israeli Defence Forces, and its role in transporting military materials and other covert goods is as such no secret.

When an El Al Boeing 747 crashed on an Amsterdam residential area on 4 October 1992, causing 43 official deaths, it was hardly surprising that most of its cargo was of a military nature. Dozens of witnesses, including many police and fire brigade officers, have stated on record that within hours a team of Israeli officials equipped with fireproof 'astronaut-like' suits was present at the crash site. They forced their access and were seen carrying away several large pieces of material from the site. Rescuers and police personnel were during that period kept at a distance to allow the Israelis to work unhindered. Later, the presence of these 'men in white moon suits' was fervently denied by the Dutch authorities, which tried to explain them away as 'Red Cross people', even though the genuine Red Cross has stated that their personnel wore overalls of a different colour and had also reported the unknown 'men in white'. A number of mysteries surrounded the El Al crash, and the only reason that the case would not go away is that a large number of people present at the crash site (including police and fire brigade officers) are very motivated to get to the truth because they still suffer from unexplained but serious health complaints, believed to be caused by unidentified chemical substances from the plane's cargo. This cargo was confidential, and although parts of the freight list have since been released, the fire brigade has found several pieces of ammunition that officially was not on board. There have been many allegations of a government-approved cover-up, based on enigmas and unexplained coincidences such as the fact that both the civilian and military air traffic controllers have deleted all records and radar images of the disaster night. MPs from the largest coalition party have tried time and again to unearth evidence of what went on that night, but they got nowhere, until Parliament finally decided to hold a formal parliamentary enquiry in 1998. The inquiry after several months of investigations concluded that there was no proof of any conspiracy. The plane's cargo was certainly of a military nature and had not been reported and handled as it should have, and individual officials were found guilty of covering up damaging information on the understanding that El Al deserved a special treatment. In spite of this, a concerted government cover-up operation was not found.[30]

Not surprisingly, any role of the Dutch security service in the El Al affair has consistently been officially denied, even when the BVD's director at the time, Mr. Arthur Docters van Leeuwen (after having left in disgrace following a conflict with the Justice minister) confirmed in April 1998 that the BVD had worked together with Mossad agents at the crash site to investigate a possible terrorist involvement. Anonymous sources from within the police also confirmed that BVD officials had arranged that Mossad personnel had immediately been given access to the crash site on the night of the disaster. Several vital pieces of evidence, such as the plane's black box, were never formally recovered.

A third and final example of 'state interest' could be covert military operations by Dutch personnel in foreign countries. Obviously, the troubled former Dutch colony of Surinam comes to mind. It has become clear that Dutch military operators over the last eighteen years have repeatedly worked under cover in the country with the objective of reconnoitring the possibilities for military intervention, although this has so far never been officially confirmed. But also in other, less obvious countries in Latin America, North Africa and the Middle East Dutch military reconnaissance specialists have been (and still are) active, often in relation to drug intervention programs. The fact that the lives of such men and women as well as the international reputation of the nation would be jeopardised were such facts ever to become public justifies that the 'interest of state' doctrine comes into play here to guarantee secrecy.

The question of whether or not such situations constitute a breach of human rights and civil liberties is a legitimate one, but also one that on a fundamental level is politically loaded. In most cases, the rights and freedoms of Dutch citizens are hardly affected, although the right to good health could certainly be relevant in relation to the victims of the El Al disaster who still do not know what could have caused their health complaints. But in the cases of the government-approved covert drug lines and the small-scale covert military operations abroad, the principal matter is much more whether citizens have the right to be fully informed on their government's doings, even when such operations would be unfeasible were such a right recognised and acted upon. Is a state allowed to set up and carry out secret operations while withholding information on it even from members of parliament? If the answer is yes, then no rights have been violated with the possible exception of the health risk situation related to the El Al disaster. If the answer is no, the consequence would be that covert (and possibly effective) operations against drug traffickers, terrorists, arms proliferation and other evils would be almost impossible to carry out in a responsible manner. There is clearly a balance between openness and effectiveness, a matter that all governments in the world are well aware of. At the end of the day, it boils down to the question of whether one trusts one's own political rulers to be honest and competent. Indications of cover-ups and foul play like those uncovered by the parliamentary commission on investigative methods do not help to boost such public confidence.

Assessment and Forecast

One of the main things an intelligence service is expected to possess is foreknowledge of the world around it, and the BVD is no exception. Since about five years, it too has tried some modest attempts to producing forecasts and scenarios. All intelligence specialists agree that such predictive efforts constitute in fact the most difficult of analytical tasks. To a relative outsider without full access to information and sources, it is even more difficult to write an assessment of likely future developments relating to the intelligence services themselves. However, the fact that we are dealing with bureaucracies which are required to produce working plans and which usually behave according to familiar administrative 'laws' and traditions helps to predict at least to some extent what can be expected.

One of the things which immediately strikes an academic researcher is that increasingly, the BVD attempts to co-operate with academics, although an actual exchange of information is still a rare occurrence. In most cases the BVD restricts itself to financing research projects by universities into topics such as migration or the violent potential of 'house dance music' fans and proponents of extreme right ideologies. Actual exchanges of information and opinions still appear to be a bridge too far for the time being.

This approach to get in touch with selected parts of the academic world is part of a wider policy to become a more open and responsive, almost 'normal' institution, a direction which is certainly favoured especially by parts of the new cadre that the BVD has hired since the late 1980s. There is still much internal debate over these matters however: certain off-the-record remarks by those few BVD employees allowed to participate in congresses both in Holland and abroad indicate that their eagerness to get in contact with, for example, open sources specialists from other organisations and analysts with an academic or journalistic background is frowned upon by much of the older and more senior staff. For these conservatives, who still populate the corridors of the BVD in considerable numbers, such contacts are risky by definition. Even the mere suggestion in articles such as this that innocent information from inside the BVD 'leaks' to the outside world for them is cause for concern and prying questions. The hard-headed intelligence dinosaurs resist the very idea of harmless information, let alone a need to engage in a debate with outsiders about intelligence policy and practices.

One can imagine that such attitudes clash with the opinions of the dozens of newly-arrived latter-day BVD staffers, who include some bright and rather liberal students just out of university as well as a former National ombudsman legal counsellor and a specialist in modern Islamic culture. Women at the more senior levels are still a rarity in the BVD, but overall about one third of the posts are taken by female personnel, mainly administrative.

Some signals of a delicate internal balance between the 'old' and the 'new' BVD appear on the surface every once in a while. One example of this was the unexpected change in its leadership in January 1997, when the former Vice-Admiral Nico Buis who had taken over as chief in May 1995 was succeeded by Mr. Van Hulst, a chief police commissioner. Mr Buis himself had been a compromise figure: while it was unprecedented for a military officer to become head of the civil security service, it had taken exceptionally long to find a new chief who would be acceptable to all parties involved both within the BVD and in departmental circles. As an outsider with no partisan allegiances and extensive international experience, the vice-admiral seemed perfectly suited to run the BVD in a professional manner and to represent Dutch interests in the increasingly important international security and intelligence arena. Still, his rigidity and lack of experience in the subtleties of the political arena that the BVD is part of, soon made it clear that his reign would be brief.

The first major problem occurred when in February 1996, Interior Minister Hans Dijkstal decided to form a BVD oversight committee following severe criticism of the BVD for poor covert work by the Van Traa Parliamentary Commission, and a negative appraisal by Van Traa of the public prosecutor's capability to oversee BVD activity because in fact the service itself was deciding what to report and what to withhold. Mr. Buis apparently resisted having to answer to a single inspector general, as Mr. Dijkstal intended, but later agreed to a three-man oversight committee to which he would personally answer. By then however, his political credit had been all but exhausted. The Admiral had already been labelled by critical insiders as just another cold warrior, who gave free rein to the BVD's long-time penchant for all sorts of 'dirty tricks' and close co-operation with the CIA, to the detriment of more modern intelligence association with academia, the business sector and open source information. In September 1997 police commissioner Sybrand van Hulst, a soft-spoken and intelligent man, became the BVD's new head, a new departure considering that no policeman has ever before been put in charge of the BVD.

The increasing dominance of the 'new school intellectuals' within the security service coincides with a development in the wider Dutch society, one in which the BVD has successfully invested. Under the influence of the alarming signals of growing organised crime and increasing corruption, there is a great need to develop methods and means to guarantee the integrity of public administration. A stream of reports, investigations, seminars and directives on the subject of 'integrity' has put the BVD firmly on the map as the nation's centre of expertise in honest administrative practices. Although the cynical implications of this exercise is not lost on some commentators ('the fox guarding the hen house'), BVD employees have managed to convince the senior management of several ministries, police forces and municipal administrations that they have the most professional expertise on offer to help reinforcing their organisation's integrity. For the BVD's officials involved this appears to be a rewarding role: less than a decade ago, they were looked upon by many 'decent people' as shady operators who could not really be trusted and should be avoided as one avoids a pimp or a sleazy yellow press reporter. In their respectable new function as integrity consultants, they can help identify 'weak spots' in bureaucracies and advise public servants on how to avoid falling prey to criminal schemes. They can write neat reports, and sit in on commissions. In short, they are finally taken seriously.

For the BVD's organisation as a whole, the effect has been that there is a reduced demand for 'foot soldiers' while more and more Internet whiz kids and students of administration have entered the ranks. Typical BVD work used to include running nihilist informers wearing 'no future' buttons; new BVD staff would be required to sit in dirty outposts for days on end observing squatted houses. Nowadays, only some radical environmentalist groups and animal rights campaigners seem to merit the service's continued attention, and of the numerous squats under surveillance in every major city throughout the 1980s, only perhaps three objects in Amsterdam are still regularly monitored with police personnel doing most of the legwork.

While the BVD's public image has improved considerably over the years and undesired publicity has largely been avoided, there are now those who question the service's competence in traditional intelligence tradecraft. Police covert surveillance teams have always considered their counterparts in 'The Service' to be inferior, but some old hands in the BVD itself are reportedly also blaming the orientation to desk work for what they perceive as a dangerous loss of operational capabilities. Is the BVD losing its edge? In a recent unpublished incident for instance where prime minister Kok was threatened with blackmail on the eve of an important EU meeting, the BVD was not even brought into the action with the police quickly solving the case. Only years ago, this would have been unthinkable.

Also, an old legacy still resurfaces from time to time: when nobody knew how to deal with the mysterious RaRa group that exploded bombs near ministries and even destroyed the home of a junior minister in the early 1990s, the BVD chief boasted that he knew exactly who was behind it and that he would eventually catch RaRa red-handed. Nothing has been heard of this since and RaRa has long gone the way of the dodo, but inside observers suspect something odd has prevented the police from simply solving the case, and that a certain intelligence outfit still has some questions to answer.

The functioning of a security service is very much a reflection of the societal circumstances in which it finds itself. In the contemporary Dutch society, crises seem far away and political extremism a thing of the past. It is therefore hardly surprising that the sharp edges of political intelligence work seem to have eroded, just as there are no more police goon squads beating up activists in dark alleys. The Netherlands has by and large become a more decent society, although some would still disagree with that, pointing to the fate of asylum seekers. An analysis of the post-modern Dutch security and intelligence apparatus can only conclude that the visible signs of manipulation and outright repression have disappeared. Simultaneously however, the juridical and technical capacities of government institutions to monitor citizen behaviour in other domains such as fraud and crime control have increased impressively, an issue in itself which we leave untouched here. Also Europeanisation in many aspects has worrying dimensions for civil liberties and freedom, something of which even mainstream liberals and social democrats are increasingly becoming aware. Years ago the BVD started to invest heavily in European co-

170 *Democracy, Law and Security*

operation, and understandably so. One can only hope that the European project contributes to a more equal, democratic and stable society, and that the economy holds its course in the decade ahead.

Notes

1 The authoritative official publication on the history of the Dutch domestic security services is D. Engelen, *Geschiedenis van de Binnenlandse Veiligheidsdienst*. Den Haag: Sdu uitgeverij Koninginnegracht, 1995. The author is himself a BVD employee, and this dissertation manages to avoid most of the embarrassments the BVD has experienced in its 50–year history. Critical publications on the BVD are scarce, although progressive researchers and activists over the years have produced about a dozen books and brochures on the topic, often based on their own observations and experiences, statements made by former BVD informants, stolen documents and press publications. Examples of publications in the latter category are: Jansen and Janssen, *Regenjassendemocratie. BVD-infiltraties bij aktievoerder/sters*, Amsterdam: Ravijn, s.a. (1990); *De tragiek van een geheime dienst. Een onderzoek naar de BVD in Nijmegen*, Nijmegen, 1990; Jansen and Janssen, *De vluchteling achtervolgd. De BVD en asielzoekers*, Amsterdam: Ravijn, 1991; Buro Jansen and Janssen, *Opening van zaken. Een ander BVD-jaarverslag*, Amsterdam: Ravijn, 1993; Buro Jansen and Janssen, *Welingelichte kringen. Inlichtingendiensten Jaarboek 1995*, Amsterdam: Uitgeverij Ravijn, 1995; *Onderzoeksburo Inlichtingen- en Veiligheidsdiensten* (OBIV), *Operatie Homerus. Spioneren voor de BVD*, Breda: Papieren Tijger, 1998. On the other side of the political spectrum there is a study group on Dutch intelligence history, the Netherlands Intelligence Studies Association (NISA), which consists of selected academics and current and former members of the intelligence services. This group produces a newsletter, the NISA *Nieuwsbrief*. Some other publications on the history of the BVD between the 1940s and the late 1980s are: P. Brijnen van Houten, *Brandwacht in de coulissen. Een kwart eeuw geheime diensten*, Houten: De Haan/Unieboek, 1988; P. Klerks, *Terreurbestrijding in Nederland*, Amsterdam: Ravijn, 1989, P. Koedijk et al (Eds.), *Verspieders voor het vaderland. Nederlandse spionage voor, tijdens en na de Koude Oorlog*, Den Haag: Sdu Uitgevers, 1996.

2 ECHR Report of 3 Dec 1991 re. Applications Nos 14084/88 *et al*. of R.V. *et al*. against the Netherlands.

3 The Council's ruling in the Van Baggum case of 16 June 1994 was published in AB 1995, 238.

4 The Intelligence and Security Bill (Handelingen II 1997–1998, 25 877 No. 2, revised in Handelingen II 1999–2000 No. 9) is taking an unusually long time to pass through parliament. This is probably due to its complicated legal nature, also because some of the laws to which it refers such as the privacy legislation is itself undergoing revision.

5 Cf. Intelligence and Security Bill (Handelingen II 1997–1998, Bijlagen 25 877 No. 2, amended in No. 9), articles 17–29. Article 30 states that the application of a new operational method to obtain information which has not yet been legislated, can only be undertaken after the minister responsible for the service has given his or her permission. Also, within a year after first carrying out the activity involved, new legislation covering the activity must be introduced in parliament.

6 Cf. 'BVD GETS WHAT IT WANTS ... COMING AND GOING', Intelligence, N. 79, 4 May 1998, p. 32.

7 Handelingen Tweede Kamer 1997–1998, Bijlagen 25 877, Nos. 2 and 9, articles 35 and 54. Later, the Council of State advised the Cabinet to introduce stricter limits to the 'persons and bodies' to which intelligence could be supplied ('Advies Raad van State en nader rapport', *Handelingen Tweede Kamer 1999–2000*, Bijlagen 25 877, No. B, p. 8).

8 *Besluit organisatorische inrichting BVD 1999*, Staatscourant 1999, 17.

9 This does not mean the BVD has become a modern and efficient organisation yet. In a confidential report in 1998, investigators from the Algemene Rekenkamer (General Accounting Office) came to the conclusion that the BVD still lacked quality in a number of vital domains (*Handelingen Tweede Kamer 1999–2000*, Aanhangsel 888).

10 Budget Bill for the year 2000, Ministry of the Interior and Relations in the Kingdom, 1999.

11 BVD's Annual reports for 1997 and 1998.

12 Cf. parliamentary questions in *Handelingen Tweede Kamer 1999–2000*, Aanhangsel 500.

13 Cf. P. Klerks, 'Veiligheidsdiensten in verandering'. Pp. 99–138 in: A.E. van Almelo and P.G. Wiewel (eds), *Politiezorg in de jaren '90*. Arnhem: Gouda Quint, 1991.

14 *Ontwikkelingen op het gebied van de binnenlandse veiligheid. Taakstelling en werkwijze van de BVD*. Ministerie van Binnenlandse Zaken, Binnenlandse Veiligheidsdienst, 11 februari 1992.

15 *Binnenlandse Veiligheidsdienst. Jaarverslag 1991*. Ministerie van Binnenlandse Zaken, Binnenlandse Veiligheidsdienst, oktober 1992.

16 In 1998, the commission decided it would try to meet at least five times a year (Handelingen II 1998–1999, Bijlagen 26279 No. 2, p. 11).

17 The National ombudsman is charged with investigating and ruling on all complaints by civilians regarding alleged wrongdoings of public bodies that operate above the local level, such as the ministries, the police and the BVD.

18 The best current research source on the Dutch foreign intelligence services (IDB and predecessors) is: Bob de Graaff and Cees Wiebes, *Villa Maarheeze. De Geschiedenis van de inlichtingendienst buitenland*, Den Haag: Sdu Uitgevers, 1998.

19 Sources for this and the following paragraph: BVD annual report over 1998.

20 Currently, the best research source for the history of the Dutch military intelligence services (which also supplies ample data on the other services) is F.A.C. Kluiters, *De Nederlandse inlichtingen- en veiligheidsdiensten*. 's-Gravenhage: Sdu Uitgeverij Koninginnegracht, 1993, and its supplement, 'Crypto – en trafficanalyse, Sectie 2, TRIS' (same author and publisher, 1995).

21 The publications were: 'Dossier CID 001 – 004', published with various activist magazines in 1985.

22 'Nieuw evenwicht' (New balance), a confidential 1998 MOD report evaluating the MID's flawed performance and detailing the urgent need for reform currently forms the basis of a thorough reorganisation.

23 Two military officers, personal communications to the author, 1999.

24 The MID's annual report is available on the World Wide Web at the MOD's website (www.mindef.nl). More detailed information on the Dutch military intelligence structures can be found in Peter Klerks, chapter 'Königreich Niederlande', in: Schmidt-Eenboom, Erich (Hrsg.), *Nachrichtendienste in Nordamerika, Europa und Japan: Länderporträts und Analysen*. Weilheim: STÖPPEL-Verlag 1995 (CD-ROM, ISBN 3–89306–726–4).

25 Personal observations and discussions with police officers, 1994–2000.

26 In 1999, the BVD in the secret version of its annual report as it is presented to the commission began to provide some details on the number of taps, bugs and burglaries it conducts. Based on estimates made off-the-record by insiders, it can be assumed that the Dutch security service operates at least 3,000 phone and Internet taps, bugs, tracers, mail

cover ops and surreptitious entries per annum. The number of individuals registered with a personal file is given by the BVD as more than 100,000 (*Handelingen II 1999–2000*, Bijlagen 25877 No. 8, p. 84).

[27] In 1999, the BVD's management estimated that the obligation to notify surveillance targets afterwards would occupy at least 15 of its staffers (BVD mid-level manager, personal communication to the author, 1999).

[28] *Handelingen Tweede Kamer 1999–2000*, Bijlagen 22 036 nr. 15, 24 februari 2000.

[29] Inside observers believed the police in fact acted on a tip-off supplied by either a foreign intelligence service or a BVD informant. Cf. 'A BUSY FORTNIGHT FOR "CRIME BUSTERS"', Intelligence, N. 105, 18 October 1999, p. 21; 'MINK "K" TRIAL LEADS TO DEA and CONTRAS', Intelligence, N. 111, 7 February 2000, p. 1; 'MINK KOK'S "SECRET" PUBLIC TESTIMONY', Intelligence, N. 114, 27 March 2000, p. 23.

[30] Enquête vliegramp Bijlmermeer, *Handelingen Tweede Kamer, 1998–1999*, Bijlagen 26241 nrs 9–11.

Chapter 8

Internal Security in Sweden

Iain Cameron and Dennis Töllborg

Introduction and a Note on Citation

The structure of this chapter is as follows. We will first give some relevant background information on Sweden, and then deal with the organisation of the Security Police, *Säkerhetspolisen*, commonly known as Säpo. We will then examine the statutory functions of the Security Police, its powers and working methods. Thereafter, we will analyse in detail its most important tool, the intelligence files. We will begin by looking at the open and secret government instructions that governed filing of security intelligence from 1969 until the end of 1998. An official investigation in 1998 revealed a great deal of information on filing practices during this period. We will proceed to look at the changes that have been made in the statutory framework for police databanks and the new, post-Cold War targets of the Security Police. Thereafter we examine the past and present system of security vetting and the operation of the recently established oversight body, the Register Board *(Registernämnden)*. Finally, we make some concluding comments on the system of control and oversight of the Security Police.

Translations are our own unless otherwise noted. As regards citation, references to Swedish statutes or government ordinances are to *Svensk författningssamling* (SFS) by year followed by the relevant number (for example, *Personalkontrollkungörelsen* is SFS 1969:446). A statute is divided into chapters (if it is a large statute) and sections. References to *travaux preparatoires* are either to the number of the public inquiry responsible for investigating and proposing law reform, *Statens offentliga utredningar* (SOU) and the year of its report or to the draft bill put before parliament together with its accompanying documentation (*proposition,* prop.). The copious references to *travaux preparatoires* can be explained by the fact that in Sweden the *travaux preparatoires* to a statute are usually taken very seriously by courts and administrative agencies when it comes to interpreting and applying it.

Some Relevant Background Information on Sweden

Sweden has a population of just under nine million, which is concentrated heavily in the southern third of the country. This population was very homogenous until the early 1960s, when immigration increased. Immigrants came mainly from the other Nordic countries (particularly Finland), but also other European countries such as Italy, Yugoslavia and Turkey. Sweden also (until recently) pursued a fairly generous policy towards asylum seekers. Relatively large groups of immigrants came during the 1970s from the Middle East (Syria, Iran) and, in the 1990s, from former Yugoslavia. Now almost one million residents of Sweden are first, second or third generation immigrants.

Sweden is a constitutional monarchy. Since 1945, for most of the time, the Social Democratic Party has been the party of government, either alone or in coalition. The exceptions to this were in 1976–1982 and 1991–1994, when a coalition of centre and right wing parties formed the government. Sweden has not been at war since 1809. It remained neutral during the two world wars. During the Cold War, it applied a formal policy of neutrality, maintaining large, and relatively strong, defence forces. There was, however, secret intelligence co-operation with NATO. Despite joining the EU in 1995, Sweden officially attempts to maintain a policy of neutrality. With the developments in cooperation in justice and home affairs and in security/defence cooperation under the EU common foreign and security policy, including the creation of EU 'crisis management' military forces, the official Swedish policy is becoming less and less credible.

The Organisation of the Security Police

Sweden does not have a separate internal civilian security agency, as exists in a number of other states. Internal security is a matter for the Security Police who have full police powers. However, during the 1960s and early 1970s, a part of the military intelligence agency, *Informationsbyrån,* IB, engaged in extensive collection of data and amassed files. Different estimates exist as to how extensive this military intelligence gathering was. It has been said that these files were on 5,000, 20,000 and even on 100,000 people, depending on who gave the information. Subsequent official investigations concluded that all these files were later destroyed.[1] The existence of a parallel internal security agency led occasionally to the familiar phenomenon of turf battles with the Security Police. The friction between these two agencies was exacerbated by the suspicion which the ruling party, the Social Democrats, then felt towards the Security Police and its consequent favouring of IB. Investigative journalists revealed the activities of IB in 1973. The full extent of the co-operation between IB and the leadership of the Social Democratic Party has only recently become apparent. The military intelligence agency was reformed in 1974 and its mandate to monitor only military, as opposed to civilian, threats to security was reaffirmed.[2] In March 2000, legislation was enacted providing for a statutory mandate, and the appointment of an oversight board.[3] However, this essay focuses on the Security Police, not on military intelligence. This is due mainly to the fact that military intelligence work mainly abroad and do not deal with internal security.

The Swedish police was centralised in 1965, and organised as a National Police Board (NPB) accountable to the Department of Justice. The National Police Board is placed under the leadership of a national police commissioner appointed by the government, with the head of the Security Police as vice chairman, and a board of directors fetched from the political parties represented in the Parliament. Until recently neither the Left Party (formerly the Communists), nor the Green Party nor the Christian Democrats was represented in the NPB – now it is only the Green Party that lacks representation. It should, however, be stressed that neither the NPB nor the government is allowed to make decisions in operational police work. Sweden is unusual in having a constitutional provision (Instrument of Government, Chapter 11, section 7) which prohibits the government from interfering in administrative agencies' decision-making in individual cases. It is still possible, however, to steer decision-making more generally in a number of ways, for example by means of rules (government ordinances, formerly called *kungörelser*, nowadays *förordningar*). It should also be pointed out that Sweden does not have a system of ministerial responsibility, so formally speaking the police are not accountable to the Minister of Justice as such, but to the government as a whole.

The different rules that apply to the police in general also apply to the Security Police. The Security Police is, however, in organisational terms, a separate agency, albeit under the overall control of the NPB, with special responsibility for certain types of crime. And in practice, the Security Police operate with a high degree of autonomy from the ordinary police and from the National Police Commissioner. The chief of the Security Police has the status of 'Director General', and is, like other heads of administrative agencies, appointed directly by the government. A Director General cannot usually be sacked by the government during the period of his or her employment contract (usually four or six years) but a special provision in the Employment Act allows the government to transfer to other duties persons engaged in work of significance to national security. Sten Hecksher, a former under-secretary of state at the Department of Justice as well as a former minister in a social-democratic government, is the present National Police Commissioner. Anders Eriksson, a former first secretary at the Justice Department, was until recently head of the Security Police. Eriksson was appointed by the conservative Minister of Justice in the former government and Hecksher some years later by the social-democratic government. Eriksson had little or no experience of security or police work before being appointed head of the Security Police. In 2000 Eriksson was replaced by Jan Danielsson, a prosecutor engaged *inter alia* in the investigation of the assassination in 1986 of the Swedish prime minister, Olof Palme. As a result of this investigation, and of the investigation of other security crimes, Danielsson obviously has some experience of the work of the Security Police.

The Security Police are organised into a central staff unit and four other main units: an administrative unit, a unit for counter espionage, a protection unit and a unit for technical assistance etc. The central staff unit handles inter alia questions concerning co-operation with foreign security services.[4] It can be noted here that Sweden ratified both the Europol and Schengen agreements in April 1998, and that the latter entered into force for Sweden in April 2001. In the administrative unit there is a personnel section, a financial section and a computer section. The unit for counter-espionage includes a staff for analysis functions and sections for counter-espionage and counter-subversion. The protection unit has a staff section, a security protection section and sections for VIP protection and counter-terrorism.

There are approximately 800 employees in the Security Police, and it is claimed that the number has gradually been reduced since the beginning of the 1990s.[5] By 1 January 2000, 65.7 per cent were men and 34.3 per cent women. The average age was 44.9 years. The figures for previous years cannot be presented 'for reasons of national security'.[6] The total number of police in January 2000 was 16,199. There were also 5,808 civilian employees in the police.[7] The official budget of the Security Police is publicly known as it is specified in the annual bill on the budget submitted to parliament. It should, however, be mentioned here that the true cost of internal security functions could be somewhat higher, as the Security Police also have the right to call upon the assistance of the CID – costs that fall upon the main police budget. The official budget for the period 1990–2000 shows that the Security Police has increased its budget by almost 85 per cent (from 300 million crowns to over 550 million), a substantial increase in real terms at a time of cutbacks in public expenditure. The Security Police share of the total police force budget has also increased from 3.8 to 4.6 per cent during the same period.

The Security Police and internal security policy in Sweden has been relatively free from major scandals since the IB affair in the early 1970s. Two exceptions should, however, be mentioned. In 1986 in a (vain) effort to obtain evidence against persons suspected of the murder of Prime Minister Olof Palme, a number of officials, including the National Police Commissioner, the head and deputy head of the Security Police and the chief of police in Stockholm, either approved or failed to prevent the use of a variety of unlawful methods of obtaining intelligence. These included assisting private persons to engage in parallel investigations and the importation and use of (illegal) bugging equipment. When the customs caught a former policeman attempting to smuggle bugging equipment into Sweden, the responsible officials resigned and, in some cases, were prosecuted and convicted of certain minor offences. The Minister of Justice also resigned. An extensive official inquiry was made into the activities, functions and powers of the Security Police, (the Säpo committee) and informative reports were published.[8] Even though no major organisational changes were proposed, the new head of the Security Police, Mats Börjesson – a former judge, widely respected from his leadership of the National Courts Administration – got rid of many of the oldtimers and created an organisational structure whereby the chief of the Security Police, and not just the head of the investigation department, was in a position to exercise real control over the Security Police as a whole, and their operations.

Again, in 1987, the European Court of Human Rights decided the case of *Leander* v. *Sweden*, concerning the Swedish security vetting system, more particularly the question of whether the Security Police monitored lawful political activity. Sweden won the case (by a one-vote margin). However, allegations of systematic Security Police monitoring of (mainly leftist) political activity persisted throughout the 1980s and 1990s. In 1997 the contents of Leander's file were finally revealed to one of the authors of the present article, Dennis Töllborg, in his capacity as Leander's lawyer. This showed that, contrary to the assurances given by the Swedish government during the Leander case in Strasbourg, the only information stored on Leander was information concerning lawful political activities. Leander was granted ex gratia compensation and a public apology from the state in 1997.[9] The public outcry the Leander revelations caused has resulted – so far – in a number of measures designed to allay public concern. There have been two investigations from the body earlier created to monitor police files, the Register Board (see below pp.194–98). Its first report, in late 1998, concluded that there had been extensive registration of lawful political activities. This report is analysed in detail below at p.185.

Another report was made by the newly established oversight body for military intelligence. The Government also initiated a national wide research-project on post-war intelligence and security policy, supported with a budget of 20 million Swedish crowns. This research project is widely regarded as having been a fiasco, the government refusing the researchers necessary access to secret files, contrary to previous assurances.[10] A further independent inquiry (*Säkerhetstjänstkommissionen*) into Swedish intelligence against internal threats from 1945 up to 2001 has been appointed. This latter investigation was designed to meet criticism that Sweden needed a detailed, general and independent investigation into internal security practice on the lines of the Norwegian Lund commission.[11] However, it is doubtful whether *Säkerhetstjänstkommissionen* can add anything of significance to the previous investigations made by the Register Board, as it has no members with any detailed knowledge of security matters and, to our knowledge, it has taken relatively little evidence from independent experts in the field. The commission was originally requested to report in September 2001, one year before the next general election. However, this has now been postponed to December 2002. A public campaign complaining about the composition of the commission, and the timing of its report, has (at the time of going to print in December 2001) obtained signatures from individuals and organisations representing more than 350,000 people. Thus, ever since the Leander-file became public, the Security Police have suffered certain legitimacy problems.

The growing integration of the work of the Security Police with the work of the ordinary police (dealt with below pp.188–91) has led to an official inquiry being appointed to investigate whether the Security Police and the National Criminal Investigation Division (CID) should be amalgamated. This inquiry reported in Spring 2000, and was in favour of merging the Security Police and the CID into one organisation.[12] The National Police Board has agreed to the suggestion, although the CID and other bodies such as the Chief Public Prosecutor are highly critical. There is still (December 2001) no governmental bill in the matter, but the greatly increased emphasis on anti-terrorism, as a result of the events of 11 September 2001 will probably act as a further spur in this direction.

The Functions of the Security Police

The main purpose of the police force in Sweden is set out in the Police Act (Polislag 1984:387). Section 1 states that:

> As a component in the activity of society in its efforts to support justice and maintain public safety, the purpose of the work of the police is to maintain public order, protect the public and provide it with other assistance.

Section 2 specifies these duties as being among the tasks of the police:

- prevent crime and other disturbances of public order;
- monitor public order, stop disturbances of this order and react whenever such disturbances happen;
- carry out searches and investigations as far as concerns crime subject to public prosecution;
- give the public protection, information and other kinds of help, whenever suitable and proper; and
- fulfil the other duties which might be placed on the police through special regulations.

The primary function of the Security Police is mentioned very briefly in section 7 of the Act, namely to prevent and discover crimes against national security (mainly those crimes set out in the Criminal Code, chapters 18 and 19). The Act does not specify this primary function further, but other acts and government ordinances have specified and complemented it. The Security Police also have the main responsibility for dealing with terrorism.[13] In this respect one can note that refugees and other immigrants create two types of problem for the Security Police; as the perpetrators, or possible perpetrators, of terrorist acts, and as the victims of violence or threatened violence. They can carry out, or assist, in acts of terrorism, against their home state or third states. They can also be subjected to attacks and intimidation by their home state or extremist groups. There are thus two sides to the monitoring of the political activities of refugees, although it can be argued that protecting refugees and immigrants has usually been of secondary importance to the function of combating terrorism. It can also be noted as regards terrorism, that the Security Police itself emphasises the importance of international co-operation, in order to be able to receive the information needed. Much of the existing and proposed exchanges of information with other police agencies comes from, or is channelled through, the Security Police. Another function of the Security Police is to provide personal protection for VIPs, in accordance with instructions issued by the NPB. A fourth function is to fulfil the responsibilities of the police in relation to the system of physical security and security vetting controls *(registerkontroll,* earlier labelled *personalkontroll)* established by the Security Protection Act (Säkerhetsskyddslag 1996:627). A fifth, more recent, function is to play a co-ordinating role in relation to crime against citizens' democratic rights and freedoms. Here the main focus appears to be on organised racist crime.[14]

The opinion of the Security Police is also sought in all applications for citizenship. The Security Police can, and do, take the initiative in suggesting to the government that foreign citizens who are suspected terrorists or spies be expelled from the country. A further activity of the Security Police, which is alleged to be of growing importance, is preventing the proliferation of components and technology for the production of mass-destruction weapons.[15] In this respect, the Security Police work in close co-operation with the intelligence services of other European states.

Since the beginning of the 1990s, the Security Police have submitted an annual report to Parliament. This is one effect of the drive for greater openness following the bugging scandal in 1986. These reports are, however very brief and, with one exception, lacking in substance. The exception is the section on the vetting system, which is presented in some detail. The Register Board, not the Security Police, is responsible for this new openness. As the Register Board presents statistics on the vetting system in its own report, the Security Police can hardly refuse to follow suit. This is a radical change – also, of course, affecting the reports from the Security police as far as concerning the vetting system – of policy from the 1970s and 1980s when much of the system was classified. It was only in 1990, when the Säpo-committee produced its report, that the extent of the system became known, something which had been kept secret even from the European Court of Human Rights.

Security Police Methods

It is an internationally well known fact that intelligence is largely (c 90 per cent) gathered from open, public sources. The category of open sources as far as the Security Police is concerned includes not only information in election pamphlets, newspapers, journals and other mass media but also information obtained from applications for demonstrations and public meetings and from open filming of such demonstrations and meetings. Otherwise, as with most police work, information comes from informers and confessions. Secret guidelines govern police recruitment of informers. To our knowledge there are no instructions specifically applicable to the Security Police. There are occasional allegations that the Security Police have employed heavy-handed tactics such as blackmail to recruit informers particularly in immigrant communities.

Covert physical surveillance, infiltration of agents and use of electronic surveillance play, quantitatively speaking, a much lesser role, although these methods are still claimed to be of great importance from the perspective of obtaining quality (that is, reliable) intelligence.[16] As is certainly the case for all intelligence agencies, the emphasis is switching more and more from the collection of information to the analysis of it. The information-society means that there is raw material in abundance: the problem is now how to obtain useful answers from it.

As regards searches of computerised data files, revealing confidential personal data held by an administrative agency is in general prohibited by the Secrecy Act (1980:100). However, in general, an agency in possession of confidential data can be permitted or obliged to reveal the information to another agency by another law (chapter 1, section 3). Moreover, there are specific provisions under the Secrecy Act (chapter 14, sections 2 and 3) under which data can be transferred to the police when a preliminary investigation *(förundersökning)* has been started. Under chapter 23, section 1 of the Code of Judicial Procedure, a preliminary investigation can be started by the police or a prosecutor as soon as there is suspicion that a crime has been or is being committed. Where the police start the investigation, the prosecutor is to be brought in as soon as evidence emerges that is sufficient to link a specific person with the crime in question. On the other hand, the level of suspicion to start a preliminary investigation can be small. Ordinarily it is necessary that the suspicion relates to a concrete crime, but this is interpreted relatively liberally in security matters. Thus, once the preliminary investigation has been started, a request can be made to an administrative agency to reveal data relating to the suspect(s). The police must nonetheless still prove to the satisfaction of the administrative agency that the information is necessary for their investigations. Although it can be assumed that a request from the Security Police will invariably be complied with in practice, the way the system is constructed means that the Security Police do not have carte blanche to come in and rummage in any and all government files at random, still less to have on-line access to files without the agency holding them even being aware of the fact that the Security Police has accessed them. As regards access to information in private databanks, where the holder of the data does not voluntarily give it to the police, this can be compelled by the issue of a judicial warrant to search and seize material under chapter 28 of the Code of Judicial Procedure. Such a warrant will usually be issued *ex parte*, and the controller of the data will be placed under a duty not to reveal this, in order not to damage the ongoing investigation. Nonetheless, such a warrant will only be issued if a specified person is *reasonably suspected* of crime. It is not enough that a preliminary investigation has been opened.

As regards secret surveillance, it can be noted that, in common with a large number of other countries, the Security Police have in general greater powers than do the ordinary police. There is, however, no 'strategic' mass telecommunications interception capability within the Swedish Security Police such as exists in the USA (NSA) or the UK (GCHQ). The military signals intelligence agency, *Försvarets Radioanstalt*, FRA, is believed to have relatively sophisticated strategic telecommunications interception capability, but on nothing like the same scale as NSA or GCHQ. The extent to which this capability is or can be used for non-military intelligence gathering is unknown.

Special legislation from 1952 (1952:98) regulates the use of telephone wiretaps in investigating crimes against national security. Authorisation is granted by a court, on application by a prosecutor. In an emergency, the prosecutor can seek court approval retroactively. It would appear that very few security applications are, or have been, refused.[17] Although telephone tapping is supposed to be limited to investigating on-going or completed offences, the practice is this respect is fairly liberal. Other special legislation, from 1973, now consolidated in the Act on Special Monitoring of Aliens (1991:572) allows the Security Police to engage in more 'proactive' telephone tapping, but only against foreigners. Figures are published on 'ordinary' law enforcement tapping, but are not available for security tapping. Around 400 people per year are subject to law enforcement taps. The majority of investigations concern narcotics offences.[18]

There have been a number of changes in laws relating to secret surveillance. Legislation has been introduced making it easier for the police to use tele-controlled video surveillance equipment, which also can pick up audio signals (Secret Video Surveillance Act, 1995:1506). In the Code of Judicial Procedure, there are new rules for telephone tapping and 'metering' information. Permission to tap phones applies to a given telephone number, code or other telecommunications address, not a specific telephone or physical place as was the case before. Permission can also be given to tap outside the publicly owned telecommunications system. Telephone companies using digital equipment are obliged to allow the police to understand/decode the communications intercepted. These changes are largely only bringing the regulation of telephone tapping in line with changes in technology and changes in the telecommunications market (which has gone from a public monopoly to mixed public/private ownership). The increased use of mobile phones does, however, increase surveillance capability. It is now easier both to keep track of someone (either by simply following the cells which the target's activated telephone is in continual contact with or, if pinpointing them is important, by using the above information combined with radio tracking equipment). It is also possible to get some idea of a target person's contacts, or the people who frequent a particular suspect location, by identifying the active mobile telephones in the cell in question.

At present, electronic surveillance using so called 'bugs' is not lawful. Having said this, one of the usual means of tapping a telephone is to bug it, which means that it can serve as a microphone even when it is not being used.[19] In 1996, the government once again appointed a commission of inquiry to investigate the issue of electronic surveillance through the use of bugs. The commission reported in April 1998 (SOU 1998:46) and, not unexpectedly, as this was more or less its mandate, proposed allowing this kind of electronic surveillance subject to certain conditions. It also proposed making permanent the law from 1952 (which has been renewed yearly). Legislation on this issue was expected in 2001. But due to massive criticism from the public, mass media and lawyers, including official bodies such as the Ombudsman, one of the first decisions by the new minister of justice, Thomas Bodström, was to postpone the bill. However – probably soon after the election in September 2002 – most probably electronic surveillance will be allowed in accordance with the recommendations of the commission of inquiry. If these recommendations are followed, a court would be allowed to authorise bugging for a maximum (renewable) period of one month in order to investigate more serious offences, that is, those punishable by a minimum sentence of two years imprisonment. Swedish sentences being relatively low by international comparison, bugging would thus not be available for the investigation of any crime. Bugging would not be allowed for proactive purposes, where there is no concrete suspicion of an offence. A security-screened advocate would attempt to safeguard the interests of the suspect in the secret proceedings before the authorising court in all bugging and telephone tapping cases. The advocate would be able to appeal against a decision to authorise surveillance. However, unlike the foreign legislation on which this proposal is based (sections 784 and 785 of the Danish Code of Procedure) there would be no general requirement to notify the target after the bugging or telephone tapping had ceased. The awareness amongst the police that notification will occur is an important deterrent against overuse, and the present authors see no reason for this not being the general rule, albeit subject to exceptions, especially as Security Police targets are no longer simply the 'traditional' ones of foreign intelligence officers.

Security Police Targets and Security Files

The Public and Secret Government Instructions on Security Files

As indicated, the most important instrument in the work of the Security Police is their security intelligence files. The purpose of these files is to identify people who pose an actual or potential threat to the internal or external security of the state; subversives in a broad understanding of the concept.[20]

By way of introduction to this subject, one can say that, in any state, it is activities carried out in secret that scare those in power the most. The job of the Security Police is to provide those in power with information concerning real and potential threats to the state. In order to gain access to, or even control over, secret activities, the Security Police are forced to resort to undercover activities and the use of methods which give rise to fear, and even hatred, within the groups that already consider the Security Police as repressive, and as evidence of the undemocratic nature of the state. Surveillance can result in dissenting groups going underground. However, the very fact that a group has begun to work secretly is used as a justification by the Security Police for seeing their activities as being of an especially dangerous character. And information once gathered will inevitably be used, and not simply for identifying groups and planning responses, but in employment matters, and in other preventive contexts.[21] The use of vague information, based on infiltration and other kinds of undercover activities, which causes people to be denied citizenship, lose their jobs or be pilloried in the press as suspected terrorists confirms for these marginalized groups that their fears were justified and can give rise to countermeasures – propaganda of course, but also physical activities such as demonstrations, or even the violent activities the surveillance was meant to prevent. Propaganda directed against the Security Police, often using extreme language, is used as a justification for the state and the police that the groups really are dangerous, and so on. Thus, the system itself can generate the security problems it was established to remove. In the end democracy can risk committing suicide in fear of death.

Until 1998, the registration of subversives was governed by public and secret government instructions. An entry in the files of the Security Police, however, may never be founded *solely* on the fact that the registered person is a member of a certain organisation or has expressed a particular political opinion. This rule, which has been in force since October 1969, corresponds to an identically worded provision in the constitution (Instrument of Government, Chapter 2, section 3) which was inserted following the IB scandal.[22]

In December 1998, the Register Board published its report on the operation of the security filing system during the period 1969–1996.[23] The report made public all the secret government instructions to the Security Police on surveillance and registration of subversives. These instructions named political groups and parties on which the Security Police was to collect information. It was the Security Police itself that proposed the political groups and parties. In practice, the government invariably approved the proposal. The great majority of the organisations listed were on the left wing.

Collecting information on political groups and parties meant, in practice, opening individual files on the members. The public government instructions stated that mere membership of a 'revolutionary' party was not sufficient to lead to the opening of a personal file. However, the secret instructions identified a number of different grounds for registering members in certain 'extremist' political groups and parties. As well as such relatively uncontroversial factors as a conviction for a crime of violence connected to political activity or bearing weapons during a demonstration, these included 'building or participating in secret cells in the work place', taking part in a political (re)education course and, most general, 'having, or having had, a leading position in the party'. All three of these grounds for registration were criticised by the Register Board as being vague. As regards the second ground, all of the left wing political parties listed as potentially subversive required, as a condition of membership, that an applicant participated in a 'political education' study circle. This meant that registration of members of these parties was automatic. As regards the third ground, the Security Police criteria for determining 'leading position' included acting as a member in a working group, receiving an invitation to attend a national party conference, counting votes in an internal election, acting as a steward in a demonstration organised by the party and being responsible for receiving applications to attend a summer camp or to join a study circle.[24] The vagueness of the 'leading position' requirement meant that the Security Police itself decided whether a person had a leading position.

The report of the Register Board confirmed the allegations made by certain commentators, and by Leander himself before the European Commission and Court of Human Rights, that the prohibition was in practice interpreted so narrowly as to be almost meaningless. The figures revealed by the Register Board show that in 1980, 3,998 Swedish citizens were filed in the register *solely* because of their membership of or sympathy with a left or anarchist organisation and 158 citizens for membership of, or sympathy with, a right wing extremist organisation (that is, if the person were suspected of a security related crime he or she was not included in these figures). The figures for 1990 were left-wing/anarchists 3,467, right-wingers 118, and for 1998, left-wing/anarchists 2,062 and right-wingers 98.[25]

The contradiction between the law and the secret instructions to the Security Police was well known to the different governments (at least the different ministers of justice) since 1969, whether social democratic or centre/right. It was also well known to the different supervising authorities and committees. The most stunning example is the investigation from 1989/90 by the senior government law officer, the Chancellor of Justice. In his public report (submitted in January 1990) he stated that he had checked both the secret instructions and approximately 1,000 different files (including the Leander file!), and that no prohibited political surveillance had occurred. At the same time, he submitted a secret report to the government that stated his opinion that this kind of registration was not only common but also in accordance with the secret government instructions.

This kind of information was used in vetting applications. The Security Police did not make the formal decision to reveal information from its files (though it could decide that information should not be revealed on grounds of irrelevance). It was the National Police Board that decided whether information should be revealed to an employer or prospective employer. However, the NPB almost invariably decided to do so. According to the report of the Register Board, the release of information from the Security Police files almost always led to a negative result for the filed person. One of the main purposes with the investigation by the Register Board was to see if there were any more 'Leander-cases', that is cases in which individuals had suffered because of the release of information on lawful political activity from the files. The Register Board found at least 1,001 possible 'Leander-cases', not of all whom were still alive.

In March 1999, the Government gave the Board a mandate to continue its investigation into security screening between 1969–1996. However, the Government authorised the Board only to investigate cases in which the person involved had requested this, and excluded certain categories of security screening (the main one being recruitment to part-time defence forces). The Board placed two advertisements in some national newspapers. However, this was done during the summer, and arguably only a few of the 1,001 of the suspected 'Leander-cases' (those still alive that is) actually saw them. The Board also decided that such an investigation would take place only if the applicants filled in a special form and allowed the Board to publish their full names and year of birth. A total of 204 people applied to the Board, but two of these withdrew their applications, and ten applications related to a time period outside of the investigative mandate of the Board. Of the 192 applications, only 22 came from people who the Board had earlier identified on a preliminary basis as being a 'Leander-case'. This figure can be compared with the – already at this early time – almost 1,500 people who had so far asked the Security Police to see their files. In many of the applications, it transpired that no security screening had occurred (120 cases), or no information had been disclosed from the Security Police files (42 cases) or the information disclosed concerned screening which did not fall within the Board's mandate to investigate (3 cases). Of the remaining 27 cases, the Register Board found that in 16 of these, that is more than 50 per cent, some mistakes had been made in the procedure, and in 6 cases, about 20 per cent, the security screening had damaged the applicant in an unreasonable way.[26] The Register Board stated in other cases that the decision not to employ had been reasonable in the circumstances, thus implicitly agreeing that had been correct to regard these people as 'security risks'. All of them were identified in the public report, by their full name and year of birth. In no case had there been any allegations of criminal behaviour, simply active membership of groups regarded as extremist. The Register Board considered that the security situation at the time of the decisions to release information must be decisive, not later events tending to show the lack of any concrete danger posed by the organisation in question. Opinions differ on whether such an approach is correct. Nonetheless, the fact remains that people were denied employment because they were on elections lists for local elections or the parliament, had been arranging open political meetings, participated in demonstrations or summer-camps, sold political newspapers on the streets or had been writing letters to the press supporting Charter 77 or arguing against the Pinochet regime.[27] The report of the Register Board, and its conclusions, were heavily criticised in some quarters. In the summer of 2001 the Government decided that the Register Board was to further investigate if there are any more citizens who have been unreasonable victims of security screening.[28]

It is unclear how many active personal files exist today. The figure is secret. It has been estimated that the total number of personal files in 1970 was approximately 250,000.[29] Even if this figure is correct, many of these files can be assumed to have been weeded out during the period 1969–1996.[30] A qualified guess as to the total number of active files today can be made on the basis of publicly available information,[31] the total number of posts subject to vetting and the total number of 'positive' responses from the Security Police files, taking into account the fact that only Swedish citizens of working age may apply for a security classified post. This would give us a figure of between 13,500 and 28,000, probably closer to the former figure.[32]

Reform of the Security Police Files and Changes in Targets

Even before the real facts of the Leander case were published in 1997, it was recognised that a system allowing registration so easily is problematic. There was an official inquiry headed by a former chief of the Security Police into the registration system in 1994 (the Register Commission). The report of this Commission led to the enactment of the Security Protection Act (*Säkerhetsskyddslag* 1996:627).

The Security Protection Act should now be read in conjunction with the new Police Databank Act (*Polisdatalag* 1998:622) which entered into force in April 1999. According to section 5 of the Police Databank Act, a file may not be opened on a person solely on the ground of what is known about the persons 'ethnic background, political opinion, religious or philosophical conviction, membership in trade union, health or sexual character'. Such information may however be attached to a file, created because of other reasons, if this is absolutely necessary. The main impetus behind the Act was not so much the report of the Register Board as the Swedish ratification of the Europol Convention Article 10 of which contains a similar prohibition.[33] The Security Protection Act contains general rules, codifying what would appear to be internal practice, as to when a security risk should be seen as ceasing. Under section 35, if no new information is found about the filed person for ten years, his or her file is to be weeded out (except when extraordinary reasons exist).

It is an open question what will be the result of these new rules. Some anxiety might of course arise out of the interpretation of the word 'solely' which the Register Board has promoted (see note 18). It is, however, intended that the natural tendency to open individual files too easily will be partly counteracted by the requirement (set out in the *travaux préparatoires* to the Security Protection Act, but not the Act itself) to provide information on the source's reliability and the likely reliability of the information as such, except where this is clearly unnecessary. Still, information on the membership of extremist organisations is still likely to be a very important part in mapping out presumptive security risks. It is also clear that personal files cannot, and will not, be limited to suspected internal subversives (and, naturally, suspected foreign spies and terrorists). It is also necessary to have files on informers and people working in senior (vetted) positions. The purpose here is to be alert to these people being approached from foreign intelligence agencies or for other reasons risk finding themselves in situations that might mean that they might become security risks, for example as a consequence of double loyalties. This actually is a reflection on co-option that comes naturally after comparing the special reports on security screening in 1998 and 2000 from the Register Board.[34]

In the past, registration was more or less routine concerning visitors from certain countries, and Swedish visitors to certain (communist) countries, as well as Swedes' contacts with certain foreign consulates and embassies.[35] Even today, registration of information on asylum seekers occurs without any concrete suspicion of crime or subversive activity. This is done simply in order to obtain a picture of the contacts within groups of people who previously had been active in political opposition in their home states. Another reason is to work as a help to identify whether an asylum seeker has in fact been sent by the regime to spy on the exile community.[36] Such routine registration is likely to continue.

As indicated, the degree of suspicion of subversive activity that needs to exist before registration occurs seems to have been non-existent for foreigners and very low for Swedes. The normal standard for registration in the police criminal intelligence files is 'reasonable suspicion' of involvement in crime. But the official inquiry into registration in 1994 took the position that such a test is too demanding for the Security Police, and it should be sufficient that there is 'reason to believe' involvement in crimes against national security, terrorism or the constitution.[37] The *travaux préparatoires* to the recent bill on police databanks refer however to the standard 'suspected' involvement in crime as well as allowing registration even in other cases 'where there are special reasons for this'.[38]

As with other European states, the end of the cold war has led to a shift in targets and intelligence gathering priorities. The annual reports of the Security Police – largely uninformative documents – state that there has not been any reduction of illegal intelligence activity. On the contrary, it is claimed that this activity has increased, because many countries believe that the reduction in military forces has to be compensated for by increased intelligence gathering. The intelligence gathering tends to concentrate on political questions, technology and military capacity. According to the Security Police, there is a certain amount of espionage directed against refugees, initiated by foreign countries.[39] There are also direct attempts from foreign countries to 'influence Swedish citizens with powerful positions as well as Swedish opinion in a more general sense.'[40] Some of these activities are performed under the cover of doing private business. It is also suspected that some of the organised crime in Sweden is connected directly to foreign intelligence activities. Among the foreign intelligence organisations active in Sweden may be found organisations from countries which are members of NATO, in other words countries with which Sweden has good relations. It is at the same time pointed out that Swedish businessmen who try to establish businesses in the former Soviet Union are the objects of interest of the Russian intelligence organs.[41]

As regards Swedish refugees' or immigrants' involvement in terrorism abroad, the Security Police consider that the majority of refugees who are dissidents in their home-countries and who work actively in Sweden against their home-countries' regimes, only engage in ordinary propaganda and the collection of money. However, a small number of different groups with members or sympathisers in Sweden, or more generally, in Europe, are identified in the Security Police's annual reports as engaged in terrorist activities.[42] Resources devoted to this will undoubtedly increase as part of the UN and EU counter-terrorism response to the terrorist acts of 11 September. More generally, this counter-terrorism response is a challenge to European civil liberties generally. Swedish legislation and police practices dealing with terrorist crime is usually less, and in most cases, much less, severe than similar legislation and practices in other European states. EU harmonisation of practices and legislation in this area is hardly to be welcomed from a civil liberties perspective.

As regards purely internal subversive threats the position is taken that, while extremist political groups that wish to destabilise the Swedish democratic system continue to exist, they no longer pose a serious threat to it. There is no evidence that extremist groups active in Sweden are supported by foreign powers. The main focus of the Security Police's attention as regards radical political groupings is now said to be on extreme right-wing-groups that have frequently committed crimes disturbing public order. The racist groups active in Sweden have not been considered to be so powerful or numerous that they can constitute a threat to national security, but they threaten others' peaceful exercise of their constitutional rights and freedoms, in particular Swedish citizens of foreign origin. Moreover, the relatively strong constitutional protection of freedom of speech has had the unwelcome effect that Sweden has become something of a centre for racist music. More recently, however, there has been evidence that the threat from fascist and racist groups has been underestimated. During 1998 and 1999, several journalists and politicians were injured in neo-Nazi bomb and firebomb attacks. The Security Police also consider that anti-racist and anti-fascist groups are worthy of attention because of the threat they can pose to public order. Associations involved in systematic criminal activity, such as certain motorcycle clubs, are also said to be a legitimate object of Security Police attention on the basis that they attempt to intimidate witnesses, prosecutors etc. and therefore constitute a threat to the *Rechtstaat*.[43]

It is further noted that there are other groups engaged in a particular cause, which occasionally resort to violent or unlawful actions (for example environmental groups and animal rights groups), but that these groups are not involved in subversion as such. On the other hand, the Security Police 'follow the activities of such groups, in order to keep themselves informed in case more violent groups emerge from them'.[44] The Security Police also monitors the activities of extremist environmental activists who have occupied and damaged different industrial areas and communication facilities, especially those belonging to multinational companies, and militant vegans who have been responsible for a number of firebomb attacks on dairies and food packing centres. The common theme is opposition, mainly against the political establishment but also against big companies.[45] These targets cannot be described as traditional national security concerns. However, the fact that Sweden has a Security Police, rather than a separate civilian security agency, makes it organisationally speaking easier to transfer attention to such targets.

The most obvious example of this was during the EU summit meeting in Gothenburg, in June 2001. The police raided several different buildings where demonstrators were staying (mainly different schools) and forced everyone in the buildings to state their name, personal identity number and address in front of a video camera, handled by the police. The vast majority of these people had no involvement in any of the violent demonstrations, and were not suspected by the police of being so involved. Many have afterwards, quite reasonably, difficulties in ridding themselves of the suspicions that this information is being gathered for reasons of general registration of 'fringe' political groups.

The Security Vetting System

Which People Are Subject to Vetting and What Does This Involve?

In this paper it is not possible to give a detailed picture of the Swedish vetting system. We will only give an overview of the system.[46] The main rule is to be found in section 7 of the Security Protection Act that states that only those who are regarded as 'reliable from the security perspective' are authorised to have access to secret information.[47]

There are three security classifications. Class 1 covers about 1,000 people. This classification is limited to posts and tasks where the incumbent to a large extent comes in contact with very secret material. Class 2 covers around 10,000 people. This classification applies to posts and tasks where the incumbent to a not insignificant extent comes in contact with very secret material.[48] The government decides which appointments falling within classes 1 and 2 within the public-sector, although this is on the basis of proposals from the employer concerned, that is the relevant administrative authority or public company.[49] In cases of defence contractors (so-called SUA contracts) the Defence Authority decides appointments falling within the classes 1 and 2. Class 3 applies to posts and tasks in which the incumbent comes into contact with secret information the unveiling of which can involve more than minor damage to national security.[50] The government has delegated to the administrative authorities and companies concerned the authority to employ people to class 3 posts and tasks. At the beginning of the 1990s, the number of class 3 posts and tasks was about 400,000.[51] There are no definite publicly available figures on the total number of security classed posts today, but the Security Police have stated that the above figures give a 'rough idea' of the present levels.[52] Notwithstanding the very large numbers of posts involved, bearing in mind Sweden's population, the Security Police consider that by no means everyone involved in very security sensitive work is subject to vetting.[53]

In addition to security classed posts, vetting can be done ad hoc, for anti-terrorism purposes, or under certain circumstances, at the request of another state or an international organisation. In the latter cases, the National Police Board decides whether or not to accede to the request (Security Protection Act section 15 and Security Protection ordinance section 22). The envisaged exchanges of information are primarily within the framework of the Europol convention.

Vetting always involves a check of the security files and the police criminal records. However, with vetting for purposes of protection against terrorism, without connection to national security, there are restrictions on the release of information from the criminal records. Only information on certain crimes can be revealed. However, as the list of crimes includes assault, this means that information on minor offences can be made available to an employer.[54] In the vetting procedure information in police registers other than the files of the Security Police can also be checked and disclosed, for example the CID intelligence files. In addition, a special investigation is made, whenever the vetting is made for a post in security class 1 or 2, into the subject's personal circumstances (Security Protection Act sections 21 and 22). This can also include an investigation into the personal circumstances of the individual's spouse or cohabiting girlfriend/boyfriend. The person vetted is to submit, in writing, details of his or her personal circumstances. These are forwarded to the National Police Board, which checks whether these are accurate and complete. Incomplete or inaccurate information is obviously a significant factor in determining whether the vetted person is a security risk or not.

As indicated, there must be vetting when a decision is made to employ a person, or otherwise involve them (for example as a consultant) in security classed work. There must also be vetting when a person already in security classed work is moved to a higher security classification (Security Protection Ordinance sections 23–24). The two higher security classifications are to be 're-vetted' at least every five years, as well as whenever the person in question has got married or begun cohabiting with someone or whenever there are 'special reasons' for a new control (Security Protection Ordinance section 25). The Security Police itself considers that continual follow-up of changes in personal circumstances is preferable to periodical five-yearly updating but that this is out of the question, taking into account its present capabilities.

The applicant for a security-classed post must be informed that vetting will be carried out and thus has the right to withdraw his or her application for the job. In such a case, in principle, this person should not be vetted. But there is no prohibition on this. The Security Police has stated that systematic attempts to infiltrate the vetting system occur, so it would be surprising if the Security Police did not request employers (administrative agencies and companies) to provide information about applicants who withdrew their applications.

During 1990–1999 there were 1,167,302 vetting controls in Sweden, in other words approximately almost 120,000 every year. The total number of controls has however lessened recently, and during the last three years of the period there have been between 60,000 and 80,000 a year. In 2000 the figure reduced further, with 52,641 controlled persons. (The real figure each year is about five per cent higher each year, due to the fact that in some cases also the controlled person's wife/husband/cohabitor/cohabitee is subject to control). As a point of comparison one can mention that there are in total, including those made during vetting cases, about 1,300,000 checks in the criminal records register every year.

Functions and Composition of the Register Board

The decision whether or not to reveal information contained in the Security Police files to prospective employers is now taken, not by the National Police Board, but by a body specially established for this purpose, the Register Board. The Board is also to exercise continuous monitoring regarding the Security Police's registration of information in files, especially as regards the constitutional prohibition (for Swedish citizens) of registration purely on the basis of political opinions.

According to its mandate as set out in the relevant government ordinance (1994:633) the Board consists of a secretariat and a maximum of eight members. One cannot apply for a position on the Board. The government instead appoints members. During the two first periods (July 1996–June 1999 and July 1999–June 2002) there were (and will be) five members, three lawyers[55] and two serving MPs, one from each of the two largest parties, the social democrats and the conservative party. In November 1998 the social democrat member was replaced by a party colleague since he was to become a government minister.

The government does not consult with Parliament before it appoints the members of the Board, although it probably consults with the leaders of the major parties. The fact that not all political parties are represented was criticised by the Green Party.[56] Both the politicians who served during the first mandate period had been earlier involved with monitoring the Security Police. The first social democratic member, Lövdén, was formerly on the National Police Board and he was also the former chairman of the parliamentary inquiry into the Security Police, the Säpo Committee. The conservative member, Hellsvik, was also formerly Minister of Justice during the centre/right government of 1991–1994.[57]

The lack of parliamentary input into appointments, and the fact that the Board is only answerable to the executive, might be seen as implying a lack of independence from the executive, and a lack of meaningful control. However, as already mentioned above, administrative authorities in Sweden may not be subject to direct governmental control in taking decisions in individual cases. We have no reason to doubt that the Register Board in practice is functioning with the required degree of independence from the government, strange though this might seem to readers from some countries with a (justified) tradition of greater suspicion towards the executive. Still, the fact remains that the Board can easily become a club for 'insiders'.

Procedure before the Register Board

Where there is no entry for the vetted person in any police file whatsoever, or where the Register Board (or, where applicable, the Government) determine not to reveal information, the employer is simply informed, on a printed form, that there is no information to reveal. Once an entry exists, irrespective of whether it is in the Security Police or any other police files, the information is always to be forwarded to the Register Board. In order to fulfil its functions, the Board has the right to see the files or obtain excerpts from them.[58] In addition, each case is orally presented to the Board. The Board and the National Police Board decide who should make these presentations. So far, the task of making presentations has usually been entrusted to a member of the Security Police.

The quorum for the Board in making decisions on revealing information is the chairman and three other members. A decision to reveal information can only be made if everyone is unanimous. If the Board is not unanimous in its decision to reveal the information, the chairman may decide to hand over the decision to the government, should he consider that the information should be revealed. This means that, even where there is a majority against revealing the information, the chairman can refer the case to the government which can decide to reveal the information.[59] If a preliminary decision is taken to release, the Board must first decide whether the information can be revealed to the person vetted, either in extenso or summarised/sanitised or through a so-called 'security dialogue'.[60] This involves a meeting between the vetted person and a member of the Security Police who will, if deemed necessary without revealing in detail the negative information involved, attempt to obtain the vetted person's views. Initially, there were comparatively few cases during 1996–1998 in which the Register Board communicated the filed information from the security files even to the vetted persons. After the earlier classified instructions for political registrations were revealed, such security dialogues started to occur more regularly. In 1999 the Register Board refused such communication only in 9 cases, and in 2000 only in 8 – hence, nowadays one can state that a vetted person as a rule has the chance to comment on the substance of the information in the Security Police files, before a decision is made to release this information. This – which was the main legal question in the Leander case – is a significant improvement of the system. You can with no doubt claim that this new transparency at least towards the vetted subjects must be regarded as the single most important fact to explain the major reduction (see below Table 8.1) in the number of vetting cases where the content of the files of the Security Police *de facto* is handed out. Once again, this more than anything else confirms that the most important safeguard for democracy and the *Rechtstaat* is transparency.

If the Register Board decides to reveal information from the Security Police, or other police, files, there is no possibility for the vetted person him or herself to appeal against this decision (Security Protection Ordinance section 50). The way the vetting system is constructed means that, as the Security Police or the Register Board take no formal decision regarding employment, the usual basic right of appeal under Swedish administrative law is not applicable. It is the employer who takes the employment decision. Where an existing employee (in either the private or public sector) is dismissed, he or she will usually have the possibility of claiming unfair dismissal. In some cases however, a private employer will act (will be forced to act) after an administrative authority has taken the decision to withdraw a security clearance. In such cases, the employee will not be in a position to invoke unfair dismissal against his or her employer.[61] The Register Board has criticised certain employers, in particular, the Air Transport Authority, for automatically withdrawing security clearances from employees who have criminal convictions for crimes of violence, however minor these might be.[62]

Analysis of the Impact of the Register Board

The Register Board produces an annual report to the government. As there are no special rules on whether or not this document should be public, in accordance with ordinary Swedish rules on official information, it is available to the public unless the government decides that it should be classified. So far the government has not classified any of the reports. The reports tend to be short, usually ten pages, with the same number of pages in appendices. Nonetheless, they are relatively informative. The reports set out the total number of vetting cases and then break down these figures in a number of ways; by security classification, by requesting authority (defence and other authorities), by number of 'positive' responses from the Security Police files and other police files and by number of decisions to reveal this information to prospective employers. The vetting statistics are displayed in Table 8.1.

Table 8.1   **Personnel Vetting in Sweden 1992–2000**

Year	Number of personnel vetting cases (not including vetting of co-habitees)	Percentage of cases in which Register Board* revealed information from Security files in a vetting case
1993–93	243,000	76.0
1993–94	133,249	94.2
1994–95	128,250	70.3
1995–96a	118,133	79.6
1995–96b	77,426	34.0
1997	69,303	9.9
1998	79,733	9.1
1999	63,485	4.8
2000	52,641	3.1

* The Register Board came into effect in July 1996.

This shows the clear drop in the number of cases in which information was revealed from the Security Police files. Since 1996 security information has been revealed in less than ten per cent of the cases in which it could have been revealed. This appears to show that the Register Board is well aware of the crucial distinction between intelligence which the Security Police can gather for general surveillance purposes, which may be highly speculative, and intelligence which is sufficiently certain to be used in vetting cases, with serious consequences for an individual's career. When the question about handing out information from the intelligence files was decided by the National Police Board, the information the Security Police regarded as relevant was handed out in between 70 per cent and 95 per cent of all cases. Nowadays, in the vast majority of vetting applications that lead to material being revealed, the information revealed is not 'soft' intelligence from the Security Police files, but 'hard' intelligence, namely that the vetted person has a criminal conviction. The conclusion appears to be that the Register Board is taking its job seriously, and that it is functioning as a proper control.

    As to why there is an improvement in scrutiny, the reasons are the integrity of the members of the Board, the time they have to devote to the job and the competence the lawyers, in particular, have in determining whether intelligence is too speculative and unsupported to be used to a person's detriment in a job application. The fact that the Board has received

198 Democracy, Law and Security

a certain amount of mass media, and academic, scrutiny can also be assumed to have bolstered its resolve to show that it was capable of exercising effective scrutiny over Security Police files.

Of course, experience shows that a security agency is well capable of circumventing improved scrutiny mechanisms and continuing to collect intelligence on targets an oversight body has told it to keep away from. But, even before the end of the Cold War, there were indications that the Security Police itself seem to have been aware that much of its intelligence on internal threats was irrelevant or overly speculative and that changes in collection and filing routines were necessary. The substantial weeding of files, which occurred in the 1980s and 1990s, is evidence of this. Senior staff changes following the debacle of the Palme murder investigation can also be assumed to have had some significance here. The main motivation for the Security Police as regards improving the files can be assumed to be a desire for improved efficiency. Still, there is no reason to believe that either senior staff or the rank and file are totally unreceptive to being reminded by the Register Board of the importance of respecting human rights in their work. In other words, although we naturally cannot be certain of this, the Security Police as a whole does not appear to have resented the scrutiny of the Board, or have attempted to undermine it.[63]

The Board itself has expressed the opinion that it has both the time and the competence to do a better job than its predecessor. The critical approach of the Board comes across in both its annual reports and at least in the first special report it produced on the operation of the government instructions on filing. It states, for example, that it has occasionally come across information noted in a file, or the database itself, which it considered was of questionable continuing relevance for the work of the Security Police, or even whether it was ever relevant to file this information. While it considers that the relevance or otherwise of information is, in the first place, a matter for the police involved in the investigation of the subversive activity in question (that is, it leaves them a margin of discretion) it has had occasional discussions on the matter with Security Police and there have been some changes in registration criteria made as a result of these discussions.

A Right of Access to Security Files

On 1 April 1999 the statutory requirement of absolute secrecy for Security Police files was abolished. Instead, the normal test in the Secrecy Act now applies, that is the responsible administrative authority (in this case, the

Security Police) is to determine whether revealing the information might cause damage to certain protected interests (in this case, national security). The onus of proof is, however, reversed. Information can only be revealed if it can be proved that this can occur without negatively affecting the work of the Security Police in preventing or discovering crimes against national security or terrorist offences (Secrecy Act Chapter 5 section 1), or damaging relations with foreign powers (i.e. foreign intelligence agencies or Europol, Secrecy Act Chapter 2, section 2).

There has been some debate in the press about the advantages (for historians) of retaining the files intact as opposed to the disadvantages for the personal integrity of the persons concerned, or their next of kin.[64] Up until 31 December 2000 there had been 4,219 applications to see files. Of these, 995 of the applicants were, according to the Minister of Justice, filed in the computerised files of the Security Police (whenever such an application is made, the check is only made against these files). No applicant was allowed to see their whole file, and 144 denied all access.[65] Critics have also pointed out that these figures give no idea of whether a person has in the past been registered. Bearing in mind the extensive weeding operations that took place at the end of the 1960s and 1980s, it is quite possible that files had existed. Critics have also pointed out that, in the cases where partial access was granted, it mainly consisted of giving the individual in question copies of his or her own correspondence with the Security Police, together with newspaper clippings detailing, for example, his or her participation in a public meeting. To call this 'partial access' to a file is true, but misleading. In November 2000, four applicants complained to the European Court of Human Rights, where the case now is pending.[66]

A decision to refuse access can be appealed to the administrative courts. Since the entry into force of an amendment to the Police Databank Act (1999:622), occasioned as a result of Sweden's ratification of the Europol Convention, an individual who has suffered from the filing of inaccurate data can apply for damages. This might, conceivably, be of some use where an applicant can prove a case of mistaken identity, although this is no easy matter when he or she is probably unaware of the fact that such information is filed on him or her in the first place. It is likely only to be a remedy on paper as far as the Security Police is concerned, as the courts are hardly in a position to criticise them for operational decisions made on available evidence, even if these later turn out to have been badly wrong. The only way we see in which such a remedy could be made real is if the courts commissioned an expert independent witness or body to assess, in camera, the reasonableness of the filing of the data. Outside of the academic world, the only body which we consider is both expert and independent is the Register Board.

In all cases of non-access which have so far been appealed, the administrative courts, and the administrative courts of appeal have rejected the applicant's appeal with a standard formulation. This is hardly surprising. The Stockholm Court of Administrative Appeal, which has dealt with the majority of requests for such information, signalled a very restrictive attitude towards revealing any information on the Security Police in its comments on the legislative proposal to amend the Secrecy Act.[67] The Supreme Administrative Court did finally decide not to allow review dispensation, and this independent of whether the application had been totally or only partly denied.[68] The legality of the decision can, however, be discussed. The same court also decided that the number of employed at the Security Police 1965 could not be made public, because of reasons of national security, and this even though there was no danger for the national security to release information about the number of employed 2000![69] All this must be understood not only as something that goes to show that the ordinary and administrative courts rarely have the expertise to evaluate critically government claims that national security would be endangered by the release of certain information, it most importantly shows how blinded you can be by the light of power, if you have done all – as in the Swedish context of employment of posts as higher judge – of your career in the corridors of the ministry.[70]

Some Concluding Remarks on the System of Control and Accountability

The main characteristic of the Swedish system of control and accountability for the Security Police is that it has not been a 'system'. There are different bodies – executive, judicial and parliamentary – each have different areas of responsibility. One of the most significant conclusions that can be drawn from the facts of the Leander case is that all the supervisory bodies failed to provide effective oversight.

To deal first with executive accountability, the main mechanism of supervision here is the occasional meetings the Minister of Justice has with the head of the Security Police and the head of the National Police Board. There are also contacts between civil servants in the Ministry of Justice and the Security Police. But, as already mentioned, the Minister of Justice is not entitled to give directions in specific cases to the police. Having said this, it is possible to steer the activities of the Security Police through the power of appointment of the head of the Security Police and the head of the NPB, by budgetary means, by government ordinances of general character and by encouraging the NPB to issue instructions or supervise particular matters in more detail. As regards the last of these, the Leander case, and the report of the Register Board in December 1998, have shown that the lay members of the NPB have inadequate time and expertise to investigate the activities of the Security Police.

The government is also able to steer activities by initiating, or threatening, investigations by the Chancellor of Justice or an independent inquiry. But the Chancellor of Justice is not an expert in security matters. Living as they do in a sort of grey zone, it is easy for individual members of the Security Police to evade governmental control and the oversight of the supervising authorities when the lawfulness or the justifiability of their activities can be questioned. No minutes of legally dubious decisions are waved before the face of the Chancellor of Justice on the few occasions when this official has undertaken inspections of the Security Police. The Register Board report of December 1998 confirmed the inadequacy of scrutiny by the Chancellor of Justice at least as regards monitoring the security files.

The government can also decide to appoint special commissions of inquiry, consisting of MPs and/or lawyers. The value of such *ad hoc* commissions can also be questioned. Bearing in mind the arcane, closed world of the Security Police, it is not surprising if amateur investigators, probably even the on-going *Säkerhetstjänstkommissionen*, fail to discover any dubious or illegal decisions or procedures by listening to reports from officers at the Security Police or by going through their documents. And the Security Police have hardly been encouraged to volunteer information of measures of doubtful legality either. The special investigator appointed by the Säpo committee, Carl Lidbom, noted that at least with some of the lawyers whose task it is to investigate the legality of the activities of the Security Police, there has been an attitude that 'it is probably better not to know so much. When it comes to an activity that ultimately is concerned with the security of the nation, it might not always be possible to maintain normal standards'.[71]

At least since the IB surveillance was revealed in 1973, it is difficult to say that there has been party political abuse of power by the government or the Minister of Justice, in the sense of spying on other major political parties. Rather, it seems that during the 1970s and 1980s there has been a (quiet) political consensus to watch the extreme left-wing parties. There has not been a total abdication of political responsibility either, but the conclusion is nonetheless that the Security Police have been allowed too much autonomy in practice in their day to day work.[72] Especially significant from the point of view of political responsibility seems to be the seemingly instinctive avoidance of going into structural problems and instead reducing scandals to isolated individual incidents. Here one can recollect Hannah Arendt's words:

> the point is that they lied not so much for their country – certainly not for their country's survival, which was never at stake – as for its 'image'.[73]

The Register Board is a form of quasi-judicial mechanism.[74] As mentioned, it is accountable to the executive but operates with a large degree of autonomy in practice. The appointment to the Board of politicians from the two major parties serves to reassure the mainstream of the parties represented in Parliament that the filing and vetting systems are not being used against the rank and file of these parties. As mentioned above, we consider the Register Board to be a great improvement on the earlier system. However, the Register Board's jurisdiction is limited. It has no competence to look at how the Security Police handles citizenship or deportation issues. It has no competence to look at Security Police operations as such, only filing practices. Moreover, two question marks still exist regarding the depth of its scrutiny. Firstly comparative experience in this area, most notably the work of the Canadian SIRC, indicates that there is a 'long learning curve' in security matters.[75] None of the legally qualified members of the Board appointed during its first mandate period had any experience in security matters. Secondly, the Board has no staff of its own, but relies on people seconded from the Security Police. Again, the Canadian experience shows the crucial role independent staff have in building up knowledge of the areas where the security agency is capable, for good reasons or bad, of stretching the letter of the law, and the ways it has of doing so. The staff thus gets to know the right questions to ask, and how to ask them. The staff is also crucial to building up a co-operative as opposed to confrontational relationship with the agency. Finally, the staff plays an important role in maintaining continuity of expertise when the membership of the oversight body changes.

There is another body charged with monitoring police files, including Security Police files. Following ratification of the Schengen and Europol conventions, the Data Inspectorate has been given the formal role in monitoring compliance with the requirements of these conventions relating to accuracy, relevance etc. of stored information. The Data Inspectorate is an administrative authority, and thus answerable to the executive. However, like other Swedish administrative authorities, it operates independently from governmental control. But the Data Inspectorate is unused to looking at 'soft' intelligence, and is likely to focus simply on formal matters, leaving the task of 'quality control' to the body which has been specifically entrusted with it, the Register Board.

Another form of quasi-judicial scrutiny is the Parliamentary Ombudsman. The jurisdiction of the Ombudsman[76] extends to the police, including the Security Police. The Ombudsman has in fact criticised the Security Police on occasion, but will usually refrain from investigating what can loosely be called operational decisions. The same criticism of lack of expertise made against the Chancellor of Justice can also be levelled against the Parliamentary Ombudsman.

To turn now to parliamentary controls. Obviously, the type of government in a state (presidential or parliamentary), the type of organisation (part of the police, or with police powers, or a separate civilian organisation) and the constitutional structure of the state (unitary or federal) influence the extent of parliamentary controls. A presidential system will, generally speaking, need more in the way of powerful committees than a system where the government is drawn from the party or parties with a political majority in the parliament, and so is (usually) accountable to parliament. In contrast to for example Norway, there is no specialist organ that takes overarching responsibility for monitoring the work of the Security Police. However, there are two standing parliamentary committees that have the competence to investigate the police, including the Security Police. These are the Committee on the Administration of Justice (JuU) and the Committee on the Constitution (KU). Both these bodies have on occasion investigated the Security Police. The Committee on the Constitution in particular is a useful mechanism for discovering and highlighting alleged governmental abuse of power. But the problems in this area have been not so much governmental abuse of power, but lack of effective governmental (and parliamentary) control of the Security Police. The same criticisms can be made of these committees as have been made regarding the Chancellor of Justice and the Parliamentary Ombudsman. They do not consist of experts in security matters, their staff resources are limited and they have limited time to devote to investigations of security matters. Neither can these committees take evidence under oath. The inadequacy of these committees in this respect is shown by the fact that they investigated the security vetting system on a number of occasions without ever discovering the extensive practice of registration of lawful political activity.

Finally, there is judicial control over certain Security Police methods, in particular, telephone tapping and search and seizure. One should point out in this respect that the requirement to involve a prosecutor in such matters is itself a safeguard. Swedish prosecutors operate independently from governmental supervision and control and are trained to gather all the evidence, not simply evidence in favour of the prosecution. Still, the closed world of security crimes and the small number of prosecutors involved in security matters means that this control function can easily be eroded. The same can be said for judicial involvement in telephone tapping. Training and experience as a judge is designed to give impartiality, care and indeed scepticism, in weighing evidence, an overriding interest in getting to the truth of the matter and an awareness of the importance of taking account of the rights of the individual. The Swedish judiciary has, for good and ill, a bureaucratic nature.[77] Most senior judges have long experience of working in government departments and this naturally colours their approach to the question of the 'proper role' of the judiciary in a democracy, as well as the issue of what questions are justifiable and what are not. The main problem here is that the group of judges to whom warrants are submitted is very small and they have operated in total isolation from supervision. At least in the past, some of these judges have shown themselves capable of renewing security telephone tapping warrants for very long periods.[78] Transparency is the only reliable guarantee against abuse. As three of the members of the commission of inquiry into bugging (all judges) stated, arguing for a general rule of post-hoc notification of a suspect:

> It is inevitable that a system without any transparency sooner or later will lead to that the those who takes the decisions adapt themselves to each other, developing a mutual view on what is demanded to allow for example telephone-tapping. In this fact there is a risk that the decisions will be all to routine. Knowing that the suspected citizen later will be informed about the decision will automatically lead to that the decision maker being more cautious.[79]

We can conclude by saying that in our experience the value in practice of any supervisory mechanism depends only partly on its formal structures and powers. The personal convictions and integrity of those involved are also extremely significant. This in turn is at least partially conditioned by the legal culture, in particular, the unqualified acceptance of, and wholehearted commitment to, the values of the material *Rechtstaat*, even in the most sensitive area of state activity, and the incumbent's views on his or her function. If these personal qualities are lacking then even the most impressive mechanism on paper will not be worth much. If they exist, then even less powerful mechanisms may be satisfactory, especially when one bears in mind the fact that Sweden is a country with a strong investigative press and strong protection of press freedom.

Notes

1   See, in particular, the most recent investigation, Försvarets Underrättelsenämnd, Redovisning av vissa uppgifter om den militära underrättelse- och säkerhetstjänsten, 26 November 1998.
2   The Military intelligence agency went through a succession of name changes, GBU, USK, SSI, KSI and is now known as Militära Underrättelsetjänsten, MUST. A Commission of Inquiry recently recommended improved control and oversight of the service (Underrättelsetjänsten – en översyn, SOU 1999:37).
3   Defence Intelligence Activity Act (SFS 2000:131) and Ordinance (SFS 2000:131). The commission of inquiry report is SOU 1999:37, Prop. 1999/2000:25.
4   SOU 1990:51, p 45 and 50f and Annual Report of the Security Police 1995/96, p. 8.
5   The Security Police have refused to give one of the authors of the present article, Dennis Töllborg, the figures on a number of occasions, claiming national security. Töllborg finally told them that he could find out the figures in other ways, did so and showed it to the Register Board. A month later, the Security Police publicly announced the figures in their annual report for 1998.
6   Säkerhetspolisen SA 187–2140–98.
7   Polisens årsredovisning 2000, page 41.
8   See SOU 1988:16, SOU 1989:18, SOU 1990:51.
9   The background to the case can be found in D. Töllborg (ed.), National Security and the Rule of Law, (Centrum för Europaforskning, Gothenburg, 1998) and I. Cameron, National Security and the European Convention on Human Rights, (Iustus/Kluwer, 2000).
10 See Christer Jönsson, Truth and Consequence.
11 Lund Commission Document nr. 15. Rapport til Stortinget fra kommisjonen som nedsatt av Stortinget for å granske påstander om ulovlig overvåking av norske borgere, avgitt till Stortingets presidentskap 28 mars 1996 ('Lund Report').
12 SOU 2000:25.
13 The national security offences in Chapters 18 and 19 of the Criminal Code are not seen as encompassing terrorist offences unless these are aimed directly at the government or state of Sweden, so the two categories of crime are treated separately.
14 Annual Report of the Security Police 1995/1996, p 3, SOU 1994:149 and below, section 5.2.
15 This is alleged to have occurred several times during 1995/96.
16 We will not go into detail regarding surveillance methods. See further, D. Töllborg, 'Under Cover. The Swedish Security Police and Their Modi Operandi'. In C. Fijnaut and G. Marx, Under Cover. Police Surveillance in Comparative Perspective (Kluwer, 1995).

[17] This was the conclusion of an official inquiry, SOU 1989:18, p. 64. Even applications for ordinary law enforcement taps are very rarely refused. E.g. in 1997, only one application was refused (JuU 10 1998/99).

[18] See, e.g. the report on telephone tapping for 1997/98, JuU 10. For a deeper analysis on wire tapping in Sweden, see Töllborg, Report on Wire Tapping Legislation in Sweden.

[19] This was criticised as 'unsuitable' by the senior government law officer, the Chancellor of Justice (See dnr 172–97–21, decision of 2 April 1998).

[20] SOU 1994:149, pp. 57 and 88.

[21] A recent graphic example of this was the freezing of bank accounts of people in the EU who are suspected of supporting the Al Qaida terrorist network. See EU Council regulation 467/2001, Commission regulations 1996/2001 and 2062/2001 (which in turn are based upon a Security Council resolution, 1373 of 28 September 2001).

[22] NB This restriction only applies to Swedish citizens. Also, it must be underlined the new – actually a complete new, earlier absolutely denied – interpretation of this ban, made by the Register Board when discussing the files of the Security Police. We quote: 'Whenever interpreting the rule in the Constitution, the emphasis must be put on the word solely. To register someone only on the basis of his or her membership in a political organisation must be regarded as forbidden, at least against her or his expressed will. However, if a person is regarded as a security risk, that is if it might be suspected that he or she is prepared to participate in actions against the society, his or her membership in a political party may be filed. Then it is a question of allowed political registration by the Security Police.' Register Board II 1999, p 18.

[23] Personalkontroll den 1 oktober 1969 – den 30 juni 1996. Rapport till regeringen av Registernämnden beslutad den 16 december 1998, hereinafter, 'Register Board Report'.

[24] Register Board report, p. 75.

[25] Register Board report, appendix 16.

[26] Register Board II, 1999.

[27] In the summer 2001 the Government decided to grant SEK 100,000 each to these six new 'Leandercases'.

[28] Ju2000/4972/PÅ, Ju2000/4983/På. The Board is to present their new report not later than March 2002.

[29] This information was in a newspaper, without source (Dagens Nyheter, 28 February 1998), moreover, without further references. Thus, we do no consider it to be reliable. Most probably, the figure is stolen from another newspaper article, written by Björn Kumm, published in Aftonbladet in the sixties.

[30] Some 100,000 entries were weeded out as a result of the reform of the vetting system in 1969. This statement has later been repeated both by Superintendent Therese Mattson at the Security Police (Göteborgs-Posten November 4th, 2000) and by the Register Board (2000, Report II, p 25 f), at least as concerns the computerised files. At the same time, we must consider that there are supposedly 2,000 meters of files still left, and these have not been professionally checked in individual complaints.

[31] See below, section 7.4.1.

[32] This figure is obtained by multiplying the highest and lowest percentages with the number of the working population, thus, $0,0027 \times 5,000,000 = 13,500$, $0,0056 \times 5,000,000 = 28,000$.

[33] Treaty on the Establishment of a European Police Office (Europol Convention), OJ 1995 C 316/2. Article 10 refers to safeguards set out in the Council of Europe Convention for the Protection of Individuals with regard to Automatic Processing of Personal Data, 1981, ETS No. 108.

[34] See Register Board II, 1999, p. 139 f.

[35] SOU 1997:65, p. 205.

[36] Ibid. According to section 19 of the Act on Special Monitoring of Aliens, the police are authorised to take fingerprints from foreigners, if the government or a court have so decided, and keep these in computerised files, if this is deemed necessary to find out if a foreigner, an organisation or a group this person belongs to or works for is planning or preparing a deed which involves violence, threats or force to achieve political goals, and this activity is an offence punishable by imprisonment for two or more years.

[37] SOU 1997:65, pp. 315–317.

[38] Prop 1997/98:97, pp. 152–154.

[39] Security Police, Annual Report for 1995/1996, p. 13. Espionage on behalf of a foreign power directed against refugees is a crime under Chapter 19, section 11 of the Criminal Code.

[40] Ibid. p. 10.

[41] It should be mentioned that during this period we know of only one case where a person was prosecuted and convicted as a result of the activity of the Swedish Security Police, namely a former Moroccan citizen who was spying on former countrymen on behalf of the Moroccan intelligence agency. During the same period three North Korean diplomats were declared persona non grata, when they had been caught trying to smuggle tobacco into Sweden. One Swedish businessman received a suspended sentence and a fine for breaching the Swedish law on export of war material. An Iraqi citizen, who had been living in Sweden for eight years, working as a doctor, was expelled in 1997. He was later allowed to return to Sweden on humanitarian grounds after a long and intensive debate in the Swedish mass media.

[42] According to the former chief of the Security Police, Anders Eriksson, there are 20 foreign organisations represented in Sweden which are regarded as terrorist by the Security Police. Those which are still active but do not necessarily use violence, at least not in Sweden, are: Sendero Luminoso and MRTA (Peru), Aissif, Harakat Ul Ansar and JKLF (India), FLNC (Corsica), ETA (Spain), LTTE (Sri Lanka), GIA (Algeria), PKK (Turkey), the provisional IRA (Northern Ireland), 17 November (Greece), FARC (Colombia), Abu Nidal, Islamic Jihad and PFLP-GC (Palestine) and finally Al Jama al Islamiya (Egypt).

[43] This explanation for the Security Police involvement in monitoring motorcycle gang criminality seems a bit thin to us. It certainly marks a departure from traditional Security Police targets. It can probably be explained partly by directives from the government, channelled through the NPB (there was a bloody feud between rival motorcycle gangs in Scandinavia during 1996 and 1997) and partly by post Cold War excess in capacity.

[44] SOU 1997:65, pp. 261–263.

[45] Security Police, Annual Report for 1998, pp. 3–4, 30 and 32–3 and SOU 1994:149, p. 110.

[46] For the history of the system, see, D. Töllborg, Personalkontroll, (Symposium, 1986). For the most recent research see D. Töllborg, Medborgerligt pålitlig? (Norstedts juridik, 1999).

[47] It should be noted that there is a requirement of Swedish citizenship for a number posts, inter alia, in the government, as a general director of an administrative agency, prosecutor, policeman or member of the armed forces. See Instrument of Government Chapter 11, section 9 and Public Employment Act (1994:260) section 5.6 Security vetting is take place before a person is employed or otherwise participates in, activities of significance to national security, or activities that are important regarding protection against terrorism.

[48] Security Protection Act section 17.

[49] Security Protection Act section 20.

[50] Security Protection Act section 17.

51 SOU 1994:149, p. 86, referring to SOU 1990:51, p. 233.
52 Säkerhetspolisen SA (Official Diary of the Security Police) 189–307–98.
53 SOU 1997:65, p. 260. The justification given for such a large number of posts being subject to vetting is national security – the 'total defence' policy of a state that pursued, and still, formally, pursues, a policy of neutrality. Still, we consider that the figures are still very high, even allowing for the need to screen, for anti-terrorism purposes, e.g. everyone working at international airports. Parallels might be drawn to another neutral state, Switzerland, which has had a 'fortress' mentality, but this is outside the scope of the present article. It can be recollected that part of the justification advanced by the Swedish government in the Leander case for the lack of adequate safeguards in the security system was that the number of posts covered was relatively small (verbatim record of the hearing in the Leander case, 26 May 1986).
54 A case concerning this problem has in August 2000 been forwarded to the European Court of Human Rights. For the Register Board criticism of this, see below, section 6.3.3.
55 A former senior judge (male), a serving senior judge (female) and an advocate (male).
56 Motion 1996/97:Ju918.
57 Even prominent social democrats have criticised the fact that no politicians who have taken a critical stance to the question of security files have been appointed to the Board. See H.G. Franck, 'SÄPO: Medborgarkommission behövs för att nå full klarhet', Advokaten nr 2/98.
58 Here one can note that simply providing an excerpt from a security file can give a misleading picture of the seriousness of a particular threat.
59 Ordinance with instruction for the Register Board (1996:730) section 9.
60 Security Protection Ordinance, sections 32 and 36.
61 See a recent decision of the Labour Court to this effect, AD 1999 nr. 17.
62 Register Board Report, 1998, p. 7.
63 See also in this respect, an interview from 1997 in the Swedish magazine Försvarets forum with the former chief of the Swedish Security Police, Anders Eriksson, 'we have a strategy aiming at allowing more insight into the work of the Security Police. I also work for a better democratic control over the Security Police, and think it is fair that there exists a special board to control us.'
64 Eriksson, ibid. gave his view on secrecy and openness: 'People who give information to the Security Police must have the same right to have their identities kept secret as those who give information to the mass media. Even the identities of those who work at the Security Police must be secret in order for them to be able to fulfil their duties.(On the other hand) There is also a lot of very interesting historical material in our archives, which I think people ought to be allowed to look into. With some few exceptions, we are not allowed to show this today.'
65 Ju2001/226/PÅ. For discussion of the issue in the travaux préparatoires see SOU 1997:65, pp. 101–102, 268–270 and 344–345.
66 Application No 62332/00, Ingrid Segerstedt-Wiberg et al v. Sweden.
67 See Prop 97/98:97, p. 68.
68 RÅ 2000, ref. 15.
69 Regeringsrättens underrättelse, mål nr 1808–2000.
70 See below, section 8, regarding the bureaucratic nature of the Swedish judiciary. For criticism of the system of appointment and training of senior judges see the Swedish Helsinki Committee.
71 SOU 1988:18, p. 30.

72 This was the conclusion of the Register Board in its report pp. 58–59. It did not consider that the same degree of political neglect had existed in Sweden, as compared to that revealed in Norway by the Lund Commission.

73 Hannah Arendt, 'Lying in politics, Reflections on the Pentagon Papers' in Arendt (1972).

74 There is an equivalent body with competence to monitor the work of the military intelligence agency, Försvarets Underrättelsenämnd, FUN, headed by a former minister of defence in a Conservative Government, Anders Björk.

75 See, e.g. L. Lustgarten and I. Leigh, In From the Cold, (Oxford, 1994) pp. 461–462.

76 There are five Ombudsmen, collectively known as the Ombudsman.

77 For a short discussion of the role of the Swedish judiciary in the protection of human rights, see I. Cameron, Protection of Constitutional Rights in Sweden, (1997) Public Law, p. 491.

78 See Svenska Dagbladet, 27 January 1999, which disclosed the information that a tap had been placed on the Gothenburg office of the Communist Party between 1953 and 1966, renewed every month.

79 SOU 1998:46, s 518.

Chapter 9

The Globalisation of Security and Intelligence Agencies: A Report on the Canadian Intelligence Community

Jean-Paul Brodeur

Introduction

The purpose of this paper is to present the structure of the Canadian intelligence community in its main aspects. The paper is divided into two parts. The first part deals with facts and thus provides a description of the Canadian security intelligence network in respect to its history, the main agencies of which it is comprised, and their respective mandates, budgets and manpower. In so doing, it addresses the normative issue of the transition of the Canadian security and intelligence apparatus to a more democratic stance, partly understood here as a move beyond the Cold War mentality. The second part is devoted to specific issues: the doctrine underlying the action of these agencies, their secrecy and accountability and the risks for human rights stemming from their activities.

The Canadian intelligence community has been the object of numerous scholarly descriptions, few of them being truly exhaustive. This is in part explained by the fact that the mechanisms for making the Canadian Security Intelligence Service (CSIS) accountable have been hailed as unique and have consequently been the focus of some interest both within Canada and outside of the country. In particular, the Inspector General and the Security Intelligence Review Committee were the object of a significant body of literature (see for example, Gill, 1989a, b and 1991; Lustgarten and Leigh, 1994; Lustgarten, 1995 and 1997; Robertson, 1989; Starnes, 1991). We feel in this regard no need to repeat in detail what is already well acknowledged in the literature. Instead, we shall focus on theoretical concerns in respect to the theory of accountability.

The issue of *secrecy* takes a new meaning in the context of sophisticated technology. In order to make a security agency accountable you must know at least that it exists; you also have to know what it actually does and can potentially do. Trying to assess what can be achieved through the use of electronic surveillance can be a complex undertaking even under the best of circumstances, when no wall of secrecy surrounds the technology being used and its power. When technological complexity, which is a problem in its own right, is cloaked in secrecy, determining its potential for abuse may raise insuperable difficulties.

Historical Background: The Quest for Democracy

The complexity of the Canadian national security apparatus is difficult to grasp without addressing aspects of its history. We shall say nothing of the Communications Security Establishment (CSE) in this general historical survey, because its history will be the object of a separate analysis below. Up until 1984, Canadian law made no difference between politically motivated crime and common delinquency. Consequently, it was the police who were tasked to protect the national security of Canada. Although some police forces played a key role in counter-terrorism,[1] it was the Royal Canadian Mounted Police (RCMP) which had the main responsibility for the repression of terrorism and of what was perceived to be political deviance (for example communism). Canada being a federation of ten provinces and two territories, the RCMP is the Canadian federal police force.

From 1910 to 1984, the RCMP was the political police in Canada and its Security Service (RCMP/SS) had the mandate to protect Canada's national security. The RCMP/SS eventually developed as a separate entity within the RCMP and increasingly abused its vast powers. From 1966 to 1981, there were no less than six major commissions of inquiry that investigated the RCMP's Security Service – the Wells Commission (Canada, 1966a), the Spence Commission (Canada, 1966b), the Mackenzie Commission (Canada, 1969), the Krever Commission (Ontario, 1980), the McDonald Commission (Canada, 1981a and b) and the Keable Commission (Quebec, 1981).[2] These abuses are also well documented in the literature (Brown and Brown, 1978; Dion, 1982; Mann and Lee, 1979; Sallot, 1979; Sawatsky, 1980, Whitaker, 1991).

During the height of Quebec terrorism (1968–1973), the RCMP/SS tried to destabilise all dissidence in Quebec, whether or not it advocated violence or resorted to it, through a program of aggressive 'disruptive tactics' patterned after the infamous FBI's COINTELPRO (Blackstock, 1976). These excesses, which were simultaneously investigated by two commissions of inquiry (Canada 1981a and b; Quebec, 1981), proved to be the RCMP/SS' undoing. Repeating a recommendation that had already been made by Commissioner Mackenzie in 1969, the McDonald Commission recommended that the RCMP/SS be abolished and replaced by a civilian (non-police) agency. The civilianisation of the RCMP/SS had one far-reaching implication. The fact that the members of the security intelligence agency to be created were *not* to be police meant that they were not to be granted *police powers.*[3] As expected, they were granted huge powers of intrusion in order to collect intelligence. However they were forbidden to act upon the intelligence that they had collected (for example to perform an arrest). For any operation that went beyond the collection, analysis and dissemination of intelligence, the new civilian agency was to rely on the police and, more particularly, on the RCMP. In other words, the civilian agency would be the brain of national security and the police the arm. Needless to say, neither the new agency nor the police were satisfied with this arrangement.

Canada has never officially developed a foreign intelligence capacity, at least with respect to HUMINT. In theory, it does not spy on its friends nor on its enemies: the standard belief is that Canada has no enemies except for the ones that it indirectly makes through the support of its allies, the US and the UK; as for spying on friends, it is as much distasteful in the eyes of Canadians as gentlemen reading each other's mail.

The National Security Apparatus

The Canadian national security apparatus is comprised of several components, which we shall briefly review.

The Government Bureaucracy

In 1987, the Security Intelligence Review Committee (SIRC), a body which we will later describe, issued a fairly lengthy paper on 'the security and intelligence network in the government of Canada' (SIRC, 1987). The paper is 60 pages long and although it is no longer accurate in its details, the broad picture that it provides is still valid. National security reaches into the highest levels of government such as the Cabinet and the Privy Council Office (PCO).[4] Its scope is comprehensive, several ministries having a stake in it, namely the ministry of the Solicitor General (the Canadian equivalent to the Home Secretary in the UK), the Ministry of Foreign Affairs, the Department of National Defence, the Ministry of Employment and Immigration, the Ministry of Transports, Customs and Excise and the

Ministry of Revenue. According to the SIRC document, each of these Ministries has an intelligence unit. However, it would be a mistake to confuse these units – most often consisting of a committee of bureaucrats – with a field agency. Nevertheless, the SIRC document is revealing of the scope of national security. Both the report of the Thacker Committee, which conducted in 1989–90 a review of the *CSIS Act*, and the report that presents the government's response to the recommendations of the Thacker committee offer an updated picture of the main government committees involved in policy-making in the field of security and intelligence (Canada, House of Commons [Thacker Committee], 1990: 44–45; Canada, Solicitor General, 1991: 52–53).

The Lead Agencies

The lead agencies are the bodies immediately responsible for the protection of Canadian national security. The best known of these agencies is the Canadian Security Intelligence Service (CSIS). CSIS is the civilian agency that replaced the RCMP/SS. The least known of these agencies, but no less important than CSIS, is the CSE.

The Back-up Agencies

The powers of CSIS were limited to the collection of intelligence, when it replaced the RCMP/SS in 1984. When the intelligence thus collected needs to be followed by law enforcement, CSIS must rely on police forces. Part IV of the *CSIS Act* is in itself a separate act (*Security Offenses Act*) and is devoted to solving the problems of law enforcement. Section 61 of the Act asserts that the primary responsibility for enforcing the law in respect to security offences lies with the RCMP, which is CSIS' main policing partner. Following the creation of CSIS, the Solicitor General of Canada issued ministerial direction spelling out the expected relation between the two agencies. In 1986, the RCMP/CSIS Liaison Officer Program was also established by ministerial direction and the Minister also approved a Memorandum of Understanding between the two agencies (Canada, Solicitor General, 1991:47). In order to meet its responsibilities, the RCMP created special units: National Security Enforcement Units (NSEU) which belong to the National Crime Intelligence Sections (NCIS).[5] Despite all the ministerial direction, the relationship between the two partners remains tangled and strained (Brodeur, 1991; Farson, 1991; Clèroux, 1990).

Depending on the seriousness of the problems it must face, the municipal police of a large city may develop significant expertise in policing politically motivated deviance. As was shown by an extensive report by SIRC, officers of the Toronto Metro police department worked closely with CSIS agents in monitoring the development of the far right and of racist activities in that city (SIRC, 1994). The difference between politically motivated violence and common criminality is increasingly blurred, as is shown by the example of narco-terrorism. Consequently there is an increasing interface between criminal and security intelligence (Farson, 1991). In the French-speaking province of Quebec, the provincial police (*Sûreté du Québec,* SQ), which would become the national police force of Québec in the event of the province's secession from Canada, has developed a security intelligence capacity of its own; because of the present political tensions between the governments of Canada and of Québec, the SQ is a reluctant partner of federal agencies such as CSIS, which may be spying on Quebec separatists.

Military and Other Agencies

Very little is known on this subject. According to SIRC (1987) there is a Chief for intelligence and security in the Canadian Armed Forces. There are two directors working under this chief, namely the Director General for Intelligence (DGI) and the Director General for Security (DGS). The DGI is assisted by 6 directorates (defence intelligence, current intelligence, imagery exploitation, intelligence plans and doctrine, scientific and technical intelligence and intelligence and security automation). This apparatus looks impressive on paper, but may not be as much in reality. Following the disastrous 1992–93 peace-keeping mission of the Canadian Forces in Somalia, the Canadian government appointed a commission of inquiry to report on this failed mission. The findings of the commission and of its researchers on the state of intelligence and security in the Canadian Forces were dismal. The Canadians were sent on this mission with almost no intelligence on the situation in which they were to intervene as peacemakers (Brodeur, 1997a: chapter 3).[6] Furthermore, the Armed Forces security units completely failed to assess the extent to which the Airborne regiment that was sent to Somalia was penetrated by extreme right-wing and racist elements (Canada, 1997: vol. II, c. 18 and Brodeur, 1997a).

Besides the military, there are other government agencies that harbour intelligence units. In the field of internal revenue, the departments concerned with the collection of taxes have acquired huge powers to compare the information contained in a large number of government data-banks. Because of a Canadian paranoia with social welfare and unemployment fraud, the relevant agencies have also been granted similar powers. This field of state surveillance is still very much a *terra incognita*, although we have good reason to suspect that much is happening there.

The Canadian Security Intelligence Service (CSIS)

In comparison to other intelligence services, there is no dearth of information on CSIS. The main source of information is to be found in the annual and special reports of SIRC. There are also other government reports, including CSIS' annual reports, CSIS' own public newsletter entitled *Commentary*, the *Report of the Special Committee on the review of the CSIS Act and the Security Offenses Act* (the Thacker Committee: Canada, 1990) and the agency's site on the Internet.[7] There is in addition an academic and an investigative literature on CSIS (for references, see Brodeur, 1997c).

CSIS: Its Mandate

The mandate of CSIS is defined in the *CSIS Act*. This mandate is threefold and is comprised of what we shall call a primary, a secondary and a problematic component.

The primary component: warning and advising the government on security threats According to section 12 of the Act CSIS' first duty is to collect, analyse and retain information respecting activities that may constitute a threat to the security of Canada and, in relation thereto, to report to and advise the government of Canada. The threats to the security of Canada are defined in s. 2 of the Act as (a) espionage or sabotage, (b) foreign influenced activities detrimental to the interests of Canada, (c) politically motivated violence (terrorism) and (d) subversion.

The problem with the mandate relates to the threats of category d (subversion). In Bill C-157, which initially attempted in 1983 to define the mandate of CSIS in Canada, subversion was defined thus:

> activities directed toward undermining by covert unlawful acts or directed toward or intended ultimately to lead to the destruction or overthrow of the constitutionally established system of government in Canada.

This definition of subversion raised a furore in Canada for it implied that any political agitation for constitutional change (for example, Quebec separatism) would fall within the ambit of CSIS' mandate, whether or not it was carried through peaceful, public and democratic means. The uproar was such that the government appointed a special committee of the Senate to propose amendments to Bill C-157. The Special Committee recommended that the clause 'by violence' by added after the word 'overthrow' (...*to lead to the destruction or overthrow* **by violence** *of the constitutionally established system of government in Canada*; Canada, Senate, 1983: 15, para. 40). This recommendation was accepted and the clause 'by violence' was duly added to s. 2 (d) of the *CSIS Act*. Although a significant victory for the rights and freedoms of Canadians, this amendment introduced some fuzziness into the definition of the security threats and, to this extent, into the mandate of CSIS. In particular, category 'c' and 'd' of the security threats overlap to a significant extent. This ambiguity was reflected in the operations of CSIS, which maintained for several years a counter-subversion arm. It was finally abolished in November 1987.[8]

The secondary component: security assessments According to s. 13 and s. 14 of the *CSIS Act*, the agency is to provide security assessments in support of the government's security clearance program and to provide information and advice in support of government citizenship and immigration programs. Enforcing s.13 of the Act implies vetting government employees and persons under contract. It also implies determining through interviews and investigations whether a person working for the government should be authorised to operate at a particular level of security clearance (there are many levels of security clearance, the higher levels giving access to classified information).

The problematic component: foreign intelligence Unlike Australia, for instance, Canada does not have a foreign intelligence service. CSIS is a domestic agency and, with the exception of liaison officers in a few other countries, it is tasked to operate in Canada. This is a problematic feature of the mandate of CSIS in several respects. Section 16 of the *CSIS Act* allows CSIS to conduct investigations on foreign states or groups thereof and on foreign citizens or corporations in relation to the defence of Canada or the conduct of the international affairs of Canada. This is alleged to be the basis for the activities of CSIS in the field of foreign intelligence (Canada, House of Commons, 1990:37; Canada, Solicitor General, 1991:35). However, s. 16 limits these investigations on foreign powers and their agents to take place *within Canada*. This limitation is perceived by many to be a contradiction in terms: CSIS can be involved in foreign intelligence, but only within Canada. Actually, CSIS has moved beyond this limitation. In response to a question by a member of the Thacker Committee as to whether the Service has legal authority to send officers outside Canada to gather intelligence, the Hon. Pierre Blais, who was then Solicitor General, answered:

> The answer to the question is clear and is based upon the nature of CSIS as a defensive security intelligence service. It does not seek to conduct offensive intelligence operations abroad. However, CSIS does have the power to investigate threats to the security of Canada. Under the Act we have not only the power but also the duty to send informants or Service employees abroad. It is a known fact, there is no secret about it. Our foreign operations always relate to investigations of a threat to Canadian security. That is something we must remember. (Canada, House of Commons, 1990:39)

The Canadian intelligence community resents the fact that Canada depends on its allies, most notably the US, for foreign intelligence. There have been repeated calls in Canada to create a foreign intelligence service or to give CSIS the mandate to become Canada's foreign intelligence service (Russell, 1988; also see Starnes, 1987). In particular the Thacker Committee recommended that the government consider the implications of enlarging the foreign intelligence mandate of CSIS by repealing the words 'within Canada' from s. 16 of the *CSIS Act*[9] (Canada, House of Commons, 1990:42). These calls have been so far resisted. According to our inquiries, the ministry of Foreign Affairs would view a foreign intelligence service as a threat to its turf. Intelligence activities are in theory openly performed by various diplomats and attachés through the network of the embassies, although neither the quantity nor the quality of the information thus provided were ever submitted to any kind of public appraisal.

The latest component: transnational crime   According to an operational audit of the CSIS conducted by SIRC (1999: 5), a 1993 Department of Justice legal opinion concluded that certain forms of transnational criminal activity could be construed to represent a threat to the security of Canada. Hence, they would fall within the legal ambit of CSIS' mandate. CSIS' involvement in countering transnational crime did not immediately result from this legal opinion. Yet, over the ensuing years, its involvement in this field of operation was increasingly made public through its public reports. The Cold War being all but ended, it is not surprising that organisations such as CSIS would be looking out for new 'markets' for its services (Brodeur, 2000).

Budget and Personnel

Interestingly enough the number of persons officially working for CSIS appears to have been a well kept secret until recently. In the course of this research, we consulted the budget estimates of the ministry of the Solicitor General from 1989 to the present time (Canada, Solicitor General, 1989–1997). Although the budget estimates also contain the size of the personnel with the budget figures of all mentioned agencies, it does not do so for CSIS.[10] However, the 1994 *Annual Report* of CSIS discloses the number of CSIS personnel from its creation in 1984 up until 1997–98. These figures were updated in each subsequent report and we now have projections for up until the year 2,000.[11] For certain years – and, in particular for the peak year of 1993–94 – the budgetary figures in the budget estimates of the Solicitor General and in the CSIS' annual reports do not coincide. According to the Solicitor General estimates, CSIS' budget peaked at 228.7 million in 1993–94, whereas the corresponding figure in CSIS' 1996 Annual Report is 244 million.

Budget CSIS' budget for 1997–98 is 165.6 million dollars (Can.).[12] In themselves, budgetary figures are not significant and have to be compared with other figures in order to reveal their meaning. For the same year, the budget of the RCMP is 1,201 billion dollars, the difference between the budgets of the two agencies being explained by the fact that the RCMP's manpower is ten times the size of CSIS'. The important finding that can be made in comparing the budgetary figures of CSIS with those of the RCMP and of the CSE is that the cuts in CSIS' budget have been and will be much more drastic than those affecting the RCMP and the CSE. We compared the RCMP's and CSIS' budget from 1987–88 to year 2,000, for which we have estimates. The RCMP's budget increased from 1987 to the peak year of 1992–93, after which it started to decline. CSIS' money increased from 1987 to its peak year of 1993–94, after which there was a marked decrease. Comparing the estimate for year 2,000 to its peak year of 1992–93, one finds a decrease of 13.9 per cent in the RCMP's budget. The same comparison yields a much higher decrease of 32.7 per cent for CSIS, using the estimates of the Solicitor General, and 37 per cent (rounded), using the figure given in CSIS' 1996 Annual report. Comparing the years 1995 to 1998 for CSIS and the CSE, it is found that CSIS' budget decreased 12 per cent between these years whereas the CSE's budget only went down by six per cent. What these figures are telling us is that the kinds of concern which fall under CSIS' mandate do not seem to have the same level of priority as what is covered by the respective mandate of the RCMP and of the CSE. Another explanation for the more significant decrease in the budget of CSIS is that its budget was provisionally increased to cover the cost of building new headquarters. Indeed from 1988–89 to 1995–1996, part of CSIS' budget was devoted to construction capital, this part being significant in the peak year of 1993–94. Both factors – the lower priority given to CSIS' activities and the cost of building new headquarters – played a part in the decrease of CSIS' budget but it is premature to assess which of the two played the greater part.

Personnel   As we previously said, information on the size of CSIS' personnel was withdrawn from various government reports as of recently. It is now available in its annual report and on the agency's Internet web site. The statistical curve representing the changes in the number of persons working for CSIS is shaped like a bell. The personnel of CSIS numbered 2,153 persons, three years after its creation in 1984. It reached its highest point in 1992 (2,760 employees), after which it started falling. It is now slightly over two thousand (2,030) and it is estimated that it will actually be two thousands persons in year 1999. The downsizing of the personnel reflects the budgetary cuts. In comparison, the civilian staff of the CSE remained fairly constant, as we shall see, even increasing between 1996–1997 and 1997–98.

The Communication Security Establishment (CSE)

In the opening of his classic book on the US National Security Agency – the agency devoted to the collection and analysis of signal (SIGINT) or communication intelligence (COMINT) – Bamford tells us that it is the most secret of all the publicly acknowledged US intelligence agencies (Bamford, 1982:15). This is still true today. In the second edition of his book on US intelligence, Lowenthal confirms Bamford's statement and provides an illustration for it by devoting only three pages of his book to the NSA (Lowenthal, 1992:134–36; the much more recent report of the US Congress Committee established to conduct a review of the whole US intelligence community devotes a whole chapter to the CIA (c. 6) and less than two pages to the NSA. See US, Congress, 1996: c. 6 and 11). The CSE is the Canadian counterpart of the NSA and is even less well known, no equivalent of Bamford's study having been published in Canada. The Hon.

Allen Lawrence, who was Solicitor General of Canada in 1979 under the short term government of Prime Minister Joe Clark, confided that he had never been told of the existence of the CSE when he was a Cabinet minister (Noël, 1989). In an arrogant display of disingenuousness, the diagram on the 'major component of the national security system' provided in the government's response to the Thacker Committee report does not even mention the CSE (Canada, Solicitor General, 1991:3).

The CSE and its Historical Background: A Failed Transition to Democracy

The history of the CSE is intertwined with that of the NSA and, albeit to a lesser extent, of its British counterpart, the Government Communications Headquarters (GCHQ). The first embryo of the NSA was a small US cipher unit – Military Intelligence 8 (MI-8) – created in 1917 by American-born Herbert Osborne Yardley. MI-8 remained active after the war under the rather melodramatic name of the Black Chamber. The Black Chamber enjoyed its greatest success in 1919 by breaking the code of previously intercepted Japanese radio messages. It was to continue its activities of interception and decoding of radio messages, Japan being a favourite target, until the new Secretary of State, Henry L. Stimson, who believed these activities to be highly illegal, cut off all funding of the Black Chamber by the State Department in 1929. Yardley's unit had to close and he retorted by writing a book in 1931 – *The American Black Chamber* – which proved embarrassing for the US government (Bamford, 1982:20–46).

Yardley fell in great disfavour in the US for having written this book and for threatening to retaliate with a second one, but he was recruited in 1941 by two Canadian mathematicians on a recruitment mission in Washington.[13] He was to recreate the equivalent of his US black chamber in Canada, during the war. His unit was first known by the name of the Canadian Examination Unit (XU) and it engaged in the same activities that Yardley[14] had previously pursued in the US – interception and decipherment of enemy communications; the French communications under the Vichy regime were a high priority target (Lester, 1998:111–112; also see St. John, 1984 and Wark, 1987). The XU became permanent and was eventually nested in the Canadian National Research Council, where it operated under the utmost secrecy as the Communications Branch of this council (CBNRC). The CBNRC continued to operate under this innocuous cover until 1974, when the true nature of its operations were disclosed on television by a Canadian Broadcasting Corporation (CBC) program – entitled *The Fifth Estate*. The following year, the CBNRC was transferred to the department of National Defence, where it became the CSE by Order-in-Council PC 1975–95. It is of paramount importance to stress that the government never went beyond the level of an order-in-council and that to this day there is no enabling legislation for the CSE. Even in 1975, the existence of the CSE was not publicly acknowledged; it was to be so acknowledged only in 1983 in the context of the public storm over Bill C-157 (the first CSIS Bill).

We must now briefly regress in time to review other weighty developments. After its abolition, Yardley's Black Chamber was succeeded by the Signal Intelligence Service (SIS). Although the SIS had intercepted Japanese messages that indicated that Pearl Harbour was to be attacked, it did not succeed in communicating this intelligence in time to counter the attack. After the US had entered the war, the SIS went through a thorough reorganisation, its name apparently changing by the week (Bamford, 1982:63 and ff.). The Americans were being prompted by the British who had acquired a vast expertise in cryptology and in the interception of radio communications. After the war, the US COMINT/SIGINT community went through a period of turmoil. On the one hand, its funding was drastically reduced and the community seemed to dissolve through fragmentation. On the other hand, important moves were being made. In 1947, the UKUSA Agreement between the US, the United Kingdom, Australia, Canada and New Zealand was signed. According to a report cited by Bamford (1982:399), the US was designated as the first party to this agreement and the other four nations as second parties. This agreement, which was never officially acknowledged (Bamford, 1982:392), split the globe between its signatories for the purposes of COMINT/SIGINT and brought the agencies of the participating nations under a single umbrella (on co-operation in the field of intelligence see, Richelson and Ball, 1985; Richelson, 1988 and 1990). Canada was awarded the Soviet Arctic. In the end, the importance of COMINT/SIGINT was recognised in the US and the NSA was created on November 4, 1952, by a Presidential Memorandum signed by President Harry Truman. Unlike the CIA, which was created by the *National Security Act of 1947*, the NSA was not created by legislation. The creation of the Canadian CSE followed a similar pattern. In the early seventies the CANAKUS agreement brought the US, the United Kingdom and Canada into a closer partnership for the collection of COMINT/SIGINT. The extent of the existing relationships between intelligence agencies was explicitly acknowledged in 1996 by the Aspin Commission, which was chartered by the US Congress in October 1994 to conduct a comprehensive review of American intelligence (United States, Congress, 1996). According to the Aspin Commission report, the 'general' existing relationships between the US and other countries in the field of

Security intelligence are the following (note that many of these relationships take their full meaning within the context of the collection of SIGINT):

- another country may agree to undertake collection and/or analysis in one area and share it with the US in return for the US reciprocating in another area;
- another country may permit the US to use its territory for collection operations in return for the US sharing the results of such collection;
- the US may help another country acquire a collection capability for its own purposes with the understanding that the US will be permitted to share in the results;
- joint collection operations may be undertaken with US intelligence officers working side-by-side with foreign counterparts;
- exchanges of analysts or technicians between the US and other services may occur; or
- the US may provide training in return for services rendered by the foreign service, for example translations of particular foreign languages, where a foreign service brings unique skills to the endeavour. (US, Congress, 1996:c. 12, p.2 of 4)

All of these relationships can be applied to describe the co-operation between the NSA and the CSE.

For the purposes of our general argument, Herbert Yardley is the emblematic figure of the beginnings of COMINT/SIGINT. Despite his short term in the Canadian XU, he should be considered the originator of both the NSA and the CSE. It is also important to stress that what was to become the CSE was originally founded by an American and staffed by British officers after the Yardleys' early dismissal in 1941 (see note 14). Whether the CSE ever succeeded to come into its own and rid itself of foreign tutelage is still very much an open question.

The CSE: Its Mandate

Since the CSE's mandate is not enshrined in any Canadian legislation and that the deepest secrecy shrouds this agency, there is considerable ignorance of its mandate. There is also a recurrent puzzlement over what it actually does pursuant to this mandate.

Canadian Privacy Law   One contentious issue concerns wiretaps. According to Part VI (*Invasion of Privacy*) of the *Canadian Criminal Code* (C.C.), the interception of interpersonal private communications – including telephone conversations – is a criminal offence. Only police officers and agents from CSIS can intercept private communications, but they have to get a judicial authorisation for the intercepted communications to be admissible as evidence in a court of law. A 'private' communication is legally protected *only if there is a reasonable presumption of its private nature*. Section 183 of the C.C. defines 'private communication' thus:

> 'private communication' means any oral communication or any telecommunication made under circumstances in which it is reasonable for the originator thereof to expect that it will not be intercepted by any person other than the person intended by the originator thereof to receive it.

There are further conditions for *telephone conversations* to be protected. Telephone conversations are defined in the C.C. as 'radio-based telephone conversations'. Such conversations are made through a device – a telephone – connected to a 'public switched telephone network', which is defined thus in section 183 of the C.C.:

> 'public switched telephone network' means a telecommunication facility the primary purpose of which is to provide a *land line-based* telephone service to the public for compensation. (our emphasis)

These definitions have significant implications with respect to the notion of privacy. A very thorny issue is whether the interception of private conversations carried by cordless or cellular telephone requires judicial authorisation. Not only are these conversations not transmitted through land lines, but because their interception is so easy to effect – all that is needed is low-cost electronic equipment sold in public stores – it would follow that there can be no reasonable presumption that these conversations are private. The Canadian courts have not yet produced consistent and comprehensive jurisprudence on this question. At the present time, the landmark case is *R. v. Solomon* (1996), which is a ruling by the Quebec Court of Appeal that was affirmed the following year by the Supreme Court of Canada. The Quebec Court of Appeal reversed a lower court ruling to the effect that telephone conversations made through or received by a cellular phone were not private conversations within the meaning of section

224 *Democracy, Law and Security*

183 of the C.C.[15] However, the substance of this case was not whether conversations using a cellular phone were private or not according to Part VI of the C.C. but whether the police ought to get a judicial authorisation to intercept such conversations. The Court of Appeal ruled that *even if* a conversation made from a cellular phone was not a 'private conversation' – a matter which the Court saw no need to settle –, its interception violated section 8 of the Canadian Charter of Rights and Freedoms, which protects Canadians against unreasonable search or seizure. The police therefore had to be authorised by a magistrate to carry the interception.[16] That much is clear: recordings by 'agents of the State' of conversations made from or received by a cellular telephone need to be judicially authorised in order to be admissible as evidence in a court of law. This restriction is of no real consequence for security intelligence organisations such as the CSE, because the intelligence collected by them is not intended for supporting public criminal prosecutions, which they systematically shy from. However, as the Court of Appeal did not decide whether such conversations were to be construed or not as private according to Part VI of the C.C., it is not clear whether their interception is *per se* illegal according to the privacy law. Hence, as long as it does not initiate court proceedings, the CSE may scoop up all the radio and other electronic emanations travelling through the air without violating any privacy law.

A further question would be to examine whether the CSE has the technological capabilities to intercept any telephone conversation – indeed any communication – through its antennas. If it did, we would be faced in Canada with the following legal predicament: if all communications can be intercepted by the CSE as easily as a citizen can intercept conversations on a cordless or cellular phone, then there might be no more reasonable assumption of privacy at all and the legislation making the intrusion upon 'private' communications into a criminal offence would be completely obsolete. There is a great deal of confusion in Canada on this subject. In a series of newspaper articles, a *Globe and Mail* journalist implied that the CSE could intercept **any** domestic telephone conversation that it wishes (Moon, 1991); in his book, Mike Frost, an ex-employee of the CSE, said that the CSE 'can pipe into a phone line without even having to plant a "bug" in it' (Frost and Gratton, 1994:21).

CSE's technical capabilities Because of the secrecy that surrounds the CSE, we cannot know what it is precisely tasked to do and what it actually does. It then becomes reasonable to assume it does everything that it technically can, *to some degree*. Agencies like the NSA and the CSE operate in a legislative vacuum and their only limitations are those of the technology that they use. We have used so far the acronyms – COMINT and SIGINT – to generally refer to the activities of NSA and the CSE. Here are their respective definitions, as stated in the US National Security Council Intelligence Directives (NSCID):

> COMINT: Communications intelligence; the interception and processing of foreign communications passed by radio, wire, or other electromagnetic means, and by the processing of foreign encrypted communications, however transmitted. Interception comprises search, intercept, operator identification, signal analysis, traffic analysis, cryptanalysis, decryption, study of plaintext, the fusion of these processes and the reporting of results. Excluded from this definition are the interception and processing of unencrypted written communications, press and propaganda broadcasts. (from NSCID No. 6, quoted in Bamford, 1982:620)

> SIGINT: Signals Intelligence; comprises communications intelligence (COMINT), electronic intelligence (ELINT),[17] foreign instrumentation signals intelligence (technical and intelligence information derived from the collection and processing of foreign telemetry, beaconry and associated signals), and information derived from the collection and processing of non-imagery infrared and coherent light signals. (From Senate Bill S. 2525, *National Intelligence Reorganisation and Reform Act of 1978*, quoted in Bamford, 1982:624)

Apart from the obvious fact that COMINT and ELINT are sub-categories of SIGINT, the one thing clearly standing out of these definitions is the emphasis on the *foreign* character of the communications and signals to be intercepted. This emphasis is directly connected to what is publicly disclosed about the mandate of agencies such as the CSE and the NSA and does not reflect an intrinsic limitation of the technology itself, which is blind to the fact that communications are taking place between US or Canadian citizens or between foreigners.

With respect to these definitions, our inquiries would indicate that the CSE collects COMINT and that in contrast with the NSA its activities do not cover the full spectrum of SIGINT. However, even limiting ourselves to COMINT, its definition does not rule out the interception of telephone conversations of the kind that is protected by the Canadian privacy laws: the definition of COMINT quoted above explicitly mentions the interception of communications passed by *wire*, 'wire' being used both to refer to telegraph and telephone communications. Since it does collect COMINT, has the CSE the technical means to intercept private telephone conversations? The answer to this question depends on the kind of channel through which the telephone communication is transmitted. If the communication is transmitted through a landline, as most non long-distance telephone communications are, it would seem that the CSE cannot intercept it by using its present technical means, which only pick up electromagnetic emanations travelling through the ether (as opposed to being transmitted through a cable).[18] This means that the CSE can intercept telephone communications by cordless, car and cellular phone and more generally all telephone conversations transmitted through microwave towers. Microwave towers are used for long-distance telephone communications both within one country or between two or more countries. When, however, the landlines are overloaded, telephone systems automatically switch from the landlines to microwave transmission. In sum, although landlines are technologically out of reach, the CSE can still intercept a great deal of the telephone traffic within Canada (all the microwaves communications) and all conversations between Canada and other countries. Even if microwaves transmit them, there is no question that the Canadian privacy laws protects a significant part of these conversations and that the CSE would need in theory judicial authorisation to intercept them.[19] As the trend is now to move from landlines to microwaves transmissions (car, cordless and cellular phones, not to mention electronic mail), the capabilities of agencies like the CSE or NSA to intercept private communications is ever increasing.

What the CSE should do according to its publicly stated mandate There is no enabling law for the CSE. Hence, what we call its publicly stated mandate was pieced together from public declarations by relevant authorities on the nature of the CSE's mandate. In 1991, the present director of CSIS, Mr. Ward Elcock, was deputy clerk for security and intelligence and legal counsel to the PCO. It was he who testified on the CSE before the Thacker committee who was reviewing the *CSIS Act* and related issues. Mr. Elcock's testimony was extremely cryptic. He stated the two component of the CSE's mandate, that is the protection of classified federal government communications and the collection of signals intelligence 'intended to provide the government with foreign intelligence on the diplomatic, military, economic, security and commercial activities, intentions, and capabilities of foreign governments, individuals and corporations' (quoted in Moon, 1991:A4). He added that the CSE collected radar and other emanations but he was 'not prepared to go into the operations of CSE beyond that, and how it may do that, *and where it may do it from*' (quoted in Moon, 1991a:A4, our emphasis). The last clause of Mr. Elcock's statement implies that the CSE operates from a variety of bases, which is indeed the case.

The closest thing to a statement of the mandate of the CSE is to be found in the response of the Canadian government to the Thacker Committee report (Canada, Solicitor General, 1992:54–55) and in the first report of the recently appointed CSE Commissioner, who performs the duties of an independent Inspector General (Communications Security Establishment Commissioner, 1997). Both statements closely parallel Mr. Elcock's testimony quoted above. The most explicit formulation is expressed in the first report of the CSE Commissioner:

> Today CSE is Canada's national cryptologic agency. In its SIGINT capacity, CSE collects and analyses foreign radio, radar and other electronic emissions; it is assisted in this activity by the Canadian Forces Supplementary Radio System (CFSRS), a component of the Canadian forces, which operates from a number of stations around the country.
>
> Through the provision of signals intelligence, CSE contributes to the government's foreign intelligence program. Foreign intelligence refers to information or intelligence about the capabilities, intentions or activities of foreign states, corporations, or persons in relation to the defence of Canada or the conduct of international affairs. It may include information of a political, economic, military, scientific or social nature that could have security implications.
>
> Through its ITS program, CSE provides technical advice, guidance and service on the means of assuring government telecommunications security and on aspects of electronic data processing security. CSE's objective is to help the federal government achieve an appropriate level of security for its telecommunications and automated information systems. CSE meets this objective by providing departments with both the means and advice to ensure the protection of classified and designated information. In this capacity, the service provided by CSE is intended to prevent access to sensitive information carried on government telephone and computer systems by any unauthorised person or organisation, and to protect the integrity and availability of government information. (CSE Commissioner, 1997:5–6)

The CSE is then responsible for two programs. Of these two programs – the defensive ITS and the more aggressive COMINT/SIGINT – it is clearly the first one on which the CSE is willing to give public information. For instance, the CSE's Internet Web[20] site is entirely devoted to its ITS program and does not even mention COMINT/SIGINT.

As mentioned above, the CSE is assisted in its operations by the CFSRS, which operates from a number of stations around Canada. The two main stations are the ALERT base in Ellesmere Island in the Arctic and Leitrim in the province of Ontario; the training school for the CSE is at the Armed Force base of Kingston. There are also stations in Argentina and Gander (Newfoundland), in Moncton (New Brunswick), in Deben (Nova Scotia), in Grande-Prairie (Alberta), Ladner and Masset (British Columbia), Whitehorse (Yukon), Frobisher Bay and Inuvik on the coast of the Beaufort Sea in the Arctic. Canada has also a listening station in Bermuda (Frost and Gratton, 1994:35). The stations of Gander and Masset are linked with the US Navy Bullseye network (Lester, 1998:117).

What the CSE actually does Although it does not publish an annual report, we must at least presume that the CSE does everything that falls within the scope of its publicly stated mandate. Its Internet Web site does invite government departments and private corporations to participate in its ITS program, which then cannot be conceived as just a smoke screen. The situation in respect to its COMINT/SIGINT program is more difficult to assess. The CSE's mandate puts an emphasis on *foreign* intelligence and excludes any domestic spying on Canadian citizens. However, it was claimed in 1984 that the CSE compiled national security files on individuals. This claim was made on the basis of an examination of the official federal index of personal information data banks, which said that a CSE data bank contained 'personal information relating to sensitive aspects of Canada's international relations and defence', this information being used 'to advise the Government with respect to international affairs, security and defence' (Sallot, 1984). As the information stored in the data bank is highly classified, there is no way to know whether the information it contains is limited to foreign individuals or whether there are files on Canadian citizens. There have been numerous allegations that the CSE spied on Canadian citizens (Sallot, 1984; Noël 1989; Moon, 1991a,b and c; Frost, 1994; Lester, 1998). Excluding for the sake of discussion that the CSE is or was deliberately flaunting Canadian law, how can the CSE legally spy on Canadians? There are two main ways of doing it. The first one has actually been officially acknowledged by Mr. Ward Elcock when he testified before the Thacker Committee: in intercepting foreign communications, the CSE may 'incidentally' and only 'on rare occasions' learn something about Canadian citizens. How incidental and rare are these occasions cannot at the present time be assessed. The other way of doing it has been strenuously denied by the CSE, although it keeps surfacing in what ex-CSE officers are saying to the media or, in one case, in a book (Frost, 1994). These officers stress the fact that the CSE is part of a pool of agencies, linked through UKUSA, CANAKUS or other such agreements. The agencies thus linked have the technological capability of intercepting communications on the territory of its other partners. Hence, Canada can intercept communications transmitted in the US and vice-versa. Since these agencies share at least a part of the intelligence that they collect, they can easily trade intelligence on their respective nationals, thus circumventing the privacy laws in force in their own country. This trading of intelligence is not limited to countries that have signed an intelligence sharing agreement. For instance, Frost (1994:241) reports that the Norwegians intercepted telex communications between France and Quebec, after the separatist party headed by René Lévesque won the provincial Quebec elections in 1976.

The truth of these allegations was denied by the CSE. In view of other pronouncements by the CSE, it would seem that these denials are in great part perfunctory. We previously quoted a Privy Council official – Mr Ward Elcock – to the effect that he would not testify on wherefrom the CSE may conduct its communications interceptions. It is generally assumed that these interceptions are conducted from stations located on Canadian territory and serviced by the CFSRS. This assumption has been put in serious doubt by the allegations of ex-employees of the agency. For instance, Ms. Jane Shorten employed by the CSE as an analyst by the CSE from 1986 to 1994 declared on TV and in the written press that she spied for the CSE on friendly countries such as South Korea, Mexico and Japan (Canadian Press, 1995). Ms. Shorten did not indicate from where she conducted eavesdropping on friendly governments. However, another long-time employee of the CSE, Mr. Mike Frost, co-authored a book on its activities for the CSE (Frost and Gratton, 1994). Frost and Gratton described several operations – code names: Stephanie, Julie, Daisy, Sphinx and Pilgrim – that were conducted in Canadian embassies or consulates in the former USSR (Moscow, at least twice), Venezuela (Caracas), the Ivory Coast (Abidjan), Morocco (Rabat), Rumania (Bucharest), Brazil (Brazilia) and Costa-Rica (San José). Most of these operations were instigated by the NSA and to a lesser extent by the GCHQ (Frost and Gratton, 1994:40). The NSA considers the CSE as part of its organisation and in the case of the Arctic base Alert on Ellesmere Island it provided the money, the expertise and the equipment. It also gave the orders and Frost and Gratton refer to an 'abrogation' of Canadian sovereignty in respect to the ALERT base (Frost and Gratton, 1994:14 and 41–43). Frost and Gratton (1994:234–239) also recount an operation that was conducted in London (UK) at the instigation of Prime Minister Thatcher who suspected that two of her Cabinet ministers were not 'on side'. As the GCHQ could not chance spying on British government ministers, it made a request to the CSE to this effect; the CSE obliged the GCHQ and conducted the operation from an intercept post inside Canada's McDonald House in London.

Needless to say, the Canadian government again denied the truth of these allegations. The CSE's ex-employees never recanted, stressing that they had personally partaken in the operations they described. Given the wealth of details provided on these operations, particularly in Frost and Gratton (1994), it is difficult to believe that all the information is fabricated unless some of the CSE's ex-employees are involved in a large-scale operation of deception. Although these ex-employees may exaggerate the rogue character of the CSE's operations out of vindictiveness, the broader picture that they provide – the use of Canada's embassy network and the crucial role played by Canada's main allies, the US and the UK – is according to our own verifications true (or was until very recently).

The paranoia generated by the secrecy that shrouds such an agency as the CSE and its partners in the UKUSA agreement was vividly exemplified by the recent ECHELON affair. According to a report solicited in 1998 by the European Parliament and echoed in Canada, there is an internationally co-ordinated electronic surveillance system (ECHELON) that intercepts global land-based and space-based communications networks such as the Internet and telephone, data, cellular, fax and email transmissions, regardless of whether they are communicated through satellite, microwave, cellular or fibre-optic channels. According to an article quoted on the *Wired News* Internet site, 'by co-ordinating across national boundaries, governments can monitor each other's traffic and circumvent laws prohibiting governments from spying on their own citizens'.[21] The American Civil Liberties Union launched the *Echelon Watch*, following the disclosures contained in the report to the European Parliament.

We quoted the *Wired News* article because it tells us anew something that was publicised by the media and officially denied by the governments implicated at least since 1991 in Canada and since 1988 in the US (Moon, 1991a, b and c): members of the UKUSA agreement use fellow members of the covenant to spy on their own citizens (see our remarks above). Actually, there is almost nothing known about ECHELON that goes beyond the standard information fare on the activities of the UKUSA allied agencies. The one striking and ominous exception is a list of key words, which triggers the interception of any communication containing one of the words in that list.[22] Apart from this detail, ECHELON is as far as we can know little else than a belated discovery in Europe (and in Australia) of the activities of the UKUSA agencies, with the attendant mediatization of this 'sudden' awareness in the rest of the Western democracies. These remarks do not imply that ECHELON is a benign threat to privacy rights, but rather that this threat has been with us for the past ten years, at the very least.

Budget and Personnel

Both the budget and personnel of the CSE are difficult to estimate, because the agency has two components. The first component is comprised of the civilian experts who perform a variety of tasks ranging from cryptology to covert operations. The second component consists of the military who operate the CFSRS.

The budgetary figures given by the Department of National Defence are respectively 123.85 million dollars for year 1995–96, 117.14 million for 1996–97 and 115.7 million for 1997–98 (Canada, Department of National Defence, 1997). For the same years, the figures concerning the CSE's personnel are respectively 911, 870 and 892. Unfortunately, neither the budgetary nor the personnel figures for the military side of the CSE (CFSRS) are to be found as such in the National Defence estimates. Lester (1998:115) quotes figures that a CBC journalist was able to get through the Canadian legislation on the access to information: for year 1994–95 the budget of the military arm of the CSE was estimated at 81.3 million, whereas the civilian arm was costing 113 million. The total budget of the CSE for year 1994–95 would then be 194.3 million, as compared with 182.8 million for CSIS for the same year.[23] As we already noted, the decreasing trend in their respective budgets is steeper for CSIS than for the CSE. It would then seem that in terms of budget, the CSE is and will be the primary security agency in Canada. With respect to personnel, the figure most often cited for the CSE's total civilian and military staff revolves around 2,000 persons. This figure coincides with the present and projected staff of CSIS.

Questions and Issues

Focusing on CSIS and the CSE, we will now review issues that are pertinent to a discussion of the activities of security intelligence agencies in Canada. Four issues will be discussed, namely the present *doctrine* of the Canadian intelligence community, *accountability* and *secrecy*, which will be jointly addressed, and *human rights* violations. In the context of this paper, 'doctrine' is used as in 'military doctrine' and refers to a set of principles which are taught at the CSIS and CSE academies and transmitted throughout these organisations. They jointly determine their world outlook and their framework for defining Canada's national security problems and for solving them.

CSIS: The Doctrine

We shall begin with CSIS, on which we have much more information than on the CSE. The report of the House of Commons review committee on the *CSIS Act* is entitled *In Flux But Not In Crisis*. This report was published in 1990 and the hearings of the Committee took place in 1989–90. The Berlin wall having collapsed by the end of 1989, there were strong intimations of a thaw in the Cold War, even if the USSR had not yet dissolved. Although it would have been a most appropriate forum to reassess the role and mandate of Canadian security and intelligence agencies in the post-Cold War period, the Committee did not at that time appreciate how pressing this reassessment had become. If the report were to be written today, its title might be 'Adrift and In Jeopardy'.

I will briefly recount a story that I told elsewhere in detail (Brodeur, 1997b) and which indicates that CSIS is presently operating in a doctrinal vacuum. In 1994 I was president of the Canadian Association for the Study of Intelligence and Security (CASIS) and also director of a research centre that specialised in issues of intelligence and security. With the help of two other colleagues, I put together in 1995 a workshop on the theme of 'Canadian needs in security intelligence in the post-Cold War era and their consequences for the future role of CSIS'; this workshop was a follow-up for the benefit of CSIS, which had agreed to participate in it, of an international conference organised by CASIS in 1994. The 1995 workshop was not open to the public and in addition to members from CSIS its participants were academic experts (a minority), police and civilians with a knowledge and a practical experience of intelligence and security (a member of SIRC, a former Solicitor General of Canada, a former member of PCO). Needless to say, all the persons invited to the workshop were above suspicion with regard to leaking its proceedings. The workshop was scheduled to begin on Monday 15 May 1995. On Friday 12 May at the very end of the working day (17h00),[24] a senior officer reached me in my office to tell me that all CSIS members had been ordered to withdraw from the workshop. The alleged reason for CSIS' withdrawal was that the questions prepared for the different sessions of the workshop (in short briefing notes) addressed issues unresolved within the Service. It was not prepared to discuss these issues within the forum provided by the workshop, which allowed for external input. Since the workshop had been explicitly put together for CSIS, the agency's withdrawal precipitated its cancellation. Among the many lessons to be drawn from this incident, we will stress only one: the inner core of the intelligence community – which includes CSIS, its respondents within PCO and the CSE – had not succeeded in 1995 in defining its new mandate, such a redefinition being the essential topic of the workshop. This situation, we believe, has not substantially improved even today.

This being acknowledged, there are indications of CSIS' priorities.

Counter-terrorism When SIRC held a workshop on the mandate of CSIS in September 1992, the agency was devoting about 60 per cent of its efforts to counter-terrorism, according to Raymond Protti who was then its director. According to a June 1998 submission by the director of CSIS to the Canadian, this figure has remained exactly the same until today (CSIS, 1998b). Given the fact that there are very few acts of terrorism perpetrated on Canadian soil, CSIS' involvement in counter-terrorism needs to be explained. The explanation presented by CSIS is that Canada respects its international commitments and, most crucially, its commitment to the US. Terrorism being transnational, Canada can be a crucial link in setting up an operation that will ultimately be carried in another state.[25] Thus the importance of curbing the action of foreign terrorist organisations on Canadian territory, even if Canada is not the target of their action.

Weapons proliferation This aspect of CSIS' activities is related to its traditional mandate (counterterrorism). It is given a new urgency by the threat of nuclear terrorism, which is perceived to be very real.

Trans-national criminal activities We would list under this label all the interfaces between politically motivated deviance, which falls under the traditional mandate of the intelligence and security services, and organised crime (particularly drug trafficking), which is claimed by these agencies to be within the scope of a renewed mandate. When the Department of

National Defence recently purchased new submarines from the UK, it partly justified their usefulness as a means to intercept boats running drugs into Canadian shores.

Economic intelligence   This is perhaps the most hotly debated subject around which there is considerable confusion (Lowenthal, 1992:90–91; Potter, 1998). There is now a consensus that CSIS and other agencies should perform at least a defensive role in this regard. For instance, they are fighting against industrial espionage and briefing private corporations on how to avoid being spied on during business travels to certain countries. The CSE offers through its ITS program advice on communications protection and private industry can be admitted to parts of this program. The really thorny question is the development of an offensive capacity. Two difficulties are frequently mentioned. First, security agencies operate by definition on behalf of the State and not of private industries; because of the number of businesses involved in the development of new technology, equal treatment from security and intelligence agencies could not be provided to every one of them. Second, there is the even more difficult question of the foreign corporations operating in Canada. If, for instance, a Japanese company operates several car plants in Canada, should it then be made privy to intelligence on the US automobile industry that might be collected by a Canadian security and intelligence agency? Such companies may argue that they contribute as much to the Canadian economy as the national corporations and that consequently they are entitled to the security and intelligence agencies' services, when they engage in economic intelligence. These issues are far from being resolved.

Foreign intelligence   This is a telling issue for Canada since the country does not legally have a foreign human intelligence capability. Again two questions come to the foreground. First, the Thacker Committee, in line with many Canadian intelligence experts, recommended that the *CSIS Act* be modified to allow the Service to operate abroad as a full-fledged intelligence agency (Canada, House of Commons, 1990:42–43, rec. 19–24). These recommendations have not so far been acted upon. Second, in view of the disclosures and persistent rumours about the CSE's foreign operations, a report or a White Paper should be tabled before Parliament describing the present involvement of all Canadian intelligence agencies in foreign intelligence. This would allow the present debate on foreign intelligence to proceed in a more judicious fashion.

Needless to say, CSIS will continue to perform its legal duties in counter-intelligence, the screening of immigrants and the vetting of government employees through the process of security clearance.

CSIS: Accountability and Secrecy

As we previously said, there is a significant amount of literature on this subject, because the accountability mechanisms for CSIS are fairly elaborate and in stark contrast with the relative lack of controls over the CSE. The basis of our description of the structure of accountability for CSIS rests in great part on a very detailed presentation of this structure, which is to be found in Canada (House of Commons, 1990 – the Thacker Committee report) and in Canada (Solicitor General, 1991 – the government's response to the Thacker report).

The Thacker report makes a distinction between accountability and control (Canada, House of Commons, 1990:83, section 8.1). Accountability is viewed as an information process through which an agency is made answerable for the activities for which it is responsible. In other words, being accountable means to provide accurate answers. Control is the set of constraints from various sources under which an agency is labouring. This set of controls is *open*, because new constraints may be introduced pursuant to the provision of answers by an agency, which may indicate a new problem to be solved (Stenning – 1995:50–57 – also distinguishes between accountability and control). Although we also argued for this distinction (Brodeur, 1997:200), holding on to it in the context of this presentation would only make it more ponderous. Consequently, we will present at the same time instruments of accountability and of control. Generally speaking, the exercise of control by the responsible authorities is dependent upon their being truly informed; it entails for the official in a position of authority the power to request needed answers and for the agency under such authority the obligation to provide them. Control is a top down process, whereas accountability is bottom up. This being said, the instruments for making CSIS accountable and for controlling it are the following.

Internal accountability: the minister Subsections 6(1) and 6(2) of the *CSIS Act* state that the Director of CSIS is under the authority of the Solicitor General, who may issue written directions to him. In addition to his power of issuing policy guidelines, the Minister also exercises his authority through the power of approval. Under the normal rules of government, the Minister must be consulted for all important matters related to his portfolio.

In addition, the *CSIS Act* stipulates that the Minister must personally approve (i) all CSIS applications for judicial warrants, (ii) all CSIS arrangements with other federal agencies and departments, provincial authorities, and foreign governments and (iii) the nature of the assistance to be provided by CSIS in the collection of foreign intelligence in Canada. The Minister is himself accountable to Parliament.

Internal accountability: the deputy minister   Section 7 of the *CSIS Act* stipulates that CSIS' director must consult with the Deputy Minister on the general operational policies of the Service and on any other matter with respect to which a ministerial direction makes consultation with the Deputy mandatory.

Internal accountability: committees   In the spirit of the McDonald report recommendations which distinguished between levels of intrusiveness in investigative techniques and requested that the levels of authorisation within the government be consonant with the levels of intrusiveness, two important committees were established, namely, the Target Approval and Review Committee (TARC) and the Warrant Review Committee (WRC). TARC consists of senior CSIS officers and representatives of the ministries of Justice and of the Solicitor General. Its role is to authorise the targeting of special individuals for specified periods of time and to approve the use of various investigative techniques, including the use of human sources which does not require a judicial warrant and can lead to the most serious abuses. The WRC reviews CSIS warrant applications under Part II of the *CSIS Act*. The WRC is chaired by the Director of CSIS. Other members include the Assistant Deputy Solicitor General for the Police and Security Branch, senior members of the Department of Justice and an 'independent counsel' engaged by the Justice Department.

   Despite the elaborate aspect of these control mechanisms, a word of caution is not out of place here. According to our own research based on government reports on electronic surveillance, the number of authorisations given to CSIS for the interception of voice transmissions was in excess of 200 each year after its establishment in 1984, including new and renewed warrants. As we shall see, voice interception is not the only form of intrusion for which CSIS may require judicial authorisation. It thus follows that the number of warrants applications may be well over 200 every year. Persons such as the Director of CSIS and other senior civil servants sitting on the WRC are generally quite busy. It can be questioned whether a committee staffed with such members really has the time to do more than perform an assiduous rubber-stamping of all these warrants applications.

Internal control: the Inspector General The role of the Inspector General (IG) is specified by s. 30 of the *CSIS Act*. This officer is responsible to the Deputy Minister and its functions are threefold: the IG monitors the compliance by the service with its operational policies; he or she reviews the operational activities of the Service and, finally, submits 'certificates' to the Minister. Subsection 33(1) of the Act obliges the Director of CSIS to submit a report to the Minister at least every year and also, upon a specific demand by the Minister, reports on the operations of CSIS. A copy of the report(s) is given to the IG, who must inform the Minister in written certificates on the extent of his or her satisfaction with the Director's report(s), particularly in three respects: (a) whether any act or thing done by the Service was not authorised by the *CSIS Act*, (b) contravened any directions issued by the Minister or (c) involved any unreasonable or unnecessary exercise of the powers of CSIS.

The role of the IG is aptly summarised in Canada (Solicitor General, 1991: 21): 'the Inspector General conducts independent internal reviews for the Minister'. The Solicitor was lied to so many times by the former RCMP/SS that it was felt that the Minister needed to have additional eyes and ears, the IG performs this role for the Minister to whom he or she has direct access. The fact that the IG is the shadow of the Minister on CSIS may be a bad omen for its independence and was criticised by Lustgarten, who stressed that 'the IG is neither a whistle blower nor in any sense an avenue of public accountability' (Lustgarten, 1995:174). This criticism is in part justified by the fact that no document originating from the IG is public. However, saying that the IG is not *in any sense* an avenue of public accountability overstates the case. The IG may be an *indirect* avenue of public accountability through his or her working relationship with SIRC, which definitely is such an avenue. According to ss. 33(3) of the *CSIS Act*, the IG's certificate must be transmitted to SIRC, which may then direct the IG to conduct a review of specific activities of the Service (s. 40 of the Act). A diligent IG – as Dr. Richard Gosse, the first IG, was reputed to be – may include something in his certificate with a view of having it bounced back to him by SIRC for further inquiry. As such an inquiry would now be under the direction of SIRC, its findings may publicly disclosed.

Another problem is caused by the limitations on the IG's access to all the information needed to perform his or her functions. The IG has access to any relevant information from CSIS and may interview any of its members. However, he or she was not granted access to the 'confidences of the Queen's Privy Council for Canada', that is to the Cabinet documents. Both Dr. Gosse and Professor Peter Russell, who was director of research for the McDonald Commission, testified before the Thacker Committee that this limitation was crippling (Canada, House of Commons, 1990:145). The Committee eventually recommended to amend the *CSIS Act* so that the IG be granted a right of access to all Cabinet documents under the control of CSIS (recommendation 76). This recommendation was not followed by the government.

Judicial control The powers of CSIS to collect intelligence and to conduct investigations are quite extensive and they are far from limited to the interception of audio communications. Under the *CSIS Act*, the Service may intercept any communication or obtain any information, record, document or thing [ss. 21(2) c and ss. 21(3)]. For achieving these ends, it may (a) enter any place or open or obtain access to any thing (for example it may open mail); (b) search for, or return, or examine, take extracts from or make copies of or record in any other manner the information, record, document or things; (c) install, maintain or remove any thing (ss. 21(3) a, b and c of the Act). These powers can only be exercised under judicial authorisation (s. 21 of the *CSIS Act*). This is a fairly elaborate process implying pre-screening mechanisms such as TARC and the WRC. As was shown in Brodeur (1997c:88), the number and duration of the authorisations both decreased after 1984, when these authorisations began to be granted by the Federal court. Before 1984, these authorisations for intruding upon privacy were granted to the RCMP/SS by the Solicitor General of Canada under the *Official Secrets Act* (OSA). From 1976 to 1983, 3,369 warrants were granted by the Minister, that is a mean of 421 per year, with an average duration of 253 days.[26] From 1985 to 1996, a sum total of 1491 warrants were signed by the judges of the Federal court, the yearly mean being 124 and the average duration 192 days. We should hail SIRC's warning in deriving a naively optimistic interpretation of these data. SIRC is 'concerned that aggregate warrants statistics under the *CSIS Act* do not give as accurate a picture of the level of intrusive activities as did the statistics that used to be published under the *Official Secrets Acts*' (SIRC, 1987:11). For example, the Solicitor General's reports on electronic surveillance gives both the number of applications for warrants and the number of refusals, whereas the CSIS' statistics do not reveal the number of refusals.[27] More importantly, we cannot directly compare the number of authorisations given before and after 1984. Under the OSA, each warrant authorised the use of only one covert technique – in general electronic audio surveillance – against only one target. Under the *CSIS Act* one warrant can authorise the use of many devices against many targets. Such warrants contain 'basket clauses', according to which an individual whose name is not mentioned in the warrant authorisation may be submitted to intrusive techniques of investigations if an on-going inquiry shows that he or she is suspiciously connected to the original target of the warrant (SIRC, 1987:10). SIRC submitted proposals to close the loopholes in the judicial control and to get the Service to provide more detailed information on the warrants granted by the Federal Court to the Thacker Committee in its 1989 review of the *CSIS Act* (SIRC, 1989b:6–7). Although these proposals were retained in the Thacker Committee's report (Canada, House of Commons, 1990:121–124), they were ultimately rejected by the government in its response.

External review: the Security Intelligence Review Committee SIRC is the independent review body that was created to oversee CSIS, following the recommendations of the McDonald report (Canada, 1981a and b). SIRC consists of a Chairperson and between two to four other members. All appointments are made after consultation between the government and the opposition parties that have at least twelve elected members in Parliament (*CSIS Act,* s. 34). This consultation usually results in the fact that multi-partisanship is respected in the appointments to SIRC. SIRC also has a small staff that is headed by a director of research.

SIRC acts mainly in two ways. It reviews the performance of the Service (s.38), specifically in order to ensure that its activities are carried out in accordance with the *CSIS Act* and, more generally, according to the rule of law (s.38 and s. 40). This oversight function is performed by reviewing, among other things, CSIS' annual reports, the Certificates of the IG, Ministerial direction, CSIS arrangements with domestic and foreign governments and agencies, CSIS' regulations and, finally, reports that may be submitted by the Director of the Service on unlawful conduct on the part of its members. SIRC also acts as a complaint board that receives and investigates complaints from citizens against the service (s. 41). In this capacity, SIRC receives two different kinds of complaints: complaints with respect to 'any act or thing done' by the Service and complaints concerning denials of security clearances, and denials of citizenship or of permission to immigrate to Canada based on security considerations. SIRC's action is not only triggered by an external complaint or demand, as it can conduct inquiries out of its own initiative or directs the Service or the IG to conduct such inquiries (s. 40). SIRC submits an annual report on its activities and findings to the Solicitor General of Canada, who must table it in Parliament within 15 days of its reception (s. 53). SIRC is the sole master of the content of its annual report and of determining what part of its findings is going to be publicly disclosed. However, when SIRC conducts a special inquiry, it is the Solicitor General who ultimately decides what part of its report is going to be made public (s. 54; see Lester – 1998: 18 – for criticism of this feature). From 1984 to 1989, SIRC has forwarded 15 section 54 reports to the Minister, three of who were based either in whole or in part on reports that the IG had been directed to submit to the Committee.

SIRC's powers of investigation are considerable: it is granted access to any information under the control of CSIS, or its Inspector General or any deputy head that controls the access to information relevant to a SIRC inquiry (s. 39). Furthermore, SIRC can require from any member of CSIS (verbal) explanations deemed necessary for the performance of its duties and functions (s. 39). However, SIRC is barred from access to the Cabinet documents – 'the confidences of the Queen's Privy Council for Canada' – just as much as the IG is [ss. 39(3)]. *Per contra*, all members of SIRC and its staff are held to the strictest code of confidentiality in relation to the information that is not publicly disclosed in its reports. This requirement is particularly stringent in connection to the disclosure of the identity of a CSIS operative or informant (s. 18). Since its establishment in 1984, SIRC has not been publicly known to be embroiled in any security leak.

There is one particular feature of the *CSIS Act*, which deserves a discussion, despite its technicality. All members of SIRC are selected among Privy Councillors and cannot belong either to the House of Commons or the Senate during their tenure (s. 34). The Privy Council is the Prime Minister's own ministry. In order to belong to it, one must have been elected to Parliament. All government ministers belong *ex officio* to the Privy Council. A Privy Council member retains his or her title after returning to private life. Hence, there is a pool of Privy Councillors who no longer sit in the House and have not been appointed to the Senate from which the members of SIRC are selected. They may belong to any political party that once formed the government (with the exception of minority governments which are infrequent in Canadian politics, all past Canadian government have been formed either by the Liberals or the Progressive-Conservatives). This makes it at least possible to have a bi-partisan representation among the members of SIRC. A person may be appointed to the Privy Council by an order of the Governor in Council (the government), although this is rather exceptional.[28] In this latter case, any appointment of a member of the *Official Opposition* to the Prime minister's ministry – the Privy Council Office – is politically ruled out. This did not forbid the appointment of members from the New Democratic Party (NDP) to the PCO, since the NDP never had enough elected MPs from its ranks to form the official Opposition. Nevertheless, this condition has so far excluded MPs from the *Bloc Québécois* (BQ) or from the Reform Party (RP) from being appointed to SIRC, both of these parties having formed (the BQ) or presently forming (the RP) the Official Opposition in the federal House of Commons.

The largely unforeseen consequence of this requirement of being a Privy Councillor for membership of SIRC was to create a serious gap between SIRC and Parliament after the elections of 1993 and of 1997. In the 1993 election, one of the two traditional Canadian political parties – the Tories – was not only swept from government but very nearly extinguished, its representation going from 157 MPs to only two. With only one exception, all members of the new opposition parties had never been previously elected to Parliament. *A fortiori*, had they also never been part of any past government with the title of minister. Consequently, there was *no one* from these new opposition parties that had belonged to the Privy Council, nor was there anyone that could be exceptionally appointed by the newly elected Liberal government, which would not appoint political opponents to the PCO. The ultimate result of this predicament was that the new opposition parties – the RP and the BQ – were not represented within SIRC. The situation has remained essentially the same after the 1997 election, the only difference being that it is now the RP instead of the BQ which is forming the official Opposition to the Liberal government. This was not an auspicious context for a partnership between SIRC and the Sub-Committee on National Security, which was then the instrument of parliamentary control.

Some government documents stress that 'SIRC's review role is an *ex post facto* one' (Canada, Solicitor General, 1991: 69). This is actually a very contentious issue in Canada, part of the intelligence community viewing SIRC as an oversight body and the other part as a review mechanism (the French version of the law, where SIRC is described as a *surveillance committee/Comité de surveillance des activités de renseignement de sécurité*, could be interpreted in favour of the oversight view).

External control: parliamentary review   The government did not implement the recommendations of the McDonald Commission on the creation of a Joint Committee of Parliament – from the House and the Senate – on security intelligence. This was not surprising in view of the reservations of the Canadian establishment in relation to the appointment of such committees for controlling intelligence agencies (Franks, 1979:67).[29] This lack of enthusiasm for involving parliamentary committees in sensitive issues such as defence and national security stems in part from the British parliamentary tradition as it is interpreted in Canada and was again strongly evidenced in the recent report of the Somalia inquiry (Canada, 1997).[30] A sub-committee on National Security (SCNS) was established belatedly in 1993, by the Liberal government of Prime Minister Jean Chrétien, as an appendix of the Standing Committee on Justice and Legal Affairs. This solution has proved to be considerably frustrating for MPs, who have repeatedly asked for the appointment of a fully-fledged committee of Parliament on national security (Canada, House of Commons, 1990: 193 and ff., rec. 107). Not only has the government not responded to this grievance (Canada, Solicitor General, 1991), but also it abolished the SNCS after its reelection in 1997. The SCNS did not have any constraining powers over CSIS, least of all the power of determining its budget, as similar bodies have in the US. Its biggest shortcoming in the Canadian context was that the SCNS members did not hold a high level security clearance and that they were consequently barred from access to confidential security intelligence information. In this regard, they were wholly dependent on the information fed to them by CSIS, SIRC and any other agency involved in the secret collection of security intelligence. This was a crippling limitation on its action.

The impossibility of having within SIRC representatives from the newly elected parties to the House – the *Bloc Québécois* and the Reform Party – eventually generated a conflict between SIRC and the SCNS (Brodeur, 1997c). This conflict was serious enough to be decried by the Auditor General of Canada in one of his recent reports (Canada, Auditor General, 1996; also see Whitaker (1996) for another view of this conflict). Needless to say, strained relations between the two principal mechanisms for external accountability were detrimental to Canadian rights and freedoms. It is doubtful that the abolition of the SCNS will put an end to the strains between Parliament and SIRC. It may actually increase parliamentary frustration.

Human Rights Issues

We saw that one of SIRC's functions was to receive and to process complaints against CSIS. One way to address the human rights issue is to go through all of SIRC's annual reports, which always have a section on complaints, and see whether the complaints received by SIRC would indicate serious abuses of human rights. Complaints are not however a perfect indicator of abuse in the case of security services: persons may have their rights being abused without knowing it, because of the secrecy in which security services operate. Consequently they are not in a position to complain. However, SIRC does not only investigate complaints from the public. It also investigates any allegation made in the media against CSIS, when it does not appear to be *prima facie* frivolous.

There are basically six grounds on which to complain to SIRC.

Official languages There are two official languages in Canada, English and French. After CSIS was created, SIRC was swamped with 600 complaints made against the Service's practices regarding the use of French and of English. SIRC eventually investigated this whole issue, producing a separate report on it and making recommendations. The number of such complaints decreased sharply after two or three years and there are now very few.

S. 41 of the CSIS Act complaints According to this section Canadians may complain in respect to 'any act or thing done by the service'. This is a very mixed bunch of complaints ranging from the delays involved in making a security assessment to claims by persons that they are illegally under surveillance by CSIS. SIRC never confirms or denies that someone is under surveillance, its answers bearing on whether CSIS is abusing its powers or acting illegally with respect to the complainants. A great number of s. 41 complaints are either frivolous or cannot be supported by evidence. They are dismissed without a formal inquiry or hearing. More than half of the complaints received by SIRC are s. 41 complaints. From 1984 to 1991, SIRC received 179 s. 41 complaints.

S. 42 of the CSIS Act complaints These are complaints about unjustified denials of security clearance. This is the other large category of complaints processed by SIRC (102 s. 42 complaints from 1984 to 1991).

Immigration and Citizenship These are distinct but closely related categories of complaints. An immigrant's application to come to Canada may be refused for security reasons; an accepted immigrant may also be expelled from Canada or refused his or her citizenship for the same kind of reason. In all cases a person can complain to SIRC, if he or she believes that they have been wronged by CSIS' security assessment. There are very few complaints of this nature (10 with respect to immigration and 12 with respect to citizenship for the period 1984–1991).

Human rights complaints This is a special category and does not refer to an abuse of power by CSIS. These cases generally concern discrimination (sex, age, ethnicity etc.) and are referred to SIRC by the Canadian Human Rights Commission, when discrimination occurs within an agency operating in the field of national security (for example discrimination within the Department of National Defence). These complaints are very infrequent: there were only seven from 1984 to 1996.

Between 1984 to 1991 SIRC received 306 complaints, 32 of which were found to be supported and 274 unsupported. These early figures are somewhat inflated because of the high number of complaints on the use of the official languages. According to our own calculations, there were 349 complaints from 1987 to 1996, with an average of 38.7 complaints per year (all categories). The distribution of these complaints was the same as in the SIRC figures for the period between 1984 and 1991, s. 41 and s. 42 complaints being by far the most numerous. The more serious complaints are dealt with through formal hearings. From 1984 to 1992, there were 66 cases that required formal hearings. Thirty-six of these cases were resolved in support of the complainant and 30 against him or her. There were several special inquiries conducted by SIRC from 1984 until today, the most important bearing on the use of the two official languages, the early recruitment and training practices of CSIS (Canada, SIRC, 1986), the investigation by CSIS of Aboriginal extremism in northern Canada, the use of bombs by an agent of CSIS infiltrated within a labour union in Quèbec (see Lester, 1998:c. IV) and, most importantly, the alleged surveillance and infiltration of the Reform Party by a CSIS informant acting under the cover of being an extreme-right winger (see Canada, SIRC: 1994, Whitaker 1996 and Brodeur, 1997c).

The CSE

In striking contrast with CSIS, there are almost no public sources on the CSE. As short and relatively uninformative they may be, the 1996–97 and the 1997–98 *Annual Report* of the CSE Commissioner are the most extensive documents that we now have on this organisation.[31] Accordingly, we will begin by raising the issues of secrecy and accountability; we will afterward address the issues of doctrine and of human rights.

Accountability and secrecy: background   We shall briefly describe the background against which the Honourable Judge Claude Bisson was appointed Commissioner of the CSE for three years. We shall afterwards describe his functions.[32] Before retiring from the bench, Judge Bisson was Chief Justice for the province of Québec. When the Thacker Committee issued its report, it stated that the CSE 'clearly has the capacity to invade the privacy of Canadians in a variety of ways. It was established by Order in Council, not by statute, and to all intent and purposes is unaccountable.' (Canada, House of Commons, 1990:153). The Thacker Committee recommended that Parliament formally establish the CSE by statute and that SIRC be appointed as the body responsible for monitoring, reviewing and reporting to Parliament on the activities of the CSE concerning its compliance with the laws of Canada (Canada, House of Commons, 1990: 153, rec. 87). The government ignored this recommendation, like most others that the Committee formulated.

In its response to the Thacker report, the government stated that 'a broad accountability system for CSE is in place' (Canada, Solicitor General, 1991:55). This broad framework then consisted of the following elements: (a) the presence within the CSE of an in-house legal counsel from the Department of Justice; (b) frequent consultations between the CSE and various senior officials from the departments of Justice, External Affairs, National Defence and of the Privy Council Office; (c) internal administrative review of the CSE by the Department of National Defence; (d) review of its strategic plan and new policy proposals by the Cabinet and by the Interdepartmental Committee of Security and Intelligence. Benefiting from legal advice, from consultations with government bureaucrats and having its policies reviewed by two committees minimally qualifies an agency as being accountable, if it does at all. The only element bearing some resemblance with a true element of internal accountability is the CSE's being subject to the Department of National Defence's administrative review mechanisms. The royal inquiry on the failed peace-keeping mission of a Canadian regiment to Somalia found that the greatest shortcomings of the Department of National Defence and of the Canadian military lay in the weakness of their leadership and of their accountability mechanisms (Canada, 1997:vol. II, c. 16–17). Hence, the Thacker Committee was right in stating that the CSE was to all intent and purposes unaccountable.

How unaccountable the CSE really was came to be revealed by a book co-authored by an ex-employee of the Service (Frost and Gratton, 1994). The publication of this book apparently convinced the government that some action was needed and a motion was passed in March 1995 in the House of Commons calling for the establishment of an independent external review mechanism.[33] In a statement delivered on May 2 1995 before the House Standing Committee on National Defence and Veterans' Affairs, the Deputy Clerk of the Privy Council Office[34] Ms. Margaret Bloodworth, acknowledged that the Minister of Defence would 'be looking into ways to supplement (the) existing structures with external oversight'

(Bloodworth, 1995:12). According to the Honourable Claude Bisson, who was to be appointed Commissioner of the CSE in June 1996, that is, one full year after the Deputy Clerk's statement, the government was quite reluctant to appoint an independent commissioner. It took several other calls, in particular from the Privacy Commissioner and from the Auditor General of Canada, to move the government to action (CSE Commissioner, 1997:6–7).

Accountability and secrecy: the CSE commissioner There are two crucial facts to bear in mind in respect to the CSE commissioner. The first one is that the government *did not create a permanent office* – the office of the CSE commissioner – but appointed a person, retired judge Claude Bisson, for a period of three years, ending in 1999, as the CSE Commissioner. We have no guarantee that an independent review mechanism such as the present CSE Commissioner will continue to operate after the termination of Judge Bisson's appointment (CSE, Commissioner, 1998: 10). The possibility that SIRC will succeed the CSE Commissioner after June 1999, as was recommended by the Thacker Committee, is now being raised, but it is nothing more than an option among many others. If there is no pressure for external review of the CSE when Judge Bisson will cease his activities, accountability may quietly evaporate.

The second fact is that in apparent contradiction with Mr. David Collenette, the Minister of Defence who appointed him, Judge Bisson interpreted his mandate as bearing *exclusively* on the *current and future activities* of the CSE and that examining the past of the agency was outside his competence (Gauthier, 1993). Since all the allegations in respect to the CSE's abusing its mandate have been made before the judge's appointment, we will never know through him whether there was any truth to them. However justified it may be, given the scarcity of his resources, this decision may nevertheless cause prejudice to the Commissioner's credibility, despite his acknowledged dedication and personal integrity. For instance, baldly asserting that the CSE operated lawfully from 1996 to 1998 and neither targeted Canadian citizens nor permanent residents of Canada may not appear to be fully convincing (CSE Commissioner, 1997:10 and 1998: 4).[35] CSE's operations were indicted as unlawful by former employees as late as 1995; organisations do not generally change as abruptly. At issue here is not whether the Commissioner is misrepresenting the facts, but whether he knows them all and puts the right interpretation on what he knows. In his annual report, the Commissioner himself wrote: 'Obviously, it was not possible to review all aspects of CSE's complex operations within the first ten months of my mandate' (CSE Commissioner, 1997:12).

The Commissioner was appointed pursuant to Part II of the *Inquiries Act*, which gives him wide powers to access CSE documents and summon persons to testify before him. His only limitations in this regard are the limitations of the IG of CSIS and of SIRC: he has no access to cabinet documents. The Commissioner devotes part of his time to his task, which is approximately six days per month. He is assisted by a permanent staff of two and by experts in security intelligence who occasionally act as consultants. These experts belong to the intelligence community, being for instance ex-members of CSIS. Due to his publicly stated lack of experience in security intelligence, the Commissioner must rely to a significant extent on these experts.

The commissioner's mandate is essentially to review the activities of the CSE for the purpose of determining whether they are in compliance with the law and to advise the Minister of National Defence and the Attorney General of Canada of any CSE activity that may not comply with Canadian legislation. The Commissioner fulfils this mandate by communicating to the Minister of Defence his findings in reports containing classified information, which are not made public, and by tabling his annual report in Parliament. Before being submitted to the House, the annual report is groomed by ministry officials to make sure that it does not unintentionally disclose classified information. Although the Commissioner of the CSE is an independent reviewer, the difference in scope between the efforts to make CSIS accountable and the provisional attempt to make the CSE less opaque in its operations is quite manifest.

CSE: Doctrine

Very little is known on the perspective that the CSE takes on Canada's national security, on its intelligence priorities and on its principles of operation. Frost and Gratton (1994:260–61) list a series of priorities which does not differ significantly from what is known about the priorities of CSIS: counter-terrorism and economic intelligence topping the list. However, they must be considered at best as a speculative source in this respect.

In the absence of any authoritative statement on the CSE's intelligence priorities, we will state the CSE's doctrine on the interception of communications. This doctrine can be found in the Statement by the Deputy Clerk of the PCO (Bloodworth, 1995:11) and in the CSE Commissioner's annual reports. It is of overwhelming importance to note that for both of these sources, the CSE is acknowledged to be part of an international agreement between the US, the UK, Australia, New Zealand and Canada (the UKUSA agreement). Given this premise, the doctrine consists of the following statements:

- The CSE does not target Canadian citizens nor, apparently, permanent residents of this country. *Both* the *originator* and the *recipient* of a communication must be foreigners in order for the CSE to intercept their communication in accordance with its mandate.
- There is an agreement between the parties of the UKUSA treaty that they do not target each other's communications.
- It follows from the latter statement that no party to the agreement asks another party to target its own citizens on its behalf. Such targeting would imply by necessity a violation of clause number two (for example, in order to intercept Canadian communications at the behest of Canada, the US would have by definition to target Canadian communications, which violates the second clause of the doctrine).

There are three important difficulties with this doctrine. First, it was repeatedly contradicted by serious investigative reporters[36] and by ex-employees of the CSE. Although it may be claimed that these ex-employees had an axe to grind with the CSE, it should also be considered that they knowingly made themselves vulnerable to prosecution according to the *Official Secrets Act*. If all one wants to do is to get even by spreading lies, this would seems to be an unreasonable risk. Furthermore, it seems to us that CSE officials do lack credibility in some of their pronouncements. For example, in the May 1995 Statement by the PCO Deputy Clerk, it is said that 'Canada needs and uses such (the CSE's) information for obvious defensive reasons, such as support to peacekeeping missions involving the Canadian Armed Forces' (Bloodworth, 1995:6). Having ourself conducted a study into the dreary absence of any intelligence – excepting medical advice – for the failed peace-keeping mission of the Canadian Forces in Somalia, we believe that the Deputy Clerk's statement is either misinformed or deliberately misleading for the Canadian public.

Another serious problem is that statement 2 of the doctrine may have made sense during the Cold War, when all the good guys were bunched together and supposed to be mutually supportive. In the post-Cold War world of economic intelligence, this notion seems outdated. Why should we rule out having to investigate our friends, because we believe that the parties to the UKUSA agreement are unconditional allies of Canada and would never undermine any aspects of its national security?

The last glitch involves our conception of legality. Discussing the issue of the legality of the CSE's interceptions of private communications with lawyers, we came to the following conclusions. First, the CSE never requires judicial authorisation for intercepting private communications, as it is mandatory under Canadian privacy laws. Why is this? Because (a) the intercepted communications are between foreigners at both ends and (b) because they are transmitted through microwave towers instead of landlines. If we raise the question of whether the *Canadian police* would need a judicial warrant to intercept communications between foreigners when at least one party is on Canadian soil, it would definitely appear that they would, the only possible qualification being that a warrant may not be needed when the communications are transmitted by microwaves (like cordless or cellular phones; see endnote 18 on this issue). The overall conclusion is that we are in a legal no man's land when it comes to the legality of the CSE's interception of private communications, even when they take place between non-Canadian citizens. The basic question boils down to this: why is it that the CSE does not need judicial authorisation for intercepting private communications when the police definitely would in similar circumstances?

CSE: Human Rights Issues

Much was said in the course of this paper on the possible abuses by the CSE of the rights and freedoms enjoyed by Canadians and there is no need to repeat what we said previously. There is however one ominous development that needs to be mentioned. It might be asked why ex-employees of the CSE, such as Mike Frost and others, who blew the whistle on the agency, were not prosecuted. The answer is that their prosecution may have revealed even more damaging facts for the CSE, since trials are public in Canada. According to our inquiries, the government of Canada is contemplating amendments to the *Official Secrets Act*, which would authorise the prosecution of whistle blowers in trials held *in camera*. The traditional designation for such confidential trials is 'Star Chamber' proceedings. It is to be hoped that Canada will not regress to that.

We will finally mention one last development, although it is not related to human rights issues. The CSE will have to spend large sums of money to effect the transition towards (the interception of) digital communications. This transition is necessitated by the changes in communication technology and, despite its costs, must be made, if the CSE wants to avoid becoming obsolete.

Conclusion

There are several conclusions to be drawn from the preceding analyses. The first one is, we believe, that the much vaunted structure established to make CSIS accountable is now showing signs of wear. SIRC is apparently having difficulty to recruit enough members to operate with a quorum. Furthermore, the Sub-Committee on national security was abolished in 1997 and it has not been replaced by anything else. Finally, it would seem that these mechanisms work to the extent that committed and energetic persons staff them. The first Chairman of SIRC, the Hon. Ron Atkey, was such a person and so were Michel Robert, legal counsel to the Solicitor General, and Jean-Jacques Blais, an ex-Solicitor General of Canada. All three have now left SIRC. Mr. Atkey's successors – John W.H. Bassett and Jacques Courtois – had either little experience with government and/or no real knowledge of the intelligence community. Since he had never been elected to the House, Mr. Bassett, a successful businessman with ties to the Progressive-Conservative party, had to be made a special member of the Privy Council, before becoming SIRC's chairman. Mr. Courtois' health became a serious concern during his tenure and he died on 3 July 1996, while still Chairman of SIRC. He was replaced by Mr. Edwin A. Goodman, who was already a member of SIRC. The present chairperson of SIRC is Mrs. Paule Gauthier.

Second, we argued that there were strong indications that CSIS was operating in a vacuum of doctrine. Instead of repeating what we already said in this regard, we will give another indication of this vacuum. On 1 May 1998, the Montreal daily *The Gazette* released a *Canadian Press* release quoting the Hon. Andy Scott, who was then Solicitor General, to the effect that the terrorist threat was still very real in Canada[37] (Canadian Press, 1998). Mr. Scott's speech had been given the previous day on the occasion of the release of CSIS' 1997 Annual Report, which claims that contrary to expectations at the beginning of the 1990s, the end of the Cold War has created more – not fewer – threats to national security. On the very same day, the Montreal daily, *La Presse*, printed a press release from Washington to the effect that according to a recent US report terrorism was in sharp decline all over the world (Associated Press and *Agence française de presse*, 1998). Not only is CSIS operating without a new set of orientations, but recent breaches in internal security indicate that the service may be experiencing serious problems with its personnel.[38]

The recurrent theme of this paper was the contrast between CSIS and the CSE in the present Canadian context. We first suggested that with respect to budget and personnel, the CSE was poised to become Canada's first security and intelligence agency, in the same way that the NSA had become the US' foremost agency in this field. There is presently a trend to disparage HUMINT, when it is compared to SIGINT, and there have been calls to abolish agencies that specialise in HUMINT, like the CIA (Draper, 1997; Eichner and Dobbert, 1998 and Ulfkotte, 1998). This development actually compounds the problem of accountability, because the traditional obstacle to it is secrecy. Now, in the field of SIGINT, the sheer pace of the development of technology is in itself a major source of opacity.

In terms of doctrine, the contrast between CSIS and the CSE is also sharp. CSIS is the Canadian domestic agency, whereas government officials heavily stress that the CSE only collects intelligence on foreign powers. There is one thing with this emphasis on the CSE's foreign intelligence mandate that we find rather opportunistic. As we saw, there has been a very lively on-going debate in Canada about extending CSIS' mandate to give it a foreign intelligence capacity in an official way. This debate started with the establishment of CSIS and the government always resisted extending CSIS' mandate. It is both interesting and surprising to note, in view of the government's opposition to granting CSIS a larger role, that it never actually argued – at least to our own knowledge – that there was no pressing necessity to involve CSIS in foreign intelligence *because the CSE was already deeply implicated in the collection and analysis of foreign intelligence*. It would seem that the CSE's focus on foreign intelligence was a rather late discovery by the Canadian government, which happily coincided with the multiplication of the allegations by former employees that the CSE was spying on Canadians and was operating abroad at the behest of its two main partners in SIGINT, that is the US and the UK.

The biggest contrast of all lies between the number of public checks on CSIS and the near absence of public control in which the CSE is operating. We stressed this contrast throughout the paper. There is, we believe, a direct relation between the lack of accountability of the CSE and its heavy involvement in international co-operation in the field of security intelligence. We would like to propose the hypothesis that the strength of the linkages between security services belonging to different countries acts as a common shield against accountability. Indeed, it can reasonably be argued that no national agency should answer to the government of another state than its own. By stressing the closeness of the operational links between two agencies respectively connected to different sovereign states, it might be claimed that you cannot make one of them accountable without also putting the other one under scrutiny, at least indirectly. Such scrutiny being equivalent to a form of oversight, its exercise would result in a situation where one state would then hold the security service of another country accountable to itself, albeit indirectly.

We do not claim that such an argument was overtly presented to the Canadian government by other governments. However, as we have seen, it is publicly acknowledged that the CSE has a very close relationship with its counterparts in the US and in the UK. Secondly, it was repeatedly objected to SIRC's oversight of CSIS that it jeopardised its relationships with the intelligence services of other states. The same line of reasoning would apply all the more to the CSE, which is joined by the UKUSA treaty to like agencies in other countries. Lastly, there is no doubt that close co-operation between different services provides them with insights into each other's workings. The report of the Aspin Commission can be quoted in this regard:

> liaison relationships provide insight into the activities of other intelligence services, as well as provide important contacts that may be essential to the ability of the United States to influence events during a crisis. (US, Congress, 1996:c.12, 2 of 4)

The Aspin report also notes that by far and large its relationships with its partners in security intelligence 'have remained confidential'. Finally, officials or ex-officials from the Canadian intelligence community have claimed several times that the external controls on CSIS were so tight that they jeopardised its capacity to get the full co-operation of other countries' security and intelligence agencies, which were not accountable to external bodies to such a degree.

Despite numerous calls to make it more accountable, the CSE has so far eluded these pressures nearly successfully, the exception being the provisional appointment for three years of an independent Commissioner. Our contention is that the transnationalisation of security and intelligence is intrinsically bound with the issue of the accountability of the Canadian intelligence community and of its partners. Indeed, how should we view the increasing international linkage between the security agencies of different countries (for example the members of NATO)[39] in relation to their respective accountability?

At the end of his study on accountability in relation to security intelligence in Australia and Canada, Lustgarten proposes that review or oversight should be *functional* rather than *institutional*, as it presently is (Lustgarten, 1995:182). This means that instead of having a one-on-one match between a security agency and its watchdog committee, there should be a general body with the authority to review and/or to oversee all agencies performing the same function. The increasing linkages between various national intelligence and security agencies raises the issue of whether Lustgarten's argument should not be pushed one step further to reach the level of transnational functionality. While the usefulness of overseeing CSIS can be doubted, when the CSE can do relatively unchecked what CSIS is being restrained from doing, it can also be asked what is the point of putting the CSE under scrutiny, when, judging from past experience, its liaison officers and special envoys can do in partnership with the NSA or with GCHQ what the agency is forbidden to do by itself. This line of argument, which ultimately leads to the need of an international oversight authority, may be viewed as being at best as wishful thinking. The problem with security intelligence is that we consider it normal for dystopia to spread – after all, the international networking boldly going on between the security and intelligence agencies under US tutelage is no figment of the imagination – while we remain so timid in contemplating utopia.

However, just asserting utopia as did Ernst Bloch in *The Hope Principle* will no longer do in our time, grown justifiably suspicious of wishful thinking. So, how should we proceed to make into a reality the international functional accountability that we just referred to? A first step would be to co-ordinate the efforts made by several non governmental organisations (NGOs) devoted to the protection of human rights, such as Amnesty International, Human Rights Watch and the numerous civil liberties associations that exist in all democratic countries and many others. We briefly saw that while the ECHELON surveillance system was brought to the attention of the European Parliament, it was also denounced by NGOs such as Human Rights Watch, the American Civil Liberties Union and similar organisations in Canada, Australia and in Europe. There should be a mechanism for bringing together the fragmented efforts of all these organisations. Such a mechanism could be under the aegis of the United Nations – the UN High Commissioner for Human Rights has an institutional budget to fund organisations devoted to the protection of human rights and could therefore sponsor the co-ordinating mechanism. The warnings and indictments of a UN sponsored co-ordinating mechanism on the actual or potential abuses of security intelligence agencies would be more influential than the dispersed efforts of present NGOs. This would be but a first step towards global accountability, but it would be in the right direction.

Post-scriptum

In the wake of the 11 September, 2001 terrorist attacks against the World Trade Centre and the Pentagon, the Canadian government has taken steps to increase its capabilities to fight terrorism. Some of these steps are in line with the main thrust of the argument developed in this chapter. The federal government has thus allocated 47 million dollars (Canadian) to the agencies involved in protecting Canada's national security: the CSE was given the lion's share of these monies, that is, 37 millions as opposed to only ten for CSIS.

There is, however, one major innovation. On 15 October 2001, the government tabled an enabling law for the CSE in the House of Commons. This law was buried into an all-embracing package of high profile counter-terrorist measures submitted to Parliament (Bill C-36; this bill is over 180 pages long). Because of the general ignorance surrounding the CSE and its operations, the government proposal generated almost no public reaction. The law was passed in a hurry on 28 November, with only two minor amendments, the government having used a gag order to keep the debate in Parliament to a minimum. This haste contrasts direly with the repeated advice of the CSE Commissioner to tread cautiously in developing enabling legislation for the CSE. Compared to the 1984 CSIS Act, the legal framework developed for the CSE is quite sparse, consisting of some ten sections to be integrated into the *National Defence Act* (as Part V.1 of the Act; this integration was made very much on an *ad hoc* basis, Part V of the Act dealing with peripheral issues of military justice). At the time of writing, the Canadian Senate must still approve Bill C-36, before it becomes law. However, senatorial approval is normally only a formality in Canada.

The Act first appoints a Commissioner to oversee the CSE. The commissioner's duties are to review the activities of the CSE to ensure that they comply with the law, to investigate complaints against the agency and to inform the Minister of Defence and the Attorney General of any activity that may not be in compliance with the law (section 273.63). The Commissioner is to report to the Minister at the end of each fiscal year and the latter must lay a copy of the report before each House of Parliament. The appointment of a commissioner to oversee the CSE enshrines in law what has been past practice since 1996, when the first CSE Commissioner was appointed by an Order in Council. Although it provides a safeguard against the infringement of the rights of Canadians, the appointment of a Commissioner definitively seals in secrecy the operations of the CSE. During the last five years, the CSE Commissioner issued no less than 17 confidential reports (classified as SECRET and TOP SECRET Codeword/CEO) as compared to five (yearly) public reports. His public reports have infallibly been a short 13 pages (some 4,000 words) – by comparison, SIRC's last public report of 2000–01 was, with appendices, 70 pages long – and disclose minimal information. Their main purpose is to blandly assert that Canadian laws were not violated. Furthermore, the appointment of a separate commissioner for the CSE violates the requirement of having a systemic approach to security intelligence accountability, whereby not only agencies are held accountable on a fragmented basis, but the whole intelligence function is the subject of comprehensive oversight.

The main part of the new CSE Act is the definition of the agency's mandate and of its relationships with the Minister. With respect to past practice, the Act broadens the CSE's mandate. In the past, this mandate had two basic components. First, the agency was to provide the government with foreign intelligence by collecting, analysing and reporting on foreign radio, radar and other electronic signals (in short, signals intelligence or SIGINT). Second, it helped insure that the Canadian government's telecommunications and information technologies were secure from interception, disruption, manipulation or sabotage (it provided information technology security or ITS). According to the new Act, the CSE is also 'to provide technical and operational assistance to federal law enforcement and security agencies in the performance of their lawful duties' (subsection 273.64 (1) c). SIGINT and ITS activities shall not be directed at Canadians or any person in Canada and shall be subject to measures to protect the privacy of Canadians in the use and retention of intercepted information. However, it is not altogether clear whether the privacy of Canadians will be fully protected in the CSE's law enforcement assistance operations. The Act states on the one hand that these operations are subject to the legal limitations imposed on federal law enforcement and security activities (273.64, subsection 3). On the other hand, the Minister can in certain circumstances – the gathering of foreign intelligence and the protection of the Canadian government telecommunications system against abuse – authorize the CSE to intercept private communications outside the legal framework currently limiting electronic surveillance by police agencies (section 273.69). These ambiguities may have been dispelled through a public debate, but the government was in such a haste to enact its legislation that this debate was drastically curtailed. In this instance as in many others, the 11 September crisis was used as an occasion to provide a quick fix to previously identified 'collateral' problems.

List of Acronyms and Abbreviations

BQ	The *Bloc Québécois* (a federal political party)
CASIS	The Canadian Association for the Study of Intelligence and Security
CBNRC	Communications Branch of the Canadian Research Council
C.C.	Canadian Criminal Code
CFSRS	Canadian Forces Supplementary Radio System
COINTELPRO	The FBI's Counter-intelligence Program
COMINT	Communications Intelligence
CSE	Communications Security Establishment
CSIS	Canadian Security Intelligence Service
ELINT	Electronics Intelligence
FBI	Federal Bureau of Investigations (US)
GCHQ	Government Communications Headquarters (UK)
HUMINT	Human Intelligence
IG	Inspector General
INFOSEC	Information Security (Canada: a CSE program)
ITS	Information Technology Security (Canada: a CSE program)
MI-8	Military Intelligence 8 (US)
NCIS	National Crime Intelligence Sections (Canada, RCMP)
NSA	National Security Agency (US)
NSEU	National Security Enforcement Units (Canada, RCMP)
NSCID	National Security Council Intelligence Directive (US)
NSID	National Security Investigations Directorate (Canada, RCMP)
OSA	*Official Secrets Act* (Canada)
PCO	The Queens' Privy Council Office (Canada)
RCMP	Royal Canadian Mounted Police
RCMP/SS	Royal Canadian Mounted Police Security Service
SCNS	Sub-Committee on National Security (Canada)
SERT	Special Emergency Response Team (RCMP)
SIRC	Security Intelligence Review Committee
SQ	Sûreté du Québec (Quebec provincial police)
RP	The Reform Party (a federal political party)
TARC	Target Approval Review Committee (Canada)
WRC	Warrant Review Committee (Canada)
XU	Examination Unit (cryptology unit, Canada)

Notes

1　For the period during which Canada was plagued by terrorism (1963–1973), the municipal police of the city of Montreal in the province of Quebec played a major role in counter-terrorism, as most terrorist incidents occurred in Montreal.

2　As in other countries, commissions of inquiry are designated in Canada by the name of their respective chairperson.

3　The reasoning of the Commission was the following. The RCMP/SS had not seriously abused its powers in respect to the collection of intelligence but in respect to its actions ('disruptive tactics') against groups and individuals (for instance, members of the RCMP/SS stole dynamite to plant it into the vehicle of a suspected terrorist who was planning to cross the US border for legitimate purposes). The Commission believed that granting the future agency the power to collect intelligence, while at the same time withdrawing from it the power to act upon the intelligence thus collected (e.g. destabilising subversive organisations), would cut down at the root the kind of abuse which the former RCMP/SS had been responsible for.

4　In Canada, the Privy Council Office is the highest body of government and can be viewed as the Prime Minister's own ministry. The PCO's documents have the highest level of confidentiality and no review committee has any access to them.

5　The name of these sections and units may have changed since their identification in SIRC (1987). According to a report issued by the Solicitor General, the RCMP created in 1988 its National Security Investigations Directorate (NSID), which comprises national security investigations sections (also see Farson, 1991:204). In the same period the RCMP also established its Special Emergency Response Team (SERT), which can be described as an elite SWAT team analogous to the German GSG-9 (*Grenzeschutzgruppe No. 9*) or the French GIGN (*Groupe d'intervention de la Gendarmerie nationale*). As it proved too difficult for a police force to maintain the emergency unit in a constant state of battle readiness, SERT is now in theory part of the Canadian Armed Forces (it may have been altogether disbanded, because there has been up until now no real need for such an assault group in Canada).

6　When the intelligence officer for this mission learned that the Canadians were to be deployed in Somalia under Chapter VII of the *United Nations Charter*, he consulted the Encyclopaedia Britannica to prepare for his intelligence briefings (Brodeur, 1997a:191).

7　The address of CSIS' Internet Website is http://www.csis-scrs.gc.ca. For an extremely useful source of information on CSIS and, more generally, the Canadian Intelligence community, the reader should consult the CASIS Intelligence Newsletter, which is currently in its 33rd issue. CASIS stands for the Canadian Association for the Study of Intelligence and Security and its website can be accessed at http://www3.sympatico.ca/andr.lapointe.

8　In its discussion of the abolition of the counter-subversion arm of CSIS, the 1987–1988 Annual report of SIRC provides us with these rather chilling details. Following the abolition of this arm, which SIRC had recommended the year before, 'a *residue* of counter-subversion targets are now monitored by the Analysis and Production Branch' (Canada, SIRC, 1988:13, our emphasis). The SIRC 1987–1988 annual report goes on to say: 'In total, slightly more than 3,000 of the files that had been actively pursued in the counter-subversion program remain open.' (Canada, SIRC, 1988:13) These quotations raise an obvious question: if *3,000* files are the *residue* of the counter-subversion targets, how many of these files were actually alive in the heyday of the counter-subversive arm of CSIS and of the previous RCMP/SS? The answer is to be found in the 1989–1990 Annual Report of SIRC: there were 57,562 files (Canada, SIRC, 1990:44). What were called their 'residue' in 1988 was actually *all the files (among the original 58,000) that were still active.* This residue was reduced to 1,400 files following further examination. SIRC eventually changed its mind about keeping this residue independently alive and suggested that these files be redistributed among the Counter-Intelligence and Counter-Terrorism arms of the Service, after having been carefully re-examined to see whether they could be documented as referring to a genuine threat (Canada, SIRC, 1990:48–49).

9   This was initially proposed by Peter Russell. Professor Russell was the research Director of the McDonald Commission, which recommended the abolition of the RCMP/SS and the creation of what was to become CSIS.

10 The mention in the column for personnel in the case of CSIS always reads 'NA' (non applicable).

11 All these figures are also given on the Internet site of CSIS.

12 Unless otherwise specified, all figures are given in Canadian dollars. Our figures on budget and manpower come from the 1996–97 and the 1997–98 Expenditure Plan of the Ministry of the Solicitor General of Canada (Canada, Solicitor General 1996 and 1997).

13 The beginning of the XU is a complex story first told in St. John (1984) and afterwards in Wark (1987:644–46).

14 Following the publication of his book, *The American Black Chamber,* Yardley and his wife had been branded in the US as security risks. Shortly after setting up the XU in Canada, Yardley and his wife were identified as its main cryptologists by the Americans and the British. Bowing to US and UK pressure, the Canadian government had to dismiss the Yardleys, who were replaced by British cryptologists. Lester B. Pearson, who at the time was the first assistant to the Deputy Minister at the Canadian department of External Affairs, was the government official responsible for the XU. Mr. Pearson was to become a Nobel peace laureate in 1957 and the Prime Minister of Canada from 1963 to 1968. On the XU, see his memoirs (Pearson, 1972, Vol. 1, p. 198).

15 The reasoning of the trial judge rested on the lack of a reasonable presumption of privacy. '...Part VI of the Criminal Code did not apply to the interception of conversations made from or received by a cellular telephone. The trial judge held that these telephone conversations were not private within the meaning of the C.C., because the ordinary user knows or ought to know that the communication is likely to be intercepted by a person other than the person to whom it was intended.', *R. v. Solomon* (1996), 110 C.C.C. (3d) 354 at 355 (Que. C.A.). The court rulings are somewhat inconsistent. *R. v. Cheung* held that at least in 1990 conversations over a cellular phone were private (*R. v. Cheung* (1995), 100 C.C.C. (3d) 441 (B.C. S.C.). *R. v. Lubovac* held that pager messages were not private communications (*R. v. Lubovac* (1989), 52 C.C.C. (3d) 551, Alta C.A.).

16 'If a conversation made from a cellular telephone is not "a private conversation" within the meaning of s. 183, *which need not be decided here,* its interception by agents of the State is nonetheless a search and seizure within the meaning of the Canadian Charter of Rights and Freedoms... The interception and recording, by the State, of conversations from a cellular phone will therefore never be valid unless authorised.' *R. v. Solomon* at 356, our emphasis. As we said this judgement was reaffirmed by the Supreme Court of Canada [1997] 3 S.C.R., 118 C.C.C. (3d) 351, 151 D.L.R. (4th) 383.

17 ELINT is defined thus: Electronic Intelligence; the collection (observation and recording) and the processing for subsequent intelligence purposes of information derived from foreign, noncommunications, electromagnetic radiation emanating from other than atomic detonation or radioactive sources (from NSCID No. 6, quoted in Bamford, 1982:621).

18 Ex-employees of the CSE who blew the whistle on the agency tend to confirm this limitation. Although he believes that the CSE can get 'whatever it wants, from

anywhere', Mike Frost acknowledges that is much more difficult to get into a land line (Frost, 1994:21). When he was asked to listen in to the telephone conversations of Margaret Trudeau, the Prime Minister's wife who was then suspected of using drugs, Mike Frost could do nothing but try to intercept her *car phone* conversations with the technical means at his disposal (Frost, 1994:95). We should remember that according to this paper, Canadian privacy law legally protects only communications transmitted through landlines.

[19] At least one thing is altogether clear: under Canadian law, police need judicial authorisation to intercept a telephone conversation going through a landline. Let us assume that a telephone conversation going through a landline is automatically switched to microwaves towers because of system overload of the landlines. Would this imply that the CSE could now intercept it without a warrant just because it has technically been switched to another channel of transmission, which can easily be picked up by the CSE? A positive answer to this question would make a mockery of Canadian privacy laws, the need for legal authorisation being, as it were, switched on and off depending of the mode of transmission of a private communication.

[20] The address of the site is http://www.cse-cst.gc.ca.

[21] See 'ACLU to Spy on Echelon' by Chris Oakes, www.wired.com/news/politics/. There are several articles on ECHELON to be found at this Internet address.

[22] Here is for instance the list cited by Chris Oakes in 'Monitor This, Echelon' (www.wired news/politics/0.1283.32039.00.html): ATF, DOD, WACO, RUBY RIDGE, OKC, OKLAHOMA CITY, MILITIA GUN HANDGUN, MILGOV ASSAULY RIFLE, TERRORISM BOMB, DRUG, KORESH, PROMIS, MOSSAD, NASA, M15, ONI, CID, AK47, M16, C4, MALCOLM X, REVOLUTION, CHEROKEE, HILLARY BILL CLINTON, GORE, BUSH, WACKENHUT, TERRORIST (the parsing of this key word list is admittedly tentative). An expanded list was given in James Glave's 'Hackers Ascend Upper ECHELON' (www.wired.com/news/politics/0.1283.31726.00.html).

[23] Moon (1991a) estimates the budget of the CSE to be 250 million for the year 1991 and its total staff (civilian and military) to number 2,000 persons. Moon does not cite its source(s) for these estimates. Although the budget estimate may be high – it is generally believed to be closer to 200 million – the figure for the total staff seems more accurate. A staff of approximately two thousand is the most frequently cited.

[24] I remember the exact time vividly because I told the CSIS officer who reached me in my office at the university that he was lucky to catch me on a Friday night at 17h00, just before I was to leave for my home. To which the officer casually replied that he would have found a way to reach me regardless of where I was for the weekend.

[25] An example would be the known availability of bomb detonators in Canada. Although bombs are not exploded in Canada, CSIS must keep foreign terrorist organisations from finding their supplies in bomb detonators in Canada.

[26] This number varies from the one given in Brodeur (1997c:86), because we added the year 1983 to our calculations.

[27] The number of refusals for criminal police operations is very low. From 1974 to 1994, 13,488 authorisations were granted by the courts, which refused only 19 applications, that is less than one every year, on average. (Brodeur, 1997c:88). We hypothesise that the number of refusals must be even lower for the applications made by CSIS. It is not unreasonable to assume that given the pre-screening mechanisms the bad applications are weeded out and that *all* applications made to the Federal court are accepted.

[28] The second Chairman of SIRC – Mr. Bassett – was a businessman connected to the Progressive-Conservative party. The Tories who were then forming the government appointed him to the Privy Council by an order of the Governor in Council, just before

he became chairman of SIRC. The same applies to the present chairperson, Mrs Paule Gauthier, who was appointed to the PCO by the Liberal government.

29 C.E.S. Franks, who was commissioned by the McDonald inquiry to prepare a study on parliament and security matters, concluded his study in the following way: 'It is not recommended that a new standing committee on security be established. There are already too many committees, and they demand too much of members' time and energy. Security falls already within the ambit of the Justice and Legal Affairs, and the External Affairs and National Defence committees.' (Franks, 1979:67). Franks' advice was ambiguously followed. No new standing committee was established, but a national security *sub*-committee was appointed, under the umbrella of the Standing Committee on Justice and Legal Affairs.

30 The Commission completely endorsed the position of law professor Martin L. Friedland, who had been commissioned to write a study (Friedland, 1997:108–110). Friedland's position, deeply influenced by the British, is that Parliament can better play its role in receiving reports from bodies reporting to it than in appointing committees to produce such reports. This position was entirely endorsed by the Somalia inquiry, which quotes it approvingly in its final report (Canada, 1997, Vol. 2:397).

31 Both reports that have been so far published have exactly the same length, that is 12 pages and one paragraph. The pages have wide margins and little text on them.

32 The Honourable Claude Bisson was between 1984 and 1987 the Vice-Chairman of the Canadian Sentencing Commission. I was myself the Director of Research for this commission and developed a friendly relationship with Judge Bisson. He graciously granted me an interview in the course of my research for writing this paper. Needless to say, I bear the sole responsibility for the content of this paper.

33 This motion was presented by Liberal MP Derek Lee. Mr. Lee was a member of the Thacker Committee.

34 The Deputy Clerk of the PCO for intelligence and security affairs is one of the two officials holding immediate authority over the CSE, the other being the Deputy Minister of the Department of National Defence.

35 The Commissioner stated: 'Based on the results of my own review and analysis, I am of the opinion that CSE has acted lawfully in the performance of its mandated activities during the period under review. I am also satisfied that CSE has not targeted Canadian citizens or permanent residents.' (CSE Commissioner, 1997:10)

36 When Sallot (1984) referred to a CSE data bank on Canadian citizens, he actually quoted the description of this data bank in Canadian government official documents.

37 This does not mean that terrorist violence is expected to rise in Canada, but that there may be foreign terrorists who are operating in Canada either to raise funds to pursue their homeland conflicts or to look for weapons and similar activities (e.g. bomb components).

38 It was thus revealed in several articles published in November 1999 by the Canadian daily *The Globe and Mail* that two significant breaches of security had recently occurred. In the first one, a CSIS agent lost in a phone booth a CD-ROM that listed criminal organisations – motorcycle gangs – being targeted by the Service. The CD-ROM apparently fell from the agent's briefcase and was found by a citizen who reported his find back to CSIS, but admitted having first considered selling it to the intended CSIS targets. In the second breach, deemed even more serious, another CSIS agent went to a hockey game and left her briefcase on the back seat of her car in the parking area of the arena. The briefcase contained highly secret information on CSIS targets and on the restructuring of the service. The agent's car was burglarised by two drug addicts who stole the briefcase. They were shortly picked up by the Toronto police and claimed that they had disposed of the briefcase's content in the bin of a garbage truck. Despite police and CSIS searches, the content of the briefcase was never found. According to the *Globe*

and Mail, the two CSIS agents were not disciplined by the organisation. SIRC was not informed by the Minister of these mishaps and only learned about them through the press reports. After an investigation the agent in the second case was fired from the Service.

[39] For example, despite pressures from the Canadian public, the Canadian government is refusing to demilitarise the Arctic in order to abide by its international commitments to NATO and NORAD (Coulon,1998:a 2).

PART IV

SECURITY INTELLIGENCE IN OLD AND NEW 'SUPERPOWERS'

Chapter 10

Security and Intelligence Services in the United Kingdom

Peter Gill

Introduction

The pan-European coverage of our enterprise recognises that in the last few years there have been some spectacular political changes in the nature of states that, at least rhetorically, represent a convergence towards the two central concepts of this project: the rule of law and democracy. In the most general terms, the first of these has come to refer to the subjection of governments (both ministers and state officials) to the same laws regarding conduct as those relating to citizens in general and the second refers to the fact that, at regular intervals, citizens exercise some choice of governments through competitive elections conducted in the context of freedoms of speech and association. A third dimension to the convergence must be acknowledged since it has profound implications for the issues we are examining: the central position of market economies.

The development of the rule of law, democracy and market economies in Western and Southern European countries (WSEC) over the last two or three centuries was by no means a story of steady and even progress and therefore it is hardly surprising that the attempt to install all three simultaneously in the Central and East European countries (CEEC) is a process fraught with numerous strains. This applies to all state policy sectors, yet the specific area of state security intelligence is, in a number of respects, quite different from other policy fields (cf. Anderson, 1995, 57). Primarily, although the differences between state security intelligence agencies in the various European states were significant (especially in terms of their size and the extent of their penetration into civil society), they shared a common immunity from the mainstream legal and policy-making processes of their respective states (however polyarchic or otherwise they were). This common feature can be summarised in the notion of the 'national security state' that is discussed further below.

In considering, as we are, the issues of transition in states, it is important to question the extent to which the state can be usefully considered as a single unitary actor. Certainly this was the assumption in much traditional analysis of international relations that was carefully criticised by Graham Allison (1971). Now, it is much more likely to find state theorists acknowledging the fragmented structure of states with no necessary coherence to their operations (Jessop, 1990, 366; Buzan, 1991, 349). Security intelligence agencies exist within these fragmented states; often they are seen as being at their 'core' as in this author's earlier characterisation of the 'Gore-Tex' state. Here, security intelligence agencies defend their autonomy from intrusion by society and other levels of the state, on the one hand, while, on the other, seeking to penetrate those other levels in search of information and to implement policies (Gill, 1994, 80).

However, there is another factor that did not really touch the agencies while the national security architecture remained frozen in the Cold War, but which is now becoming far more obvious. This is the fact that 'security' (rather than 'national security') has become a modern totem that simply cannot be provided adequately by states facing fiscal crises of varying dimensions and which therefore is offered also by an increasing variety of both private and what have been described as 'hybrid' agencies (Johnston, 1992). To be sure, Les Johnston was discussing 'policing' rather than security intelligence work but since 'serious' or 'organised' crime is increasingly the target of both sets of agencies, the differences between police and security work are not as great as perhaps they once were. So, it is not just that the state itself is now viewed more realistically as a fragmented structure but that state bodies now find themselves in ever-increasing relations of co-ordination and/or competition with non-state agencies.

Privatisation may not have proceeded as fast in security intelligence matters as elsewhere but, taken together with the increasing 'marketisation' of security, it does mean that we need now to examine a plethora of security agencies and the nature of their interaction. In this task the most reliable concept is the *network*. When our concern was concentrated upon a few state agencies operating within a context of legalised sovereignty then it was entirely appropriate to seek to explain their policies in terms of *hierarchies*: to a greater or lesser extent modern states sought to maintain legitimacy via their organisation as hierarchical bureaucracies in which policies were determined at the top and implemented downwards through the hierarchy. As a formal model this was always a better description of large police agencies than of (in the

West) relatively small security intelligence agencies but as a description of how those agencies actually operated the hierarchical model was always flawed. Hierarchies impede rather than facilitate the flows of information that are at the very heart of security intelligence work and the organisational form that best describes these is the network (cf. Powell, 1991, 272). When we take into account the increasing variety of external agencies with which any particular organisation needs to deal then this reinforces the shift to the network form. The other facilitating factor is communications and information technology (CIT): whereas networks existed thirty years ago, they were slow and marginal to most agencies, now with rapid data processing and transfer their significance increases exponentially.

Organisation

The main elements of the security architecture in the UK were erected in their present form in the late nineteenth and early twentieth century and have remained more or less intact ever since. Prior to this there were certainly official efforts at domestic spying but they lacked any continuity or systematic structure apart perhaps from the section responsible for mail interception from the very beginnings of the Royal Mail. Political surveillance was most extensive during periods of greatest concern, for example the fear of revolution at the turn of the eighteenth century but practically nil at other times, for example, between 1850–80 (Porter, 1989).

MI5 – the domestic security intelligence agency – and MI6 – the main HUMINT foreign intelligence agency more correctly known as the Secret Intelligence Service (SIS) were both established in 1909. What has become the SIGINT agency – Government Communications Headquarters (GCHQ) – originated during the first world war and the Defence Intelligence Staff (DIS) represents since the 1960s (when the Ministry of Defence replaced the individual service departments) the central location for the bringing together of military intelligence.

Security intelligence agencies have always been loath to publish their budgets (Gill, 1994, 227 summarises some historical estimates) but during the 1980s they apparently increased under Thatcher's benign gaze; in the early 1990s they were cut back (Urban, 1996, 183). The government now publishes a single figure budget – the Single Intelligence Vote – that covers GCHQ, SIS and the Security Service but does not give a figure for each agency. The SIV for the current period is shown in Table 10.1.

Table 10.1   The UK Single Intelligence Vote (£m)

1996/97	740.7
1997/98	707.8
1998/99	693.7
1999/00	743.2

Source: Intelligence and Security Committee, 1998, §19

GCHQ has always absorbed the lion's share of this budget, the Security Service budget for 1997/98 was 'less than' £140m (MI5, 1998, 9). The inclusion of the agencies in government's general reviews of public expenditure symbolises ministers' desire to integrate the agencies better and the fact that they are now in greater competition for resources with other departments.

The process of assessing and disseminating the product of foreign, SIGINT and defence intelligence to ministers has, since 1936, been centralised in the Joint Intelligence Committee (JIC). Since 1957 this has been part of the Cabinet Office. The Assessments Staff (seconded from various departments, military services and intelligence agencies) prepare all-source assessments for submission to specialist sub-committees (called Current Intelligence Groups) that include members from interested government departments. The reports of the CIGs are passed to the JIC itself that consists of the heads of the security intelligence agencies and of the Foreign, Defence and Treasury ministries, plus others as appropriate. The weekly survey that is agreed by the JIC and circulated throughout Whitehall is known as the Red Book. The other main Whitehall 'player' is the Co-ordinator of Intelligence and Security who advises the Cabinet Secretary on the co-ordination of the intelligence machinery and reviews annual intelligence requirements and agency budgets (Central Intelligence Machinery, 1993). However, the domestic security agencies have, historically, operated more or less independently of this overall intelligence structure.

Special Branch

In 1883 Irish Nationalist bombs in London precipitated the birth of what became the Metropolitan Police Special Branch. From 1961 onwards provincial forces started to establish special branches but they were not, at least until recently, well-integrated into the criminal investigation departments of which they were officially part let alone mainstream policing. This was because their central role was primarily laid down by the Security Service (MI5) for whom special branch officers have been seen as 'foot-soldiers'. Numbers of SB officers have fluctuated, especially upwards in wartime, but in, for example, 1984 there were 446 in London and 870 elsewhere in England and Wales (Gill, 1994, 228). A high proportion of these, especially outside London was allocated to Port Duties that are essentially concerned with policing the Prevention of Terrorism Acts.

The Home Office first issued guidelines on what special branches should be doing in 1970 but they were never published. They were revised and published in 1984, largely in response to the establishment by the House of Commons Home Affairs Select Committee of the first parliamentary inquiry into any aspect of domestic security intelligence. Special branches' functions are the investigation and surveillance of individuals and groups suspected of a variety of offences (including against election law) or by way of 'threat assessments' in advance of political meetings and demonstrations. The latter was what provided the police with part of their rationale to surveille any group involved in political activity; the rest was provided by their role of assisting the Security Service in 'defending the realm' against espionage, sabotage, terrorism and subversion (Home Office, 1984, para. 6). It is the last of these – never defined as a criminal offence – which historically enabled security intelligence agencies to cast their surveillance nets wide into areas of entirely lawful and peaceful political activity:

> Subversive activities are those which threaten the safety and well being of the State, and which are intended to undermine or overthrow Parliamentary democracy by political, industrial or violent means. (Home Office, 1984, para. 20)

Revised guidelines were issued in 1994 and retain the same basic definitions and responsibilities with the additions of 'counter-proliferation' (regarding weapons of mass destruction) and the responsibility for gathering intelligence on 'animal rights extremist activity' (Home Office, 1994, para.12).

Security Service

The Secret Service Bureau was established in 1909 as a small department for domestic political surveillance at a time when there was a 'spy-scare' with respect to Germany. By the end of the first world war the staff of what was now MI5 was over 800 but by 1925 had fallen back to 30. In 1931 it was re-named the Security Service (though MI5 is still used) and by 1939 had steadily grown back to 83 intelligence officers and 253 support staff. Growth continued throughout the war and, because of the Cold War, the rundown after 1945 was never as great as it had been in 1918 (Gill, 1994, 226). Never much bigger than 2,000 personnel, after budget cuts in the 1990s staff now number 1,900 (MI5, 1998, 9).

One of the functions of the JIC is to 'task' the collection agencies. This applies particularly to the SIS and GCHQ. However, although the Director General of the Security Service sits on the JIC, the Service retains a greater degree of autonomy from these procedures. Historically, MI5 has been self-tasking: to the extent that there has been 'all-source' analysis of domestic threats it has been MI5 that has carried it out. Since there was no official source of domestic security or political intelligence other than MI5 (or their special branch helpers) ministers had no real means by which to direct MI5 otherwise. Therefore, one of the consequences of changes in the 1990s has been greater integration of MI5 within the central system: the passage of the 1989 Act and the greater involvement of the Security Service in counter-terrorism and 'serious crime' mean that, although it remains largely self-tasking, since 1991 its 'strategic operational objectives' have been in line with JIC requirements (Warner, 1998, 149 fn2). Some uncertainty remains, however, as to how extensively the security service has modernised itself. Internal management was severely criticised by the Security Commission in the case of Michael Bettaney (1985, 25–7) and David Shayler submitted to the Cabinet Office a critique of the Service's outdated management, deployment of CIT and consequent low morale and efficiency (Shayler, 1999).

The first non-statutory mandate for MI5 was written in 1945 but never published; a directive from the Home Office superseded it in 1952 though this was not made public until Lord Denning published it in his 1963 report on the Profumo security scandal. MI5's 'task' was described as the 'Defence of the Realm' from espionage, sabotage and subversion. This was not elaborated upon until the Security Service Act 1989 for the first time gave a statutory mandate to MI5. The primary motivation for this Act was the perception that the complete lack of a statutory mandate or any provision for the receipt and handling of citizen complaints meant, in the light of the *Leander* decision, that it was almost certain that the UK would lose the case being brought before the European Court of Human Rights by two former civil liberties' workers because of their surveillance. Another motive for the Act was the fear that a subsequent Labour government might introduce more radical reform than the minimal measure preferred by the security establishment (Robertson, 1998, 145).

The first section of the Act defined the function of MI5 as the protection of national security, especially against espionage, terrorism, sabotage and subversion but also to safeguard the 'economic well-being of the UK'. In 1992, after an apparently fierce 'turf war' in Whitehall, MI5 took over from the Metropolitan Police Special Branch the lead role regarding Northern Irish Republican paramilitary activity (it already was the main agency regarding all other 'terrorist' groups) and then in 1996 a further move on to police turf came when the Security Service Act added to the 1989 mandate:

> It shall also be the function of the Service to act in support of the prevention and detection of serious crime. (s.1(1) – this new role is considered in more detail below)

In 1993 MI5 published its first account of itself, followed by further editions in 1996 and 1998. An increasing proportion of the Service's resources – now over 40 per cent – is allocated to protective security work, communications, training etc., while the allocation of intelligence work is shown in Table 10.2.

Table 10.2   Security Service Priorities (percentages)

	1990/91	1993	1995/96	1997/98	1998/99	2000/01
Counter espionage	50.0	n/a	n/a	21.1	24.4	23.5
(and counter proliferation)	n/a	(25.0)	(25.0)	3.5	4.2	3.5
Counter terrorism:						
– international	20.0	26.0	33.0	27.2	26.8	25.9
– Irish and other domestic	17.5	44.0	39.0	43.9	36.3	35.3
Counter subversion	12.5	5.0	3.0	–	–	–
Serious crime	–	–	–	4.4	8.3	11.8

Source: adapted from MI5, 1993, 1996, 1998; interview.

Northern Ireland

It would be misleading to write even a brief account of security intelligence in the UK without making reference to the distinctive situation in Northern Ireland, especially since 1969. Despite official secrecy, it is possible to construct a broad account of the organisation of intelligence there, thanks mainly to the work of journalists and occasional court cases and document finds. (Unless otherwise referenced, the following account is based primarily on Geraghty, 1998, 130–68; Statewatch 2(5), Sept-Oct 1992; Urban, 1992, 93–8. See also Maguire, 1990). The intelligence structure in Northern Ireland is a three-pronged affair in which police, security intelligence and military have provided proportionately the most intensive surveillance of the population (1.5 million) anywhere in Europe.

The Royal Ulster Constabulary (RUC) Special Branch ('E' Department) has been the main police department concerned though at various point's efforts have been made to break down their self-imposed isolation from the rest of the force. For example, when Kenneth Newman took over as chief constable in 1976 he brought from London the idea of targeting and sought to establish a new criminal intelligence system to support the work of a new Headquarters Crime Squad drawn from both CID and Special Branch. When Jack Herman took over in 1980 he believed this squad had in turn become a 'force within the force' and imposed a greater circulation of officers (Ryder, 1989, 150, 232). The main sections into which Special Branch is divided are: E1 administration, E2 legal, E3 intelligence (E3A Republican, E3B Loyalist, E3C Left), E4 operations (E4A watchers, E4B technical, E4C/D specialist photographic). Working closely with E4 are the Headquarters Special Mobile Units (HQMSU) used for both public order and covert operations.

The second prong is provided by the Security Service, almost half of whose resources have been devoted to Northern Ireland and connected operations in Britain since 1993 (see Table 2), the Service having taken over the lead role in respect of Republican paramilitary operations in Britain from the Metropolitan Police Special Branch in 1992 (MI5, 1998, 12). It has about 70 officers actually serving in Northern Ireland and one of its Deputy Director Generals serves as the Director and Co-ordinator of Intelligence (DCI) at Stormont advising the Secretary of State for Northern Ireland. In 1994 the then DCI, John Deverell was one of the 29 police, military and RUC intelligence officers killed in the Chinook crash in Scotland (*The Guardian*, June 4 1994, 1). MI5 personnel tend to be attached to specific police or army operations as and when their specific expertise is appropriate.

The third prong is the army. Broadly speaking, one set of intelligence specialists are integrated into the mainstream of army operations while another serve in units that enjoy a high degree of autonomy from the first. In the first group were such as a Weapons Intelligence Unit, a Joint Surveillance Group that was responsible for the management of the product of the multiple computer systems being used, RAF and Army Air Corps providing aerial reconnaissance, and the Field

Reconnaissance Unit (FRU – sometimes referred to as the Field Research Unit) that was based at army HQ at Lisburn and was a centralised handling group for informers. Special Military Intelligence Units (SMIU) provided for liaison with RUC Special Branch and had officers at RUC HQ as well as about 30 officers in each police division. The principal of this liaison was that the RUC provided the local knowledge and the military provided follow-up action. The main players in the second group were the SAS and 14 Intelligence Company. The latter started life as 4 Field Survey Troop and were 'watchers' providing covert surveillance and including also 'Dets' who provided more aggressive information gathering and countering operations.

Given the numbers of agencies on the ground and the lethal nature of the conflict in Northern Ireland in the 1970s, it is perhaps not surprising that the period was characterised by 'intelligence wars' as different agencies competed in terms of their perception of the problem, preferred remedies for dealing with it and sources of information. In an attempt to bring about peace and greater co-ordination of intelligence operations at the end of the 1970s Tasking and Co-ordination Groups (TCGs) were set up in each of three regions (Belfast, South – Gough and North – Derry) with representatives of each of these three prongs. In recognition of the 'police primacy' that had been established in 1976 as part of the overall Government policy of seeking to 'de-militarise' the conflict, an RUC officer was in the Chair. Given the different *modus operandi,* bureaucratic interests and degrees of political autonomy of the three contributors, it is not surprising that this model of hierarchical co-ordination worked only partially. For example, 14 Intelligence Company is not represented on the TCG (Dillon, 1990, 469) and the FRU's system of informers run parallel to that of the RUC. Geraghty concluded that there was no unified intelligence command in NI and that if 'synthesis' occurred it was primarily through the SAS or the Intelligence Corps (1998, 134).

The case of Brian Nelson illustrated very well the longevity of turf wars and the dangers that could result. Nelson joined the UDA – the largest loyalist paramilitary group – in 1972, having been discharged from the army, and became an intelligence officer in 1983. He went to live in Germany in 1985 but returned to Belfast in 1987 having been re-recruited by the FRU as an informer and rejoined the UDA as a senior intelligence officer. However, the RUC were not told of his re-recruitment and MI5 were told but argued against it. Nelson's job included compiling details of Republican targets for UDA gunmen and, in turn, he supplied the army with information as to imminent UDA attacks. His relations with the army were exposed by John Stevens' inquiry into allegations of collusion

rity forces and the loyalist paramilitary groups and he was
uary 1990. Only some limited part of Nelson's activities and
,ications were revealed at his trial in 1992 (*The Guardian*, January
, 1992, 2; Panorama *Dirty War*, BBC1, June 6, 1992).

Doctrine

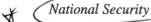

National Security

The Cold War may be over but the extremely broad definition of national
security still pertaining in the UK is a potential pretext for widespread
political surveillance: 'the safeguarding of the state and the community
against threats to their survival or well-being' (HC Debs. March 23, 1984,
col. 591). Outside the UK inquiries into security intelligence abuses have
resulted in a number of efforts to *narrow* similarly broad national security
mandates but this has been resisted in Britain. First, there has been no
public inquiry; second, when ministers have been invited to narrow the
official definition they have declined. Douglas Hurd, for example, during
the passage of the Security Service Act said that the Government did not
want to exclude *anything* from the Service's mandate which might one day
become a threat (HC Debs. Jan 17, 1989, cols.213–4).

It is not, in fact, impossible to define this concept in such a way
that it would concentrate security intelligence resources on genuine threats
and reduce the risk of interference with legitimate political activities.
Laurence Lustgarten and Ian Leigh argue that, contrary to notions of
'balance' between security and rights that predominate in the security
intelligence literature, political and civil rights are actually a major
constituent of national security. Consequently the national security of any
state that fails to protect human rights is not worth defending. Therefore
governments must elaborate precisely what they see as threats, respond to
them proportionately and with appropriate mechanisms of oversight. The
core security task to which, they argue, governments must be confined, is
to defend democratic practice from foreign manipulation along with the
ability to defend the nation's independence and territory against military
attack (Lustgarten and Leigh, 1994, 4–26)[1]. This 'minimalist' definition of
national security provides a significant critique of officialdom's preference
for 'maximalism' but it is difficult to see UK judges actually implementing
it given their ability simultaneously to affirm the importance of rights *in
general* while denying them in *individual* cases (McBarnet, 1983, 154–68).
Once domestic security intelligence threats are enumerated more

specifically, espionage, subversion, terrorism, foreign influence and, more recently, 'economic well-being' are the main categories normally identified.

From Espionage to 'Economic Well-being'?

Espionage, we are told, has not ended with the end of the Cold War. There are some residual areas in which the traditional concern with protecting military secrets still applies, but officials are now more likely to refer to 'illegal technology transfer' and 'proliferation'. For example, the UK Security Service claims its interest is in the 'leakage of selective technology' (1993, 16). But there is reason for scepticism as to the security intelligence role here in that security agency action regarding 'technology transfer' will not be unambiguously determined by any legal prohibitions. Organisational interests must be considered: if an agency's primary mandate is intelligence-gathering then it may well connive at illegal technology transfers if, as a consequence of those transfers, it is receiving useful information. Thus the very utility to the SIS and Security Service of those who became the Matrix Churchill defendants was the access they gained to Iraqi factories and officials through supplying them illegally with machinery (Scott, 1995–6; *Public Law*, Autumn 1996 contains a series of articles discussing the Scott Report).

Yet, especially with foreign intelligence, espionage has been to some extent supplanted by the protection of 'economic well-being'. This is less true of domestic intelligence: MI5 devotes less than half the resources to counter-espionage now compared with the early 1990s (see Table 10.2 above p. 271) but is understood to have only a minimum of resources devoted to economic well-being *per se*. Since all states will define protection of the basic socio-economic structure as a fundamental task of governing, and in modern times governments expect their performance to be judged by the electorate largely in terms of the economy, we should not be surprised if 'national security' is viewed increasingly through the prism of 'economic well-being'. Both GCHQ and SIS have a role here (for example, Smith, 1996, 248–53) but that of domestic security intelligence agencies is minimal.

From 'Subversion' to 'Terrorism'?

Historically, security agencies within liberal capitalist states have regarded 'subversion' as synonymous with left-wing dissent – that never was justifiable in any terms other than the self-interest of the political elites themselves and maintaining this mandate perpetuates the risk of improper state surveillance of political activity. As was shown above the proportion of resources that the Security Service claim to apply to 'subversion' is now very small (half of a person) and in 1998 there was only one British-based organisation that it regarded as 'subversive' – Combat 18, a right-wing group.

The shift has clearly been to 'terrorism' (see Table 10.2, p. 271). What impact a continuation of the Irish peace process will have on these figures remains to be seen but a crucial question will be: how to ensure that there is some legitimate state structure for the gathering of information as to threats of serious political violence while preventing 'terrorism' simply replacing 'subversion' as the pretext for the widespread surveillance of political dissidents? This tendency within security intelligence agencies has been brought about not just by the conservatism of their personnel but also by the logic of targeting and surveillance. Any individuals who are planning illegal political violence will do so covertly and thus be harder to detect. By comparison, political activists organise and propagandise openly and thus are relatively easy to surveille – so agencies develop large banks of data on the latter but frequently struggle to identify the former (Brodeur, 1985, 7–9).

Potentially this problem has been aggravated by the passage of the Criminal Justice (Terrorism and Conspiracy) Act through Parliament in just 48 hours in September 1998. In the wake of the Omagh bombing the Government recalled Parliament during the Summer recess in order to pass the bill to facilitate the conviction of members of groups still using violence in Northern Ireland. But it took the opportunity to include also provisions that had failed to get parliamentary approval in 1997, namely, to make it an offence to incite or conspire in activities in foreign countries that would be unlawful both there and in the UK. This was an attempt by the Government to placate foreign governments such as Egypt and Turkey who have criticised Britain in recent years for harbouring those active opponents of their regimes labelled as 'terrorists'. (*The Guardian*, 26 August 1998, p. 3; 3 September, p. 9; 4 September, p. 5).

'Foreign Influence'

Historically, this has been closely related to subversion and terrorism because western elites have assumed not only that domestic political conflict will arise only as a consequence of conspiracies (Hall *et al*, 1978, 309–10) but also that they will most probably be foreign-directed (Porter, 1989; Thurlow, 1994, 396). Again, the Left has been particularly vulnerable to this because it has explicitly avowed the centrality of international solidarity to its struggles. Although there have been isolated cases of members of the Communist Party being involved in espionage and after 1956 the Soviet Government did provide financial support to the CP, this category for surveillance has been particularly pernicious because, in its most extreme form, there is no way in which an individual can 'disprove' the proposition that she is an agent of foreign influence. The only 'evidence' required for a positive threat-assessment is that someone takes public positions that are consistent with those of a foreign state. Typically, during the Cold War, therefore, arguing for British unilateral disarmament was 'evidence' simply because that was consistent with Soviet aims to achieve military superiority. Currently this will remain a pretext for surveillance primarily in connection with foreign political struggles, especially where they may fall foul of the new terrorism laws referred to above.

From 'Domestic Security' to 'Law Enforcement'?

Although not seen historically as matters of 'national security', the final collection of threats that are currently receiving increased attention from domestic security services relate to law enforcement. The UK Security Service Act 1989 did not include a role for MI5 regarding crime, except permitting it to pass on 'collateral' information, but the Intelligence Services Act 1994 that sets out for the first time in statute the jobs of the SIS and GCHQ specifically included 'the prevention or detection of serious crime' as a function in addition to those regarding 'national security' and 'economic well-being' and the Security Service Act 1996 added 'serious crime' to the Security Service mandate. On the face of it, this represented a rapid change for, in her Introduction to the corporate brochure, the then MI5 Director General, Stella Rimington, wrote in July 1993:

> ...the work of the Service is strictly limited to countering activities that are assessed as threatening national security, or safeguarding the economic well-being of the United Kingdom. *There are*

therefore no plans for the Service to become involved in the investigation of, for example, the misuse of illegal drugs, or organised crime. (1993, p. 5, emphasis added)

But by October 1995 (when the first IRA cease-fire was still holding) the Security Service had successfully positioned itself to take on an increasing role with respect to 'organised crime' (Urban, 1996, 197–209, 280–5 provides some details). Stella Rimington's public lecture to the English-speaking Union offered 'the same strategic approach, the same investigative techniques' to counter the threat of organised crime as had been developed to deal 'with the more familiar threats' (4 October, 1995, p.13). Initially the Service was understood to use 15–20 officers working on crime issues as and when it accepted tasking from the law enforcement community, in particular the National Criminal Intelligence Service (NCIS), but this commitment has certainly increased since given the continuing Irish cease-fire and rising significance of 'organised crime'.

Secrecy and Openness

These are best viewed within a context of 'information control' that has four interacting processes: gathering (both overt and covert), persuasion (providing others with the information you want them to have), secrecy and evaluation (getting more from information than those providing it may want you to have) (Gill, 1996 discusses this in detail). The first two are 'offensive' and are more or less equivalent with Giddens' notion of 'surveillance' that also has two elements: the collection and storage of information (gathering) and the supervision or superintendence of people and/or objects (Giddens, 1985), of which 'persuasion' is clearly one example.

On the defensive side of the equation, secrecy is deployed against the gathering efforts of others, and evaluation is deployed against others' persuasion. Thus there is a dialectical relationship between these processes of information control that is directly analogous to the relationship between power and resistance:

There is always a dialectic to power, always another agency, and another set of standing conditions pertinent to the realisation of that agency's causal powers against the resistance of another. (Clegg, 1989, 208)

This framework provides a context within which to examine a number of recent changes in the UK. First, official secrecy legislation was modernised in 1989. Prior to that, since 1911, the Official Secrets Act contained two main sections of relevance to the security intelligence area. The first section in effect criminalises the communication of information to enemies and has not proved to be particularly controversial in its application over the years. The second section of the 1911 Act, however, proved highly controversial since it criminalised the communication of *any* state information to *anyone* without authorisation. It was the 'catch-all' nature of this section that provided the basis for the notion that secrecy has been the 'cement of the British constitution' (Harden and Lewis 1988, 143–5). Although a series of official reports from the later 1960s onwards recommended the abolition of section 2, in the 1980s it was used on several, uniformly controversial occasions against civil servant 'whistleblowers'. The acquittal of a senior civil servant who had leaked information to an MP revealing the misinformation provided by ministers to Parliament regarding the sinking of the Argentinean ship *General Belgrano* during the Falklands War effectively laid to rest section 2 as an instrument of government and a few years later what became the 1989 Act was introduced.

This was hailed by the government as a 'liberalising' measure on the grounds that it de-criminalised the disclosure of *any* official information (though that remained subject to internal civil service discipline codes) and defined more precisely those areas the disclosure of which would remain a criminal offence, one of which is security and intelligence. This new section has conspicuously *not* been used against some people who have rather obviously been in breach of the law, for example, Robin Robison who worked as an official at the JIC and resigned as a matter of conscience, later talking on TV and elsewhere about aspects of his work.

However, recent cases indicate that the Official Secrets Act will still be used if and when the State chooses although they also demonstrate how the Internet reduces the ability of states to suppress information. Former SIS officer, Richard Tomlinson, was convicted of an official secrets offence in December 1997. He had been dismissed from SIS in 1996 and, having failed to successfully challenge his dismissal or obtain the reasons for it, he planned to write and publish a book about his time in SIS. Since his release a Government injunction has sought to prevent him from publishing any further information but in May 1999 the names of 100 SIS officers (perhaps 30 per cent of the total) appeared on an Internet site. Tomlinson denied having posted it but the list apparently originated with him. Second, David Shayler, who worked in MI5 for 5 years until leaving in 1997, successfully challenged an attempt to extradite him from France where he was arrested on 1 August, 1998. His revelations regarding MI5 first appeared in the *Mail on Sunday* in August 1997 and amounted to two main critiques: the unnecessary retention of redundant counter-subversion files and the Service's incompetence in countering the more serious threat of terrorism (24 August, 1997, 31 August, 1997). Shayler's allegations can be read on www.shayler.com.[2] In a third case, Tony Geraghty has become the first writer to be charged under the Act, along with a former Army officer, Nigel Wylde as a result of his book *The Irish War* (*The Guardian*, 11 May 1999, 6). The charges against both men have subsequently been dropped.

Files

The core of security intelligence work is the files. Three issues are considered here: first, the principles upon which, as far as we know, the security agencies generate and keep files, second, the issue of the destruction of files and, third, the circumstances under which, if any, files are released. As far as the Security Service is concerned, what we know about the first is based upon the report of the Security Services Commissioner. In 1992 the Commissioner outlined the procedures: a file may be 'temporary' and have a maximum life of 3 years. Once a permanent file is opened it is coded 'green' for an indefinite period while there is active investigation of the subject. Once active inquiries are no longer perceived as necessary it will be coded as 'amber' during which time any further information that the Service receives about the subject may be added to the file. At the end of this period the file will be coded 'red' during which no further information may be added to the file. After a further period the file is microfilmed, the hard copy is destroyed and reference to the file is transferred from the Live Index to the Research Index (Cm1946, 1992 [original misdated as 1991], para. 19). Given that the Service started computerising in the mid-1970s and by 1990 was said to have the capacity for 20 million files (Gill, 1994, 190), the failure of the Commissioner to make reference to computerisation is interesting. The Service itself first referred to it in 1998. It says that the paper files remain the main working documents but that computer-based documents increase in significance. Also the Service maintains computerised indices of individuals and organisations that have 'come to notice' in the course of investigations. Such references may or may not subsequently develop into files (MI5, 1998, 24; Intelligence & Security Committee [ISC], 1998, para.41).

The main headings and numbers of current holdings were published in 1998. The Security Service presently holds 440,000 files. Of these 150,000 relate to administration, subjects and organisations who have been 'studied' by the Service and individuals or groups who have not been studied but who have for example, been offered protective security advice. The other 290,000 files are on individuals who 'may have' been subject to investigation. Of these, 40,000 have been microfilmed and are available only for specific research purposes, 135,000 'red' files are closed but have been retained for research purposes, and 97,000 'amber' concern individuals into whom there are no active inquiries but to whose files collateral information may be added. There are 20,500 'green' files (of which 3,000 are temporary), 13,000 of them on British citizens (MI5, 1998, 24–5; ISC, 1998, paras. 41–51).

The ISC has now published also the first details of SIS file-holdings. There are 86,000 records relating mainly to staff, agents, former agents and other potential sources about half of which are on British citizens. 75 per cent of these are closed in the sense that no papers have been added to them for three years and the 'vast majority' is retained because of their potential operational value (ISC, 1998, para. 52).

Regarding file-destruction, the security and intelligence services may, like any other government department, destroy whatever files they wish up to 25 years after closure. The Security Service had opened 725,000 files since 1909; by 1970 175,000 of these had been destroyed, mainly after the two world wars. The process of destruction was halted in 1970 when the Service encountered problems in a counter-espionage investigation because of files that had been destroyed. Destruction resumed in 1992 since when a further 110,000 (mainly subversion) files have been destroyed or earmarked for destruction. So far the review of these has been limited to individuals aged 55 or over (ISC, 1998, para. 47).

When the continuing destruction of those most contentious of files regarding counter-subversion was made public there was vigorous parliamentary opposition and in July 1998 the Home Secretary announced a review of the criteria on which the Security Service selects files for preservation. The review criticised the Service's existing criteria for retention for their emphasis on 'major' investigations and 'important' individuals. Instead it said that the interests of future historians should be met by preserving a wider range of material showing the Services activities within their social, economic and political context. The findings of the Review were accepted by the Government (HC. Debs. 3 February 1999, cols. 619–20) and can be accessed at www.pro.gov.uk/advisory council/.

Third, until very recently MI5 files were never released. However, in November 1997 MI5 handed over to the Public Record Office (PRO) the first of its files covering the period 1909–19 and it was expected that about 98 per cent of its *remaining* files for the period would be released. These are now available on CD-ROM. The names of employees are intact but those of agents (informers) are excised. In 1999 and 2000 further files were published, mainly covering the two world wars but including also an internal history of the period 1908–45 that has also been published by the PRO as a book.

So, as it is, those files that do become available having been selected by the Service, while they may give some insight into the past, will, in terms of our model, be part of an information control strategy aimed at the 'persuasion' of society that Service operations have always been necessary and proportionate. Only full access to the historical files would enable researchers to judge whether that strategy is best described as 'education' or 'deception'.

The 1997 Labour Government announced its intention to introduce a Freedom of Information Act and the White Paper published in 1998 set out plans that went further than many reformers had hoped. However, the Act passed in 2000 after the Home Office took over responsibility for the legislation has been a comparative disappointment (for example Frankel, 1999). National security matters and the work of the intelligence agencies are exempt, as they were in the White Paper. But, in general, the damage test has been weakened from one of 'substantial harm' to 'prejudice' and, where departments have the discretion to publish information 'in the public interest' but decline to do so, the Information Commissioner will be unable to challenge their judgement.

Accountability

Until 25 years ago little could have been written about the accountability of security intelligence agencies apart from its absence. In the US congressional committees had a formal role reviewing programmes and budgets but carried out no serious inquiries. In the UK the Security Commission had been established in 1965 but it operated only when set up by the Prime Minister to investigate and report on some security leak. Much has changed now but fundamental questions remain: specifically, for what are security intelligence agencies accountable and to whom?

It is important to distinguish 'accountability' from 'control'. The first refers to the liability of an agency to explain or justify its actions to some other body. The second refers to the situation in which some outside body manages or directs the actions of the security agency (cf. the discussion in Brodeur, 1997, 83–5).[3] Both are crucial dimensions on which to measure the autonomy of the agency: the most autonomous agency will be that which determines its own policies and accounts to no-one for its operations; the least autonomous will be both directed in its policies and have to explain its actions to others. The normal liberal democratic doctrine is that permanent state officials should not be autonomous, in other words, they should be both directed in their policies by elected ministers and be accountable to those ministers for their actions. In turn those ministers should account for their actions, in a parliamentary system, to the assembly. Historically, however, security intelligence agencies have been granted virtual immunity from these arrangements: they have normally been established by political executives rather than assemblies and mandated to defend the state itself. Consequently executives felt no pressure to subject the agencies to the usual democratic restraints.

Since 1989 a series of new structures enabling outsiders to review aspects of Security Service work have been installed but these have actually been intended to improve the management of the Service rather than its accountability (for example, Robertson, 1998). The first innovation was the appointment of a Commissioner and Tribunal. These offices had actually first been introduced in the Interception of Communications Act 1985 and the model has now been extended to cover also SIS and GCHQ. The procedures under which they operate are quite complicated; indeed, it might be argued that this is the direct result of the search for a minimalist structure of accountability that would pass the scrutiny of the European Court of Human Rights but go no further. The Tribunal (three lawyers) receive complaints from the public and determine whether they are justified. They enlist the help of the Commissioner if the complaint relates to 'an interference with property' for which the Service would have required a ministerial warrant. The Commissioner, either at the request of the tribunal or on his own initiative, examines the granting of warrants and subjects the process to the standards of judicial review (that is, deciding whether the action of the minister was 'reasonable'). The only public product of all this is the Commissioner's annual report to the Prime Minister which is subsequently (and suitably censored) placed before Parliament. Since 1989 the Tribunal has received something like 200 complaints, none of which have been upheld. The Reports of the Commissioner amount to very brief (the first five averaged four pages) and highly legalistic discourses on the minutiae of procedures by which warrants are obtained and, occasionally, reveal errors that have been made.

But the whole edifice has produced nothing remotely as significant or informative as, say, the annual reports of the Canadian Security Intelligence Review Committee (SIRC).[4]

The other innovation, and one that is potentially of much greater significance, is the Intelligence and Security Committee (ISC) that was established by the passage of the Intelligence Services Act 1994. The main objective of this Act was to place SIS and GCHQ on similar statutory footings as the Security Service had been in 1989. The mandate of the ISC is to examine the expenditure, administration and policy of the three agencies. Now, potentially this is a wide remit, certainly by comparison with that of the Commissioner whose remit is the procedural legality of issuing warrants, and the ISC has already produced some quite interesting reports, for example, regarding the issue of the Security Service taking on 'serious' crime and the implications of this for co-operation with police (ISC, 1995).

The main flaw in the ISC structure (from the point of view of outsiders) relates to its access to information. First, the committee consists of parliamentarians whose *raison d'être* is their role as public representatives but they have been taken within what ministers refer to as 'the barrier of secrecy'. This is symbolised by the fact that the committee's staff is drawn from the Cabinet Office (the heart of executive government in the UK) and not from Parliament and that it meets in the Cabinet Office, not at the Houses of Parliament. However, having been thus embraced by Whitehall, the ISC has still not been granted the complete access to security information that would be necessary for them to do a thorough job. Interestingly, both the Commissioner and the Tribunal do have complete access: the relevant legislation places a legal duty on members of the agencies to provide all documents and information that they require. But the Government that brought in the legislation said that the ISC did not 'need to know' as much as the Commissioner and the Tribunal (Lords Debs, January 13, 1994, cols. 285, 293) and the procedures by which it obtains information boil down to the fact that the minister is the crucial gatekeeper in determining whether the ISC does or does not receive information for which it asks (Gill, 1996 discusses these procedures in detail). In its 1998 report the ISC acknowledges that it has problems in being authoritative and thus establishing public confidence in the oversight system:

> ...we are conscious that, in comparison to other countries, we lack the ability to investigate directly different aspects of the Agencies' activities...We believe that enhancement of the present

arrangements can be achieved without necessarily changing our remit or the law, at this stage, but by extending the Committee's reach with an additional investigative capacity. Such a person would need access to the Agencies' staff and papers…we have not had the capability to conduct independent verification ourselves. (ISC, 1998, §69)

In its response the Government said that it would view 'sympathetically' ISC requests for information and would be prepared to discuss strengthening of its staff but it was equally clear that it had no intention of giving up ultimate control of the information available to the Committee (Prime Minister, 1998, para. 21). Subsequently an investigator with previous experience in Defence Intelligence Services was appointed.

It is too early to draw firm conclusions regarding the ISC; it is only now that some research is being undertaken into its performance. Marc Davies (1999), for example, notes the significant change in tone that is evident in the Report for 1997–8. While this may well have been partly due to the Labour majority on the Committee, he suggests it also showed the fruits of a committee that had started slowly but had successfully developed trust among the agencies and avoided provoking them into resistance to the new oversight mechanism. However, parliamentarians continue to criticise the relative non-accountability of the agencies, especially regarding financial matters (*Sunday Telegraph*, 6 June 1999, 8) and, in June 1999, the Commons Home Affairs Committee recommended that the ISC be reconstituted as a select committee. However, acknowledging the advantages of one committee reviewing all the intelligence agencies, it proposed the establishment of a special rather than a departmental select committee (1999, 3rd Report, paras. 31–48).

Currently, the structure of accountability in the UK is a ramshackle affair: whether by accident or design is hard to determine. On the one hand, it is possible to see the structure as a triumph of English empiricism with governments responding to successive pressures from Europe or the agencies themselves by 'bolting-on' structures as circumstances appeared to require. However, sometimes a different image appears as governments seek to minimise accountability while increasing their own precarious grip on security intelligence matters. For example, the resources available to review bodies are always small and, if there is more than one such body, then it makes sense from the point of view of maximising their effectiveness if these bodies are able to co-operate, share expertise and so on. This is, for example, the situation in Canada where SIRC and the Inspector General have different places within the structure and different

ose co-operation and sharing of information is required by
:r, the Government specifically excluded this; indeed it has
ed the accountability structures by, for example, rejecting
ports from the Tribunal and Commissioner go direct to the
; can only be directed intentionally at reducing rather than
.... accountability. The ISC appreciates this problem and has sought
to establish co-operation between itself, the National Audit Office and the
Public Accounts Committee (ISC, 1998, paras. 21–3).

Human Rights Dangers

The May 1997 election of a Labour Government committed to the
incorporation of the European Human Rights Convention into UK law
clearly marked a significant break with the past yet nothing so far indicates
that 'eternal vigilance' will be any less needed in the future. Although
British lawyers and politicians played a significant role in writing the
convention after 1945 and Britain signed up to the Convention, individuals
have normally had to go to Strasbourg to challenge adverse Government
decisions. The Human Rights Act 1998 makes it illegal for public
authorities to act incompatibly with the Convention but, while courts will
be able to declare Acts of Parliament 'incompatible with the Convention',
they will not be able to overrule them. Thus the Government has sought to
maintain parliamentary supremacy, indicating their hope that laws deemed
incompatible will be changed by Government and Parliament (Home
Office, Cm 3782, quoted in *The Guardian*, 25 October 1997, 10).

The HRA only came into effect in October 2000 and it remains
uncertain just what difference incorporation will make. On the one hand, as
we have seen, the security intelligence agencies have spent the last ten
years erecting a new, statute-based security architecture that was designed
with the Convention in mind and therefore incorporation is unlikely to have
a dramatic effect. There are several specific areas of the security
intelligence 'process' that give rise to particular dangers for human rights,
especially in the context of the convergence of 'national security' and
'crime' issues. Just three are discussed here: targeting, sources and
networks. Historically, the traditional 'targeting' practices of security
intelligence agencies led them inexorably towards the surveillance of
dissent, usually based on membership or association with some group
(union, peace etc.) or already targeted individual. Targeting is the crux of
the intelligence process; given the large variety of behaviours that might be
targeted, the process leading to the designation of some as targets but not

others is crucial. Much of what security agencies do thereafter involves efforts to confirm hypotheses, a similar process to the 'case construction' conducted by police (McConville *et al*, 1991). Thus targeting is not a process of 'rational' decision making; rather, it is heavily influenced by official discourses and stereotyping. 'Recipe' or 'cybernetic' theories describe better how targeting decisions are initially relatively constrained and then tend to be reinforced by organisational processes. (Gill, 1998 discusses the use of cybernetic models in analysing intelligence processes).

The current significance of this is that 'organised crime' – increasingly cited as a central target for security intelligence – has always been viewed by police in essentially ethnic terms, for example, 'Italian', 'Asian', and, most recently, 'Russian'. For example, a recent survey of the impact of transnational organised crime on Canada acknowledges the unsurprising point that its foremost advantage for criminal organisations is its provision of unparalleled access to and from the US market, the original and largest centre of organised crime. But this point and the significance of NAFTA receive scant analysis or official recognition compared with what are identified as the main consequences of 'global modernisation' – the increases in criminal activity originating from the third world and Eastern Europe (Jamieson *et al*, 1998, 306; Rioux and Hay, 1995, 173–92). Similarly, the new European security architecture is dominated by official concerns with population movements and defined largely in terms of ethnicity (for example Bunyan, 1993, 15–33; Busch, 1997, 51). Didier Bigo characterised this as a paradigm shift in which previously disconnected issues (drugs, hooliganism, extreme right, smuggling, illegal immigration, asylum) are brought together along what he calls a 'security continuum' (1994, 163–4). Hence, as 'crime' replaces 'subversion' as the target, then widespread surveillance of ethnic minorities may well replace that of dissident minorities.

Police and security agencies have always relied on some mix of 'technical' and 'human' sources for their information. Various legal changes since 1985 have sought to provide some structure for both the authorisation and oversight of the former (Interception of Communications Act 1985, Security Service Act 1989, Intelligence Services Act 1994, Police Act 1997) but the latter remain essentially unchecked other than by internal guidelines. This may seem odd given that human sources are by far the more extensively deployed and productive source of information yet precisely because of that the Home Office has shrunk from attempting to provide greater controls. In some jurisdictions the courts have sought to apply some check but in the UK the courts have taken a lenient view of police information gathering practices even for example, tolerating the employment of *agents provocateurs* if the resulting information provided useful evidence (*R* v. *Sang*, 1980).

The Regulation of Investigatory Powers Act 2000 (RIPA) provides for the first time a more-or-less comprehensive statutory umbrella for all forms of surveillance including the up-dating of IOCA to take account of recent technological developments such as the Internet. It includes provisions for the authorisation of informers and undercover operations but these will still only be internal. RIPA's provisions for the external oversight of other surveillance practices replicates the inadequate Commissioner/ Tribunal model discussed earlier. This suggests that the overall objective of RIPA was to construct a legal edifice that would pass muster with the European Convention rather than genuinely enhance oversight. In the wake of 11 September 2001 it seems very unlikely that the HRA will provide enough political 'space' for such practices to develop with respect to covert surveillance where recent developments have compounded the lax and state-centred regime in the UK.

For example, since 1993, police have been seeking to make greater use of intelligence techniques not just against 'serious' and 'organised' crime but at all levels of policing. This has meant that all police officers (frequently with little if any training and inadequate supervision) are being encouraged to recruit informers. A second development was the passage of the Criminal Procedure and Investigations Act 1996. The major miscarriage of justice cases that were resolved from 1989 onwards included a significant number where the police and/or prosecution had failed to disclose material evidence to the defence. As a result the obligations on the prosecution had been increased and this Act reflected the Government's desire to 'redress the balance'. It sets up a procedure whereby the prosecution, first, disclose to the defence what they believe to be 'relevant' to the prosecution and then the defence must disclose their case to the prosecution. Then the prosecution must disclose any further material that might be reasonably expected to assist the defence case (Leng and Taylor, 1996, 7–33).

The Act retains broadly the same rules regarding the withholding of 'sensitive' material from the defence – Public Interest Immunity (PII) certificates. The judge makes the decision as to whether a prosecution request for non-disclosure will be upheld after a hearing in which the defence may be involved or not. In the case of 'super-sensitive' information, for example, when disclosure would directly threaten national security, the defence may remain unaware even of the application. Given that prosecution disclosure is based on the decisions of prosecution and police in a system that remains adversarial, it is assuredly only a matter of time before we hear of fresh miscarriages. Indeed, recent surveys by the Law Society and

Criminal Bar Association found a 'widespread and fundamental series of failures' by police and prosecutors to comply with the Act and even the Director of Public Prosecutions has warned of the implications of these failures for generating fresh miscarriages (*The Guardian*, 15 July 1999, 8).

As the Security Service becomes involved in the preparation of cases for trial there are further dangers because of the gulf between the agencies' traditional practices and the requirements for open and fair trials. For example, when Security Service officers have appeared to give evidence it has been anonymously, and, in some cases, appearing behind screens. The increased use of informers by police similarly results in an increased tendency to use PII to prevent disclosure of their identities to the defence. JUSTICE – the British section of the International Commission of Jurists – has published a comprehensive review of the human rights issues involved in the growth of covert policing (JUSTICE, 1998, pp.62–9 discusses disclosure issues in particular).

The third problem illustrates in a very practical way one of the more conceptual ideas with which this paper began. Until relatively recently the fears of civil libertarians regarding the activities of police and security agencies were most likely to be encapsulated in the notion of a highly centralised state structure incorporating extensive surveillance and information-banks. The most-used metaphor for this was George Orwell's 'Big Brother' in *1984*. It was suggested early in the paper that this model of the state as unified, centralised, hierarchical and sovereign was being increasingly replaced by a more pluralistic view of state structures seeking to 'guide' or 'steer' varieties of other organised groups in pursuit of policy goals. The idea of networks of governance can be seen most clearly in the process by which information is now gathered, processed, analysed and disseminated. The problem for civil libertarians now is less the development of *centralised* databanks because they are no longer necessary, but rather the rapid extension of surveillance and information networks in both the public and private spheres. Manuel Castels has characterised this invasion of all realms of life as the replacement of 'Big Brother' by a myriad of 'little sisters' (1997, 301).

The sisters interact increasingly: 'data matching' – the exchange of personal data between government departments without the consent or knowledge of the data subjects – is progressing fast. For many years police and security agencies have relied much on the unofficial exchange of information between officers who know and trust each other (the defining characteristic of an effective 'network') and these informal exchanges will always remain highly significant. But CIT enables much more systematic and rapid exchanges of data between agencies and renders centralised databases obsolete.

In the UK the Social Security Administration (Fraud) Act 1996 for the first time permitted computerised cross-matching of personal data as between tax, immigration, social security and local authorities (*The Guardian*, 17 July 1997, p.7). Security intelligence agencies are not yet formally included in that network but there is a UK Intelligence Messaging Network incorporating the Agencies (MI5, MI6, GCHQ), Ministry of Defence and the Foreign and Commonwealth Office and connections with other departments, for example, the Department of Trade and Industry (ISC, 1996, para. 40).

The UK Data Protection Registrar had until recently failed to insert any data protection for the citizen into these developments but the Data Protection Act 1998 does extend her powers. The 1984 Act allowed the exemption of any system on 'national security' grounds if validated by a ministerial certificate to that effect. This meant that the security intelligence agencies refused to even register their systems with the Data Protection Registrar but she did warn them that their move into the area of 'crime' meant they must be subject to the same rules as police, that is, systems must be registered even if specific areas of data remain exempt from subject access (*The Sunday Times*, 1 February 1998). The new Act retains ministerial certificates as conclusive evidence that a system may be exempted because of its national security nature but with the slight modification that such certificates may be subject to judicial review by a special Data Protection Tribunal.

Of course, this networking is not happening only within nations. Prior to the 1990s most discussion of transnational intelligence structures revolved around the security networks erected as part of the Cold War and, in the West, under US hegemony (Whitaker, 1998, 417–21). Otherwise transnational policing co-operation was relatively underdeveloped – since the 1920s it had been manifest in Interpol which was little more than a rather insecure post-box for information and did not develop any more significant role hampered as it was by the lack of trust which is necessary for any meaningful intelligence network to develop. Within Europe the attempt to develop more systematic frameworks began in 1976 with the institution of TREVI as an inter-governmental structure (separate from the then EC institutions) aimed particularly at intelligence regarding political violence and public disorder (Bunyan, 1993, 15–28).

The Maastricht Treaty 1992 for the first time brought aspects of these developments within the third pillar of the EU treaty (justice and home affairs) though there remained a considerable democratic deficit in that the opportunity for elected representatives to contribute was highly restricted. The most formalised attempt to transnationalise policing in Europe came with the introduction of the European Police Office (Europol) which was envisaged by most EU countries as essentially an intelligence office that would, for the first time, provide a central pool of law enforcement intelligence, though Germany, and especially Helmut Kohl, retained the ambition that Europol would become an operational police force throughout Europe. The official view in UK seemed to be that this was extremely unlikely for a number of reasons, including the lack of a common criminal code that Europol might enforce, as well as the obvious political difficulties (Interview with Home Office official). Yet at the Amsterdam summit in 1997 an agreement was reached which clearly envisaged a role for Europol in the operations of European police forces (*Statewatch*, 7(2), 1997, 2), and so it came about when Europol 'went live' in 1999.

However, in general it is clear that the movement towards formal co-operative networks of law enforcement has been relatively slow. There are a number of important reasons for this. Whitaker suggests that one reason is the extensive bi-lateral agreements already in existence from the Cold War that have been developed from below by practitioners with minimal involvement of ministers and which, therefore, suit practitioners very well and make the search for grand international agreements less urgent (Whitaker, 1998, 431). A long-standing but still developing example of this is the use of liaison officers, for example Customs and Excise has a network of 41 Drugs Liaison Officers (DLOs); by 1997 they also had eight Fiscal Liaison Officers to deal with tax and excise matters, mainly in Europe but also in Hong Kong (Interview with member of Customs & Excise National Intelligence Division).

Even if formal multilateral agreements are seen as, in some respects, preferable, their negotiation is fraught with difficulties since internal security and law enforcement are precisely those areas of traditional state power where politicians are most wary of being seen to give up their 'sovereign' powers. Formal bi-lateral arrangements are further augmented by informal networks that have developed within the law enforcement and security intelligence communities. The Club of Berne, Trevi and Vienna Group are all examples of informal multilateral networks between European security agencies (Bunyan, 1993, 173–81). One organising framework for law enforcement co-operation is the International Working Group on Police Undercover Activities that provides a forum for mutual assistance in undercover operations (Penrose, 1996). Another is a 'Group of 20' – the 15 EU states plus the US, Canada, Norway, Australia and New Zealand – that is said to be seeking the creation of a global system for the surveillance of telecommunications – phones, faxes and e-mail (Statewatch, 7(4/5), 1997, 1–2). One wonders how this network will interrelate with the similar UKUSA network co-ordinated by the US National Security Agency.

There is now an extensive literature regarding many of the issues raised by these transnational developments (Hebenton and Thomas, 1995; Anderson *et al*, 1995). For present purposes it is important to note that intelligence process are absolutely central: networks of information exchange can develop *sub rosa* in a way that joint operations cannot. The former can be conducted quietly, informally with no other requirements than mutual trust between donor and recipient since there need be no public manifestation of the exchange at all. The latter, however, require *action* that, even if conducted covertly, carries with it the much greater risk of becoming public knowledge and therefore something for which an agency might be held to account. Therefore, intelligence networks are always likely to be far in advance of operational networks and informal ones will always will be far more extensive than the formal.

Conclusion

The current rapid development of security intelligence networks both within and between nations raises profound problems of control and accountability. Some of these problems are not new but are aggravated by these developments. For example, existing accountability arrangements tend to be 'institutional' rather than 'functional' and therefore, if only some agencies are subject to review, the possibility arises of operations being 'sub-contracted' to unreviewed agencies elsewhere in the network (cf. Lustgarten, 1997, 78–9). Furthermore, there is extensive interchange of personnel and, under certain conditions, information between public and private sector security agencies who deploy similar intelligence methods in developing their targets and 'risk assessments' (Johnston, 1992, 183–203; Marx, 1987). The steady growth of the number of agencies now performing security intelligence functions and the increasing sophistication of their CIT resources seem to render older models of institutional review redundant. The problem is not that the agencies together represent some panoptic 'Big Brother' because the networks reflect bridges across which some data is transferred but much is not and remains, unshared, in the 'ownership' of one agency.

Rather it is that, given the apparent extent of current 'threats' to security, these (usually quite small) agencies select those who are to be targeted and, as long as the law is as permissive as it is in the UK, there will be no real check on those selections. Such checks as do exist in the UK are on processes of information gathering although, as we have seen, they are concerned essentially with procedural regularities. Where there are no checks at all is in relation to the quality of intelligence analysis and dissemination. There is no external review body in the UK that could conduct an independent audit of these crucial functions – they are not within the mandate of the Commissioner or Tribunal and the Intelligence and Security Committee lacks the necessary access.

It might be thought that the move of the security agencies towards the 'crime' area would potentially increase the check on their activities since such operations are more likely to end up in the public arena of a court than was usual with traditional security intelligence work. This will be so only in a minority of cases because, increasingly, both police and security agencies seek not the arrest and prosecution of their targets but the *disruption* of their enterprises. This can take a variety of forms but what they have in common is their low visibility (compared with arrests and prosecution) and therefore their relative immunity from traditional forms of accountability. If we are to start to tackle this immense problem of securing greater democratic control and accountability of the security intelligence community, then, we are going to have to do so by developing appropriate ways of auditing the networks of security information and intelligence processes.

Notes

[1]   See also Lustgarten's contribution to this volume.
[2]   Shayler returned to Britain in August 2000 and currently is on bail awaiting trial.
[3]   See also Brodeur's essay on Canada and Brodeur/Dupeyron on France in this volume.
[4]   See Brodeur in this volume.

Chapter 11

Parliament, Media and the Control of Intelligence Services in Germany

Shlomo Shpiro

Introduction – German intelligence and its controls

Intelligence services have been an integral part the German state organisation since the founding of the Second Reich in 1871.[1] Different and often competing services formed the backbone of the Nazi party security apparatus during the Third Reich. After the end of World War Two Germany was divided into two parts, the Soviet controlled zones establishing their own intelligence services as extensions of their larger Soviet counterparts. In the western part the CIA undertook the establishment of a German intelligence services, in the form of the 'Organisation Gehlen (OG)', run as a private venture by General Reinhard Gehlen, former head of the Wehrmacht's military intelligence on the eastern front. Only in the mid-1950s was the OG instituted as an official government body, accountable to the Chancellor, and renamed *Bundesnachrichtendienst* (BND). In parallel to that, the Federal Republic of Germany established an internal security service (BfV) and a military counter-intelligence arm (MAD). These three organisations were augmented by a nascent military intelligence service only truly established in the late 1980s.

Throughout the Cold War, the German intelligence services were often viewed through a cloud of myths and an atmosphere of 'James Bond'-like dimensions, often encouraged by these very services themselves, while their inherent secrecy made comparative analysis difficult. The German unification, the end of the bipolar conflict and the need to redefine the roles of intelligence services in Western democracies exposed some of the basic parameters in the intelligence debate, which in Germany is far from over. These parameters, in the German context, clearly present intelligence services as an integral and 'normal' part of the democratic state mechanisms, performing various assigned functions for the defence and protection of democracy, being regulated by legislation, financed by public funds and providing a service for the community at large like any other government department.[2]

Unlike some of their western counterparts, throughout the years of the Cold War the German intelligence services enjoyed only a very limited level of public legitimacy and support for their perceived role within the East-West conflict. Media coverage of intelligence was far less limited by legal restrictions than in other European democracies and developed into an important element in both creating the public image of the German services as part of government and limiting their activities in the more extreme aspects of intelligence work. Following the collapse of the Soviet Union and the German unification, questions began to be raised both in the German political and media spheres over the efficiency, economy and even actual need for intelligence services. German intelligence chiefs began a hard battle for the survival of their organisations, a battle that necessitated the adoption of new roles and new targets for their activities. Various cost-cutting measures implemented in the defence budgets, often referred to as the 'dividends-of-peace', forced sharp measures within the intelligence community to reduce expenditure and increase efficiency, while new parliamentary debates and legislation lifted some of the veil covering their activities and compelled them to adopt a new posture towards the issue of parliamentary controls and media coverage. Despite intense debate following the 1998 election victory of the SPD/Green coalition under Chancellor Gerhard Schroeder, the multilateral system of parliamentary controls remains in place, the new government being satisfied with minor changes in the individual competencies of the different controlling bodies.[3]

This chapter examines the mechanisms that exert official control or democratic oversight functions over the intelligence services in Germany. It analyses the different parliamentary committees and their specific functions, as well as the role of the media as a public 'watchdog' in influencing the services to adapt their internal workings and operations to more public scrutiny in the information age.

The Structure of the German Intelligence Communities

The origins of the Federal German intelligence services date to the early years of the Federal Republic and the end of the Allies occupation of Germany.[4] This community comprises three services:

- The Federal Intelligence Service – *Bundesnachrichtendienst* (BND),

- The Office for the Protection of the Constitution – *Bundesamt für Verfassungsschutz* (BfV),
- The Military Counter-intelligence Branch – *Militaerischer Abschirmdienst* (MAD).

The BND was established in 1955.[5] It is responsible for the collection and analysis of information from a variety of clandestine sources outside Germany, as well as through the monitoring of telecommunications (SIGINT), carried out through listening stations and state-of-the-art technologies.[6] It provides intelligence information to the government and its various branches, to assist in the carrying out of their official policies. Ministerial responsibility for the BND is in the hands of the Federal Minister at the *Bundeskanzleramt*.[7] The BND central headquarters is located in Pullach, on the outskirts of Munich.[8]

The BfV, established in 1950 as a security body to protect the new Federal German constitution, is responsible for counter-espionage activities within the geographical boundaries of Germany.[9] It is also tasked with monitoring a wide range of extremist political organisations and movements that are considered capable of posing a violent threat to the democratic order of the Federal Republic.[10] These include terrorist organisations, extremist political movements and racially-motivated groups as well as foreign organisations active in Germany.[11] The BfV works in co-operation with its counterparts on the Land level – the LfVs – in collecting information through a variety of agents, informers and technical clandestine methods. The BfV works under the ministerial authority of the Federal Ministry of Interior – *Bundesministerium des Innern* (BMI) – and is based in Cologne.[12]

The MAD was established at the same time as the Federal Armed Forces – the *Bundeswehr* – in mid 1950s.[13] It is responsible for military counter-espionage and internal security within the armed forces.[14] Its work is restricted to the military and it does not conduct work concerning civilians, which is referred to the BfV or appropriate police force.[15] The Federal Ministry of Defence – *Bundesministerium der Verteidigung* (BMVg) – is responsible for the MAD.[16]

Parliamentary Control

The parliamentary control system developed in Germany is multilateral, with four distinctly separate parliamentary bodies operating side by side. The different roles assigned to each body in this multilateral system represent separate aspects in the work of intelligence, which require different mechanisms and capabilities for their effective control. The activities of all four controlling bodies are anchored in parliamentary legislation establishing their powers and limits. However, often in issues not specified by legislation various forms of administrative practical norms, or 'operational tradition', have developed in the relations between government and the intelligence bodies on the one hand and the controlling bodies on the other.

The system of parliamentary controls in Germany draws on over three decades of development. The main body to exercise this control is the Parliamentary Control Commission – *Parlamentarische KontrollKommission* (PKG) – that is tasked with examining political and operational issues.[17] Beyond the PKG, three other parliamentary committees control different professional aspects of intelligence activities. The G-10 Committee (*Gremium*) and the G-10 Commission (*Kommission*) deal with issues where the privacy of the individual citizen, enshrined in the Basic Law, are encroached upon in the form of mail interception and electronic monitoring of communications.[18] The 'Committee of Confidants' (*Vertrauensgremium*) examines the budgets of the intelligence agencies and authorises their expenditure and accounting.[19] All these bodies depend for their administrative support on the Office of the Federal Chancellor which co-ordinates and regulates the executive control of the Chancellor over Germany's intelligence community.[20]

The Bundeskanzleramt

Department VI at the Office of the Federal Chancellor – the *Bundeskanzleramt* – co-ordinates the activities of the German intelligence services with respect to issues of parliamentary controls. With a staff of over twenty it is answerable to the Federal Minister in charge of the *Kanzleramt*.[21] In practice it also supports the work of the government's Intelligence Co-ordinator, with the senior rank of *Staatsminister*.[22] Ministerial responsibility over each of the intelligence services in vested in the hands of the relevant Federal Minister.[23] The Intelligence Co-ordinator is responsible for co-ordination and enhancing the co-operation between the BND, the BfV and the MAD, both among themselves and with other government departments.[24] He is also specifically tasked with the preparation of PKG meetings.[25]

The Intelligence Co-ordinator has the legal right to request any information from the intelligence services regarding their structure, methods of activity, archives, budget and personnel planning.[26] He also has direct access to the heads of the services.[27] The BMVg and the BMI are obliged to inform the Intelligence Co-ordinator of any intelligence-related matters, which are of political or public interest.[28]

Although not an elected body, the *Kanzleramt* fulfils a crucial role not only by carrying out administrative internal controls over the BND but also by affecting the activities of all the parliamentary control bodies.[29] The *Kanzleramt* carries out much of the procedural work of the controlling committees, as well as carry out the bulk of the everyday administrative work involved in this process.[30] The Intelligence Co-ordinator is the highest government representative in the different committee meetings[31] and may be called upon by the various controlling bodies to assist with any request regarding information, documents, statements or any other practical matters required by the committees in discharging their duties.[32]

The Parlamentarische KontrollKommission (PKG)

Under the 'Law over the Parliamentary Control of Intelligence Activities' of 1978 (PKG-Gesetz), the *Parlamentarische KontrollKommission* is the main parliamentary body for exercising general control functions over the Federal German intelligence services.[33] This committee consists of nine MdB's – members of the *Bundestag*, Germany's lower parliament chamber – of which traditionally five are members of the coalition.[34] PKG members are elected by the plenary session of the *Bundestag* after nominations by their respective parties, for the duration of each new parliament.[35] The PKG Chair rotates every half-year between members from the coalition and opposition.[36]

Under the PKG-Gesetz the Federal government must inform the PKG of the general activities of the intelligence services, as well as of specific operations which carry 'special meaning' (*von besonderer Bedeutung*), a rather vague definition generally accepted to mean operations which carry political risks or which, if revealed, may adversely affect the country's interests.[37] The government can deny reporting specific operations to the PKG only in extreme cases where there is an utmost need to protect intelligence sources.[38] In such a situation the PKG can request an explanation from the Intelligence Co-ordinator, the Federal Minister responsible for the *Bundeskanzleramt* or the Minister in charge of the respective service.[39]

The interpretation of '*von besonderer Bedeutung*' is a source of contention between the PKG and government, since it is often difficult to determine at what stage the government should report – often operations which are not reported initially and later develop into problems cause dissent among PKG members.

The PKG meets on average about once a month.[40] Individual committee members can and do often request that specific issues of their interest be discussed. Each member also has the right to call an extraordinary meeting of the PKG.[41] The meetings and discussions of the PKG are, as with all other German control bodies, kept secret and its members are under a legal obligation not to reveal any information gained from the PKG proceedings even after they have ceased to be members of the committee.[42] This secrecy can, however, be waived over specific cases by the vote of a two-thirds majority of the PKG members.[43] This gives the committee a potentially strong sanction against government secrecy by the threat of being able to publicly reveal misdeeds or improprieties.

The PKG is required by law to present a report on its activities to the *Bundestag* twice in each electoral period, in practice every two years.[44] It has so far presented three such reports, which have been made available to the public.[45] For its work the PKG is provided by the intelligence services and the government, through Department VI of the *Bundes-kanzleramt*, with large amounts of material relating to its work.[46] This includes highly classified material, which is deposited in a special secure reading room[47] where only the PKG members may come and read. They are, however, not permitted to copy or summarise these documents.[48]

The intelligence services perceive the PKG as not being leak-proof. This is a highly controversial issue within the intelligence leadership and inevitably affects the amount and type of information made available for its members.[49] On the other hand, some intelligence officers see the PKG as a means to protect their secrets from the general body of MdB's, since information passed on to the PKG members cannot be used publicly by them even if they receive the same information through other channels.[50] There is, however, one extreme case in which the *Bundeskanzleramt* would provide sensitive information only to one MdB from each party and not to the PKG. This would be a case where a Member of Parliament is personally under suspicion.[51] For such eventualities the parties designate one senior MdB, not necessarily a PKG member, who is then informed about the suspicions being investigated.[52]

The PKG can make requests for specific information from the services or to question specific officers over issues under its discussion.[53] In general the PKG would receive information over most issues it would inquire over. Two exceptions to this rule are information that may identify sources and information provided by the intelligence services of other countries. The BND and BfV would not present the PKG with any information that may violate the protection of their informants or agents. Regarding co-operation with foreign services, the PKG would only be informed on rare occasions over operational matters, only where there is a risk of a major political or foreign policy problem.[54] The PKG is, however, informed over financial and technical assistance awarded to foreign services.[55]

PKG members, even members of the opposition, agree that the level of reporting by the intelligence services is high and that they are informed in a full and correct way.[56] The main problem in the functioning of the PKG seems to be the lack of time for its members, all of whom are members of numerous other parliamentary committees and other bodies.[57]

The G-10 Gremium and the G-10 Kommission

Article 10 of the German Basic Law guarantees the freedom of post and communications from interference by the state.[58] This article came in response to activities carried out by the Third Reich authorities, which frequently used the interception of post and communications as political oppression tools, and became one of the most important pillars in the Basic law's attempt to prevent the creation of an all-powerful 'secret police' organisation similar to the despised *Gestapo*.[59]

But following the heightened espionage activities during the Cold War the West German legislature recognised the need of intelligence services to intercept mail and telecommunications as part of their intelligence or counter-intelligence activities. The G-10 Law, enacted in 1968, regulates the interception of post and communications by the intelligence services, without infringing any of the Basic Law's freedoms.[60] It establishes two bodies, the G-10 *Gremium* and the G-10 *Kommission*, to control intelligence activities in this field.[61]

The G-10 *Gremium* comprises nine MdBs who meet every six months to examine the general regulations regarding G-10 activities, i.e. the interception of mail, eavesdropping of telephone, fax, cellular phone, electronic mail and other forms of communication.[62] The *Gremium* is not normally informed on individual cases where such methods are used, as part of an investigation or for the procurement of intelligence, but only on the overall guidelines that prevail at the time.[63] Any changes in these guidelines must be informed by the BMI or the BMVg, within six months, to the *Gremium*.[64] The *Gremium* makes the political and 'strategic' decisions as to what type of operations may use G-10 work. With regard to the BND it decides which type of communications it is permitted to monitor.[65]

The G-10 *Kommission* is comprised of four legal experts who are not MdBs but are affiliated with specific political parties.[66] The members are nominated by the political party leaderships and formally appointed by the G-10 *Gremium*. For each official member a '*Stellvertreter*' (reserve-member) is nominated, to attend meetings when the principal member is unavailable and preserve an official quorum.[67] The *Kommission* members are usually lawyers or retired civil servants with extensive legal and political experience. They meet once a month and are informed by the BMI of individual G-10 operations.[68] The *Kommission* then examines the legality of each case, and has the right to suspend a case if they believe it infringes any law or regulation, or when it considers the evidence over a specific case presented too weak to warrant such measures.[69]

The main purpose of the *Kommission* is to make up for the lack of proper judicial controls over G-10 operations.[70] Unlike police operations, which tend to focus on very specific, individual targets, the intelligence services are sometimes required to monitor telephone calls and other forms of communications over a large geographical area or emanating from a source used by many people, satellites for example.[71] A differentiation is made in law between two types of G-10 operations: 'individual' operations, which target specific individual persons or firms, and 'strategic' operations, which cover a wide field of communications over specific issues.[72]

The law also specifies against which offences G-10 monitoring may be undertaken.[73] 'Individual' targets can be monitored for communications with relative ease.[74] But the technical monitoring of 'strategic' targets presents much greater difficulties. Since it is technically impossible in 'strategic' operations to have officers monitoring each and every call over a multitude of communications methods, much of the strategic G-10 interception is done by computers. These state-of-the-art computers are programmed to recognise certain 'hit-words', i.e. words which relate to the investigated issue, in a conversation or transmission and then record that particular conversation or communication for human monitoring later.[75] The system of hit-word monitoring is used as standard practice by many intelligence services all over the world.[76] In an investigation of nuclear proliferation issues, relevant hit-words may be for example 'nuclear material', 'plutonium', 'detonators', 'enrichment' and similar words that would indicate to the computer that the monitored communication is relevant to the subject investigated.

The G-10 *Kommission* receives detailed lists of hit-words and has the right to exclude any hit-words it considers to be irrelevant or infringing upon legal rights.[77] The issue of specific key-words is open to interpretation by the *Kommission* since the law does not, and indeed cannot, specify every word to be used. Thus as the operational requirements of the services change more requests are brought before the *Kommission* for approval. In the past frequently used key-words related to military and security issues, but as the focus of intelligence work moves more into economic and criminal issues new hit-words are being constantly introduced.

In practice the intelligence services would only submit hit-words they are almost certain will be approved by the *Kommission*. The real rejection process takes place internally by exercising regulatory interdepartmental controls.[78] Both the G-10 *Gremium* and the G-10 *Kommission* are perceived to be totally leak-proof by the intelligence services. They seem to function smoothly as long as the internal administrative controls, i.e. those within the services and the relevant ministries, are rigorously maintained. The strict 'internal filtering' of requests eliminates the need for lengthy debates in the committees since the ministry staff knows, based on past experience and legal advice, what will or will not be approved. It therefore rejects out-of-hand requests from the operational branches of the services that do not meet the legal criteria, rather than risk a conflict with the *Kommission*.[79] On average around 5 per cent of the requests are rejected on these grounds.[80]

The Vertrauensgremium

The Federal Budget Regulations concerning the dispensation of public funds to government departments stipulate that all funds are to be approved by the Budget Committee of the *Bundestag*.[81] One exception to these strict and detailed regulations is the budgets of the intelligence services, details which is required to be kept secret. These are to be scrutinised and approved by a special 'Committee of Confidants' – the *Vertrauensgremium*.[82]

The *Vertrauensgremium* is the most secret parliamentary committee in Germany. It comprises nine MdBs, all members of the Budget Committee (Haushaltsausschuss).[83] Committee members are nominated by the party leaderships taking into account their past experience in financial issues as well as their abilities to hold secrets.[84] They are elected by the plenary session of the *Bundestag* in a similar procedure as members of the PKG.[85] The *Vertrauensgremium* meetings take place about four times a year, and carry the highest security classification. Members of the *Vertrauensgremium* also visit the offices of the various services and obtain further information there.[86]

Since the main purpose of the *Vertrauensgremium* is to examine and approve budgets its members are normally required to have a thorough understanding and experience in financial and budgetary matters. The intelligence services are required to submit to the *Vertrauensgremium* detailed financial statements and budget projections, covering not only their expenditure but also income.[87] Such income may be derived from normal activities such as the sale of property, older vehicles and equipment and from a variety of clandestine sources.[88] The *Vertrauensgremium* then examines and debates these budgets for approval. The *Vertrauensgremium* informs the Budget Committee only of the total sums it approved, and these are then paid out by the state to the intelligence services.

The *Vertrauensgremium* examines and certifies the financial audits of all three intelligence services done by Federal Audit Office experts.[89] Its meetings are characterised by a high degree of professionalism, with MdBs from both opposition and coalition raising critical, informed questions.[90] Decisions at the *Vertrauensgremium* are almost always unanimous.[91] Since it is considered by the intelligence services to be absolutely leak-proof it is sometimes used as a forum to discuss unofficially matters not directly relating to finances.[92] The intelligence heads can and do reveal to the *Vertrauensgremium* issues they would not bring up in the PKG meetings for fear of leaks to the press. They may also apply to the *Vertrauensgremium* for special funds, in addition to their regular budget, for special purposes.[93] The absolute secrecy maintained over *Vertrauensgremium* meetings enables the services to reveal far more operational details than at PKG meetings, when justifying such a request.

The successful work of the *Vertrauensgremium* seems to be a function of two elements – the high level of financial proficiency of its members and the absolute secrecy all its proceedings enjoy. These enables both sides to develop a high level of mutual trust and do much to eliminate inter-party rivalry, which may otherwise turn professional discussions into party-political contests. The financial proficiency of members ensures that they are able to fully scrutinise complex financial statements and budget projections.[94] The secrecy issue is considered to be paramount to its effective performance since the committee is privy to many operational details, the disclosure of which may directly affect their success.

The Bundesrechnungshof Kollegium

The Federal Auditing Office – *Bundesrechnungshof* – is empowered by legislation to examine and audit the finances of all Federal ministries and authorities.[95] It carries out detailed annual audits examining the expenses, income and financial management of each body in relation to its assigned tasks and budgets.

Since the accounts of the intelligence services contain operational information, and are therefore deemed to be national secrets, it was recognised that these can only be revealed to a small, selected group of experts within the *Bundesrechnungshof*.[96] The financial audits of the intelligence services are therefore done by a special *Kollegium* of the *Bundesrechnungshof*, consisting of department and section heads.[97] The *Kollegium* is headed by the president or vice-president of the *Bundesrechnungshof*, and meets regularly to examine the accounts and financial management of the intelligence services.[98] Field audits are carried out by a small select group of financial controllers. The audit results are reported to the *Vertrauensgremium*, the Federal Minister of Finance, the PKG and other Federal authorities.[99] The Minister of Finance would then pass on the reports to the President of the Bundesrat.[100]

Since the *Bundesrechnungshof* is a government department staffed by professional civil servants and not a politically elected body its findings are considered objective and non-political. But in practice its work is restricted by the fact that only a small team of auditors are allowed to work on the intelligence accounts. This team has to cover not only the financial activities of the intelligence services within Germany but also those of the dozens of BND representatives at German embassies abroad.[101]

Parliamentary Investigative Committees (Untersuchungsausschüsse)

Upon the request of at least a quarter of its members, the *Bundestag* can set up an independent investigative committee – *Untersuchungsausschuss* – to examine publicly problematic issues.[102] An *Untersuchungsausschuss* has the legal right to summon witnesses and examine documents, and it reports its findings to the plenary session of the *Bundestag*.[103]

In numerous cases involving intelligence scandals and failures the *Bundestag* has initiated investigations by *Untersuchungsausschüsse* and these became a common tool used by the opposition in attempting to clear up issues which were perceived to involve 'white-wash' by the government.[104] These investigative committees included several well-known examples such as:

- in 1963 to examine the monitoring of communications by the BfV.[105]
- in 1974 following the arrest of the spy Guillaume at the office of the Chancellor Willy Brandt.[106]
- in 1977 to investigate the repercussions of the Lutze and Weigel espionage cases.[107]

- in 1985 to examine counter-intelligence work, following the defection of senior intelligence officer Hans Joachim Tiedge.[108]
- in 1994 to examine issues surrounding the discovery of a smuggled shipment of Plutonium at Munich airport.[109]

The work of *Untersuchungsausschüsse* was often perceived as sensationalist and of no practical use by the intelligence services, which were reluctant to hand over information and provide witnesses for the investigations.[110] Former BND president Gerhard Wessel complained that the intelligence services of the Soviet block were delighted to see any information emanating from such investigations, which could not, in many cases, be kept secret.[111] Others considered the work of these committees to be artificially-inflated, as backbench MdBs strive to gain political and media exposure by 'discovering' malpractice. But the work of such committees has, at times, produced evidence of misdeeds within the services and provided strong encouragement to curb such excesses. The work of the *Untersuchungsausschüsse* may often be disliked by service heads but the committees' privileges are perceived by the services to be a necessary evil in the price to pay for democratic controls. They are also viewed as powerful tools for use by the opposition in controversial intelligence-related issues.

Media Oversight and Dialogue

Beyond the official parliamentary controls, a second type of oversight over the intelligence services in Germany is applied by the mass media. The role of the media in covering intelligence issues and exercising major influence on public, and political, opinion over the activities and value of these services has been downplayed in research focusing on the legal aspects of parliamentary controls in Germany. But in everyday reality this role is one which both serves as a catalyst in bringing intelligence-related issues to the forefront of public debate, as well as one which is perceived by the services themselves to exert critical influence over political intelligence-related decisions.

The classic model of relations between the mass media and intelligence services is one of constant conflict, whereby the media's wish to publish is curbed by intelligence's inherent secrecy, backed up by legislation preventing some forms of publication on grounds of national security. Britain's Official Secrets Acts and similar media legislation in other European countries provide intelligence services with a last resort in preventing the publication of information which may damage security interests or endanger personnel.[112]

In Germany the Basic Law guarantees the freedom of the press and prohibits government censorship.[113] Furthermore, journalists in Germany are granted special legal rights and privileges in their media work.[114] These rights, which include the protection of sources and informants, immunity from police eavesdropping and searches of editorial offices, were introduced in the Federal Republic after the political experience of National Socialism and the excesses of the Nazi regime against the media. They do mean, however, that journalists can operate more effectively in investigating intelligence activities, even sensitive issues that in many other countries would have been censored or kept out of the public domain by other means.

The freedom to investigate intelligence issues, and publish them without official hindrance, provides the mass media in Germany with effective tools to detect misdeeds and bring them before the public. Intelligence issues receive high media coverage, many contend, far higher than their actual size and scope of activity merits in comparison to other government bodies. However, with few exceptions the services suffer from a low media image and are often portrayed, not only by the tabloid press but by large segments of the intellectual and conservative political press as over-staffed dinosaurs of the Cold War era.[115]

Media coverage of the intelligence services in Germany has turned into almost a ritual. The largest-distribution weekly journals, such as the *Spiegel*, *Focus* and *Stern*, feature a column on *Nachrichtendienste* almost every month, and investigative television programmes feature numerous intelligence-related issues. Editors encourage their investigative staff to focus on intelligence activities, even ones with little real political or social value.[116] Intelligence activities are perceived, and are being featured, as an integral part of government machinery, albeit one with a particular 'sexy' flavour. There is a noticeable lack of media legitimacy to the notion of intelligence agents or services being some form of 'heroes of democracy', engaged in work of a particular nature to the benefit of the state. On the contrary, the tone and structure of the media's intelligence coverage suggests that it is being treated, and expected to act, just like any other part of government. As such, they are expected to conform to the same standards of public work and being scrutinised by the investigative press to the same degree as other sensitive government issues.[117]

The unhindered media coverage ensures that the intelligence services remain under the public spotlight. It influences the services to curb activities internally that might otherwise earn them negative coverage.[118]

Thus intelligence operations within the context of the free German media are not only judged by their operational and legal merits, but also by their possible media impact. Beyond the parliamentary controls, the very high level of media freedom in Germany acts as a brake on intelligence excesses. This element gives the media an indirect, but clearly felt, role in democratic intelligence oversight. The German intelligence services do not enjoy anywhere near the public and media legitimacy for illegal actions of some similar services abroad. And whereas French military intelligence in the Rainbow Warrior affair, or the Israeli Mossad after the failed Mashal assassination in Jordan, could count on a distinct degree of media support or at least sympathy, their German counterparts must take into account the risk of media backlash even over far less spectacular events.

Negative media coverage over intelligence affects these services in several ways. Despite their Cold War political status, the intelligence services were highly sensitive to media criticism. Indeed, the BND for example, developed a wide network of media contacts in order to gain advanced warning of adverse publicity and try and moderate it, albeit on an unofficial level.[119] The problem of negative media image became more critical after the end of the Cold War, as it began to affect the quality of new recruits to the intelligence services. By 1997 over 40 per cent of the BfV officers were over 50 years old.[120] The services want to attract high quality young recruits but these are often reluctant to join because of the media image.[121]

The intense media coverage, unhampered by legal restrictions, forced the intelligence services to abandon their traditional anti-media posture and to develop new ways of interacting with the press. This relationship is perhaps best defined as the 'conflict and co-operation' model, whereby parallel to the conflict over the need for secrecy both sides realise they can better benefit from some level of co-operation. And while there is constant debate between the services and the media over just what level of secrecy must be maintained in order not to jeopardise effective intelligence work, even the more sensationalist media outlets realise the benefit of some form of dialogue with the intelligence services.

Almost unique among intelligence services in Europe, both the BND and BfV maintain press offices and official spokespersons,[122] who engage in routine media relation's work. They issue press releases, hold informal briefings and are available for comments on intelligence-related issues or reports. These offices also carry out semi-official media events, bringing journalists into what was previously an inner sanctum, to present special aspects of intelligence work. Thus a dialogue exists between the media and the services, one which is not free of its conflicts, but enables the previous one-sided coverage to be somewhat more objective. The intelligence spokespersons provide a public 'face' for services which until recently were kept in total seclusion from visual media coverage.

The role of the media in intelligence oversight complements that of the parliamentary committees. The *Bundestag* committees provide the professional, democratically elected forums for control, while the media provides the public stage for exposing misdeeds as well as heaping praise. The fear of adverse media coverage dictates internal operational decisions within the intelligence community, thus providing another set of brakes against potential misuses of power. On the other hand, attempts to come to terms with the requirements of a modern media enable the services to influence, even to a small extent, the amount of uninformed coverage, strengthening the services' public legitimacy and their role within the German democracy.

Conclusions

This study focused on the democratic control mechanisms controlling and overseeing the intelligence services of the Federal Republic of Germany. One of the major characteristics of the parliamentary committees and bodies analysed is their inherent reactive work. The committees discuss and examine events that have already taken place, operations, which were carried out, and procedures that were undertaken in the past. They generally do not deal with specific future activities, nor are they informed of impending actions and plans and therefore cannot work in a proactive way exercising control over future actions.[123]

This reactive nature of the control work may at first seem limiting. Some may argue that it would be better to clear future operations with the controlling bodies in advance, thus sparing the government potential embarrassment, parliamentary problems and adverse media coverage if anything goes wrong. But such an authority over future intelligence activities would clearly broach upon not only the professional executive authority of the service heads but also on the government prerogative to act as it deems fit within the law. Informing, or indeed consulting, parliamentary control bodies over future intelligence activities could endanger the security and secrecy of such operations and thus may threaten the lives of intelligence operatives. It may also decrease the flexibility of intelligence operations since intelligence services would be encouraged to use tried-and-true methods previously approved by the controlling bodies rather than 'risk' new approaches which might be more fitting to the specific situation but may be frowned upon or even vetoed by the parliamentary committees.

When setting out to examine the effectiveness of the control mechanisms in Germany, it is important to differentiate between procedural and operational effectiveness. Procedural effectiveness is the sum of legal and procedural powers the controlling bodies yield in respect to intelligence activities. However, these formal powers may be difficult or even impossible to exercise without the backing of the media and public opinion. Operational effectiveness may be measured by the real influence of the controlling bodies where such influence may arise not only through procedural means but through more informal means such as informal consultations with the government, the personal influence of individual members within the parliamentary system, their relations with the media and the public.

The procedural effectiveness of the intelligence controlling bodies in Germany is firmly set in legislation. Thus the controlling bodies possess an arsenal of 'official' sanctions against the government, e.g. by making their findings public (PKG) or withholding the authorisation of budgets (*Vertrauensgremium*). On the operational effectiveness level the German committees have established a set of 'working norms' which enable them to address issues not specifically set out in legislation. Legislation is also amended by responding to the requirements of the controlling bodies.[124] In Germany the government is required by law to report intelligence issues of importance to the PKG, unlike for example in Britain, where the Intelligence and Security Committee is allowed to ask questions, but no obligation is placed on the government to inform. The PKG and *Vertrauensgremium* also enjoy the privilege of being able to summon people and documents, a right denied to their British equivalent.[125]

A further element of strength for the PKG in Germany relates to its power to make an issue public, as a 'last-stand' method to force government action in case of intelligence misdeeds or problems. Such a measure can admittedly only be used in extreme situations since it may jeopardise intelligence operations, but even its threat gives the PKG an important bargaining position in matters where the government may, to protect its interests, wish to withhold certain information over illegal or even scandalous intelligence activities. German law specifically allows the PKG to make an issue public, thus waiving its legal obligation to secrecy, in a case where a majority of two-thirds of the PKG members vote in favour of such a disclosure.[126] This measure provides the PKG with a strong tool against the government if the majority of its members consider the matter to require such action. It is also a way of combining political control and indirect media oversight over intelligence.

In its overall scope the German parliamentary system of intelligence control involves 27 MdB's and six other judicial members.[127] This relatively large number of participating MdB's increases the opportunities for the parliamentary opposition to participate effectively in this process. On the other hand, it seems that in Germany a certain administrative overlap exists between the work of the PKG and *Vertrauensgremium* in regard to budgets, since the PKG is now authorised to examine the intelligence budgets that were previously exclusively the domain of the *Vertrauensgremium*.

The G-10 system in Germany is the only proactive control instance and the G-10 *Kommission* can and does prevent the use of certain 'hit-words' in intelligence operations. It is hard to assess the effectiveness of the G-10 system since every operation is unique in its operational requirements, and therefore requires different G-10 approaches, but a strong witness to its performance is the respect the G-10 *Kommission* commands within the intelligence services themselves. The tight internal controls exercised by the services themselves and the responsible ministries are essentially a manifestation of the power of the G-10 authorities to control such monitoring work effectively.

The freedom and unique legal protection from government interference enables the German media to perform an important function in the democratic control of intelligence by its investigative 'watchdog' function. Unhindered by secrecy laws or censorship, the German media is free to investigate intelligence issues and fully publish its findings. The media freedom, including a total protection of sources and the immunity from surveillance, assures that the media can perform its democratic functions without fear of the powers of the state. The effects of this media oversight is both to influence operational service decisions and force the intelligence services to conduct a dialogue with the media, minimising negative coverage and improving the public legitimacy of intelligence as a whole.

To sum up the characteristics of the German system, it seems to evolve around a distinct perception of the role of intelligence in the working of government. In Germany intelligence is perceived as an integral part of government work but one possessing unique characteristics of intelligence work which make it more prone to mishaps. These characteristics are the ones that are addressed by a complex system of parliamentary control, whereby parliamentary 'specialists' examine different aspects to ensure they are within regulations. In Germany the system of parliamentary control over the intelligence services has been honed by decades of practice. This does not prevent the occasional slip, as the 1994 'Plutonium' affair illustrates, but it does maintain the activities of the services in check by influencing the perceptions of these services themselves. Other countries are closely studying the German multilateral example as the inherent flexibility it offers can respond faster to changes in the intelligence arena.

By believing that their activities are effectively controlled by parliamentary committees and closely monitored by the media, the intelligence services themselves keep in check issues which could potentially transgress into infringements or misconduct. This is perhaps one of the strongest tools in any oversight arsenal over intelligence services. While in reality the complexity and secrecy of intelligence will often prevent foolproof parliamentary control measures, influencing the perceptions of the services goes a long way towards assuring stronger internal controls. In Germany this influence has been operating to a large degree of effectiveness for many years, as parliament an media complement each other in keeping secret intelligence under democratic control.

Notes

[1] For the early history of the German secret services see Wilhelm Stieber, *Spion des Kanzlers*, Stuttgart, 1978.

[2] For the role of intelligence services in the workings of government see Michael Herman, *Intelligence Power in Peace and War*, Cambridge, 1996, pp. 16–35 and 137–154.

[3] One of the first proposals in this field was submitted as a ministerial paper in early December 1998, calling for a new 15–member committee to take over the control functions of all four existing parliamentary bodies. Author's conversations with government officials in Bonn, December 1998. See also Frankfurter Algemeine Zeitung (FAZ), 3.12.1998. However, after two months of discussions this proposal was largely diluted into a 9–member committee similar to the current PKG but with a new name, which previously was too often confused with the Kurdish Workers Party.

[4] For a detailed history of the German intelligence services see Erich Schmidt-Eenboom, *Der BND*, Munich, 1993, pp. 40–189.

[5] Heinz Hoehne & Hermann Zolling, *Network*, London, 1971, p. 191.

[6] Ibid.

[7] *Gesetz über den Bundesnachrichtendienst* (BND Gesetz) v. 20.12.1990 (BGBl. I S. 2979).

[8] Hoehne & Zolling, p. 116.

[9] Ibid, p. 179.

[10] The issue of who poses what threat is under constant debate. For the precise legal and procedural regulations see Bundesamt für Verfassungsschutz – Befugnisse, Aufgaben, Grenzen, Bonn, undated, pp. 17–51.

[11] Such as Kurdish, Turkish, Iranian and Palestinian groups.

[12] Supra, 9, §2 (1).

[13] Hoehne & Zolling, p. 188.

[14] *Gesetz über den Militärischen Abschirmdienst* (MADG) v. 20.12.1990 (BGB1. I S. 2977).

[15] In some instances the MAD would investigate civilians who are direct employees of the Bundeswehr.

[16] Supra, 25, §1(1).

[17] Supra, 8.

[18] Gesetz zu Artikel 10 Grundgesetz (G-10) v. 15.08.1968 (BGBI. I S. 728).

[19] Supra, 39.

[20] Supra, 8, and author's interviews with senior *Bundeskanzleramt* officials.

[21] Chef des *Bundeskanzleramt*es (Head of the Federal Chancellery), who under the BND Gesetz is the minister responsible for the BND. Gesetz ueber den Bundesnachrichtendienst (BND Gesetz), v. 20.12.1990 (BGBI. 1 S. 2979), §1, 1.

[22] Author's interviews with senior *Bundeskanzleramt* officials.

[23] The Ministry for Internal Affairs (BMI) is responsible for the BfV, and the Ministry of Defence (MBVg) for the MAD.

[24] *Bekanntmachung eines Organisationserlasses des Bundeskanzlers*, v. 3.5. 1989.

[25] Ibid, §III.c.

[26] Ibid, §III. 2. (a).

[27] Ibid, §III. 2. (d).

[28] Ibid, §IV.

[29] Supra, 45.

[30] Ibid.

[31] Although in some cases the Federal Minister at the *Kanzleramt* may also attend.

[32] Supra, 45.

[33] PKG-Gesetz, §I, 1 (1).

[34] In 1997 the PKG's composition was five members from the CDU-CSU-FDP coalition, three SPD opposition members and one member of the Green party.

[35] PKG-Gesetz, §4.

[36] This arrangement is not fixed in the PKG-Gesetz but has been formalised by the committee's internal procedures.

[37] PKG-Gesetz, §II, 1 (1).

[38] PKG-Gesetz, §II, 2.

[39] The Defence Minister for the MAD, the Minister for Internal affairs for the BfV. PKG Gesetz, §II, 2.

[40] In the period between June 1994 and June 1996 the PKG met for 23 ordinary meetings and three internal discussions. See *Unterrichtung durch die PKG*, 13. Wahlperiode, 1.7.1996, Drucksache 13/5157.

[41] PKG-Gesetz, §V, 3.

[42] PKG-Gesetz, §V, 1.

[43] PKG-Gesetz, §V, 1.

[44] Elections are held in Germany normally every four years. The current *Bundestag* is the 13th Election Period, the next elections are expected to take place in September 1998.

[45] *Unterrichtung durch die Parlamentarische KontrollKommission*, Deutscher *Bundestag*, 12. und 13. Wahlperiode, Bundesdrucksache 12/5080, 12/8102, 13/5157.

[46] Author's interviews with senior BND and *Bundeskanzleramt* officials.

[47] This high-security depository – the *'Geheimschutzstelle des Bundestages'* – is located in the vicinity of the *Bundestag* building.

[48] Author's interviews with members of the PKG.

[49] For example, some intelligence officers indicated they would not wish to report to the PKG ongoing investigations over suspected spies or 'moles' in their own services, or

other serious espionage cases, for fear of leaks to the press which would then jeopardise the investigation and may preclude a prosecution.

[50] PKG-Gesetz, §V, 1.

[51] The issue of investigating MdB's has caused considerable debate, especially in the question of whether MdB's homes and offices can be 'bugged' by police and intelligence authorities. At the present it seems that a political compromise will be adopted whereby MdBs will enjoy immunity from electronic eavesdropping in their private and professional spheres.

[52] Author's interviews with Members of the *Bundestag* and officials of the main parliamentary parties.

[53] In recent years there has been one such interview of a BfV officer and twice with BND officers.

[54] Author's interviews with senior BND officials.

[55] Often such assistance is complemented by German-made high-tech electronic devices, paid for by the intelligence services out of funds allocated for external assistance. The figures and data are, however, confidential. Author's interviews with intelligence officials.

[56] Author's interviews with coalition and opposition Members of the *Bundestag*.

[57] For example, only the MdBs themselves, but not their staff, are allowed to examine secret documents deposited at the *Geheimschutzstelle*. This restricts their ability to prepare for the meetings or keep abreast of constant developments.

[58] *Grundgesetz fuer die Bundesrepublik Deutschland* (GG), §X.

[59] The Occupation Powers, which controlled Germany after the end of WWII, were not prepared to let Germany have a 'secret-police', as clearly reiterated in the so-called 'Police Letter' of 14.04.1949 authorising the creation of the BfV. See Hoehne & Zolling, p. 179.

[60] *Gesetz zur Beschränkung des Brief-, Post-, und Fernmeldegeheimnisses* (G-10 Gesetz), v. 15.8.1968, (BGBl. I S. 728).

[61] Ibid.

[62] Ibid, §IX, 2.

[63] Author's interviews with *Bundeskanzleramt* officials.

[64] G-10 Gesetz, §IV, 1.

[65] Since in principle the BND is assigned to gather intelligence overseas and not within the geographical boundaries of the Federal Republic. That is also the reason why most of the G-10 work for the BND is done by the BfV.

[66] G-10 Gesetz, §IX, 4.

[67] Author's interviews with *Bundeskanzleramt* officials.

[68] G-10 Gesetz, §IX, 2.

[69] Ibid.

[70] As demanded for by the Basic Law, Supra, 82.

[71] For a discussion of the role and means of electronic communications interception see William Burrows, *Deep Black – the Secrets of Space Espionage*, London, 1988, pp. 174–197, 297–327.

[72] G-10 Gesetz, §II and §III.

[73] The main offences listed in Paragraph II ('individual' operations) are treason, endangering democracy, threats against the security of the state, and similar crimes. Paragraph III ('strategic' operations) lists the risks of an armed attack against the Federal Republic, terrorist attacks within Germany, weapon issues and other international criminal acts.

[74] By using a multitude of electronic devices, intelligence officers can listen to the communications and determine if they contain any required information.

[75] Author's interviews with intelligence officials.
[76] For a detailed analysis of the methods of communications interception see Abraham Shulsky, *Secret Warfare*, Washington, 1993, pp. 22–40.
[77] G-10 Gesetz, §IX, 2.
[78] Author's interviews with BMI officials.
[79] Ibid.
[80] Ibid.
[81] *Bundeshaushaltsordnung* (BHO) v. 19.08.1969 (BGBl. III 63–1).
[82] Ibid, §X a (2).
[83] The regulations for electing *Vertrauensgremium* members are similar to those of the PKG, Ibid.
[84] Author's interviews with Members of the *Bundestag*.
[85] Supra, 106.
[86] Supra, 108.
[87] Author's interviews with *Bundeskanzleramt* officials.
[88] Ibid.
[89] BHO, §X a (3).
[90] Author's interviews with Members of the *Bundestag*.
[91] Ibid.
[92] Author's interviews with senior intelligence officials.
[93] Author's interviews with *Bundeskanzleramt* officials.
[94] Such proficiency is normally required from all members of the Budget Committee. Author's interviews with relevant Members of the *Bundestag*.
[95] GG, §114/2, compare also §19 of the Bundesrechnungshofgesetz.
[96] Author's interviews with federal officials dealing with the financial audits issues.
[97] Ibid.
[98] Ibid.
[99] BHO, §X a (3).
[100] Ibid.
[101] Information received from the *Bundesrechnungshof via* the *Bundeskanzleramt*.
[102] GG, §44.
[103] Ibid.
[104] In most cases it was the parliamentary opposition which called for the formation of such a committee of investigation. See, for example, the discussions in the German press over the formation of the so-called 'Plutonium Committee' in summer 1994.
[105] F. Ritter, *Die geheimen Nachrichtendienste der Bundesrepublik Deutschland*, Heidelberg, 1989, p. 127.
[106] Ibid.
[107] Ibid.
[108] Ibid.
[109] Author's interviews with German intelligence experts.
[110] The services would not withhold requested information but may be reluctant to come up with additional information that may be relevant to the committee's work. Ibid.
[111] Ritter, 1989, p. 127.
[112] For analysis on the media sensorship and preventing the publication of state secrets, see Rosamund Thomas, *Espionage and Secrecy: the Official Secrets Acts 1911–1989 of the United Kingdom*, London, 1991.
[113] Article 5 of the German Basic Law.
[114] For an extensive analysis of the rights and privileges of journalists and media personnel in Germany see Heinz Puerer and Johannes Raabe, *Medien in Deutschland*, Konstanz, 1996, pp. 259–304.

[115] Although a wide base of comparative research over media intelligence coverage is still lacking, this was the opinion of both German intelligence officials and investigative media journalists the author has consulted.

[116] Author's interviews with journalists at a major German weekly magazine.

[117] For a discussion of the media's role as democratic watchdog see John Keane, *The Media and Democracy*, Cambridge, 1991.

[118] Although this influence is difficult to measure, it was indicated to the author by the majority of intelligence officials interviewed for this study.

[119] See Erich Schmidt-Eenboom, Undercover, Cologne, 1998.

[120] Author's interview with BMI officials.

[121] 'Would you want your own son or daughter to join such a disreputable organisation?!' was the way one senior BND official defined the problem to the author.

[122] The BND press office began operating in 1972.

[123] The one exception to this is the G-10 *Kommission*, which authorises future use of 'hit-words' and can prohibit certain 'hit-words' from being used in specific operations. The use of such words may, however, be challenged as the operational requirements vary from one investigation to the other, and thus words which may not have been acceptable several years ago are now routinely approved.

[124] For example, by changing the law to allow the PKG to review intelligence budgets.

[125] A proposed amendment to the 1994 intelligence legislation calling for the ISC to be given powers to call for people and papers was rejected by government majority. See Intelligence Service Bill, House of Commons, Standing Committee E., March 3rd-29th, col. 235–255.

[126] PKG-Gesetz, §5(1).

[127] The members and substitute-members of the G-10 *Kommission*.

PART V

CONCLUSION

Chapter 12

National Security and Political Policing: Some Thoughts on Values, Ends and Law

Laurence Lustgarten

The purpose of this essay is to explore a range of issues that are too often overlooked in discussions about national security issues and institutions. These are matters, primarily normative but to some extent also empirical, that should logically precede discussions and recommendations relating to public policy. Put simply, every view expressed about what security and policing agencies should or should not be permitted to do, and what limits should be placed on how they do it, ultimately draws upon judgements about what these agencies are meant to 'secure'. Such judgements are no less real for never being expressly made or discussed: unarticulated assumptions can be equally controlling. Yet nearly always in what little public debate there is on these issues, the fundamental questions are either passed over entirely or are treated as subject to an assumed consensus. The result is to validate things as usual. This essay seeks to challenge the consensus by performing the essential first step of placing the fundamental normative questions at centre stage.

What are National Security Institutions for?

Security services and political policing exist to *prevent* harm to those interests and activities which, in *a democratic society*, deserve to be called 'national security' Both italicised phrases are important, but the latter is fundamental, and constitutes the framework of any subsequent discussion. Unless the requirement that the society be democratic is accepted at the outset, any regime exercising effective control over its territory, no matter how dictatorial its methods or how murderous its policies, may claim to be acting in defence of national security when trying to maintain itself in power. Indeed such regimes regularly make precisely that claim when faced with serious resistance from their subjects, particularly if supported by a foreign state. That claim – which confers an important international and internal legitimacy on any regime which successfully sustains it – can only be denied if the requirements of 'national security' are more rigorous than a simple Hobbesian maintenance of internal order. Hobbes equated state or regime legitimacy with the ability to maintain physical security from internal violence and external invasion. The subject's duty of absolute obedience to the Sovereign dissolved only when the latter could no longer provide that security. But the conditions of instability and terror that Hobbes dreaded and which he described in a famous phrase – a life 'solitary, poor, nasty, brutish and short'– do not in our time arise primarily from internal anarchy or external invasion. For every Somalia there are a dozen functioning states whose citizens have been terrorised by internal repression or official persecution of minorities. In the modern world the dictatorial state is the greatest threat to individuals' ability to live a peaceful life devoted to whatever activities they value.

This ability may be called physical security, yet by itself it fails to meet the expectations that are shared, indeed demanded, by the citizens of every Western state, and increasingly that of states everywhere from Latin America to China. They claim the right to participate in taking important decisions concerning their well-being to the enjoyment of democratic freedoms. We have progressed since the 17th century. Mere absence of disorder, though an essential pre-requisite for a decent life, is not enough. Now a regime which fails to provide its citizens with both physical security and effective democratic institutions has forfeited its claim to legitimacy, and hence cannot claim that its continuation in power is necessary for security of that nation or state. Indeed it may more cogently be argued that its overthrow would be justifiable as necessary for creating true national security – that is to say, the maintenance of a functioning democratic order.

If national security not only implies, but has inherent within it the notion of effective democracy, there are profound implications for what national security institutions may do, and for how they may function. A democratic society has a strong legitimate claim – it does not at all advance the argument to call this a 'right' – to preservation of its values, institutions, and processes. These may be called its democratic *praxis*. However, the task of preservation cannot be undertaken under the banner 'whatever is necessary'. Democratic *praxis* imposes its own limitations on the measures necessary for its own preservation. If this were not so, the result would be that described in Dennis Töllborg's superb phrase: 'democracy at risk of committing suicide for fear of death'.[1] Thus any measures taken by security institutions which violate democratic *praxis* are themselves contrary to national security and therefore unacceptable. This principle rules out many of the activities that security institutions have routinely engaged in, particularly throughout the Cold War, which have involved interfering with democratic rights of political dissidents and those active in industrial conflict as leaders of trade unions or other workers' organisations. But the principle is also the source of many dilemmas that will confront officials of these agencies who conscientiously adhere to democratic *praxis*. Many if not most of those whose actions they are dedicated to countering do not abide by the same standards, and the trick is to prevent any advantage the opponent may thereby obtain from leading to serious damage, without employing unacceptable means to do so. This should be recognised fairly as a serious dilemma, but it is not an impossibility, and anyone undertaking employment in these agencies must accept these limits at the outset or take up another line of work.

One major implication of the conception of national security presented here is that the language so frequently used to describe the issues raised when national security is invoked to justify restrictions on democratic *praxis* must be swiftly abandoned. The metaphor of 'balance' consistently appears in public discussion and judicial decisions. It conjures up an image in which 'national security' sits on one side of the scales and is set against 'liberty' or 'democracy' on the other. This badly distorts what is at stake, because it fails to take full account of the loss to freedom and/or the democratic process caused by the restriction. To do so requires placing that loss on both scales so that it is clear that, even as the measures purportedly protect it, democratic *praxis* is simultaneously being diminished. Purely as a matter of mathematical logic, it follows that the gain to democratic *praxis* must, at an absolute minimum, exceed twice the loss to justify any infringement.

At the very least this metaphor invites confusion to the point of incoherence. For unlike real scales, it provides no measure or metric whatever. How does one actually 'weigh' the need to prevent a certain harm – transmission of a particular piece of technology to a hostile foreign state, or acceptance as a refugee of someone involved in political violence in a friendly foreign state, to take two contemporary examples – against the invasion of many people's privacy or the suppression of freedom of expression? There is no common measure like kilogrammes or pounds (avoirdupois or sterling) to offer a ready calculation and an accepted standard of comparison. 'Balancing' is merely a rhetorical trope, and when one examines the actual decisions taken, particularly by courts, in which this language is used, the result is almost invariably to uphold some form of repressive action.

Rather than balancing, a much preferable conceptual tool is provided by the notion of proportionality. I am not suggesting that the very elaborate jurisprudence of the German administrative and constitutional courts, or of the European Court of Justice and European Court of Human Rights, be referred to in their full glory. Rather the concept should be applied in the manner suggested by the McDonald Commission in Canada, in its groundbreaking Report on security services and their governance more than two decades ago.[2] This involves giving particular weight to the idea of least restrictive alternative. In many instances where some reason or aim is invoked to justify an infringement of democratic *praxis*, it will not be wholly arbitrary or irrational, and it may be sufficient to justify some infringement. The question is how much, or to what extent. Rather than attempt the hopeless, and truly arbitrary, exercise of trying to quantify the unquantifiable, it would be more useful to ask a different question. It is not whether some infringement is justified, but whether this particular measure is necessary – not in the sense of whether it will be effective, but of whether it is truly necessary because no other measure will work. A huge mechanical digger will certainly turn over my vegetable patch, as will a regiment of gardeners, but with a common spade in my hand I can do the job nicely. In this sense, though the first two would be quite effective, their use would be unnecessary and therefore unjustified. The test is not an abstract and arbitrary calculus but whether, in each highly specific setting, no measure with a less restrictive impact could be used.

At one time the criteria for authorising telephone interceptions in Britain included the requirement that less intrusive alternate means had been tried and failed. This was abandoned in the 1980s, apparently under pressure from police and/or security agencies. It is precisely this stiffer test, rather than its flaccidly permissive replacement – that the information sought could not 'reasonably be expected' to be obtained by other means – that should be applied. It requires that the alternatives actually have been attempted, or be so obviously impossible that any attempt would be pointless, rather than letting the authorities shelter behind a weak notion of reasonable expectation which allows them to put up excuses to avoid even trying the more difficult but more carefully-tailored measures, for reasons that might range from laziness to habit to cost. The last in particular should never be regarded as an acceptable justification for a disproportionate response, for it would allow the value of money routinely to overcome fundamental human rights. If governments insist on attempting to curb democratic *praxis*, at the very least they must bear the political cost of its full financial expense. Put another way, democratic *praxis* should never be sacrificed to politicians' unwillingness to tax citizens to protect themselves.

Adoption of a working standard of least restrictive means would put a premium on innovation among those working in security agencies, for it would forbid them from continuing to employ many of the techniques, particularly in relation to surveillance, that have become standard practice. They would of course complain that their work would suffer as a result. Yet the history of security governance in the last quarter century is full of examples of restrictions in operations and changes in personnel forced on agencies from the outside, usually in response to some political scandal. It would be very hard to sustain a claim that the true national security of any Western nation has significantly suffered as a result. It was after all the Soviet Union and allied regimes, with their pervasive security police and intelligence services devoted to maintaining the ruling party, which collapsed from within.

The Role and Rule of Law

It is important to emphasise that adherence to democratic *praxis* goes well beyond compliance with the rule of law, which is only one component of it. In the context of national security governance, democratic *praxis* encompasses a) effective public decision-making in the choice of the aims and operative framework of the agencies and b) creation of oversight machinery that is capable of ensuring that they respect democratic values. Insofar as a legal charter or legal standards are one means by which this is done, then to that extent compliance with the law is important.

Strictly as an empirical or behavioural matter, it may well be sound tactics to use legal tools for this purpose. This is so for several reasons. First, putting matters such as the mandate of security agencies in legal form may give them enhanced psychological force, assisting compliance by officials. It certainly gives those in command of an agency greater leverage to ensure compliance with any limits expressed in legal form. By laying down a relatively clear standard against which compliance may be measured, use of legal standards enables those who deviate to be disciplined or dismissed in a way that cannot be portrayed as arbitrary. Use of law also provides those seeking compliance with an important symbolic and rhetorical asset. In a culture in which fidelity to law has, nominally at least, a very high value, the appeal to the necessity of obedience, even when the result is unwanted or distasteful, is a difficult argument to resist.

Second, laying down a legal structure within which institutions may operate has at least the potential to make it easier for victims of abuse of power to achieve some sort of redress. Remedies, after all, are what the legal system is pre-eminently about. But in the words of the old song, 'it ain't necessarily so', because remedies may be explicitly restricted or the procedures to achieve them strewn with deliberately placed obstacles. Regrettably the British system of complaints relating both to telephone tapping and to misconduct by the security and intelligence services is a textbook example of how this may be done. But the converse seems incontestable: in the absence of a legal structure, remedies are not possible at all.

Finally, and perhaps most important of all, placing security agencies within a legal structure has important constitutional consequences. The power of oversight can no longer remain exclusively within the executive (agency officials, senior civil servants in other relevant departments, and ministers), but is shifted at least partly to the legislature and/or to some judicial body. It may also more fully involve public opinion, primarily in the form of the media, since information is no longer kept exclusively within the executive branch but flows, under conditions of varying secrecy, elsewhere within government or into the public domain. And the media's appetite for information feeds upon itself – once the tap is turned on even to a tightly limited extent, they tend to demand ever greater access. Those within government who have tried to argue for absolute secrecy on the pragmatic grounds that it is impossible to staunch the flow once the valve is opened have had, purely as a empirical matter, a clearer-eyed view than those who have argued for limited disclosure. It is at the level of values, and the insistence upon the paramount position of democratic *praxis*, that their argument must be rejected. And there can be little doubt that in many circumstances the media are even more effective than the formal parts of the state in achieving at least some measure of public accountability of security agencies.[3] Allowing issues of governance to remain entirely a matter for the executive is to permit ministers – themselves vulnerably dependent on agency leaders for their information – the power of absolution for any activities they may deem expedient. This is unhealthy for any democracy. The question is whether contributions from the legislature or the judiciary can be expected to supply remedies. The answer turns on the political realities of any given constitutional order. In a system in which the government is formed exclusively by one dominant party, that party enjoys an unassailably large majority, and the executive dominates parliament through a tightly-controlled party discipline, the legislature is able to act only to the extent that the government will agree to statutory reform and to release information. Britain is the paradigm case of such a system. Where the government party is weaker and there is a stronger tradition of independence of parliamentarians, and perhaps particularly where government is normally formed by a coalition of parties, there is far greater scope for independent oversight. Germany and Norway are examples of the latter. Either way, the determining factors are political.

Whether the judiciary contribute significantly to the process of statutory accountability will depend largely on the understanding of justiciability that prevails in the particular legal culture. Courts which take either a limited view of their institutional capacity to consider matters in which questions of high public policy are intertwined with legal interpretation, or have a restrictive view of their constitutional role compared with other branches of government, will in general be more deferential to the executive than those which have a more activist tradition which tends to grow out of a pivotal role in protecting constitutional rights. However, the qualification 'in general' is important: the American federal courts have a long activist tradition in areas like enforcing desegregation and ensuring numerical equality of representation in legislative constituencies (a matter in which the English courts would never involve themselves), but also maintain a so-called 'political question doctrine'. This is invoked whenever they decide that a particular issue, even though raising questions under the Constitution, is more properly determined by the politically accountable branches of government. The German Constitutional Court decides matters like the constitutionality of sending troops to participate in peace-keeping missions overseas, which their equivalents in most other jurisdictions would almost certainly refuse to hear. It is a safe bet that the courts in most countries will refuse to offer any significant challenge to the definition and application of national security presented to them by the government in office. Nor, if the record of the American courts is anything to go by, will they be generally responsive to claims of violations of constitutional rights when protection of national security is presented as a justification for the restriction. The long tradition of constitutional judicial review and an elaborate jurisprudence surrounding freedom of expression in that country has been of little assistance to individuals whose rights to travel, publish or otherwise supply information have been curbed in the name of national security. It is conceivable that courts might be more forthcoming in giving effect to legislation which imposes clear procedural requirements – such as providing specified information – on a government official or agency in their dealings with other institutions, particularly the legislature itself. Yet the American experience here too suggests that this is unlikely.[4] At best, the courts' role in this sphere will remain a residual one.

Law, then, is an important element of democratic *praxis*, but is only part of a larger whole, and not necessarily the most important part.

Respect for political dissent and human rights such as privacy; establishment of a system of effective public oversight and acceptance of its legitimacy by officials; adherence to a conception of national security that is limited to core political values and societal interests and therefore unlikely to produce extravagant claims of necessity which are so often the driving force behind political repression; rigorous use of an objectively justifiable test of what constitutes legitimate grounds for withholding information from parliament and the public – these are the vital elements of democratic *praxis* in the national security context. Law is a mechanism for giving effect to them – an important component, but secondary. It is at the level of moral values and the political ideas that embody them, and in the acceptance and internalisation of these values and ideas within the political culture (and in particular by the most powerful political actors) that democratic *praxis* is most fully realised.

There is another, powerful, reason to avoid using 'rule of law' as a criterion or critical yardstick in evaluating national security institutions. The fact is that this much-used phrase, though always politically appealing, is of barely determinate meaning. If one were to be a bit uncharitable, it could readily be argued that the term has been so overused and misused that it has become virtually meaningless – a generalised Good Thing and little more.

The concept and content of the rule of law has been debated endlessly, but it seems clear from some of the most highly-regarded writing on the subject (at any rate in English) that found within it are a group of commonly-agreed core elements. Typically these include: openness, clarity, generality, prospectivity and (relative) stability.[5] The absence of any substantive content in this conception of the rule of law is quite deliberate, for it is considered of paramount importance to avoid confusing the value of legality with that of justice, fairness, equality or any other social good. Now applying this understanding may have great value in preventing retrospective criminal law or secret regulations. It would support condemnation of the Spanish practice described in Dr Salinas' essay, which allows officials to withhold information about the security services from the judicial authorities even when they are investigating possible crimes committed by members of those services. In England, some of the uses of what is called 'public interest immunity', which permits certain material evidence to be withheld from the courts on, among other grounds, those of national security, would stand condemned under the same principle. Nonetheless, though these examples may cause deep injustice to individuals in specific circumstances, they are relatively rare and marginal issues in societies that are broadly speaking democratic. The limited value of the rule of law concept as a control on the powers and their oppressive use by security institutions can be seen clearly when one examines the statutory developments described in many of the essays in this book. Indeed what emerges is a clear pattern, characteristic of 'reform' of political policing and security services in the 1990s. Often in response to extensive political campaigning, security institutions no longer operate in total secrecy. Legislation and other openly promulgated rules govern their structures, purposes and oversight bodies, in some cases replacing pure government *diktat*. Yet the law is not primarily a means of control and limitation, of safeguarding freedoms by establishing the bounds and curbing the means available to these organisations. Rather, law is increasingly used for purposes of facilitation and legitimation.

Thus, in the Netherlands,[6] a combination of constitutional amendment and a new general statute has enabled the BVD to burgle, bug and tap the telephones of targeted persons without the need to inform them subsequently, and to pass on the information received to a foreign intelligence service if this is thought necessary. Moreover certain criminal acts undertaken by the security service are explicitly identified and legalised by the statute, if ministerial or even merely official approval is granted. British legislation is similar in this respect, and may even have led the way. In Germany, the Constitution was amended, and implementing legislation followed in 1999, for the explicit purpose of relaxing previous controls on surveillance and interception of communications that the drafters of the *Grundgesetz*, working in the shadow of the Nazis after the Second World War, had insisted upon inserting. And in Belgium, Professor van Outrive describes a long historical development beginning with the origin of the state, which only produced legislation in this sphere late in 1998. Note his conclusion concerning the product of the complex coalition politics of his country: 'This "governmental democracy" also marks the kind of legal regime Belgium has achieved. To a very large extent it is a legitimation of an existing practice and/or of what important members of the executive power wanted'.[7] He makes the further, powerful point that with a 'legalistic' solution to issues surrounding the powers granted to security institutions and oversight of their exercise, the Parliament, as a political body, is the loser. What is fundamentally a political debate about how much power and for what ends an institution of the state should enjoy is recast into arcane, or at least relatively inaccessible, legal language.

In all these instances, which have parallels in other nations as well, security agencies can readily claim that they are governed by law and are according due allegiance to the rule of law. Yet if the rule of law means that private citizens can have their homes broken into and their private conversations monitored by state officials, provided other officials or a politician grants approval, then it is useless as a protector of liberty. The phenomenon of increasing legalisation of the structure and work of security agencies coupled with the expansion of their mandates and powers – the most striking new development in this realm of the state in Europe in the past decade – exposes almost cruelly the hollowness of the concept in which so many have invested such profound hopes. Those seeking to prevent abuses of power by security institutions should concentrate their energies on political mobilisation, financial limitations; and above all on strengthening the powers of the legislature and enhancing and legitimating the role of the media as agents of accountability.

Anticipating Threats

As noted at the beginning of this essay, national security institutions are distinguished by their almost exclusive focus on prevention. Their task is to protect fundamental values and institutions from harm, not punish those who perpetrate it after the damage is done. They must therefore act pro-actively, which in turn requires, to use the language of the British Security Service, constant 'threat assessment'. Long before it was discovered and developed by social scientists as a supposedly distinguishing characteristic of contemporary society, the work of security institutions was centred upon risk.

  Yet if security be defined as a state of zero risk, the result is inescapably a totalitarian society, governed by what may be called *Stasi* logic. This way of thinking is not the expression of paranoia. Indeed it is highly rational: if everyone is in fact potentially an opponent then everyone must be surveilled. Even if, indeed especially if, what is being secured is not a party dictatorship but a lively democracy, there will be persons, ideas, tendencies, trends, technologies, sects, groups, and numerous other intellectual and material manifestations of rejection of the fundaments of democratic *praxis*. The rejection may lead to opposition, latent and manifest, potential, actual, future. There will be numerous others who accept the values of democratic *praxis* but find its imperfections or particular decisions so revolting that they feel impelled to act outside the normal political processes. With this pot of pluralistic ferment bubbling away, every tendency or idea that encourages, or could encourage, active measures beyond the pale of acceptable democratic *praxis* could be seen through the prism of *Stasi* logic as demanding surveillance for what it might create. The epitome of this logic in the context of Western societies was the concept of 'subversion', with its focus on tendencies, movements and intellectual positions which though not themselves dangerous might produce. It was exemplified by the remarks of a British Home Secretary in the 1980s who stated that 'tactics which are not themselves unlawful could be used with the aim of subverting our democratic system of government'.[8] This comment was breathtaking because it was an almost casual official acknowledgement of the fact that the concept of subversion knew no bounds: almost any lawful conduct 'could' be used with an aim officials could choose to label subversive, since the concept itself had almost no boundaries. It thus made security officials arbiters of the realm of legitimate politics. Further, since careful inquiry had to be undertaken in order to determine what a particular person or organisation's aims were, and how their activities were likely to develop, widespread political surveillance became a rational necessity: *Stasi* logic indeed.

The subversion story is merely an extreme example of the problems faced by any institution whose work is organised round the concept of threat. It suggests that what democratic *praxis* command in this area is, above all, tolerance of risk. Only when a threat is of a) high likelihood of realisation, b) directed at a major societal interest and c) immediate, may countermeasures that have significant impact on democratic *praxis* be legitimately undertaken.[9]

Particularly important is the element of time. The most vivid example of immediacy is the person who is carrying a timing device which, when joined with an explosive other members of his organisation are reliably known to be transporting, is able to cause death or serious destruction. Putting that person under intensive surveillance of any and all kinds is clearly necessary – until he no longer has the device in his possession. He may, indeed should, continue to remain of interest to security officials so long as he remains active in a paramilitary organisation, but the degree of justifiable surveillance then reduces sharply. In particular, unless he is known to be in a leadership position, permanent tapping of his telephone, or bugging his home, should not be acceptable.

The emphasis on immediacy should also dictate a result quite the reverse of what increasingly is happening in Western states. Immigrants who would otherwise be accepted for permanent settlement are being deported because of participation in political organisations engaged in violent struggles thousands of kilometres away. Often the targets of their actions are dictatorial or military occupation regimes, like the Indian forces in Kashmir or the Turkish 'emergency rule' in the Kurdish area. The justification offered in law for the deportation is, in Britain and elsewhere, that of 'national security'. Now not even the Home Office would try to claim that continued Indian occupation of a disputed province is a matter of UK national security. Rather the argument is that because the UK needs Indian government assistance in containing terrorism, a world-wide phenomenon, then – as a matter of its own national security – the UK must co-operate with the Indian government in combating whatever the latter defines as terrorism and claims is essential to its national security. The truly frightening implication – that the deportation powers of the British government have been appropriated by a foreign military regime to intimidate its opponents – seemed not to trouble the House of Lords, which has shown itself willing to accept any definition of UK national security the Home Secretary chooses to put to it.[10]

It would be difficult to find an example less likely to satisfy the test of national security as democratic *praxis* than this one. It may be thought necessary by those conducting foreign policy to maintain good relations with authoritarian regimes; though a matter for public debate, that political choice is properly made by the government in office. In peacetime, however, good relations with a foreign government fall a long way short of national security. If this were not the case, every person who actively supported the violent struggle of the African National Congress against the apartheid regime in South Africa – with which Britain retained close naval and economic links until the very end – could legitimately have been labelled a threat to national security. When democratic *praxis* is understood as forming its core, the distinction between national security and other highly desirable but lesser things – good relations with foreign governments, international advantage, the furtherance of economic interests – emerges in a clear light. As the late Sir Isaiah Berlin insisted, everything is what it is, and not something else, however good. Maintenance of democratic *praxis* may require sacrifice of certain advantages, material or political, at least in the short term, since the two often conflict. An example would be adoption of a policy of curbing the extent of a nation's arms export industry, because of the evil effects on its own political process.[11] This would certainly produce an immediate loss, but its justification is grounded in the principle of putting first things first. The overwhelming priority is always to secure democratic *praxis*. To borrow a phrase, it is a matter of taking national security seriously.

Risk Tolerance and the Problem of Context

Implicit in the argument for significantly greater tolerance of risk to genuine national security is the assumption that the results will not be seriously damaging. Partly this reflects the logic of proportionality, which must take account of the gravity of the potential damage, though always discounted by the degree of its likelihood. It is also based on an empirical assessment of the stability and tenacity of established Western democratic states. One of the strange paradoxes of the abuses to which the cry of national security has been put in the last half century is that the states which have in reality been least vulnerable to threats to their democratic *praxis* and territorial integrity have often been the most hysterical in their perception and reaction to various 'enemies'. The United States during the 1950s is perhaps the best example. The Soviet Union was certainly actively engaged in large-scale attempts at espionage of American military secrets, and recruited some American citizens to assist it. This, however, is what well-trained and efficient security and police organisations should be expected to deal with. It did not require purging of public servants, infiltration of thousands of organisations, mass surveillance of anyone connected with suspect organisations, or the deportation of aliens sympathetic to Soviet ideology. Western democratic states are deeply anchored in widespread popular allegiance to their core institutions and symbols, however unpopular particular policies or leaders may become, or however disenchanted people feel with politicians as a class. This is a valuable political resource, the product of the combination of relatively widespread affluence, ideological consensus (we cannot look here into how that has been manufactured) and in older countries, habit and inertia. On any rational assessment, these are strong, secure states. Many have behaved as though they were feeble and required extraordinary measures for their survival. This extraordinary combination of irrational fear with the possession of powerful tools of repression produced far more damage to democratic *praxis* than was ever even a remote possibility at the hands of the supposed enemies, without or within.

Risks of course cannot be assessed in the abstract. What I have argued is true of established Western democracies cannot be assumed to hold for democratic regimes and institutions struggling to establish themselves in former Communist states in which there is little or no pre-Communist tradition of democracy to draw upon. Moreover, in much of eastern Europe a combination of open borders, general poverty, and unparalleled opportunities for enrichment through illegal enterprise creates the conditions for the emergence of criminal organisations rich enough to corrupt the political system to its core, to purchase immunity from prosecution and in some instances to drain a major share of public resources. This is radically different in its impact on society as a whole from even the collective impact of successful drug importers, armed robbers and major fraud operators who flourish in all Western European nations. (Only southern Italy has endured anything similar to the fusion of crime and political influence present in many of the post-Communist states.)[12] These more precarious states can therefore properly take a harder line and leave less margin for error in their identification and choice of counter-measures adopted in response to these threats. To take one concrete example: this could mean deporting major Russian 'mafia' criminals without normal procedural protections, and intensive surveillance with a view to prosecution of native officials and politicians who benefit from their largesse. The justification for such drastic measures is that the corruption is at a level so far removed from what Western democracies have shown they can reasonably live with, that it impairs the very fairness and legitimacy of the political system itself. A fragile new democracy may reasonably take measures that would be grossly excessive in a more secure political order. The practical problem they face is how to create and maintain institutions for security and high policing which are themselves outside the system of corruption, rather than major participants in it. Moreover, they must be made sufficiently independent of politicians and other officials to be able to move against entrenched high-level corruption when necessary. It is easy to state the problem in this way: to resolve it is a matter of the greatest difficulty as well as being of overwhelming importance.

Giving context its due in this way does not imply the conclusion too often and too easily reached, namely that in times and circumstances of genuine danger all normal restraints may be abandoned. Not only does the least drastic means principle continue always to govern, but at the forefront of everyone's mind should be the historical truth that those governing under emergency measures are more often responsible for the death of democracy than those who ostensibly present the threat. And even in turbulent conditions, the cure is often worse than the disease. Weimar Germany is supposed to be the classic instance of a state done in by its enemies, Nazi and Communist. Yet a more careful reading of its history establishes that democracy had been largely overtaken by rule by Presidential Decree as early as 1930, and that Hitler's accession to power was facilitated, not prevented, by the Decrees promulgated by the broadly sympathetic conservative President von Hindenberg. The post-war German constitutional settlement has in effect acknowledged this truth, for the emergency amendments enacted amidst bitter controversy in 1968 are a finely-textured and graded complex set of provisions which establish three distinct types of emergencies, each of which requires approval of special majorities within both chambers of the legislature before they may be validly proclaimed.[13]

Moreover, once a newly-democratic state has overcome its initial weaknesses, it cannot justify continued use of extreme measures on the basis that the threat might return at some point. As democratic institutions and allegiances become more deeply rooted, the tolerance of risk should steadily increase.[14] Indeed such a relaxation would be self-reinforcing, in that proclaimed official rejection of practices that are indefensible under normal democratic circumstances, would itself notably assist in the process of establishing, of bedding in, democratic *praxis*. Activities that in less fortunate places would rightly be regarded as serious perils can be treated by citizens of a secure democratic state as regrettable irritations and nuisances. Toleration of insects whose stings cause pain and occasional disease is the best response when the alternative is a programme of habitat destruction that would permanently destroy the food supply. Above all, we should recall Töllborg's warning: democracies must avoid the politics of self-destruction.

Notes

[1] D. Töllborg, 'Undercover in Sweden', in C. Fijnaut and D. Marx (eds) *Undercover: Police Surveillance in Comparative Perspective* (Kluwer, 1995), p.267.

[2] Commission of Enquiry into Certain Actions of the RCMP, *Freedom and Security under the Law*, vol. I, pp. 513ff (Ottawa, 1980).

[3] A notable example is the role of the German media in this context, as described in the essay by Dr Shpiro in this volume.

[4] See especially H. Koh, 'Why The President (Almost) Always Wins in Foreign Affairs' (1988) 97 Yale L.J. 1255.

[5] Characteristic expressions of this conception are found in the writings of Lon Fuller and Joseph Raz.

[6] See the essay by Peter Klerks in this volume.

[7] See Lode van Outrive in this volume page 54.

[8] Leon Brittain MP, speaking in Parliament on 10 July 1984.

[9] The least restrictive means principle clearly implies that the lesser the impact, the more readily can justification be established. Hence, for example, collection of open source information could not be faulted on this test.

[10] *R. v. Home Secretary*, ex p. Rehman, [2001] 3 W.L.R. [Weekly Law Reports] 877.

[11] For a detailed statement and justification of this position, see Lustgarten, 'The Arms Trade and the Constitution: Beyond the Scott Report', (1998) 61 *Modern Law Review* 499, reprinted in somewhat altered form in (1998) 69 *Political Quarterly* 422.

[12] It is precisely because of this contrast that the widespread extension of the mandate of security services in various Western states to include 'organised' or 'serious' crime is unnecessary and dangerous. Unless there is a serious risk of criminality corrupting core political institutions, it should remain a matter for the ordinary police (who may need to

expand their expertise to counter it), for the involvement of security services creates serious problems for the integrity of the criminal justice system.

[13] A good study of both Art. 48 in Weimar and the 1968 legislation, detailed without being excessively technical, is J. Finn, *Constitutions in Crisis* (Oxford Univ. Press, 1991), chs. 4–5.

[14] Spain provides an example of a state that has, initially with great difficulty, made the transition from a precariously-settled democratic regime to a relatively secure one in 25 years.

Bibliography

Agüero, F. (1995), *Militares, civiles y democracia,* Madrid: Alianza.

Allison, G. (1971), *Essence of Decision: explaining the Cuban missile crisis,* Little, Brown, Boston.

Anderson, M. et al (1995), *Policing the European Union: Theory, Law and Practice,* Clarendon Press, Oxford.

Arendt, Hannah (1972), *Lying in Politics, Reflections on the Pentagon Papers,* in Arendt, Hannah, *Crises of the Republic,* 1972, New York: Harcourt Brace & Company.

Associated Press and Agence francáise de presse (1998), 'Le terrorisme, tel que défini par Washington, serait en chute libre', *La Presse,* Montrèal, 1er mai, p. A 17.

Bamford, J. (1982), *The Puzzle Palace. Inside the National Security Agency, America's Most Secret Intelligence Organization,* New York: Penguin Books.

Barril, Paul (1984), *Missions très spéciales,* Paris: Presses de la Cité.

Beau, J.M. (1989), *L'honneur d'un gendarme,* Paris: Sand.

Berlière, Jean-Marc (1994), 'La gènèalogie d'une double tradition policière,' in Birnbaum, Pierre (sous la direction de), *La France de l'affaire Dreyfus,* Paris: Gallimard.

Bigo, D. (1994), 'The European internal security field: stakes and rivalries in a newly developing area of police intervention,' Anderson and den Boer (eds.) *Policing Across National Boundaries,* Pinter, London, 161–73.

Bigo, D. (1996), *Police en Réseaux-L'expérience Européenne,* Paris: Presse Des Sciences Po.

Binnenlandse Veiligheidsdienst (1992a), *Ontwikkelingen op het gebied van de binnenlandse veiligheid. Taakstelling en werkwijze van de BVD.* Ministerie van Binnenlandse Zaken, Binnenlandse Veiligheidsdienst, 11 februari.

Binnenlandse Veiligheidsdienst (1992b), *Binnenlandse Veiligheidsdienst. Jaarverslag 1991,* Ministerie van Binnenlandse Zaken, Binnenlandse Veiligheidsdienst, oktober.

Binnenlandse Veiligheidsdienst (1997), *BVD's Annual Report for 1997.*

Binnenlandse Veiligheidsdienst (1998), *BVD's Annual Report for 1998.*

Biuletyn Biura Informacynego Kancelarii Sejmu No 2476/II kad. Komisja Administracji i Spraw Wewnetrznych No. 102.

Biuletyn Rzecznika Praw Obywatelskich (1996), No. 3.

Blackstock, N. (1976), *Cointelpro: The FBI's Secret War on Political Freedom,* New York: Vintage.

Bloodworth, M. (1995), *Statement by Deputy Clerk, Standing Committee on National Defence and Veterans' Affairs, Communications Security*

Establishment, Ottawa, 2 May 1997 (this is a photocopy of the text of the Statement delivered by the Deputy Clerk).

Bok, Sissela (1982), *Secrets: on the Ethics of Concealment and Revelation*, New York: Pantheon Books.

Bonnet, Yves (2000), *Contre-espionnage: mémoires d'un patron de la DST*, Paris: Calmann-Lévy.

Bouchet, Paul, Lacoste, Amiral Pierre, Plenel, Edwy et Warusfel, Bertrand (1997), 'Table ronde: A propos du contrùle du renseignement,' in *Les Cahiers de la Sécurité Intérieure. Le renseignement*. No. 30, 141–154.

Brijnen van Houten, P. (1988), *Brandwacht in de coulissen. Een kwart eeuw geheime dienstaen*, Houten: De Haan/Unieboek.

Brodeur, Jean-Paul (1983), 'High Policing and Low Policing: Remarks About the Policing of Political Activities,' *Social Problems*, Vol. 30, No. 5, 507–520.

Brodeur, Jean-Paul (1985), *On Evaluating Threats to the National Security of Canada and to the Civil Rights of Canadians*, Paper presented to SIRC Seminar, October.

Brodeur, Jean-Paul (1991), 'Countering Terrorism in Canada', in A.S. Farson, D. Stafford and W.K. Wark, *Security and Intelligence in a Changing World: New Perspectives for the 1990s*, London: Frank Cass, 182–200.

Brodeur, Jean-Paul (1997), 'Parliamentary versus Civilian Oversight', D Töllborg (ed.), *National Security and the Rule of Law*, Centre for European Research, Gothenburg, 81–133.

Brodeur, Jean-Paul (1997a), *Violence and Racial Prejudice in the Context of Peacekeeping. A study prepared for the Commission of Inquiry into the Deployment of Canadian Forces to Somalia*, Ottawa: Minister of Public Works and Government Services Canada.

Brodeur, Jean-Paul (1997b), 'En être ou ne pas en ítre: telle n'est pas la question', *Les Cahiers de la sécurité intérieure*, No. 30, 155–184 (a slightly different version of this paper is forthcoming in English).

Brodeur, Jean-Paul (2000), 'Cops and Spooks: The Uneasy Partnership', *Police Practice and Research: An International Journal*. Vol. 1, no 3, 2000.

Brown, L. and Brown C., (1978), *An Unauthorized History of the RCMP*, Toronto: James Lorrimer.

Bulenda, Kremplewski, Moczydlowski and Rzeplinski (undated), *Between Militia and Reform. The Police in Poland 1989–1997*. A report submitted in March 1998 within an international project Police in Transition co-ordinated by Hungarian Helsinki Committee.

Bundesamt für Verfassungsschutz (undated), *Befugnisse, Aufgaben, Grenzen*, Bonn.

Bunyan, Tony (1993), 'Trevi, Europol and the new European state,' in Bunyan (ed.) *Statewatching the New Europe*, Statewatch, London.

Burdan, Daniel (1990), *DST : neuf ans á la division antiterroriste*, Paris: R. Laffont.

Burrows, William (1988), *Deep Black – the Secrets of Space Espionage*, London.

Busch, Heiner (1997), 'Swiss "state protection" – from scandal to law', D. Töllborg (ed), *National Security and the Rule of Law*, Centre for European Research, Gothenburg, pp.43–52.

Busch, N. (1999), 'Interception capabilities 2000: the abolition of privacy?', *Fortress Europe?* Nr 58.

Buzan, B. (1991), *People, States and Fear*, Harvester Wheatsheaf, Hemel Hempstead, 2nd edn.

Cachinero, J. and Trujillo, J. (1993), 'La guerra silenciosa: el futuro de los servicios de inteligencia', *Política Exterior*, 34, VII, pp. 115–125.

Calderón Fernandez, J. (1998), *Conference: El hoy y el mañana de los Servicios de inteligencia.*

Cameron, Iain (1997), 'Protection of Constitutional Rights in Sweden', *Public Law*, Sweet and Maxwell, 488–512.

Cameron, Iain (2000), *National Security and the European Convention on Human Rights*, Iustus/Kluwer.

Canada (1966a), *Rapport de la Commission d'enquîte quant aux plaintes formulées par George Victor Spencer* (Dalton Courtwright Wells, Prèsident), Ottawa (available in English).

Canada (1966b), *Rapport de la Commission d'enquête sur certaines questions relatives à la dénommée Gerda Munsinger* (Wishart Flett Spence, Président), Ottawa: Imprimeur de la Reine (available in English).

Canada (1969), *Abridged Report of The Royal Commission on Security* (The Mackenzie Report), Ottawa: Queen's Printer.

Canada (1981a), *Freedom and Security Under the Law* (Second Report of the Commission of Inquiry Concerning Certain Activities of the Royal Canadian Mounted Police – the McDonald Report), Ottawa: Minister of Supplies and Services, 2 volumes.

Canada (1981a), *Certain RCMP Activities and the Question of Governmental Knowledge* (Third Report of the Commission of Inquiry Concerning Certain Activities of the Royal Canadian Mounted Police – the McDonald Report), Ottawa: Minister of Supplies and Services, 1 volume.

Canada (1997), *Dishonored Legacy. The Lessons of the Somalia Affair. Report of the Commission of Inquiry into the Deployment of Canadian Forces to Somalia*, (Judge Gilles Lètourneau, Chairman) Ottawa: Minister of Public Works and Government Services Canada, 5 volumes and an Executive Summary.

Canada, Auditor General (1996), *Report of the Auditor General to the House of Commons*, Chapter 27: The Canadian Intelligence Community – Control and Accountability, Ottawa: Minister of Public Works and Government Services Canada 1996.

Canada, Department of National Defence (1997), *1997–98 Estimates. Part III: Expenditure Plan*, Ottawa: Minister of Supply and Services Canada.

Canada, House of Commons (1990), *In Flux but not in Crisis*. Report of the Special Committee on the Review of the Canadian Security Intelligence Act and the Security Offences Act 1989–1990 (report of the Thacker Committee), Ottawa: House of Commons.

Canada, Senate (1983), *Report of the Special Committee of the Senate on the Canadian Security Intelligence Service. Delicate Balance: A Security Intelligence Service in a Democratic Society.* Ottawa: Minister of Supply and Services Canada.

Canada, Security Intelligence Review Committee (SIRC 1994), *The Heritage Front Affair*, Ottawa: Security Intelligence Review Committee.

Canada, Solicitor General (1991). *On Course: National Security for the 1990s.* Ottawa: Minister of Supply and Services.

Canada, Solicitor General (1996), *1996–97 Estimates. Part III, Expenditure Plan*, Ottawa: Ministry of Supply and Services Canada.

Canada, Solicitor General (1997), *1997–98 Estimates. Part III, Expenditure Plan*, Ottawa: Ministry of Supply and Services Canada.

Canadian Press (1995), 'Canada spied on allies, former CSE agent says', The *Globe and Mail*, Toronto, 13 November 1995, A2.

Canadian Press (1998), 'Terrorist threat real: minister', *The Gazette*, Montreal, May 1st, d14.

Canadian Security Intelligence Service/CSIS (1995–99), *Public Report (1994 to 1998)*, Ottawa: Minister of Services and Supply Canada.

Canadian Security Intelligence Service/CSIS (1998b), *Submission to the Senate Special Committee on Security and Intelligence*, by Ward Elcock, Director, Canadian Security Intelligence Service, Ottawa, 24 June.

Carpentier, C. Moser, F. (1993), *La Sûreté de l'État, Histoire d'une déstabilisation*, Bruxelles: Quorum.

Castels, M. (1997), *The Power of Identity*, Blackwell, Oxford.

CBOS survey of 11–16 December, 1997.

Center for Opinion Surveys (1996), Society on the Office of State Protection. *Survey report.* Warsaw August.

Central Intelligence Machinery, (1993) HMSO, London.

Centrum Informacyjne Rzadu (1996), *The White Book. Records of an investigation conducted by Prosecutor's Office of Warsaw Military District concerning motions of Minister of Internal Affairs of 19 December 1995 and 16 January 1996*, Ref. No. PoSl 1/96. Warsaw.

Clegg, S. (1989), *Frameworks of Power*, Sage, London.

Clèroux, R. (1990), *Official Secrets: The Story Behind the Canadian Security Intelligence Service*, Toronto: McGraw-Hill Ryerson.

Comité permanent de controle des services de renseignements, *Rapports d'Activités 1994 to 1998*, 1040 Bruxelles, Rue de la Loi 52.

Commissaire Diamant (1993), *Les réseaux secrets de la police*, Paris: Éditions La Découverte.

Commission of Enquiry into Certain Actions of the RCMP (1980), *Freedom and Security under the Law*, Ottawa.

Commission Nationale du Contrôle des Interceptions de sécurité (CNCIS, 1996), *Rapport d'activité 1996*, Paris: La documentation française.

Communications Security Establishment Commissioner (CSE Commissioner: 1997–1998), *Annual Report (1996–97 and 1997–1998)*, Ottawa: Minister of Public Works and Government Services Canada.

Couëtoux, Michel, Di Ruzza, Renati, Dumoulin, Jèrôme et Gleizal, Jean-Jacques (1981), *Figures du secret*, Grenoble: Presses Universitaires de Grenoble.

Coulon, J. (1998), 'Ottawa s'oppose à la démilitarisation de l'Arctique', *Le Devoir*, Montréal, 4 mai: A2.

Council of Europe (1981), *Convention for the Protection of Individuals with regard to Automatic Processing of Personal Data*, ETS No. 108.

Cousido González, P. (1995), Comentarios a la Ley de Secretos Oficiales y su Reglamento. Barcelona: Bosch.

Davies, M. (1999), *The Intelligence and Security Committee: pawn, pussycat or tiger?* Paper presented to the PSA Annual Conference, University of Nottingham, March.

Derogy, Jacques et Pontaut, Jean-Marie (1986), *Enquête sur trois secrets d'État*, Paris: Robert Laffont.

Dewerpe, Alain. (1994), *L'espion. Une anthropologie historique du secret d'État*. Paris: Gallimard.

Dezsõ, L. and Hajas, G. (1997), *A nemzetbiztonsági tevékenységre vonatkozó jogszabályok* (Legal norms related to national security activities), HVG-ORAC, Budapest.

Diez-Picazo, L. (1996), 'El secreto de Estado en el proceso penal', *La Ley-Actualidad*, 3952, 1–3.

Dillon, M. (1990), *The Dirty War*, Arrow Books, London.

Dion, R. (1982), *Crimes of the Secret Police*, Montreal: Black Rose Books.

Dobry, Michel (1997), 'Le renseignement dans les démocraties occidentales', *Les Cahiers de la Sécurité Intérieure*. Le renseignement, Vol. 30, 53–86.

Dominiczak, Henryk (1997), *Security Agencies in People's Poland 1944–1990*, Warsaw, Bellona.

Dorn, Nicholas (1998), 'Les nouvelles formes de renseignement policier,' *Les Cahiers de la Sécurité Intérieure. Drogue*, No. 32, 137–150.

Draper, T. (1997), 'Is the CIA Necessary?', *The New York Review of Books*, Vol. XLIV, No. 13, August 1997, 18–21.

Du Morne Vert, Patrick (1987), *Mission Oxygène*, Paris: Filipacchi.

Dyson, John (1986), *Sink the Rainbow Warrior!*, London: Victor Gollancz.

East European Constitutional Review, Winter 1997, Vol. 6, No. 1.

Eichner, K. and Dobbert, A. (1998), *Headquarters Germany*, edition ost.

Engelen, D. (1995), *Geschiedenis van de Binnenlandse Veiligheidsdienst*, Den Haag: Sdu uitgeverij Koninginnegracht.

Ericson, Richard V. and Haggerty, Kevin (1997), *Policing the Risk Society*, Toronto: University of Toronto Press and Oxford: Oxford University Press.

Faligot, Roger et Krop, Pascal (1985), *La piscine: les services secrets français 1944–1984*, Paris Seuil.

Farson, A.S. (1991), 'Criminal Intelligence vs. Security Intelligence: a Reevaluation of the Police Role in the Response to Terrorism', in D. A. Charters (ed.), *Democratic Responses to International Terrorism*, Ardsley-on-Hudson NY: Transnational Publishers, Inc.

Finn, J., *Constitution in Crisis*, Oxford University Press 1991.

Försvarets Underrättelsenämnd (1998), (The Swedish Supervisory Organ for the Military intelligence) *Redovisning av vissa uppgifter om den militära underrättelse- och säkerhetstjänsten*, November 26 (A report on certain particulars regarding the military intelligence.)

Foucault, Michel (1994), *Dits et écrits 1954–1988*, Paris: Gallimard, Vol. III, 1976–1979.

France, Conseil d'État (1995), *Rapport public 1995: La transparence et le secret*. Paris: Conseil d'État.

Franck, Hans-Göran (1998), *'SÄPO: Medborgarkommission behövs för att nå full klarhet'*, Advokaten nr 2. ('SÄPO: A Truth Commission necessary to shed light on the Security Police actions').

Frankel, M. (1999), 'Abysmal handiwork,' *The Guardian*, 25 May, 19.

Franks, C.E.S. (1979), *Parliament and Security Matters*, (A study prepared for the Commission of Inquiry Concerning Certain Activities of the Royal Canadian Mounted Police – the McDonald Commission), Ottawa: Minister of Supply and Services Canada.

Friedland, Martin L. (1997), *Controlling Misconduct in the Military*, a study prepared for the Commission of Inquiry into the deployment of Canadian Forces in Somalia, Ottawa: Minister of Public Works and Services Canada.

Frost, M. and M. Gratton (1994), *Spyworld. Inside the Canadian and American Intelligence Establishments*, Toronto: Doubleday.

Frydrychowicz, Aleksander (1998), *SLD disclosing the political nature of UOP*, Trybuna 29 June, No.150.

Gauthier, G. (1996), *'Le juge Bisson contredit Collenette sur l'Etendue de son mandat'*, La Presse, Montreal, June 10, B 5.

Geraghty, T. (1998), *The Irish War*, Harper Collins, London.

Giddens, A. (1985), *The Nation-State and Violence*, Polity, Cambridge.

Gill, P. (1989a), 'Defining Subversion. The Canadian Experience since 1977'. *Public Law*, 617–36.

Gill, P. (1989b), 'Symbolic or Real? The Impact of the Canadian Security Intelligence Review Committee', *Intelligence and National Security*, Vol. 4, 550–75.

Gill, P. (1991), 'The Evolution of the Security Intelligence Debate in Canada since 1976', in A.S. Farson, D. Stafford and W.K. Wark, *Security and Intelligence in a Changing World: New Perspectives for the 1990s*, London: Frank Cass, 75–94.

Gill, P. (1994), *Policing Politics: security intelligence and the liberal democratic state*, Cass, London.

Gill, P. (1996), 'Reasserting Control: recent changes in the oversight of the UK intelligence community,' *Intelligence and National Security*, 11(2) April, 313–31.

Gill, P. (1998), 'Making Sense of Police Intelligence? The Use of a Cybernetic Model in Analysing Information and Power in Police Intelligence Processes,' *Policing & Society*, 8(3), 289–314.

Government, The Swedish, Governmental Proposition to the Parliament Prop 1997/98:97 *Polisens register* (Police Registers).

de Graaff, Bob and Wiebes, Cees (1998), *Villa Maarheeze. De Geschiedenis van de inlichtingendienst buitenland*, Den Haag: Sdu Uitgevers.

Guisnel, Jean et Violet, Bernard (1988), *Services secrets: le pouvoir et les services de renseignements sous la présidence de François Mitterrand*, Paris: Éditions La Découverte.

Hall, S. *et al*, (1978), *Policing the Crisis: mugging, the state and law and order*, Macmillan, Basingstoke.

Handelingen II 1998–1999, Bijlagen 26279 No. 2.

Handelingen Tweede Kamer, *Advies Raad van State en nader rapport*, Handelingen Tweede Kamer 1999–2000, Bijlagen 25 877, No. B.

Harden, I. and Lewis, N. (1988), *The Noble Lie: the British constitution and the rule of law*, Hutchinson, London.

Harstrich, J. et Calvi F. (1991), R.G., *Vingt ans de police politique*, Paris: Calmann-Lévy.

Hebenton, B. and Thomas, T. (1995), *Policing Europe: co-operation, conflict and control*, Macmillan, Basingstoke.

Herman, Michael (1996), *Intelligence Power in Peace and War*, Cambridge,

Hoehne, Heinz and Zolling, Hermann (1971), *Network*, London.

Home Affairs Select Committee (1999), *Accountability of the Security Service*, 3rd Report, July, House of Commons, London.

Home Office (1984), *Guidelines on the Work of a Special Branch*, December.

Home Office (1994), *Guidelines on Special Branch Work in Great Britain*, July.

Intelligence (1998), 'BVD gets what it wants...Coming & Going', *Intelligence*, N. 79, 4 May.

Intelligence (1999), 'A busy fortnight for "crime busters"', *Intelligence*, N. 105, 18 October.

Intelligence (2000), 'Mink "K" trial leads to DEA & Contras', *Intelligence*, N. 111, 7 February.

Intelligence (2000), 'Mink Kok's "secret" public testimony', *Intelligence*, N. 114, 27 March.

Intelligence and Security Committee (ISC) (1995), *Report on Security Service Work Against Organised Crime*, Cm 3065, HMSO, London.

Intelligence and Security Committee (1996), *Annual Report for 1996*, Cm 3574, HMSO, London.

Intelligence and Security Committee (1998), *Annual Report for 1997–98*, Cm 4073, HMSO, London.

Jaime-Jiménez, O. (1997), 'Politics, Security Agencies and Terrorism in Spain', Töllborg, D, *National Security and the Rule of Law*, Göteborg: University of Gothenburg, 23–42.

Jamieson R *et al* (1998), 'Economic Liberalization and Cross-Border Crime: The NAFTA and Canada's Border with the USA, Part II,' *International Journal of the Sociology of Law*, 26, 285–319.

Jansen and Janssen (1990), *Regenjassendemocratie. BVD-infiltraties bij aktievoerder/sters*, Amsterdam: Ravijn, s.a.

Jansen and Janssen (1990), *De tragiek van een geheime dienst. Een onderzoek naar de BVD in Nijmegen*, Nijmegen.

Jansen and Janssen (1991), *De vluchteling achtervolgd. De BVD en asielzoekers*, Amsterdam Ravijn.

Jansen and Janssen (1993), *Opening van zaken. Een ander BVD-jaarverslag*, Amsterdam: Ravijn.

Jansen and Janssen (1995), *Welingelichte kringen. Inlichtingendiensten Jaarboek 1995*, Amsterdam: Uitgeverij Ravijn.

Jar Couselo, G. (1995), *El modelo policial español y Policías Autónomas*. Madrid: Dykinson.

Jessop, B. (1990), *State Theory: putting capitalist states in their place*, Polity, Cambridge.

Johnston, L. (1992), *The Rebirth of Private Policing*, Routledge, London.

Jönsson, Christer (2000), *Sanning och konsekvens*, HSFR:s brytpunktserie 2000, (An english translation, *Truth and consequence*, can be ordered from Dennis Töllborg via e-mail, dennis.toellborg@law.gu.se).

Joubert, Chantal and Bevers, Hans (1996), *Schengen Investigated: A Comparison of the Schengen Provisions on International Police Cooperation on the Light of the European Convention on Human Rights*, Deventer: Kluwer Law International.

Journal of Laws, Uniform text, Journal of Laws, 90.30.180.

Justice (1998), *Under Surveillance: covert policing and human rights standards*, Justice, London.

Ju2000/4972/PÅ (Ju = Justice department, Swedish Government).

Ju2000/4983/PÅ.

Ju2001/226/PÅ *Letter to Staffan Ehnebom*.

Justitiekanslern (Chancellor of Justice), Sweden, dnr 172–97–21.

JuU 10 1998/99 (Swedish Parliament Standing Committee on Justice).

Katona, B. (1995), *Introductory speech into debates on the Bill on National Security*, Az Országgyűlés hiteles jegyzőkönyve (Authentic Records of the National Assembly), 27 February.

Keane, John (1991), *The Media and Democracy*, Cambridge.

King, Michael (1986), *Death of the Rainbow Warrior*, Auckland (NZ): Penguin Books.

Klerks, Peter (1989), *Terreurbestrijding in Nederland*, Amsterdam: Ravijn.

Klerks, Peter (1991), 'Veiligheidsdiensten in verandering' in A.E. van Almelo and P.G. Wiewel (eds), *Politiezorg in de jaren 1990*, 99–138 Arnhem: Gouda Quint.

Klerks, Peter (1995), 'Königreich Niederlande', in: Schmidt-Eenboom, Erich (Hrsg.), *Nachrichtendienste in Nordamerika, Europa und Japan: Länderporträts und Analysen*. Weilheim: STÖPPEL-Verlag (CD-ROM, ISBN 3–89306–726–4).

Kluiters, F.A.C. (1993), *De Nederlandse inlichtingen en veiligheidsdiensten*, Gravenhage, Sdu Uitgeverij Koninginnegracht.

Kluiters, F.A.C. (1995), *Crypto- en trafficanalyse, Sectie 2, TRIS*, Sdu Uitgeverij Koninginnegracht.

Koedijk, P. *et al* (eds) (1996), *Verspieders voor het vaderland. Nederlandse spionage voor, tijdens en na de Koude Oorlog*, Den Haag: Sdu Uitgevers.

Koh, H. (1988), 'Why The President (Almost) Always Wins in Foreign Affairs', 97 *Yale L.J.* 1255.

Kooiman, J. (1993), 'Findings, Speculations and Recommendations,' in Kooiman (ed.) *Modern Governance: new government-society interactions*, Sage, London.

Kozural, M. (1996), 'The problem of discipline within the UOP', *Gazeta Wyborcza*, 5 October.

Krywin, A. et Marchand, Ch. (1999), 'Le secret d'État et les droits de l'Homme', dans Comité Permanent de Contrôle des Services de Renseignements et l'Institut Royal Supérieur de Défense, *Secret d'État ou Transparence?* Colloque 20 janvier.

Kubiak, Przemyslaw (1996), 'What was the relation between SB and Lady Punk? The Counterintelligence department decided the list of radio hits.' *Super Express*, 4 December 1996, 1.

Lacoste, Pierre (1997), *Un amiral au secret*, Paris: Flammarion.

Lascoumes, Pierre (1997), *Élites irrégulières. Essai sur la délinquance d'affaires*, Paris: Gallimard.

Lecomte, Claude (1985), *Coulez le Rainbow Warrior*, Paris: Messidor, Éditions Sociales.

Lénárt, F. (1996) Nemzetbiztonsági szolgálatok ma (National security services today), *Belügyi Szemla* 12, 64–73.

Leng, R. and Taylor, R. (1996), *Criminal Procedure and Investigations Act 1996*, Blackstone Press, London.

Lenoir, Jean-Pierre (1992), *L'État trafiquant*, Paris: R. Laffont.

Lenoir, Jean-Pierre (1998), *Un espion très ordinaire: l'histoire vue du SDECE*, Paris, Albin Michel.

Le Roy-Finville (1980), *S.D.E.C.E., Service 7: l'extraordinaire aventure du colonel Le Roy-Finville et de ses clandestins*, (recueillie par Philippe Bernert), Paris: Presses de la Cité.

Lester, N. (1998), *Enquêtes sur les Services Secrets*, Montréal: Les editions de l'Homme.

L'Heuillet, Hélène (1997), 'Le renseignement ou l'impossible maîtrise de la politique', *Les Cahiers de la Sécurité intérieure. Le renseignement*. No. 30, 103–118.

Lowenthal, M.M. (1992), *U.S. Intelligence: Evolution and Anatomy*, Westport, Connecticut: Praeger, Second Edition.

Lozano, B. (1998), *La desclasificación de los secretos de Estado*, Madrid: Cuadernos Civitas.

Luccioni, Xavier (1986), *L'Affaire Greenpeace*, Paris: Payot.

Lund Commission (1996), *Dokument nr. 15. Rapport til Stortinget fra kommisjonen som nedsatt av Stortinget for å granske påstander om ulovlig overvåking av norske borgere, avgitt till Stortingets presidentskap 28 mars 1996.* ('Lund Report', the Norwegian inquiry on police and military intelligence in Norway.)

Lustgarten, L. and Leigh, I. (1994), *In from the Cold: National Security and Parliamentary Democracy*, Oxford: Oxford University Press.

Lustgarten, L. (1995), 'Security Services, Constitutional Structure, and Varieties of Accountability in Canada and Australia', in P.C. Stenning (ed.) *Accountability for Criminal Justice*, Toronto: University of Toronto Press.

Lustgarten, L. (1997), 'Accountability of security services in western democracies', In D Töllborg (ed.) *National Security and the Rule of Law*, Centre for European Research, Gothenburg, 53–79.

Lustgarten, L. (1998), 'The Arms Trade and the Constitution: Beyond the Scott Report', in 61 *Modern Law Review* 499.

McBarnet, D.J. (1983), *Conviction: law, the state and the construction of justice*, Macmillan, London.

Maguire, K. (1990), 'The Intelligence War in Northern Ireland,' *International Journal of Intelligence and Counterintelligence*, 4(2), 145–65.

Maniguet, Xavier (1986), *L'aventure pour l'aventure*, Paris: Carrère-Laffon.

Mann, E. and Lee, J.A. (1979), *RCMP vs. The People: Inside Canada's Security Service*, Toronto: General Publishing.

Marcinkowski, Adam and Zbigniew Palski (1990), 'Victims of Stalinist Repressions in the Polish Armed Forces', *Wojskowy Przeglad Historyczny*, No.1–2, 168–184.

Marion, Paul (1991), *La mission impossible. A la tête des services secrets*, Paris: Calmann-Lévy.

Markiewicz, W. (1996), 'Permanent tapping has been restored to telephone exchange stations', *Polityka*, 11 May.

Marszalek, Anna (1998), 'Plans to merge civilian and military intelligence. The Opposition on democratic oversight', *Rzeczpospolita*, 29 June, No.150.

Marx, G. (1987), 'The Interweaving of Public and Private Police in Undercover Work,' in C. D. Shearing and R. Stenning, *Private Policing*, Sage, Beverley Hills.

Melin, Karl (1997), 'Chef i det dolda', Försvarets Forum nr 8.

Melnik, Constantin (1988), *Mille jours à Matignon : raisons d'État sous de Gaulle, guerre d'Algérie 1959–1962*, Paris: Grasset.

MI5 (1993) *The Security Service*, HMSO, London; 2nd edn. 1996; 3rd edn. 1998.

MOD (1998), *Nieuw evenwicht* (New balance), a confidential 1998 MOD report .

Moon, P. (1991a), 'Secrecy shrouds spy agency', *Globe and Mail*, Toronto, 27 May, 1.

Moon, P. (1991b), 'For their eyes only', *Globe and Mail*, Toronto, 28 May, 1.

Moon, P. (1991c), 'Who's watching the watchers', *Globe and Mail*, Toronto, 30 May, 1.

Noël, A. (1989), 'Le Canada à l'Ecoute du monde...y compris peut-être de vos conversations les plus secrètes', *Journal La Presse*, Montrèal, 28 octobre, B-1.

Nyíri, S. (1997), *A titkos információgyûjtés jogi alapjai* (Legal basis of collecting secret information), BM Duna Palota és Kiadó, Budapest.

Ockrent, Christine et Comte Alexandre de Marenches (1986), *Dans le secret des princes*, Paris: Stock.

Onderzoeksburo Inlichtingen- en Veiligheidsdiensten (OBIV) (1998), *Operatie Homerus. Spioneren voor de BVD*, Breda: Papieren Tijger.

Ontario, (1980), *Report of the Commission of Inquiry into the Confidentiality of Health Information* (The Krever Report), Toronto: Queen's Printer for Ontario.

Paczkowski, Andrzej (ed.) (1994), *Security machine in 1944–1956*. Warsaw ISP PAN.

Paecht, Arthur (1999), *Rapport fait au nom de la Commission de la Défense Nationale et des Forces Armèes sur la proposition de loi (No. 1497) de M. Paul Quilès et plusieurs de ses collègues tendant à la création d'une délégation parlementaire pour les affaires de renseignement*, Paris: Assemblée Nationale, onzième législature, document No. 1951, enregistré le 23 novembre 1999 et mis en distribution le 2 dècembre 1999.

Pardarvi, Marta (1998), *Oversight of National Security Services in Hungary*, manuscript Budapest.

Péan, Pierre (1984), *'V' l'affaire des avions renifleurs*, Fayard: Paris.

Péan, Pierre (1986), *Secret d'État: La France de secret, les secrets de la France*, Paris: Fayard.

Penrose, R. (1996), interview with, December 3.

Plenel, Edwy (1997), *Les mots volés*, Paris: Stock.

Polish Official Gazette, Amendments, Polish Official Gazette 195.23.271; 96.43.419.

Porch, Douglas (1995), *The French Secret Services: From the Dreyfus Affair to the Gulf War*, New York: Farrar, Strauss & Giroux.

Porter, B. (1989), *Plots and Paranoia: a history of political espionage in Britain 1790–1988*, Unwin Hyman, London.

Potter, E. (1998 ed.), *Economic Intelligence and National Security*, Carleton: Carleton University Press.

Poulet, Y. et Havelange, B. (1999), 'Secrets d'État et Vie privée: ou comment concilier l'inconciliable?', dans *Comité Permanent de Contrôle des Services de Renseignements et l'Institut Royal Supérieur de Défense, Secret d'État ou Transparencé?* Colloque 20 janvier.

Powell, W.W. (1991), 'Neither Market nor Hierarchy: network forms of organisation,' in G. Thompson, *et al, Markets, Hierarchies and Networks: the co-ordination of social life*, Sage, London.

Prime Minister (1998), *Government Response to the Intelligence and Security Committee's Annual Report 1997–98*, Cm4089, HMSO, London.

Puerer, Heinz and Raabe, Johannes (1996), *Medien in Deutschland*, Konstanz.

Québec, (1981), *Rapport de la Commission d'enquête sur des opèrations policières en territoire* (the Keable Commission Report), Québec: Ministère des Communications.

Quilès, Paul (2000), Le renseignement: zone d'ombre de la République. Entretien avec Paul Quilès, Hommes et Libertés, No. 109, 49.

Radzinowicz, Leon (1956), *A History of English Criminal Law and its Administration from 1750. Volume 3: Cross-Currents in the Movement for the Reform of the Police*. London: Stevens and Sons Limited.

Register Board (1998), *Annual Report.*
Register Board (1998), *Personalkontroll den 1 oktober 1969 – den 30 juni 1996. Rapport till regeringen av Registernämnden beslutad den 16 december 1998* (Personnel Control 1 October 1969–30 June 1996, A report to the Government, decided 16 December 1998).
Register Board (2000), *Personalkontroll Del II. Fortsatt uppdrag av regeringen den 31 mars 1999 om utlämnande av uppgifter ur SÄPO-registret den 1 oktober 1969–den 30 juni 19996, Rapport till regeringen av Registernämnden den 3 oktober 2000* (Personnel Control Part II. Continued inquiry regarding information in personnel control matters handed out from the files of the Swedish Security Police during 1 October 1969–30 June 1996, Report to the Government from the Register Board 3 October 2000. Quoted as 'Register Board 1999').
Register Board (2000), *Annual Report.*
Register Board (2001), *Annual Report.*
Renouard, Isabelle (1997), 'La coordination du renseignement en France', *Les Cahiers de la Sécurité Intérieure. Le renseignement.* No. 30, 9–13.
Revenga, M. (1995), 'El control del secreto de Estado. Reflexiones preliminares de derecho comparado'. Paper to Conference: *El control de los secretos de estado.* El Escorial, december.
Richelson, J.T. (1988), *Foreign Intelligence Organizations*, Cambridge, MA: Harvard University Press.
Richelson, J.T. (1990), 'The Calculus of Intelligence Cooperation', *International Journal of Intelligence and Counterintelligence*, Vol. 4, No. 3, 307–323.
Richelson J.T. and D. Ball (1985), *The Ties that Bind: Intelligence Cooperation between the UKUSA Countries*, Boston: Allen and Unwin.
Rikspolisstyrelsen, Polisens årsredovisning 2000.
Rioux J-F and Hay R. (1995), 'Security, Foreign Policy and Transnational Organized Crime: a perspective from Canada,' *Transnational Organized Crime*, 1(2) Summer, 173–92.
Ritter, F. (1989), *Die geheimen Nachrichtendienste der Bundesrepublik Deutschland*, Heidelberg
Robertson, K.G. (1989), 'Canadian Intelligence Policy: the Role and Future of CSIS', *The International Journal of Intelligence and Counter-Intelligence*, Vol. 3, No. 2, 225–248.
Robertson, K. (1998), 'MI5, Policing and Serious Crime: democracy, accountability and risk management', *Intelligence and National Security*, 13(2), Summer, 144–58.
Rougelet, Patrick (2000), *La machine à Scandale*, Paris: Albin Michel.
Russell, P. (1988), *Should Canada Establish a Foreign Intelligence Agency?*, Ottawa: Typescript, December.
Ryder, C. (1989), *The RUC: a force under fire*, Methuen, London.
Rzeczpospolita (1996), 22 May, 16.
Rzeczpospolita (1998), 24 June, No. 146, 1.
St. John, P. (1984), 'Canada's Accession to the Allied Intelligence Community 1940–45', *Conflict Quarterly*, Vol. 4, No. 4, 5–21.

Sainz de la Peña, J.A. and Marquina, A. (1996), 'Los servicios de información en un Estado Democrático: las inercias del CESID', *UNISCI Papers 5*, 1–54.

Säkerhetspolisen SA (Official Diary of the Security Police), *189–307–98*.

Säkerhetspolisen (Swedish Security Police), *SA 187–2140–98*.

Sallot, J. (1979), *The Real Story of How the Mounties always Get Their Man: Nobody Said No*, Toronto: James Lorrimer.

Sallot, J. (1984), 'Secret agency keeps data on individual "security risks",' *Globe and Mail*, 21 November, 1.

San Martín, J.I. (1983), *Servicio Especial*. Barcelona: Planeta, 1983.

Santolaya Machetti, P. (1995), 'El control de los secretos de Estado; la experiencia en Derecho Comparado'. Paper to Conference: *El control de los secretos de estado*. El Escorial, december.

Sawatsky, J. (1980), *Men in the Shadows*, Toronto: Doubleday.

Scott, 1995–6, *Inquiry into the Export of Defence Equipment and Dual-Use Goods to Iraq and related prosecutions*, House of Commons Papers HC115, HMSO, London.

Schmidt-Eenboom, Erich (1993), *Der BND*, Munich.

Schmidt-Eenboom, Erich (1998), *Undercover*, Cologne.

Security Commission (1985), *Report on the case of Michael John Bettaney*, Cmnd 9514, HMSO, London.

Security Intelligence Review Committee/SIRC (1985–1998), *Annual Report (1984–85 to 1997–98)*, Ottawa: Minister of Supply and Services Canada.

Security Intelligence Review Committee/SIRC (1987), *The Security and Intelligence Network in the Government of Canada: a Description*, Ottawa: Security Intelligence Committee (also available in a much abridged form in SIRC, *Annual Report 1987–1988*, 69–75.)

Security Intelligence Review Committee/SIRC (1994). *The Heritage Front Affair. Report to the Solicitor General of Canada*. Ottawa: Security Intelligence Review Committee, File No.:2800–54.

Security Intelligence Review Committee/SIRC (1999), *SIRC Annual Report 1998–1999. An Operational Audit of the Canadian Security Intelligence Service*, Ottawa: Minister of Supply and Services Canada 1999.

SEVI (1982), *Het Labyrinth, private milities en politiewezen doorgelicht, met het officieel rapport van de commissie Wijninckx* (The Labyrinth, an analysis of private militias and of police; with the official report of the Commission Wijninckx) Brussel: Sevi-Publicatie, 1.

Shayler, D. (undated), *Management Issues*, Paper submitted to Review of Intelligence Agencies, adapted, mimeo.

Simmel, Georg (1996), *Secrets et sociétés secrètes*, traduction Sybille Muller, Paris: Circé Poche.

Smith, M. (1996), *New Cloak, Old Dagger*, Victor Gollancz, London.

SOU/Swedish Public Inquiry, Statens Offentliga Utredningar 1988:18, *Säkerhetspolisens arbetsmetoder* (The Modi Operandi of the Swedish Security Police).

SOU/Swedish Public Inquiry, Statens Offentliga Utredningar 1990:51, *Säkerhetspolisens arbetsmetoder, personalkontroll och meddelarfrihet*

(The modi operandi of the Security Police, personnel control and the right to be an informant to the mass media.)

SOU/Swedish Public Inquiry, Statens Offentliga Utredningar 1994:149, *Säkerhetsskydd* (Security Protection).

SOU/Swedish Public Inquiry, Statens Offentliga Utredningar 1997:65, *Polisens register* (Police Registers).

SOU/Swedish Public Inquiry, Statens Offentliga Utredningar 1998:46, *Om buggning och andra tvångsmedel* (Using wire-tapping, electronic surveillance and other means of coercion).

SOU/Swedish Public Inquiry, Statens Offentliga Utredningar 1999:37 *Underrättelsetjänsten – en översyn* (The Military Intelligence – an overview).

Staatscourant (1999), *Besluit organisatorische inrichting BVD 1999*, Staatscourant.

Stanley, W. (1996), 'International Tutelage and Domestic Political Will: Building a New Civilian Police Force in El Salvador', in O. Marenin, (ed.), *Policing Change, Changing Police – International Perspectives*, Garland Publ. Inc., New York-London, 37–73.

Starnes, J. (1987), 'A Canadian Secret Intelligence Service?', *International Perspectives*, July/August, 6–9.

Starnes, J. (1991), 'Review vs. Oversight', in A.S. Farson, D. Stafford and W.K. Wark, *Security and Intelligence in a Changing World: New Perspectives for the 1990s*, London: Frank Cass, 95–103.

Stieber, Wilhelm (1978), *Spion des Kanzlers*, Stuttgart.

Sveriges Riksdag (Swedish Parliament), Motion 1996/97:Ju918 *Rättsväsendet*, Marianne Samuelsson, miljöpartiet (motion from the Green Party, considering the Swedish legal system.)

Swedish Chancellor of Justice (1998), *Dnr 172–97–21*, decision of 2 April 1998.

Swedish Security Police, *Annual Report 1995/96.*

Swierczakowska H. (1996), *Promotion to higher ranks*, Gazeta Policyjna, No.21.

Szikinger, Istvan (1995), *A nemzet biztonsága* (Security of the Nation), in Társadalmi Szemle 5, 51–57.

Thomas, Rosamund (1991), *Espionage and Secrecy: the Official Secrets Acts 1911–1989 of the United Kingdom*, London.

Thurlow, R. (1994), *The Secret State: British internal security in the twentieth century*, Blackwell, Oxford.

Töllborg, Dennis (1986), *Personalkontroll*, (Personnel Control) Symposium.

Töllborg, Dennis (1995), 'Under Cover. The Swedish Security Police and Their Modi Operandi', in C. Fijnaut and G. Marx (eds), *Under Cover. Police Surveillance in Comparative Perspective*, Kluwer.

Töllborg, Dennis (ed.) (1997), *National Security and the Rule of Law*, Centrum för Europaforskning, Gothenburg.

Töllborg, Dennis (1997), 'Some Hypotheses on Significant Features for Security Policing', In D. Töllborg (ed.), *National Security and the Rule of Law.*

Töllborg, Dennis (1998), 'Report on Wire Tapping Legislation in Sweden', in *Wiretapping in Western Europe: Law and Practice*, Security Services in a

Constitutional Democracy and Open Society Institute, Ford Foundation, report Warsaw October 1998.

Töllborg, Dennis (1999), *Medborgerligt pålitlig?* (Civic Reliable?), Norstedts juridik.

Töllborg, Dennis (2000), *About this you may not speak* (Swedish version in *Festskrift to Anna Christensen* 2000, English version can be ordered via e-mail: Dennis.Toellborg@law.gu.se).

Treaty on the Establishment of a European Police Office (Europol Convention), OJ 1995 C 316/.

Tygodnik AWS, 1998 No. 48.

Ulfkotte, U. (1998), *Verschlussache-BND*, Koehler and Amelang.

Urban, M. (1992), *Big Boys' Rules: the secret struggle against the IRA*, Faber & Faber, London.

Urban, M. (1996), *UK Eyes Alpha: the inside story of British intelligence*, Faber & Faber, London.

Van Doorslaer, R., Verhoeyen, E. (1987), '*L'assassinat de Julien Lahaut, Une Histoire de l'anticommunisme en Belgique*', Anvers: Epo.

Van Outrive, L., Cartuyvels, Y. and Ponsaers, P. (1991), *Les Polices en Belgique, Histoire Socio-Politique du Système Policier. De 1794 à nos jours,* Bruxelles: Evo Histoire, Eds. Vie Ouvrière, 1991.

Wark, W.K. (1987), 'Cryptographic Innocence: The Origins of Signals Intelligence in Canada in the Second World War', *Journal of Contemporary History*, Vol. 22, No. 4, 639–665.

Warner, G. (1998), 'Transnational Organised Crime and the Secret Agencies,' *International Journal of Risk, Security and Crime Prevention*, 3(2) April, 147–9.

Warusfel, Bertrand (2000), *Contre-espionnage et protection du secret: Histoire, droit et organisation de la sécurité nationale en France*, Panazol, Lavauzelle.

Whitaker, Reg (1991), 'The Politics of Security Intelligence Policy-making in Canada I 1970–1984', *Intelligence and National Security*, Vol. 6, No. 4, 649–668.

Whitaker, Reg (1992), 'The Politics of Security Intelligence Policy-making in Canada II 1984–1991', *Intelligence and National Security*, Vol. 7, No. 2, 53–76.

Whitaker, Reg (1996), 'The "Bristow Affair": A Crisis of Accountability in Canadian Security Intelligence', *Intelligence and National Security*, Vol. 11, No. 2, 279–305.

Whitaker, Reg (1998), 'Refugees: the security dimension,' *Citizenship Studies*, 2(3), 413–34.

Wrollski, Pawel (1998), 'UOP scrutinised by SLD. A political seminar on Polish security services', *Gazeta Wyborcza*, 29 June, No.150.

Zycie   Interview with Prof. Lech Kaczyllski, President of Supreme Board of Supervision 1992–1994, 22 May, No.119.

Cases Cited

AD 1999:17 (Swedish Labour Court, Judgement 17 1999.)
European Commission on Human Rights, verbatim record of the hearing in *the Leander case*, 26 May 1986.
European Commission of Human Rights, *Appl. No 62332/00 Ingrid Segerstedt-Wiberg et al v. Sweden.*
ECHR Report of 3 Dec 1991 re. *Applications Nos 14084/88 et al. of R.V. et al. against the Netherlands.*
Leander v. Sweden, ECHR 1997.
RÅ 2000, ref. 15 (Swedish Administrative Supreme Court.).
Regeringsrättens (Swedish Administrative Supreme Court) underrättelse, mål nr 1808–2000.
R. v. Cheung (1995), 100 C.C.C. (3d) 441 (B.C.S.C.).
R. v. Home Secretary, ex p. Rehman, [2001] 3 W.L.R. [Weekly Law Reports] 877.
R. v. Lubovac (1989), 52 C.C.C. (3d) 551 (Alta C.A.).
R. v Sang (1980) AC402.
R. v. Solomon (1996), 110 C.C.C. (3d) 354, 139 D.L.R. (4th) 625 (Que. C.A.) affd [1997] 3 S.C.R., 118 C.C.C. (3d) 351, 151 D.L.R. (4th) 383.
United Nations, Human Rights Committee, Case No. CCPR/C60/D/552/1993.

Index